BOUNDARIES

·············· BANOVINA
———————— PROVINCE
—·—·—·—· INTERNATIONAL
(March 1941)

HUNGARY

RUMANIA

(BARANJA)

(BAČKA)

Subotica

VOJVODINA

sijek

Novi Sad

(BANAT)
PREFECTURE OF BELGRADE

Zemun

BELGRADE

DUNAVSKA

VONIA

SKA

INSKA

arajevo

MORAVSKA

Niš

BULGARIA

ZETSKA
MONTENEGRO

Cetinje

SERBIA

ALBANIA

VARDARSKA

Skoplje

Bitolj

GREECE

20°

22°

24°

46°

44°

42°

20°

22°

THE JEWS OF YUGOSLAVIA

THE JEWS OF YUGOSLAVIA

A Quest for Community

HARRIET PASS FREIDENREICH

The Jewish Publication Society of America *Philadelphia 5740–1979*

*Library of Congress Cataloging in Publication Data
Freidenreich, Harriet Pass, 1947–
The Jews of Yugoslavia.
(Jewish communal and public affairs)
Bibliography: p.   Includes index.
1. Jews in Yugoslavia—History. 2. Yugoslavia—
Ethnic relations. I. Title. II. Series.*
DS135.Y8F73   949.7'004'924   79–84733
ISBN 0–8276–0122–0

Designed by Adrianne Onderdonk Dudden

*Photographs of the interior and exterior of the Ashkenazic
synagogue, Zagreb, are from* Encyclopaedia Judaica *16:870, 918.
All other photographs are courtesy of
Federation of Jewish Communities of Yugoslavia, Belgrade.*

This book is a volume in the series
JEWISH COMMUNAL AND PUBLIC AFFAIRS
*in cooperation with the Center for Jewish Community Studies
Jerusalem   /   Philadelphia*

TO PHILIP

CONTENTS

TABLES*

*In text, references to percentages appearing in tables are rounded off.

PREFACE

Jewish historians know very little about Yugoslavia, and Yugoslav scholars have paid scant attention to the Jews of their country. This study of Jewish communities in interwar Yugoslavia is, then, a venture into hitherto unexplored territory. It is designed to help fill a lacuna in both Jewish and Yugoslav historiography, but it is also intended to serve a broader purpose, namely to further enrich the field of Jewish communal research.

Each Jewish community has its own particular characteristics and yet Jewish communities, wherever they may be found, tend to share at least certain elements in common. Sarajevo, Belgrade, and Zagreb represent a variety of Jewish communal experiences within the Yugoslav context; nevertheless, they demonstrate many striking similarities with one another and with other twentieth-century Jewish communities in Europe and elsewhere. It is hoped that this work will provide new insights into the organization and development of postemancipation Jewry and help confirm the importance of the Jewish community as a vehicle for Jewish survival in the modern world.

The traditional Jewish community in the preemancipation era displayed a basic uniformity, with some regional variations, wherever it occurred in the Western world. In corporate medieval society the Jewish community enjoyed a considerable degree of self-government, wielding extensive authority in judicial matters, taxation, and economic life, as well as religious affairs. With the advent of emancipation, however, conditions changed and the Jewish community was forced to undergo far-reaching adaptations in order to adjust itself to modern times. No longer could the community exercise complete control over its members in such areas as civil law and education. Instead, its jurisdiction was restricted primarily to the religious sphere, as well as charitable and cultural concerns. Emancipation meant the evolution of the Jewish community from a state within a state to a religious denomination, generally recognized by the state and often retaining the power to tax its adherents for its own purposes. Outside influences became more decisive in shaping Jewish society, and the differences among Jewish communities in diverse countries increased.

While, on the one hand, the pressures toward integration tended to undermine the strength of the community, on the other hand, the forces of tradition and continuity sought to preserve and maintain communal authority and institutions. Despite the impact of emancipation, the Jewish community nevertheless managed to retain many of its essential characteristics and institutions, albeit often in a considerably modified form. But the Jewish community did not survive into the twentieth century merely as an anachronistic remnant from the Middle Ages; it demonstrated an ability to adjust its organization and activities to the needs of the times and frequently exhibited a new vitality and creativity of its own.

The study of the modern Jewish community ideally should be conducted on a comparative basis using varied types of communities in order to determine common Jewish traits as well as local distinctions. The advantages inherent in dealing with Jewish communities in Yugoslavia can be discovered in the existence of several quite distinct types of communities within the framework of one political entity, interwar Yugoslavia; hence, one may attempt a comparative survey on a miniature scale. Here we can trace the development of traditional Sephardic communities, as in Sarajevo and Belgrade, and contrast them with modern, fairly assimilated Ashkenazic communities, as in Zagreb. Within the religious sphere, we find both Neologues (those wishing to modernize religious practices) and Orthodox, with a few shades in between. We encounter integrationists and Zionists, along with Jewish nationalists of the Sephardic brand. Not only do the Jews differ among themselves as to historical origins and outlooks, reflecting the heritage of both the Ottoman and Habsburg empires, but also their neighbors constitute separate nationalities, including Serbs, Croats, and Bosniaks, and different religions, Orthodox, Catholic, and Muslim. Thus, within one geographical unit, we are confronted with a wide variety of regional diversity and an entire spectrum of Jewish issues in the twentieth century.

For the purposes of this study the Jewish communities of Bel-

grade, Zagreb, and Sarajevo were selected, based on their size, importance, composition, and geographic distribution. They represented
the three largest Jewish communities in interwar Yugoslavia and
played leading roles in national Jewish life. Also, they encompassed
nearly all the major variations of Yugoslav Jews—religiously, linguistically, socially, and economically—and each was located in a different environment. To present a total picture of Yugoslav Jewry, however, it would be necessary at some future date to supplement this
basic outline with further research on one of the Hungarian-speaking
Jewish communities in the Vojvodina, either Novi Sad or Subotica,
and one of the Macedonian centers, Skoplje or, preferably, Bitolj.
Perhaps it might also prove worthwhile to trace the modern development of a Dalmatian community, either Dubrovnik or Split, which,
although very small, nevertheless had commercial importance in the
seventeenth and eighteenth centuries. Thus, this work does not pre-
tend to be an exhaustive investigation of the Jewish community of
Yugoslavia as a whole, but rather attempts to provide a detailed
analysis of three major communities within the Yugoslav context.

With regard to the spelling of Yugoslav words, my policy has
been to try to use the original whenever possible and to achieve some
degree of consistency in doing so. Hence, personal names, local organizations, and publications are given as they are to be found in the
primary sources, even if they are derived from Hebrew. Although
there are some exceptions (mainly for Ladino words), the reader
should be advised that for pronunciation of names with Serbo-Croatian spelling: $c = ts;\ j = y;\ š = sh;\ č = ch;\ ž = zh;$ and $ć = tch$. For
international organizations and common names, such as B'nai Brith,
Hashomer Hatzair, and Hevra Kaddisha, the common English trans-
literation of Hebrew words has been adopted.

The research and writing of this study, which began as my
doctoral dissertation, was made possible by fellowships or grants
from Columbia University, the Woodrow Wilson Foundation, the
Canada Council, the Canadian Foundation for Jewish Culture, and
the Memorial Foundation for Jewish Culture. The revision of the
manuscript was facilitated by a summer stipend from Temple University. I gratefully acknowledge the support of these institutions.

I would like to thank all the archivists at the various state and
municipal archives in Yugoslavia, as well as at the Central Zionist
Archives in Jerusalem, for their kindness and assistance in locating
materials. My special gratitude goes to Dr. Vidosava Nedomački of
the Jewish Historical Museum in Belgrade for her help and patience.
I wish, too, to recognize my indebtedness to the many Yugoslav Jews

whom I interviewed in Yugoslavia, Israel, and New York for the
valuable insights which they afforded me.

I find it difficult to put into words my feelings of sincere appreciation for the many years of guidance given me by my former advisor,
Professor Ismar Schorsch of The Jewish Theological Seminary of
America, who introduced me to the field of Jewish communities and
developed my understanding of Jewish history. I would also like to
express my gratitude to Professor Joseph Rothschild of Columbia
University for his helpful advice and criticism on both Yugoslav and
Jewish matters, and to the other three members of my doctoral defense committee, Professors Istvan Deak, Arthur Hertzberg, and Bar-
bara Kirschenblatt-Gimblett, for their constructive comments. Finally, I wish to thank Chancellor Gerson D. Cohen of The Jewish
Theological Seminary of America and my colleagues in the History
Department of Temple University for their valuable suggestions for
revising the manuscript.

H. P. F.

THE JEWS OF YUGOSLAVIA

INTRODUCTION

Before 1918 the South Slav lands, which were to comprise Yugoslavia, did not share a common history. Divided for centuries between Ottoman and Habsburg spheres of influence, the various peoples developed their own distinct identities and particular traditions. With the creation of the Kingdom of Serbs, Croats, and Slovenes at the end of World War I, East and West met and gave birth to a complex new multinational state.[1]

Twentieth-century Yugoslavia presents a wide spectrum of ethnic and religious diversity. Its native nationalities include Serbs, Croats, Slovenes, Macedonians, and Montenegrins. Among its many minorities are to be found Hungarians, Germans, Slovaks, Rumanians, Albanians, Turks, and Jews. By religion Yugoslav citizens identify themselves as Serbian Orthodox, Roman Catholic, Muslim, Protestant, and Jewish. From Austrian-like Slovenia in the northwest, populated by industrious and devout Catholics, to Turkish-style Macedonia in the southeast, inhabited by impoverished and backward Orthodox and Muslims, stretches one country composed of many different worlds.

Politically the most significant, if not the most dramatic, cultural differentiation occurs between the Serbs and the Croats. The Serbs are Eastern Orthodox Balkanites, with heroic recollections of independence and revolts against the Turks, while the Croats are Roman Catholic Central Europeans, historically linked with the West. These two nationalities share a common language, with dialectical variations, known as Serbo-Croatian (or Croato-Serbian), but they write in two different alphabets, Latin in the west and Cyrillic in the east. In addition, there exists yet another group of native Serbo-Croatian speakers, neither Serb nor Croat, but Slavic by origin, Muslim by religion, and conservative by tradition. This Muslim ethnic group, sometimes called *Bosniak,* is concentrated in the central province of Bosnia-Hercegovina, which as a result can boast of neither a Serb-Orthodox nor a Croat-Catholic majority.

The underlying causes for such extreme heterogeneity in close geographic proximity are readily discernible. Soon after the Slavic migrations to the Balkans in the sixth century, those tribes that had settled to the west, the Slovenes and the Croats, fell under the influence of Rome, whereas those, such as the Serbs, who took up residence in the east, came under the aegis of Byzantium. The cleavage between East and West was thus established early. In the middle the inhabitants of Bosnia were torn between the two conflicting powers. Many of them eventually became Bogomils, followers of a medieval Manichaean sect, that had also gained importance in Bulgaria. Later, under Turkish rule, a high percentage of these Bogomils converted to Islam.[2] In this manner the three major religions of the area struck roots in South Slav soil.

Due to historical circumstances, no two Yugoslav regions developed in a like fashion. In the Habsburg lands the Slovenian territories became part of the Austrian crownlands at an early date; Dalmatia, after centuries of Venetian domination, came under Austrian rule in the nineteenth century; and Croatia, which had formerly been an independent kingdom, accepted union with Hungary in 1102. Also under the Hungarian Crown of St. Stephen were to be found the Banat, Bačka, and Baranja, referred to jointly as the Vojvodina. These lands to the north of the Danube had been reconquered from the Turks in the seventeenth century and were inhabited by Serbs, Hungarians, Germans, and other ethnic minorities. The final expansion of Austria-Hungary into the Balkans took place with the occupation of Bosnia-Hercegovina in 1878 and the subsequent annexation of these provinces thirty years later.

Considerable differentiation had also manifested itself within the Ottoman sphere. The Serbian Empire had reached its pinnacle in the mid-fourteenth century under the leadership of Tsar Stefan Dušan. Thereafter its power declined and Serbia, along with Macedonia and the Kingdom of Bosnia, succumbed to Turkish conquest by the end of the fifteenth century. Over the years the condition of the South Slavs under Ottoman rule deteriorated greatly. In the seventeenth and eighteenth centuries frequent Austrian invasions further aggravated the general situation and Serbs migrated to Habsburg territory in large numbers. Serbia was the first among the Balkan lands to conduct a successful revolt against the Turks in the early nineteenth century. By 1830 Serbia had gained autonomy under its own prince and in 1881 became a kingdom. The only other South Slav region to enjoy independent status before World War I was tiny Montenegro, which had never been fully subjugated to Turkish masters. Macedonia remained a part of the Ottoman Empire until the Balkan Wars of 1911–13 when it was divided among its neighbors, Bulgaria, Greece, and Serbia.

The First World War provided the opportunity for the amalgamation of these diverse elements. The circumstances, however, portended ominously. The spark that set off the chain of events leading to war emanated from Sarajevo, the capital of Bosnia, and hostilities began with the Austrian invasion of Serbia. During the course of ensuing fighting, Croatian soldiers in Habsburg uniforms faced their Serbian counterparts on opposite sides of the line of fire. With the armistice in 1918 a totally new entity, a Yugoslav state, emerged from the wreckage of a collapsed empire.

The creation of the Kingdom of Serbs, Croats, and Slovenes also brought together in one political unit two distinct groups of Jews, the Sephardim of the former Ottoman territories and the Ashkenazim of the erstwhile Habsburg lands. Jewish settlements in Macedonia and Dalmatia dated back as far as Greek and Roman days, and small communities existed in Slovenia and Serbia in medieval times.[3] The first major wave of Jewish immigration to the South Slav lands, however, came as a result of the expulsion of the Jews from Christian Spain in 1492.[4] The sultan welcomed the Sephardic refugees into the Ottoman Empire and they arrived in large numbers. Initially the vast majority of these newcomers settled in Salonika and Istanbul (Constantinople), but by the mid-sixteenth century, their descendants began to spread throughout the hinterland, establishing communities in such towns as Belgrade in Serbia, Sarajevo in Bosnia, and Skoplje (Üsküb) and Bitolj (Monastir) in Macedonia. Other Sephardic communities grew up in Dubrovnik (Ragusa) and Split (Spalato) on the Dalmatian coast.[5]

The Sephardim brought their own language and customs from Spain. They continued to speak Ladino, or Judeo-Spanish, a dialect which evolved from fourteenth century Castilian. Wherever they took up residence, they formed separate communal organizations alongside those already in existence. Often, in larger Jewish centers, several Sephardic communities developed, created according to the place of origin of their membership, such as Castile, Aragon, Catalonia, and Portugal. The Sephardim considered themselves culturally superior to the native Byzantine Jews as well as to the Ashkenazim from northern and eastern Europe. Their traditions derived from their former close contact with Babylonian Jewry and the experience of the Golden Age of Jewish learning in Islamic Spain. These emigrés from Spain and Portugal soon took over undisputed leadership in Balkan Jewish life. In the sixteenth and early seventeenth centuries, Ottoman Jewry flourished both economically and spiritually. With the decay of the institutions of the empire, however, the condition of the Jews within it also deteriorated so that by the nineteenth century the Balkan Sephardim represented but a pale shadow of their former glory.

Until the late nineteenth century, the Sephardic communities in Belgrade and Sarajevo displayed an extremely traditional and patriarchal character. Jewish society was very close-knit, having little contact with the outside world, and keeping its social and cultural activities confined within the limits of the Jewish quarter. The Sephardic style of living had become strongly influenced by the oriental environment. These Jews lived in one-storied houses built around large courtyards and furnished in Turkish fashion. They wore Ottoman garb, including the fez for men, and ate eastern foods. They also retained much of their Spanish heritage in their Ladino speech and Sephardic folklore. Religious piety formed an integral part of this society and traditional Jewish customs were strictly observed.

In contrast to the Sephardic communities in the Ottoman territories, the Ashkenazic communities in the Habsburg areas were all of fairly recent origin. Until the end of the eighteenth century, Jews had been banned from residence in Slovenia, Croatia, and the Military Frontier, except for Zemun (Semlin, Zimony). During the following century, a large number of Jews from various parts of the Austro-Hungarian Empire migrated to the South Slav regions under Hungarian control. Major Jewish communities developed in Zagreb (Agram, Zagrab) and Osijek (Essig, Eszek) in Croatia-Slavonia and Novi Sad (Neusatz, Ujvidek) and Subotica (Szabadka) in the Vojvodina, and there were many other smaller towns with significant Jewish populations as well.

By the mid-nineteenth century a majority of the Ashkenazim had joined the Neologue (or Reform) group, which advocated greater leniency in religious practices, but a small number continued to adhere to strictly Orthodox Jewish beliefs. Such a split within the Ashkenazic ranks between the more observant, staunchly traditional minority and the more integrationist, reforming Neologues was characteristic of Hungarian Jewry as a whole.[6] As it extended into the South Slav lands, this division became particularly pronounced in the Vojvodina, but it was also found in Zagreb. For the most part, these Jews, especially the Neologues among them, no longer spoke Yiddish among themselves but used German or Hungarian instead.

After the occupation of Bosnia-Hercegovina in 1878, some Ashkenazic Jews moved to Bosnia, especially to its capital, Sarajevo. The Ashkenazic community in Belgrade also developed around the same time. Conversely, a small Sephardic settlement eventually appeared in Zagreb. On the whole, however, the line of demarcation between the Ashkenazim and the Sephardim continued to follow the old border between Habsburgs and Ottomans.

Thus, the Ashkenazim, who formed two-thirds of Yugoslav Jewry in the interwar period, lived in the more westernized and urbanized northern parts of the country, and the Sephardim, comprising the remaining third, were situated mainly in the poorer areas to the south and east. In 1930 there existed in Yugoslavia 114 organized Jewish communities: 38 were Sephardic (all but 3 of which were located in Serbia, Bosnia, Macedonia, or Dalmatia), 70 were Ashkenazic-Neologue (with only 4 outside of Croatia and the Vojvodina), and 6 were Ashkenazic-Orthodox (all but 1 to be found in the Vojvodina).[7]

The distinction between the Sephardic, Ladino-speaking old-timers and the Ashkenazic, German- or Hungarian-speaking newcomers is of vital importance in understanding the Yugoslav Jewish situation in the interwar period. This dichotomy mirrored to a certain extent the conflict between Serbs and Croats, the East and the West, which has always caused considerable tension within the country. Just as the Serbs accepted the Eastern Orthodox variant of Christianity and the influence of Byzantium, and the Croats accepted Catholicism and the dominance of Rome, so the Sephardim generally adopted the Babylonian model within Judaism and the Ashkenazim the Palestinian. The Sephardic experience had evolved first in Spain and then in the Balkans, whereas the Ashkenazim developed initially in Franco-Germany and later in Eastern Europe. It is scarcely surprising that significant disparities, arising as they did out of such varied historical backgrounds, existed between the two groups, not only in religious practices but also in culture, way of life, and attitudes.[8]

By the nineteenth century, the Sephardim in the South Slav lands had accepted a somewhat oriental way of life and were still living in an almost totally Jewish milieu, interacting with their Slavic neighbors only to a limited extent. The Ashkenazim, by contrast, had already begun to adopt western concepts under the Habsburgs. They had undergone a certain degree of assimilation and were no longer operating within a predominantly Jewish framework. The former were proud of their history and traditions, whereas the latter considered themselves more advanced and enlightened. Thus, the Jews, like their Yugoslav fellow-countrymen, demonstrated considerable regional variation even among themselves.

Sarajevo, Belgrade, and Zagreb were the three major cities in interwar Yugoslavia with the largest Jewish populations. Each of these centers represents a different aspect of South Slav culture; each has its own specific atmosphere. Sarajevo typifies the East, Zagreb the West, and Belgrade lies somewhere between the two extremes. Three diverse worlds—in one country. Naturally, the Jews did not react in exactly the same fashion to all of these environments. Indeed, each of the Jewish communities, whether Sephardic or Ashkenazic, was emphatically shaped by the nature of its host town.

KOŽARA ISLAND

RATNO ISLAND

DANUBE RIVER

Jevrejska St.

KALEMEGDAN PARK

CITADEL

Pančevo Bridge
Pančevo

3 4 DORĆOL

PORT AREA

2 ZEREK

Badouša St.

6

Kneza Mihaila St.

Zemun
Kralja Aleksandra Bridge

5

Poenkareova St. Hilindarska St.

SAVA RIVER

N

Central Station

8

7 9

FIŠEKLIJA

11
CEMETERY

10

Kralja Aleksandra Blvd.

Smederevo

Venizilova St.

Voivoda Misica Blvd.

Šabac

Franše Dešperea Blvd.

Kralja Aleksandra Blvd.

Voivoda Putnika Blvd.

Djordjevica Blvd.

Kragujevac

Petka

TOPČIDER

TOWN PLAN OF
BELGRADE (ca. 1937)

LEGEND

1. Federation of Jewish Religious Communities (SJVO)
2. New Sephardic Synagogue (Bet Israel)
3. Old Sephardic Synagogue (Stari hram)
4. Oneg Šabat-Gemilut Hasadim
5. Ashkenazic Synagogue
6. Cathedral (Saborna crkva)
7. Royal Palace
8. National Assembly (Skupština)
9. Orthodox Church (Sveti Marko)
10. University Library
11. Jewish Cemeteries

Laura Hollingshead

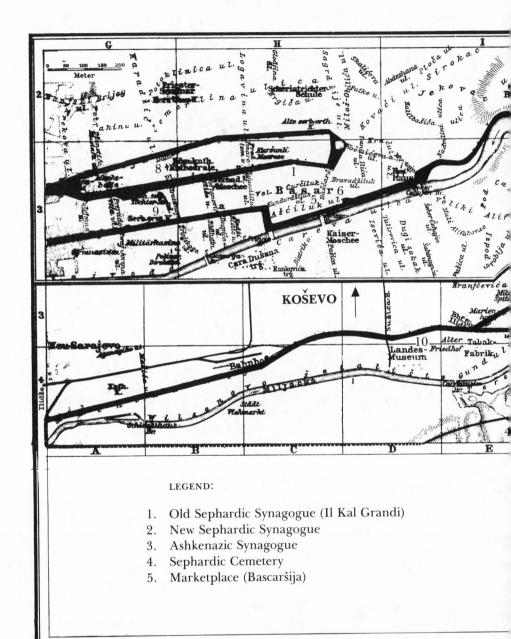

LEGEND:

1. Old Sephardic Synagogue (Il Kal Grandi)
2. New Sephardic Synagogue
3. Ashkenazic Synagogue
4. Sephardic Cemetery
5. Marketplace (Bascaršija)

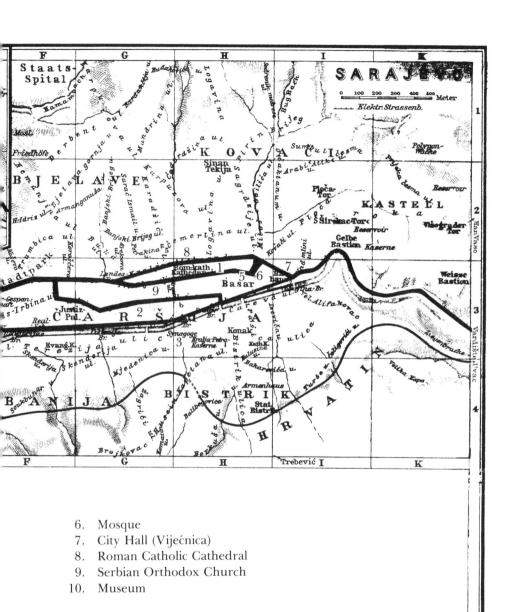

6. Mosque
7. City Hall (Vijećnica)
8. Roman Catholic Cathedral
9. Serbian Orthodox Church
10. Museum

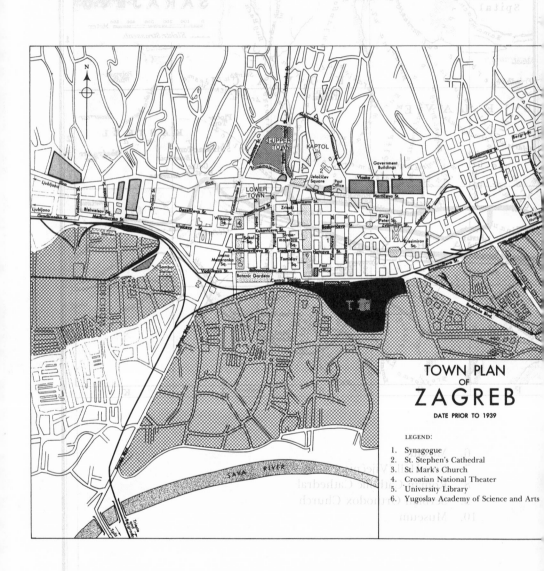

TOWN PLAN
OF
ZAGREB
DATE PRIOR TO 1939

LEGEND:

1. Synagogue
2. St. Stephen's Cathedral
3. St. Mark's Church
4. Croatian National Theater
5. University Library
6. Yugoslav Academy of Science and Arts

PART ONE

The Setting: Meeting of East and West

1

SARAJEVO: CITY OF FOUR FAITHS

Surrounded by mountains on three sides, Sarajevo lies along the banks of the gentle Miljačka River, a tributary of the Bosna near its source. The town was founded by the Turks soon after their conquest of Bosnia in the mid-fifteenth century and it served intermittently as provincial capital of this territory on the northwestern frontier of the Ottoman Empire. Favorably situated on the east-west overland trade route from Istanbul and Salonika to the Adriatic coast, Sarajevo became the major economic center of the area and played an important commercial role, especially in the sixteenth and seventeenth centuries when the Ottoman Empire was at its height. It later developed increasing significance for its artisanry.

The town itself presents a distinctly oriental impression. In the heart of the city lies the colorful and exotic Baščaršija, the old marketplace. Dotting the green hillsides all around are the graceful minarets of over one hundred mosques. In Ottoman times Sarajevo had a definite Muslim majority, made up primarily of local Slavs who converted to Islam in the fifteenth century. After the Austro-Hungarian occupation in 1878, the number of Catholics and Orthodox increased considerably, yet the Muslims managed to maintain at least a plurality. Thus it is from the Muslim sector, with its conservative nature and leisurely customs, that this Bosnian center derives its predominant flavor. The Austrians did leave their mark on the town, architecturally at least, by constructing several large and somewhat incongruous edifices, such as the rather bizarre striped Vijećnica (Town hall), ill suited to this particular setting. They also introduced railways, streetcars, electricity, and other modern conveniences. Cut off from its former Ottoman ties, however, Sarajevo gradually declined as a trade center and became economically isolated. In the period prior to World War II, then, it could boast of very little industry, only limited commerce, but considerable artisan activity. Sarajevo thus never became a major city in interwar Yugoslavia but continued to exist as a provincial town, outside the mainstream of progress.

The Jewish community of Sarajevo dates back four hundred years to the settlement of a group of Sephardic merchants from Salonika. In 1565, according to the records of the local Muslim court, ten to fifteen Jewish families were permanent residents of Sarajevo, living in one of the Muslim districts.[1] Sixteen years later, the Turkish governor erected a special dwelling for the Jews, which was officially named in his honor Siavuš-paša Daire (the Bequest of Siavuš Pasha), but which was commonly known as Čifuthan (the Jew House) by the local populace and Il Cortijo (the Courtyard) by the Jews themselves. This edifice was located on the edge of a Muslim district, close to the central marketplace, the Baščaršija. About two thousand square meters in all, with a large inner courtyard, from whence it derived its nickname, the one-storied building housed approximately sixty families, each living in one or two small rooms. Attached to the western wall was a synagogue, which the Sephardim called Il Kal Grandi (the Great Synagogue).[2]

This complex did not constitute a closed ghetto in the Western European sense but rather an Ottoman *mahala*, or quarter, such as the various religioethnic groups in the empire lived in at that time. All Jews were not compelled to live there and, in fact, probably only the poor actually did so, especially in later years. The wealthier Jews resided outside its walls, buying or renting houses and shops nearby. In 1659 a Turkish traveller, Evlija Čelebi, reported that there were two Jewish quarters, the Siavuš-paša Daire and the adjacent area; he also mentioned the existence of the synagogue. By 1841 there were five more Jewish residential districts in close proximity to one another, all in predominantly Muslim sections; three of these contained collective quarters for poor Jews.[3]

The Jews of Sarajevo in their mode of life reflected a combination of their Sephardic heritage and the influence of their Balkan environment. Jewish society was patriarchal, based on an extended family circle, with several generations and often families sharing the same household. Dwellings were not large, usually one room and a kitchen, unless the family was fairly wealthy. Furnishings were eastern style, a carpet with cushions upon which one sat Turkish fashion, eating with one's hands out of a common bowl and drinking out of a common container.[4]

The Jewish community formed a unified and tight-knit social unit. Often groups of neighbors would gather informally of an evening, gossiping, telling stories, singing, and playing games. At family celebrations, especially weddings and holidays, the older women would sing *romansas,* epic songs from medieval Spain which formed part of the Sephardic folklore heritage. They would also sing Serbo-Croatian or Turkish songs translated into Ladino.[5]

The Sephardim brought with them to the Balkans their previous form of communal organization. According to the communal statute of 1731, the earliest such official document to survive until the twentieth century, the Jewish community of Sarajevo was governed by an executive of five men, plus a *gabbai* (an overseer of the synagogue), a treasurer of Palestine funds, and a school inspector, all of whom were appointed annually.[6] There was also a permanent advisory council of three men. Persons who refused to accept communal office were fined.

Communal revenues were derived mainly from a religious tax on all Jewish residents and the sale of *mitzvot,* or synagogue honors. This money was used to pay the rabbi, teachers, and other religious functionaries, as well as state taxes and other related expenses. The communal executive was collectively responsible for balancing the budget. If expenses exceeded revenues at the end of the year, the members of the executive were expected to make up the difference out of their own pockets.[7]

The Sarajevo Jewish community maintained very close ties with Salonika, the spiritual center of Balkan Jewry. From there came Sarajevo's earliest-known rabbis in the first half of the seventeenth century, Samuel Baruh (whose grave, according to legend, is the oldest in the Jewish cemetery), Ašer Zebulun, and Macliah Mučačon. Before the eighteenth century, there is little reference to Bosnian Jews, except for the enfant terrible of the Sarajevo Jewish community, Nehemiah Hiya Hayon (born about 1650), kabbalist scholar, follower of Sabbatai Zevi, and European traveler. Sarajevo was also the temporary home from 1686 to 1697 of Hayon's chief opponent, Rabbi Zevi Ashkenazi, who, with the arrival of the armies of Eugene of Savoy, escaped from Buda and later from Sarajevo and went to Germany and finally Amsterdam.[8]

The most important figure in the cultural history of the Sarajevo Jewish community, however, is Rabbi David Pardo, who was born in Venice in 1719 and educated there. Pardo was a talmudic scholar and writer of numerous commentaries and liturgical works. He came to Sarajevo in 1765 by way of Dubrovnik and Split. The Jewish community hired him as *haham* (religious leader), *av beth din* (chief judge), and superintendent of schools. During his stay in Sarajevo, he founded a yeshiva, or higher school of Jewish learning. In 1781 he went to live in Palestine, where he continued to receive a pension from the Sarajevo Jewish community until his death ten years later.[9] The nineteenth century, however, marked a period of general decline, and the office of communal rabbi was filled only periodically.

Thus, during the lengthy period of Ottoman rule, the Sephardim in Sarajevo preserved a very traditional Jewish way of life. Although they had adapted well to their milieu, socially and culturally they remained apart, somewhat isolated from their neighbors.

The legal and social position of the Jews in Bosnia was not essentially different from that of non-Muslims, Christians or Jews, in other provinces of the Ottoman Empire. Because the empire was basically organized along religious lines, the Jews formed a separate millet, or ecclesiastical community, as did the Orthodox, the Catholics, and other religious groups. Although the general policy was one of religious tolerance, there were certain discriminatory measures against "nonbelievers," such as not being able to bear arms or ride horses in towns and having to wear distinctive clothing.[10]

More important was the limitation in legal status before Muslim courts. Non-Muslims were not admitted as equal witnesses before the *kadi,* or Muslim judge. Their testimony had full value only among their peers. In general, however, Muslim law (the *šerijat*) applied only to Muslims; Jews and Christians were governed according to their own religious and civil laws, which controlled matters of marriage, family, inheritance, and property. Except in criminal, agrarian, and tax law, where jurisdiction remained in the hands of the *kadi,* the various millets were autonomous, and legal questions were decided by their own religious leaders or judges.[11]

The Jews, like all non-Muslims, had to pay special taxes, such as the *harač,* or poll tax. This tax, levied on all males over the age of nine, was divided into three property classes: high, middle, and low. The millet was assessed as a whole and the total was divided among the members by the communal executive. The tax for the poor was paid out of the communal treasury.[12] In theory the Jews were also required to perform statutory labor on roads, bridges, and fortresses;

in practice, however, the Jewish community generally was relieved of this duty through the payment of considerable amounts of money to municipal and state authorities. Numerous other expenses, such as fines, gifts, and bribes, were paid regularly to the authorities from the communal chest and on special occasions.[13]

The mid-nineteenth century was an age of reform within the Ottoman Empire. On paper at least, the new legislation improved and clarified the legal position of the Jews as individuals and as a community. Previously, the civil-legal status of non-Muslims was not regulated by a code of law, but by tradition and customary laws. In 1839 the *Tanzimat* (Reforms) of Sultan Abdul Medjid recognized the rights of all Ottoman citizens to security of life, honor, and property, civil equality, participation in civil and military service, freedom of religious affiliation and public instruction, equal taxation, equality of witnesses before the law, and participation in regional, municipal, and judicial advisory bodies. In 1856 an act was promulgated confirming and guaranteeing the established rights of all religious communities and defining their position within the state. These measures were then incorporated into the Ottoman Constitution of 1876.[14] Shortly after these laws went into effect and before their full impact was actually felt, however, Ottoman rule ended in Bosnia and a new era began for Sarajevo Jewry.

The Austro-Hungarian occupation of Bosnia in 1878 constituted a significant turning point in the history of the Jewish community of Sarajevo. The new rulers brought with them emancipation, or full civil rights, for the Jews as individuals, but they also seemed to pose a threat to the authority and stability of the existing community. For the first time the small, unified, traditional Sephardic community was confronted directly with western culture and the arrival of significant numbers of Ashkenazim. The "natives" resented these newcomers and refused to accept them as members of their community.

The internal structure of the established Jewish community was reorganized in 1882 according to the Provisional Statute for the Sephardic Israelite Religious Community in Sarajevo, which was ratified by the regional government. An executive, composed of twelve members and four substitutes, was to be elected every three years. Suffrage in the election of communal officers was limited to those members of the community who paid three forints annually as state tax. The community had the right to tax its members for its own use up to 20 percent of the amount of direct state taxes. Membership was compulsory for all Sephardim and a register was to be kept by the communal authorities.[15] The Sephardic community of Sarajevo was thus transformed from its Ottoman millet status into a Central European *Cultusgemeinde,* subject to state control and interference.

At about the same time, a separate but parallel community of Ashkenazim developed. Unlike the Sephardim with their common origins and cultural background and unified communal structure, the Ashkenazim came from different parts of the Habsburg Monarchy, many from Slavic-speaking territories, but others from German and Hungarian lands as well. Among themselves they generally spoke German, Yiddish, or perhaps Hungarian. The main bond that drew them together, however, was religion. On September 24, 1879, the small group of Ashkenazic Jews in Sarajevo established their own religious community. They acquired temporary quarters for a synagogue and hired a *hazan,* or cantor, to lead prayers according to the Ashkenazic *minhag* (custom). Gradually they built their own synagogue, religious school, cemetery, and social-charitable organizations.[16] The Sephardim and Ashkenazim continued to maintain their separate communities and institutions into the twentieth century, with relatively little social contact between the two groups.

The Jews, whether Sephardic or Ashkenazic, constituted only one religious element within Sarajevo society. Sarajevo is a city of four faiths, coexisting side by side. In 1885 the first Austro-Hungarian census reported that the Muslims held a clear majority, or 60 percent of the total population of 26,268, while the Orthodox constituted 17 percent, the Catholics 13 percent, and the Jews 10 percent. (See table 1.) By 1910 the population had almost doubled to 51,919; but the Muslim component had declined to 36 percent, the Orthodox had maintained their 17 percent, the Catholics had jumped to 35 percent, and the Jews had increased to 12 percent. With the creation of the Yugoslav state, the proportion of Orthodox grew larger, but the other factors remained more or less constant. As no religious group retained a majority in the town, the Jews, who constituted over 10 percent of the inhabitants, were able to play a significant role in municipal politics, often holding the balance of power between the other denominations.

During the period of Austro-Hungarian rule, the number of Jews living in Sarajevo tripled. This sharp increase in the Jewish population was due not only to the relatively high Sephardic birth rate and some Sephardic immigration but also to the arrival of a sizable number of Ashkenazim from other parts of Austria-Hungary. In 1885 there were 2,618 Jews in Sarajevo; they were mainly Sephardim but included a small group of Ashkenazim. In 1895, of the 4,058 Jews who resided in the city, 3,159 were Sephardim and 899 Ashkenazim, and by 1910 there were 4,985 Sephardim and 1,412 Ashkenazim living in Sarajevo, making a total Jewish population of 6,397. (See table 2.)

During the interwar period, the number of Jews in Sarajevo remained fairly constant, 7,458, or 11 percent of the city's population, in the 1921 Yugoslav census and 7,615, or 10 percent of the total population of 78,173, according to the 1931 census. (See table 3.) Official estimates for 1939 report 8,114 members of the two Jewish communities combined, 7,054 Sephardim and 1,060 Ashkenazim.[17] This represents an increase of only 9 percent since 1921. Whatever population increase took place in the interwar years may be attributed strictly to natural growth, since Sarajevo received little or no immigration during this period. In addition, Sarajevo experienced considerable emigration to other parts of the country, in particular to Belgrade and Zagreb. As a result, Sarajevo cannot be considered a rapidly growing Jewish community on the eve of World War II.

The pattern of Jewish settlement in Sarajevo since the late nineteenth century, as illustrated in table 2, affords significant insight into the development of the community. In the early years the Jews, especially those of the poorer classes, tended to live in close proximity to one another. In 1885 over half the Jews lived in the Čaršija, the central business area, in which the old Jewish quarter had been located, and more than a quarter were found in Bjelave, a poorer section of town halfway up the mountain slope. The rest were scattered in five other districts, with the largest concentration in Kovači, a Muslim district. Ten years later, an equal number, 35 percent each, were residents of Čaršija and Bjelave, and 24 percent were now in Kovači. By 1910 they were slightly more decentralized, but 80 percent of Sarajevo's Jews were still concentrated in three areas of the city, making up 32 percent of the residents of Čaršija, the main business district, 20 percent of lower class Bjelave, and 14 percent of Kovači.[18]

The residential distribution of the Sephardim and Ashkenazim was by no means identical. In 1895 only a little more than 25 percent of the Sephardim were still living in Čaršija, their original area of settlement, but over 40 percent were now to be found in the poverty of Bjelave, with most of the others in Kovači. On the other hand, over 50 percent of the newly arrived Ashkenazim took up lodgings in the central Čaršija district; the rest were scattered, some in Bjelave and some in Koševo, a new Catholic district where very few Sephardim lived. Much the same trend was to be seen in the 1910 census, except that by then more Jews, Sephardim and Ashkenazim alike, were to be found in the outlying districts of Bistrik and Hrvatin, which housed both Muslim and Christian inhabitants. There never was any real attempt to create an Ashkenazic colony in the city, even though in the beginning most of the Ashkenazim lived in the downtown Čaršija area. Their numbers were relatively few and they settled at will, mainly according to their economic status, which tended to be higher than the Sephardic average. The Sephardic poor continued to be concentrated in Bjelave in ever-increasing numbers. The wealthier Sephardim resided in more prestigious parts of town, some remaining in the center, but not in the old Jewish quarter itself.

From the earliest years of their settlement in Bosnia, most Jews engaged in commerce. Since Sarajevo was located on the east-west overland trade route from the Balkan interior to the Adriatic coast, during the centuries of Ottoman control, the Sarajevo Sephardim maintained business contacts with their coreligionists in Istanbul, Salonika, Skoplje, and Belgrade, on the one hand, and Dubrovnik, Split, Trieste, Venice, and even Vienna on the other. They dealt in textiles, colonial goods, and other such commodities. Some Jews were involved in banking and moneylending, albeit probably on a fairly small scale.[19]

Among the Sarajevo Jews, there also existed an established tradition of artisanry. Until the late nineteenth century, certain crafts lay predominantly in the hands of one particular religious group: tanners, for example, were Muslim; furriers, Orthodox; forgers, Catholic; and tinsmiths, Jews; other trades were mixed.[20] The artisans were organized into guilds (called *esnaf*); each guild had a Muslim chief master, but non-Muslims could also belong. Artisans of the same faith usually had their own special guild section.[21] Thus, there were numerous Jewish tinsmiths, tailors, shoemakers, and so forth.

As a result of the Austrian occupation, important changes began to take place in the economic field. Capitalism was introduced, sounding the death knell for the guild economy of the old order.[22] The new Ashkenazic arrivals had a distinct advantage over the Sephardic natives because they came with a knowledge of German and with economic skills. They entered a variety of fields, mainly middle-class occupations, such as large- and medium-scale commerce, lower and middle administrators, skilled workers, and the free professions. There were a number of Ashkenazic doctors, lawyers, and engineers, but relatively few unskilled or poor among this group.[23]

In contrast, the Sephardim remained concentrated in their former occupations, especially commerce. The large-scale merchants had a virtual monopoly over the import-export business in textiles, hardware, and colonial goods. This trade was now being directed to the major centers of the Habsburg Empire and Trieste on the Dalmatian coast. Some of the old families, like the Saloms, set up private banking houses.[24] Peter Sugar concludes in his book entitled *The Industrialization of Bosnia-Hercegovina* that "we are left with only the Salom brothers [Ješua and I.G.] and [Salamon D.] Alkalaj as examples of local entrepreneurs who were able to establish industries of any significance in Bosnia-Hercegovina under Austro-Hungarian rule."[25] These men founded a successful match factory, a woolen piping plant, a tanning factory, and a flour mill. The artisan class and the petty traders, however, did not fare as well as the wealthier merchants, bankers, and industrialists. Under the impact of the new economic order, a growing polarization developed between the bourgeoisie and the proletariat within the Jewish populace.

During the interwar years, the occupational distribution of Sarajevo Jewry changed relatively little. Although complete and reliable statistics based on tax records and other such sources are unfortunately not available, it would appear that a large proportion of Jews, especially Sephardim, remained merchants. According to the estimates of Haim Kamhi, an economist and postwar leader of the Sarajevo Jewish community, approximately one-third of Sarajevo's commercial activity lay in Jewish hands, while well over half of those merchants dealing in textiles and related goods were Jews. A small class of Jewish professionals and white-collar workers, including increasing numbers of Sephardim, also began to develop.[26]

Among the several hundred Jewish artisans, the tailors, shoemakers, tinsmiths, locksmiths, and later electricians and plumbers constituted the largest groups. Jews made up 9 percent of the insured working force in Sarajevo. In 1933 there were reportedly 1,336 Jews covered by various workers' insurance programs, most of them employed in small enterprises; 609 of these were engaged in crafts and industry, 555 in commerce, and 62 in household service, and 110 were employed by the railroad. Four hundred fifty-five, or over 40 percent, of these insured Jewish workers were women.[27] Sarajevo thus demonstrates a relatively high concentration of Jews at the lower end of the economic spectrum, that is, as artisans and workers.

Such observations are borne out by the tax distribution within the Sarajevo Sephardic community. (No tax or occupational statistics exist for the Sarajevo Ashkenazic community. Based on an analysis of the Ashkenazim in Belgrade, however, the assumption can be made that it contained proportionally fewer poor and more middle class than the Sephardic community.) According to the available figures for 1928, only one-third of the Sephardic taxpayers belonged to the middle and upper tax brackets combined. Of 832 taxpayers, 136 paid over 1,800 dinars annually in communal taxes (including 5 persons who paid over 10,000), and 147 paid between 500 and 1500 dinars to the community. Two-thirds of the taxpayers, or 549 households, thus fall into the lower income bracket, a group paying between 50 and 480 dinars in annual communal taxes.[28]

But this tells only part of the story. The total membership of the Sarajevo Sephardic community in 1928 amounted to approximately 6,000 individuals, but there were only 832 taxpayers. Assuming that each head of household had an average of four dependents, about 1,200 potential taxpayers must be taken into account.[29] Evidently, close to 400 families, or one-third of the community, were tax-exempt due to their poverty-stricken condition. A quote from Isak Samokovlija (1889–1955), a Sarajevo Jewish physician and social writer of the interwar period, offers a glimpse of their dismal plight:

Only the word "Bjelave," where the majority of the Jews in Sarajevo live, is enough to give us, without further commentary, the sad picture of the typical Jewish Sephardic poor, whom we meet in Skoplje, Bitolj, Salonica, and other Sephardic centers. The poor of European countries, who claim that the bitterest of circumstances are upon them, would on the whole shudder at the conditions in which our brethren live in these quarters. In their unhygienic homes, which in most cases consist of one usually large, mouldy room, regardless of the number of members of the household, we do not find the most basic household necessities: not enough windows, chairs, or beds. And happiness is seen on their faces on that day when they are ensured bread and onions.[30]

In 1933 there were 240 Jewish families on winter relief in Sarajevo; they represented 15 percent of the total number of persons on welfare in Sarajevo at that time. An estimated 150 to 200 Jewish workers were jobless as a result of the depression. Two years later the various Sarajevo Jewish organizations formed a committee to investigate the Jewish poverty problem in the city. It reported that 398 families, with a total of 1,700 persons, were in impoverished circumstances and needed communal help. Of these 1,700 individuals, 1,116 had no income whatsoever.[31] Indeed, attempting to combat poverty became a task of increasing urgency for the Jewish community of Sarajevo. The dire straits of these Sephardim reflects the economic isolation of Sarajevo, the impact of the depression, and the lack of jobs for unskilled and semiskilled labor. To some extent, too, it is a result of the absence of diversification within the Jewish occupational structure and insufficient vocational training.

When the first public school opened in Sarajevo in the mid-nineteenth century, few Jews wanted to send their children there, because to them all secular education was profane. Hence the only official instruction received by Sephardim in the Ottoman period was strictly religious. All Jewish boys from the age of five or six attended the communal Talmud Torah, or *meldar,* as it was called in the Sephardic communities, where they learned Bible, Talmud, and Hebrew, but no secular subjects.[32] (Jewish girls received no formal education, but remained at home to do housework and embroider; they married early, at sixteen to eighteen years of age.) Thus, in the nineteenth century, virtually all Jewish males in Sarajevo were literate, if only by being able to read and write in Ladino and in Hebrew, but at the same time, very few were educated in nonreligious spheres, including the language of their neighbors.

In 1894 Serbo-Croatian was introduced into the curriculum of the Jewish school, so that Jewish children could now study secular subjects within their own educational framework. In 1910, however, the Talmud Torah ceased to exist; the new building, which it had occupied since 1903, was turned over to the state as a public elementary school.[33] Thus ended the tradition of Jewish separate schools in Sarajevo and the use of Ladino as a language of instruction in the school.

Before the turn of the century, few Sephardic children attended the state secondary school, which opened in 1879. In the first year of the school's existence, twenty-five Sephardic pupils were enrolled, of whom eighteen were in the preliminary training class for those without elementary education. In 1886/87 only seven Sephardim were listed, but there were twelve Ashkenazim. The school records in 1889/90 reveal two Sephardim and eight Ashkenazim, and in 1898 there were nine of the former and twenty-eight of the latter. In twelve years only three Sephardim graduated, the first in 1889; in the two subsequent decades there were thirty-six Sephardic graduates. By 1910 the trend had changed and there were forty-one Sephardim and nineteen Ashkenazim attending the Sarajevo secondary school.[34] In the interwar period increasing numbers of Sarajevo Jews, both Sephardim and Ashkenazim, were going on to higher education, not only at the secondary school level but also to universities, both abroad and within Yugoslavia. Nevertheless, the majority of Sephardim received little more than an elementary education. Despite efforts on the part of several Jewish organizations to encourage productive labor, vocational instruction generally proved inadequate.

Ladino constituted the dominant language of the Sephardic community of Sarajevo, at least until the beginning of the twentieth century. It was spoken in the home, the school, and the marketplace. Commercial records were kept in that language; in fact, one source even claims the existence of business correspondence between Jews and Muslims written in Ladino. According to the Austro-Hungarian census of 1910, of the Sephardim in Sarajevo 98 percent declared Ladino as their mother tongue.[35] This is not to imply, however, that they had absolutely no acquaintance with the local vernacular as an acquired second language. Many of them certainly had some facility in Serbo-Croatian, if only for business purposes, and the trend toward using this Slavic tongue in the streets, if not in the home, was definitely increasing in the twentieth century, especially since by then it was the language of instruction in the schools attended by Jewish pupils.

The 1931 Yugoslav census results show 3,950 individuals, or about 60 percent of the Sarajevo Sephardim, as native speakers of Ladino. Nearly the entire remaining 40 percent reported Serbo-Croatian as their mother tongue.[36] (See table 4.) Census data often proves somewhat unreliable for accurate linguistic analyses.[37] It appears certain, nevertheless, that during the interwar period, while a majority of the Sephardim in Sarajevo still commonly used Ladino among themselves, at the same time a growing number of them were becoming fluent in the local language and speaking it more and more frequently in their daily lives.

As for the Ashkenazim, the Austro-Hungarian census did not consider Yiddish as a separate language, nor were statistics on religious groups by mother tongue compiled for Bosnia before World War I. Hence, in the 1910 Bosnian census the Ashkenazim simply disappear among the German, Hungarian, and Serbo-Croatian categories leaving no trace whatsoever. However, in the prewar period, the majority of Ashkenazim, all fairly recent arrivals, probably considered themselves native speakers of German-Yiddish or Hungarian. By 1931, however, about 45 percent of the Ashkenazim in Sarajevo claimed Serbo-Croatian as their mother tongue, with the rest reporting German, Hungarian, or other foreign languages.[38] (See table 4.) Thus, by World War II most of the Ashkenazim, like the Sephardim, were probably bilingual, if not trilingual, with at least some knowledge of the local vernacular.

Additional insight into the relative degree of linguistic acculturation of the Sephardim and Ashkenazim of Sarajevo into their South Slav milieu may be gained through a comparative analysis of their personal and family names.[39] The Sephardim in Sarajevo rarely attempted to change or slavicize their names, and they had a remarkably small pool of last names. Hence they were usually very easily identifiable. In the communal registry of births, marriages, and deaths, less than thirty old family names constantly recurred. The largest of the "clans" were surnamed Altarac, Papo, and Levi, with Abinun, Albahary, Attias, Danon, Kabiljo, Kamhi, and Maestro not too far behind. Any new name that appeared in the record books could instantly be recognized as belonging to an outsider.

Within the Ashkenazic community, the range of family names was much greater, but they retained one common characteristic. They were almost all of German-Yiddish or Hungarian origin, with some foreign Slavic (Polish or Czech) admixtures; hence, in the context of Yugoslavia at least, they were very typically Jewish. A Sephardic surname is distinctive, but an Ashkenazic surname is often doubtful and may require additional corroboration with a first name or other evidence in order to prove definitive Jewish status. As a general rule, however, if a first name is Hungarian and a last Germanic, or vice versa, it is a relatively safe guess that the person so designated is probably a Jew rather than a member of some other ethnic group.

Sephardic first names reflected the same traditional character as their last names, with few exceptions. The Sephardic custom is to name children directly after living grandparents or even parents; hence the Sarajevo Sephardic birth registry made very monotonous reading, with identical names repeating endlessly. The boys were all called Avram, Isak, Jakov, Haim, Salamon, Ašer, Aron, Samuel, and the like—almost all straight from the Bible. Girls names were somewhat more exotic, if not more varied: Simha, Rena, Ora, Buena, Palomba, Mazel-tov, Djentila, Esperanza, Luna, along with Sara,

Rifka, Rahel, Mirjam, Debora, and Ester. Exceptionally a Cijonista (Zionist) or a Bar Kohba appeared. Such naming patterns, which lasted up until World War II, reflect a very strong sense of the Sephardic cultural heritage and a desire to remain ethnically distinct within their multinational setting. It is clear that people who continued to pass on such names to their children never became completely engulfed by the process of assimilation.

In contrast, it has become an Ashkenazic tradition to give one's child a secular as well as a Hebrew name, basing the latter at least, on the name of a deceased relative. The Ashkenazim in Sarajevo, thus, did not tend to bestow upon their offspring specifically Jewish appelations for everyday use. A random sampling from the birth registry of the Ashkenazic community of Sarajevo revealed a large selection from Henriette, Karoline, Illona, Mathilde, Marianna, and Melanie for girls to Rudolf, Oskar, Aladar, Leopold, Heinrich, Imre, and Wladimir for boys. The boys' list did include several more traditional Jewish names, such as Isidor, Max, Benjamin, Joshua, and David. Their female counterparts, perhaps, were those with names which were more common in Yiddish-speaking Eastern European circles, such as Hermine, Ettle, Fani, Mina, and Bertha; but biblical names for girls were conspicuous in their absence. Many of these names appear to be definitely outside the traditional Jewish framework, but they do not fall within the culture of their South Slav neighbors either. The Ashkenazim, then, did not seem to belong to any distinctly Jewish world, yet neither did they seem to form a part of their Bosnian milieu. They saw themselves primarily as Central Europeans; the natives, however, tended to regard them as aliens.

Linguistic and other evidence indicates that the Sephardim in Sarajevo, while well adapted to their surroundings, resisted total assimilation into their environment and preserved to a large extent their traditional Jewish society. The Ashkenazim, too, did not generally tend to imitate their South Slavic neighbors, but rather tried to retain what they considered a superior culture, their German-Magyar inheritance from Austro-Hungarian times. By doing this they maintained their Jewish identity as well. One way or the other, the Jews remained a distinct group within the body politic; only isolated individuals managed to escape completely from the Jewish fold.

On June 28, 1914, when Gavrilo Princip fired the fatal shot at Archduke Franz Ferdinand, setting off World War I and placing the Bosnian capital on the world map, the Sephardic community of Sarajevo was about to celebrate its three hundred fiftieth anniversary, and the Ashkenazic community was in its thirty-fifth year of existence. The two communities constituted completely separate entities, each with its own synagogues, cemetery, and institutions. Little social interaction took place between them and even less intermarriage.

The Sephardic majority formed an integral part of the Sarajevo scene, yet they continued to live in a Jewish world. The Ashkenazic minority represented an alien element, but they tended to try harder to become part of the general culture. Members of both groups generally spoke Serbo-Croatian as a second language. The Sephardim lived in a cluster in relatively few districts forming a close-knit society; the Ashkenazim were dispersed in various parts of the city resulting in somewhat less personal contact and interdependence. The Ashkenazim belonged mainly to the middle class, both by occupation and by wealth; the Sephardim, with notable exceptions, gravitated toward the lower end of the economic spectrum.

Bosnia-Hercegovina under Austro-Hungarian rule provided a meeting ground for Ottoman and Habsburg Jewry. Because of the differences in their backgrounds, outlooks, and economic and social status, it took time before the two groups began to mingle. With the creation of the Kingdom of Serbs, Croats, and Slovenes in 1918, Bosnian Jewry came within the larger framework of Yugoslavia developing increasing ties with the Belgrade and Zagreb communities. Nevertheless, Sarajevo retained its importance as a significant Jewish center, with its traditional, predominantly Sephardic character.

2

BELGRADE: THE SERBIAN CAPITAL

Situated at the confluence of the Sava and Danube rivers, Belgrade has always been a city of considerable strategic and economic importance in the Balkans and has experienced a very stormy political history. Even in ancient Roman times it served as a key fortress, named Singidunum. After the Turks finally captured the town in 1521, they established it as the administrative center of a separate *pashaluk,* or province. On the border between the Ottoman and Habsburg empires, the city passed back and forth several times between the two great powers in the seventeenth and eighteenth centuries, but remained primarily under Turkish control until the Serbian independence movement began in the early nineteenth century. Belgrade then became the capital of the autonomous principality, later the Kingdom of Serbia and subsequently served as the seat of government of twentieth-century Yugoslavia.

Dominating the city is Kalemegdan, the sprawling old fortress located at the northwest tip where the two major rivers meet. The architecture of public buildings gives a sense of simplicity combined with solidity, as in, for example, the massive, copper-domed Skupština (Assembly) or the rather unpretentious Royal Palace opposite it. Of the many Orthodox churches in the city, the immense Church of Sveti Marko (Saint Mark) and the impressive Saborna Crkva (Cathedral) of the Serbian Patriarch may be the most outstanding. Many private dwellings, however, did not survive the devastation of twentieth-century warfare. In the interwar period Belgrade was a rapidly expanding government town, with limited industry but considerable commerce and crafts, and with a proud tradition of resistance and independence. The local inhabitants tended to be friendly and hospitable in the true Serbian fashion, but were perhaps somewhat provincial on the European scale. Belgrade is still sometimes referred to jokingly as "the largest village in Yugoslavia."

Nothing is known about Belgrade's earliest Jewish inhabitants, and few traces remain of Jewish life there in the Middle Ages. However, individual Jews evidently did engage in trade there under the Serbian Empire in the fourteenth century; undoubtedly a Jewish community also existed, although perhaps not on a continuous basis.[1] Most of the Jewish settlers arrived after the Turkish conquest.

By the mid-sixteenth century a small Sephardic community had established itself in Belgrade. One of the earliest contemporary documents to survive refers to a fire in 1560 which destroyed a number of Jewish homes in the town.[2] The first Jews apparently lived in the western part of town near the Sava River in a Christian district, where the oldest Jewish graves have been found.[3] Most of the later arrivals, however, settled in a region near the Danube called Jalija (the shore) and later also in nearby Dorćol (Turkish for "four ways"), neighboring the Muslim section.[4] This area, several blocks square, to the southeast of Kalemegdan became known as *Jevrejska mala*, the Jewish quarter.

A German traveler named Otendorf, who visited Belgrade in 1663, reported that "the Jews have a very big two-storied house near the Danube . . . where 800 Jews live, and they have their school there as well."[5] This building, surrounding a large courtyard, was sometimes referred to as the Türkischer Judenhof and contained 103 rooms, 49 kitchens, and 27 cellars. A smaller structure, which in the eighteenth century became known as the Teutscher Judenhof, had 47 rooms, 25 kitchens, and 7 cellars.[6] Most of the poorer Jews presumably lived in these quarters and paid rent for them. Jews, however, were allowed to own property, and it is believed that some of the wealthier Jews might have lived among the Christians.[7]

Jalija/Dorćol presents the picture of a typical Ottoman Jewish quarter, with its narrow streets and old stone houses, crowded close together. Sanitary conditions were poor because the area was near the Danube and subject to frequent floods. The exterior of the houses did not look very different from other Turkish houses, with their solid stone walls, windowless lower portions and protruding upper stories. Several families lived around an interior courtyard.[8] As in Sarajevo, Jewish family ties were very strong. Families were large, since early marriages were common and young couples often lived with parents.

The whole community took part in family celebrations such as weddings and bar mitzvahs.

Religious piety was very much a part of everyday existence. Sabbath and holidays were strictly observed. Hanukkah and Purim were especially gala occasions in the Jewish quarter, with singing and dancing in the streets.[9] In fact life in Dorćol was extremely traditional with a special Sephardic flavor lent by the Ladino spoken in the home and the old Spanish *romansas* sung by the women. A touch of the local influence as well was evident in the tales told about Kraljević Marko and Nasredin-hodža (a Serbian and a Turkish folk hero, respectively) and on the menus, with Balkan specialties such as *pogačica* (little cakes with cheese) and *burekitas* (another type of pastry) for the Sabbath and *šljivovica* (plum brandy) and Turkish coffee.[10]

In the seventeenth century Belgrade became the third center of Jewish learning in the Balkans, after Istanbul ànd Salonika. There exists a considerable body of responsa in Hebrew and Ladino written by the Belgrade rabbis of this period. In 1617 Rabbi Juda Lerma of Salonika became chief rabbi of Belgrade and started a yeshiva there. He was succeeded in 1643 by Simha ben Gerson Koen, a native Ashkenazic Jew of Belgrade, and in 1662 by Rabbi Josef Almoznino of Salonika, a biblical and talmudic scholar educated in Belgrade. This cultural growth was interrupted by the arrival of the Austrians in 1688. In that year Rabbi Almoznino and his family, with a number of other Belgrade Jews, were forced to migrate north to Habsburg territory.[11]

While Serbia remained under Ottoman rule, the legal status of the Jews living there closely resembled that of the Jews of Bosnia and other parts of the empire. When the Habsburg armies captured Belgrade, however, they brought with them new restrictions and hardships for the Jewish community. The first occupation of Belgrade came to an end with the Treaty of Karlowitz in 1699, leaving the Jewish quarter with most of its houses and public buildings destroyed. Many of the wealthier Jews had fled to the interior of the Turkish Empire for safety; those who remained could not afford to repair the damages.[12] When the Austrians returned in 1717, they found only thirty-three Jewish families living in Belgrade. Two Jewish communities existed, side by side, one Sephardic, composed of the older settlers from Turkey, and the other Ashkenazic, made up mainly of newcomers who came with the Austrians. The new administration was harsher than the old and interfered more in the life of the individual Jews.

Belgrade Jews were subject to much the same limitations as other Jews in the Habsburg Empire. The number of Jews permitted in Belgrade was limited and they were not allowed to live in the Serbian interior. Jews could not own real estate or live outside the Jewish quarter. They could engage in commerce and certain other occupations, but many trades were closed to them. Jews paid a special toleration tax, as well as taxes on such commodities as wine and meat. They were allowed to have their own slaughter house outside of town. Although the building of a synagogue was officially forbidden, with the help of Josef Süss Oppenheimer, the court financier and army supplier to the Governor of Serbia, Prince Alexander of Württemberg, the Jewish community managed to gain concessions in order to rebuild their synagogue and school.[13] With the Treaty of Belgrade in 1739, the Austrians left the town, along with some of the Ashkenazic Jews, who moved across the Sava to Zemun and Novi Sad.[14]

The violent political history of Belgrade had serious detrimental effects on the Jewish community, which stood outside political life and yet was the helpless victim of the frequent military operations. The mid-eighteenth century saw a fifty-year period of quiet development and the growth of the Sephardic community, which was supplemented by new migrations from the south. In 1777 the Jewish population is estimated to have been approximately eight hundred.[15] But this peaceful interlude was shattered by the Austrian-Turkish war of 1788–89, which once again brought general property damage and population dislocation. On the whole the Belgrade Jews, especially the Sephardim, favored Turkish rule over Austrian. Nevertheless, of those Jews who remained after the Austrians came, many left when the Turks returned, fearing Turkish reprisals against them.[16] The position of the Jews was not very secure at the turn of the nineteenth century.

The first Serbian uprising (1804–13) began as a revolt against the lawlessness and violence of the local janissaries, rather than a war of independence against the sultan. The Jews did not take an active part in these events, aside from a few in Zemun on the Austrian side of the Sava who reportedly supplied wheat, animals, and weapons to the Serbs. A large number of Jews fled to Zemun and elsewhere to escape the danger. Once more, despite orders from Karageorge, the leader of the revolt, homes and stores and the synagogue in the Jewish quarter were damaged or destroyed.[17] The second Serbian uprising (1813–17), led by Miloš Obrenović, was a fight for Serbian autonomy, which was formally granted by the sultan in 1830. Now the Jews found themselves not in the Muslim Ottoman Empire or the Catholic Austrian Empire, but in an Orthodox Serbian principality, and they were not sure whether to regard the Serbs as enemies or friends.

Miloš Obrenović "remained essentially a pasha, albeit a Serbian one."[18] During his period in office, from 1817 to 1839 and again from 1859 to 1860, the Jews of Belgrade enjoyed favorable circumstances. As ruler, Prince Miloš showed a liking and respect for a number of Jews, whom he appointed to his personal service. Lazar Levenzon, an Austrian Jew, was his tailor. Josif Šlezinger, a Jew from Sombor in southern Hungary, became conductor of the military guard band. Indeed, Šlezinger is referred to as the father of Serbian musical life in the nineteenth century.[19] The most interesting example of such benevolence toward individual Jews, however, is the case of Hajim Davičo, who served as Miloš' state banker and financier for many years.[20]

In 1839 Miloš was forced to abdicate his office and go into exile as a result of pressure from the seventeen-man senatorial body which had been created under the Constitution of 1838 granted by the sultan. The same fate befell his successor, his son Michael, in 1842. The Senate elected instead Alexander Karageorgević, son of the revolutionary leader. The weakness of the new ruler, who was completely under the control of his senators, proved unfortunate for the Jews of Serbia.

In Turkish times the towns had been the domains of Turks, Greeks, and Jews, with the Serbian population living in the rural areas. This picture began to change in the nineteenth century as the Serbs joined the urban scene. The growing Serbian commercial class, in particular the businessmen in the provincial towns near Belgrade, carried on an active campaign against their Jewish competitors, who had been living in the Serbian interior, mainly in Šabac, Smederevo, and Požarevac, almost as long as they had been in Belgrade. The demands of the Serbian businessmen to help improve their economic position vis-à-vis the Jews found support among the members of the Senate. On October 30, 1846, a law was promulgated whereby Jews were prohibited from engaging in commerce or owning real estate in the interior. As a result many of the Jews in rural Serbia were compelled to liquidate their property and move to Belgrade or else leave the country entirely.[21]

Both the Serbs and the Jews welcomed the return to office of Miloš in 1859. The seventy-eight-year-old patriarch abolished the restrictions against the Jews with a government decree:

His Highness, wishing to make all the benefits of freedom equal for all subjects of Serbia, regardless of nationality or faith, orders that all former laws which are incompatible with the present decree be considered abrogated. The authorities will ensure that every inhabitant of this land, whatever his faith or nationality, may not be prevented from living where he wants or from engaging in whatever trade or profession he wishes.[22]

Miloš, however, died a year after he resumed office.

His son Michael who again succeeded him (1860–68) did not follow his father's benevolent policy toward the Jews. In 1861 a decree was passed similar to that of 1846, and during the next few years a series of expulsions of Jews from rural Serbia took place.[23]

In 1865 several scandals occurred in the town of Šabac which suddenly attracted world attention to the Jews of Serbia. On January 16 a Jew by the name of Jakob Alkalaj was murdered, the following day another Jew, Solomon Abinun, was drowned, and in April of the same year a sixteen-year-old girl was supposedly baptized by force.[24] The Jews of Šabac petitioned the Alliance Israélite Universelle in Paris for help. Appeals for diplomatic assistance were made to England, Italy, and the Ottoman Empire. England became directly involved in the plight of the Jews in Šabac after an English citizen, Israel Stern, was prevented from conducting his business activities there.[25] Due to expediency, and perhaps outside pressures as well, the discriminatory legislation ceased and Jews were tacitly allowed to remain in the interior.

None of these laws directly applied to the Jews of Belgrade, who constituted more than half of the Jewish population of Serbia. Nevertheless, these unfortunate incidents did have a considerable effect on the Jewish community of Belgrade because on the one hand, most of the Jewish businessmen who left the provincial towns came to the capital in generally impoverished circumstances, and on the other hand, some Jews left Belgrade at this time out of fear of possible future measures.

The Constitution of 1869 guaranteed the liberty and property rights of the individual and made all Serbian citizens equal before the law and eligible for public office. There were to be no religious qualifications for citizenship, and although the Eastern Orthodox Church was named as the official religion, the exercise of all other recognized religions was allowed and placed under the protection of the law. This document specified, however, that the laws of 1846 and 1861 were not to be revoked.[26] The Jews of Serbia were thus not granted full civil rights since, in theory at least, they could not live or own property outside Belgrade.

Ironically, even without receiving all the rights of citizenship, the duties of citizenship were required of the Jews. The Balkan Jews had never served in the Ottoman military establishment nor had Jews previously served in the Serbian army. In 1869, however, all Serbian subjects, including the Jews, became liable for military service. A number of Jewish soldiers fought in the Turkish wars of 1876–77 and four Jews, two of them doctors, were decorated for bravery. Nevertheless, it is doubtful whether Jews were allowed to reach officer rank before 1888.[27]

De jure second-class citizenship, however, does not appear to have had a serious detrimental effect on the actual state of Jews living in Belgrade. According to Isidore Loeb in 1877, Jews had all municipal and political rights: they could vote and were eligible for election to the municipal council; they could send two delegates to the chamber of commerce and be arbitrators in commercial disputes; they could even theoretically be named deputies to the Skupština (Assembly) or members of the Senate. Indeed, one Jew, Avram Ozerović (1848–1916), a member of an established Belgrade merchant family, took part in the Skupština debates of 1877.[28]

In 1878, at the Congress of Berlin, the Great Powers stipulated that the newly won independence of Serbia, Rumania, and Montenegro and the autonomy of Bulgaria were conditional upon the granting of full equality to all subjects regardless of religion. Article 35 of the treaty read as follows:

In Serbia, difference of religious beliefs or creeds may not stand in the way of anyone as a cause for exclusion or disqualification from that which concerns the enjoyment of civil and political rights, admission to public employments, offices and honors or the practice of different professions and occupations in any locality.

Freedom and open practice of all religions are guaranteed to all [persons] under the jurisdiction of the Serbian state as well as to foreigners, and no impediments may be raised, be they towards the hierarchical organization of the different religions, be they towards their relations with their spiritual leaders.[29]

Unlike Rumania, Serbia complied with her treaty obligations. In 1888 the civil rights of the Jews gained formal recognition in the new constitution in a clause guaranteeing full equality to all residents of the Kingdom of Serbia without distinction as to faith or nationality.[30] Thereafter, there was never to be any question as to the citizenship status of Serbian Jewry.

The legal status of the Belgrade Jewish community per se remained somewhat ill defined until the mid-nineteenth century. In 1865 in a book entitled *Les Serbes de Turquie*, A. Ubicini wrote:

The Israelite community, although it has existed in fact almost from time immemorial, has not yet been recognized by law. It possesses nevertheless a synagogue in Belgrade and enjoys full religious autonomy, in the same way, if not by the same title, as Christian churches. A committee was recently established to deliberate together with the rabbi and give the community which he represents the legal sanction which it has lacked hithertofore.[31]

Indeed, with the sanction of Prince Miloš, the community built a *beth hamidrash* (study house) in 1818 and the following year, on Rosh Hashanah, it celebrated the opening of the newly renovated Old Synagogue.[32] It was not until 1866, however, that the community was formally constituted and received an official charter. The first president, Jahiel Ruso, was reported to be a very hard taskmaster, holding board meetings which lasted over two hours every day of the week except Saturday.[33] While previously the community had conducted all its internal business in Ladino, Ruso introduced Serbian as the language of administration for Jewish affairs. In order to do this, he had to hire a Serbian secretary, named Kuzman Kuzmanović, who took charge of keeping records and correspondence until the transition was complete.[34] Thereafter, the legal position of the Sephardic community was clearly defined and regulated by communal statutes.

The Ashkenazic community in Belgrade evolved into a completely separate entity. Ashkenazim began arriving in Belgrade in significant numbers only in the second half of the nineteenth century. In 1869 they took over the old National Theater to use as a synagogue, and in 1892 the Serbian government formally granted religious autonomy to the Ashkenazic community.[35]

After emancipation, the Jewish community of Belgrade entered an era of steady growth, as did the capital as a whole. Unlike Sarajevo, Belgrade demonstrates a considerable degree of ethnic and religious homogeneity. Since the second half of the nineteenth century, over 75 percent of the local residents have been Serbian Orthodox. The remaining inhabitants have consisted of Catholics (including not only Croats, but also Germans, Hungarians and other Slavs), Jews, Muslims, and Protestants.[36] The Jewish population of the city grew from 2,599 in 1890 to 4,844 in 1921, to 7,906 ten years later. (See table 3). By 1939 an estimated 10,388 Jews, 8,500 of whom were Sephardim and 1,888 Ashkenazim, were living in Belgrade.[37] The absolute number of Jews climbed rapidly, the result mainly of a high birth rate before World War I and migration from other parts of the country in the postwar period, but their relative strength diminished against the background of the flood of newcomers to the Yugoslav capital. Thus their percentage of the population total declined gradually from 5 percent in 1895 to 3 percent in 1931.

Until the late nineteenth century virtually all of Belgrade's Sephardim continued to live in Dorćol. In the 1870s the wealthier members of the community began to move out of the Jewish quarter one by one, thereby creating the dichotomy between *los de abajo* (Ladino for "those from below"), who remained behind, and *los de arriba* (those from above), who had climbed the social ladder to Zerek, the business section up the hill and across the streetcar tracks. This geographic separation based on socioeconomic differentiation remained significant in communal life, especially until World War I when the old Jewish quarter was heavily bombed and many of its inhabitants were forced to find new homes.[38] In 1921 there were 3,171 Jews—65 percent of the city's total Jewish population—still living in Dorćol. That old Jewish neighborhood had lost much of its Jewish character, however, as only 23 percent of its population were now Jewish. The rest of the Jews were fairly evenly distributed among five other sections of town, showing some preference for the central business districts. In the wealthiest suburb of Topčider-Senjak, however, only 16 Jews were to be found.[39] Those who had escaped from the lower class Jewish district had improved their social status but apparently not yet reached the top.

The Ashkenazic Jews, most of whom arrived in Belgrade in the twentieth century, neither lived in Dorćol in significant numbers nor really formed an enclave of their own. Like their counterparts in Sarajevo, the Ashkenazim of Belgrade lived wherever their financial resources permitted, mainly in the more respectable central districts of the city. While the bulk of the Sephardim remained within the former Jewish quarter, their wealthier brethren as well as the Ashkenazim lived outside it, distributed in the various parts of the capital.[40]

The Jews in Belgrade, as elsewhere in Yugoslavia, were heavily concentrated in commercial activities and white-collar employment and, to a lesser extent, crafts and the free professions. Interestingly enough, on the eve of World War II, the occupational structure among the Sephardim and the Ashkenazim displayed striking similarities. In the Sephardic community in 1940 among the 2,002 taxpayers, 27 percent were merchants, 21 percent clerks or employees, 8 percent artisans, and 4 percent physicians, lawyers, or engineers. Among the 1,091 Ashkenazic communal taxpayers, 20 percent were merchants, 25 percent white-collar workers, 6 percent artisans, and 8 percent members of the professions mentioned.[41] Thus, while a higher proportion of professionals and white-collar workers were to be found among the Ashkenazim and more merchants and artisans among the Sephardim, these discrepancies were not very pronounced.

Communal tax records, the basis for much of this analysis, do not provide a complete picture of Jewish occupational stratification, however. They tend to include only heads of households or independent self-supporters, and they exclude all persons not earning enough income to pay taxes. Furthermore, from such sources it is impossible to arrive at an accurate estimate of the participation of Jewish women in the working market. According to the 1940 Belgrade tax lists, 405 of the 3,193 taxpayers, that is, 13 percent, were women: 235 Sephardic and 170 Ashkenazic. Further analysis reveals that 67 percent of the total—76 percent of the Sephardic, but 55 percent of the Ashkenazic tax-paying women—were either housewives, property owners, or "unemployed," while the remaining 33 percent were mainly clerks, merchants, or fashion experts. There were 6 women physicians (2 Sephardim and 4 Ashkenazim), 3 teachers and 1 engineer (all Ashkenazim).[42] From this rather limited sample, it might appear that in Belgrade a somewhat higher proportion of Ashkenazic women worked to support themselves and their families as compared to their Sephardic sisters. This data is, however, insufficient to determine how many Jewish women were actually employed outside the home.

Along with occupational diversity, the question of relative wealth should also be considered. Since tax lists supply the primary information on this subject also, there are dangers inherent in any attempt to determine financial status on the basis of such material. The major problem stems from the fact that those members of the Jewish community who did not earn enough income to pay taxes—especially the unemployed and those on welfare, but also the poorer workers—were not recorded in these sources. Hence an accurate estimate of their numbers in either absolute or relative terms is extremely difficult to determine.

In 1932, in addition to the 1,297 taxpayers in the Belgrade Sephardic community, there were an estimated 175 households of unemployed and needy poor who were tax exempt. Some 83 families were receiving aid from various Jewish communal agencies. Among those able to pay taxes, by far the largest group, 919 taxpayers, or 71 percent, were in the lowest category, paying less than 480 dinars each, while a relatively small group of wealthy at the top (104 households) paying more than 1,800 dinars comprised only 8 percent of the tax-paying membership.[43] Eight years later, by 1940, the tax list expanded by about 33 percent to 2,009 taxpayers, whereas the community as a whole grew only by about 25 percent during that period. It cannot be determined how many Jews were excluded from taxation in that year, and undoubtedly there were still a considerable number in that category. Nevertheless, in a comparison of distribution figures by wealth for 1932 and 1940, despite the fact that now 73 percent belonged to the lowest tax bracket, the conclusion cannot be that the community was growing poorer. On the contrary, more people were able to pay taxes, hence the lowest category expanded to include at least part of those formerly exempted. The wealthier element in Belgrade Sephardic society seems to have remained fairly constant.

The Ashkenazim in Belgrade, by comparison, showed a somewhat greater leaning toward the middle and upper tax brackets. While 67 percent of the Ashkenazic households belonged to the lower income category, it would appear from the high number of taxpayers relative to the total size of the community (1,085 heads of families out of 2– to 3,000 individuals) that few, if any, of the Belgrade Ashkenazim were tax-exempt due to financial circumstances.[44] The Ashkenazim included fewer poor and slightly more well-to-do than their Sephardic brethren.

Thus, Belgrade Jews, while by no means affluent as a group, were by and large gainfully employed and economically upwardly mobile. The Belgrade Sephardic community was fortunate not to have been faced with a poverty problem comparable to that of its Sarajevo counterpart. It would seem that wealth was distributed somewhat more equitably in the national capital than in the Bosnian center.

The growing trend among Belgrade Jews toward white-collar jobs and the free professions was made possible by the shift in the late nineteenth century from purely religious to predominantly secular training. As in Sarajevo, in the first half of the nineteenth century, the education of Jewish children in Belgrade lay completely in the hands of the Jewish authorities. It is unknown whether any Jewish children attended state schools at that time. The census reports of 1822 listed 239 Jewish taxpayers, with 22 individuals legally tax-exempt as religious officials, teachers, or students. By 1845 there were 6 teachers and 76 pupils reported.[45] In 1847 a fund was established for a new Jewish school, which was to serve as the office for the community officials and the rabbi and as a library and meeting place as well.[46] In these years instruction was given not by trained teachers, but by part-time religious officials, with the rabbi teaching the more advanced students. The language of instruction was Ladino; Serbian was not taught in the schools but had to be studied with a private tutor.[47] In the 1860s, however, Serbian and German were being taught, along with Jewish subjects, in the higher grades and teachers were being paid by communal tax.[48]

By the second half of the century, Jewish children were also to be found in state schools. In 1869 a total of 146 boys and 63 girls were attending elementary schools, presumably both state and private institutions, and 21 Jewish pupils were reported to be attending high school for the first time.[49] Four years later there arose a problem as to the language of instruction to be used in the public school in the Jewish quarter, since the teacher complained that the majority of his pupils could not understand Serbian.[50] Perhaps as early as 1864 the state established a Jewish girls' school with a Jewish woman as teacher.[51] Because religious instruction was compulsory in state schools, special arrangements were made for Jewish pupils: in elementary school they supposedly received eighteen hours a week of religious training and in high school, six hours. Bible was taught in Hebrew and the rest of the subjects in Serbian.[52] Thus, by the turn of the century Jewish children received their early education in public schools, which were essentially secular in nature, and used Serbian as the language of instruction. Jewish religious education became supplementary to the regular curriculum.

Until the end of the nineteenth century, Ladino constituted the dominant language of the Sephardic community in Belgrade. Almost the entire literary output of the community was published in Ladino, although some works also appeared in Hebrew. In 1837 a Jewish press was established in Belgrade, the only one in the Balkans outside Salonika and Istanbul. Among its first publications were some of the writings of Jehuda Haj Alkalaj, the rabbi in nearby Zemun, who was one of the forerunners of modern Zionism. This press also issued the translations and educational texts written in Ladino by Moša David Alkalaj, a native of Belgrade and for many years rabbi in the Sephardic community of Vienna.[53] The chief rabbi of the Sephardic community from 1886 to 1894, Simon Bernfeld, a well-known scholar from Berlin, published a Ladino translation of his *History of the Jews*.[54] The only Jewish periodical to appear in Belgrade before the end of the century was a popular monthly in Ladino called *El amigo del pueblo* (The Friend of the People). Such a preponderance of materials in Ladino is indeed striking.

In the 1895 census 80 percent of Serbian Jewry declared Ladino as their mother tongue, and only 3 percent claimed Serbian. The rest acknowledged German, Hungarian, or other languages. (See table 5.) The case in Belgrade was much the same: 77 percent opted for Ladino and only 4 percent chose Serbian. Only five years later a remarkable shift in linguistic affiliation took place. A mere 27 percent of the Jews of Serbia reported themselves as native Ladino speakers, while 46 percent adopted Serbian.[55] This fantastic jump in the number of native Serbian speakers from less than 3 percent to 46 percent over a five-year period cannot be accepted without question, however. Undoubtedly, by the turn of the century increasing numbers of Jews had acquired a working knowledge of Serbian, whether at school or in the marketplace, but it seems highly unlikely that Serbian had actually become the language most frequently used in the home at that date. According to this evidence from the 1900 census over half of the Jewish population of Serbia, and hence of Belgrade, were undoubtedly bilingual. Claiming Serbian as one's native tongue, while clearly not absolutely honest, nevertheless seems to indicate a significant change in identification with their environment for Serbian Jews especially among the Sephardim.

According to the 1931 Yugoslav census, 4,285 Jews, or about 54 percent of the total Jewish population of Belgrade and the surrounding district, considered Serbo-Croatian to be their mother tongue, 2,350 individuals (30 percent) claimed Ladino, while the remaining Jews reported German (8 percent), Hungarian (5 percent) or other foreign languages (3 percent).[56] The proportion of native Serbo-Croatian speakers proved to be considerably higher among the Sephardim than among the Ashkenazim in Belgrade, however. About one-third of the Sephardim still retained Ladino as their dominant language, but close to two-thirds of the Sephardic community had officially adopted Serbo-Croatian. By contrast over 90 percent of the Ashkenazim reported non-South Slav languages for census purposes.[57] While this Ashkenazic figure seems extremely high, it may be accounted for, in part at least, by the relatively recent arrival of the vast majority of the Belgrade Ashkenazic community. At any rate there is very little doubt that the Belgrade Sephardim were much better acculturated linguistically to their Serbian milieu than their Ashkenazic counterparts. By 1939 virtually the entire Sephardic population had definitely acquired a knowledge of the local vernacular, either as their primary or secondary language, and many, if not most, of the Ashkenazim had probably done so too.

A further possible outward sign of linguistic acculturation is the changing of Jewish names to match those of the local populace. This form of integration never occurred in Yugoslavia on any significant scale. Only on rare occasions did Jews add the South Slav suffix *ić* to their last names. Even when such an operation was performed, the Jewish origin of the name was seldom erased. In Belgrade, for example, one finds among the Sephardim such surnames as Avramović, Rafailović, Rubenović, Jakovljević, or even Čelebonović, Demajorović, and Tajtacaković. It is quite clear, however, that these Jews, in adapting their names, were merely trying to display patriotism without attempting to disguise their real identity. In general, Jewish names in Belgrade tended to retain their nonslavicized form. Among the Sephardim the most common family names proved to be Alkalaj, Almozlino, Demajo, Kalderon, Konfino, Mevorah, Pijade, Pinto, Romano, and of course, Levi and Koen, although other surnames also occurred.[58] Within the Ashkenazic community the range of family names was much greater, but they too tended to be fairly easy to identify amid the general nomenclature of the local Slavic inhabitants.[59]

The Jewish population of Belgrade, especially its Sephardic component, appears to have been more fully integrated linguistically into its environment than its Sarajevo counterpart, adopting Serbo-Croatian considerably earlier in its schools and for its communal records. According to the census data, at least, Belgrade Jews, especially the Sephardim, began to claim Serbian as their native tongue much sooner than the Sarajevo Sephardim. Belgrade Sephardim were more likely to slavicize their names, both first and last, than their Sarajevo brethren. Belgrade Jews were in general less distinct from their overwhelmingly Serbian Orthodox neighbors than the Sarajevo Jews in their multireligioethnic milieu. The evidence would seem to indicate less cultural differentiation and greater overall acculturation among Belgrade Jewry than among Sarajevo Jewry.

By the time Austria-Hungary declared war on Serbia on July 28, 1914, Belgrade Jewry had already proven themselves loyal Serbian citizens. Both Sephardim and Ashkenazim had fought bravely in defense of their country in the Balkan wars, and they continued to display their patriotism both on the battlefield and on the home front throughout World War I.[60]

The Jews of the capital, especially the Sephardim, were accepted as part of the local scene and generally enjoyed a friendly relationship with their Serbian neighbors. They spoke Serbian, as well as Ladino, sent their children to Serbian schools, and participated actively in public life.

In the twentieth century the overall population of Belgrade grew rapidly, and so too did its Jewish component. Much of this increase must be attributed to immigration rather than to a particularly high birth rate. Because of its economic opportunities, the national capital was an expanding metropolis that naturally attracted Jews as well as many others from the surrounding areas.

While as a group these Jews can by no means be considered affluent and some poverty did exist among them, for the most part, they were comfortably situated. The Ashkenazic newcomers tended to be economically somewhat better off than the Sephardic "natives," but the discrepancy between them was not very great.

The Sephardim and the Ashkenazim continued to maintain separate communal institutions, but relations between them gradually improved with the passage of time.

Belgrade and Sarajevo constituted the two largest and most important Sephardic centers in the South Slav lands. The third major Jewish community and the Ashkenazic stronghold was to be found in Zagreb.

3

ZAGREB: CROATIAN CITADEL

Located in the foothills of the Medvednica Mountains, Zagreb stands near the site of Andautonia, an old Roman settlement on the Sava River. At the end of the eleventh century, King Ladislas of Hungary established a Croatian bishopric, known as Kaptol, adjacent to the fortified Slavic town, then called Gradec. After the Tartar invasion of 1242, Gradec became a royal free city, noted for its fairs and handicrafts in addition to being an administrative center. Meanwhile, Kaptol grew in importance for its extensive feudal landholdings.[1] The two entities, the civil Gradec and the ecclesiastical Kaptol, continued to maintain a separate existence until 1850, when they officially merged with other nearby districts to form the city of Zagreb.

Zagreb appears strikingly Central European and entirely western in orientation. Situated in central Croatia, the two medieval walled towns, which have been preserved largely intact, managed to escape Turkish domination, while remaining under Hungarian control. In the nineteenth century Zagreb became a bastion of the Croatian nationalist movement. Indeed, in its main square stood an equestrian statue of Ban Jelačić, the Croatian general who had led his loyal Habsburg troops against the Magyar "rebels" in 1848. He was portrayed with his unsheathed sword pointed straight at the heart of Budapest.[2]

In the second half of the nineteenth century Zagreb commenced a period of rapid expansion. In 1848 the city once again served as the seat of the Croatian *ban* (or governor), and according to the Nagodba (or Agreement) between Hungary and Croatia in 1868, Zagreb became the capital of the semiautonomous province of Croatia-Slavonia. At the same time it developed into a major hub of the Hungarian railroad system and began the process of industrialization. During the interwar years Zagreb proved to be the leading industrial, commercial, and financial center in Yugoslavia.

Twentieth-century Zagreb comprises several distinct regions. Gornji Grad (Upper Town), the old walled Gradec, has a somewhat aristocratic air, with its upper class residential mansions and baroque administrative buildings. Its independent spirit is symbolized by the Croatian and Zagreb coats of arms atop the stately Catholic Church of Sveti Marko in its midst. To the east is Kaptol, represented by the towering spires of the majestic neo-Gothic St. Stephen's Cathedral, which was begun in the thirteenth century but not completed for almost six hundred years. Beneath lies Donji Grad (Lower Town), with its growing commercial and industrial centers built since the nineteenth century. This area gradually developed into the city's cultural district as well. Characteristic of its newer, slightly ornate style of architecture is the elegant Croatian National Theater, the Yugoslav Academy of Science and Arts, founded in 1862, and the university, established in 1874. Instead of the narrow, winding streets of Upper Town, Lower Town boasts broad boulevards and many parks and open squares. Zagreb thus lacks the somewhat oriental, Balkan flavor of Belgrade or Sarajevo, but instead in atmosphere tends to resemble Budapest or Vienna, only on a smaller scale.

The Jews did not actually enter the Zagreb scene until the end of the eighteenth century. Perhaps a few individuals did live there some three hundred years previously, but it seems most unlikely that a permanent community existed at that time.[3] After the Habsburg succession to the Hungarian throne in 1526, the Jews were expelled from Croatia. In 1729 the Croatian Sabor (Parliament) again forbade Jews to reside in this region. After 1750 Jews were permitted to remain in the territory for three days for trade purposes and to attend the annual fair, but as late as 1783 they were still not officially allowed to settle in Zagreb.[4] These regulations relaxed somewhat as a result of the Edict of Toleration of Joseph II and the subsequent legislation of Leopold I.

Jews first received permission to live in Zagreb in the 1780s. At that time the town, which was one of the largest in the area, had a population of less than 5,000.[5] To settle there each household had to obtain the right of residency from either the magistrate of Gradec or the bishop of Kaptol and then pay a special annual "toleration tax." In 1806 approximately twenty families in both parts of town formally established a joint Jewish community.[6]

The Jews who came to Zagreb were all Ashkenazim from various parts of Central Europe. A majority of the early arrivals migrated from Hungary, especially western Hungary and Burgenland; others, from Moravia and Austria and some from Galicia. By occupation most heads of households were merchants or petty traders, but a few were artisans and communal functionaries.[7]

With rare exceptions these Jews did not possess much wealth in the mid-nineteenth century. In 1842 Zagreb Jewry expended 600 forints in toleration taxes to the local authorities. This amount equaled the entire budget of the Jewish community. The Zagreb district included 103 Jewish taxpayers, of whom perhaps 70 lived in the town itself. Of these, 49 persons paid the minimum rate of 2 forints, while only 1 was assessed in the highest category at 85 forints. This same individual, David Blum by name, also contributed 200 forints in communal taxes, a sum equal to the total salary of the cantor or about half the amount which the rabbi received![8]

In 1838 a group of Croatian merchants appealed to the magistrate to ban foreign Jews from residing in the area or even attending fairs.[9] Although this proposal was rejected, the event nevertheless helped to remind the local Jews of their precarious legal status and spurred their attempt to secure the removal of all disabilities against them. The following year the Jews of Zagreb and nearby Varaždin submitted a petition in the name of all Croatian Jewry to the Hungarian authorities requesting them "to bestow the right of residency and to determine their civil status so that they might acquire property both under civil and manorial jurisdiction and maintain it, be apprenticed into a guild and pursue a craft, travel within the countryside for commercial purposes and profess their religion freely within the borders of the country."[10]

In 1840 the Hungarian Diet passed Law No. 29, which contained the following provisions: Jews might settle anywhere in Hungary or Croatia, except in mining areas; Jews were allowed to own factories and engage in trade and crafts, but might only employ other Jews; they might also enter the free professions and the arts; they could buy property in the towns where they were formerly permitted to live; they must record both first and last names in communal registry books to be kept by the local rabbi; and all legally valid agreements must conform to the language of the land.[11] Despite the fact that this law received royal sanction, it was not approved by the Croatian Sabor. In 1843 Zagreb Jews submitted another petition to the Sabor to improve the status of the Jews, but it too had no effect.

The earlier law was amended by the Hungarian Diet in 1844, thereby abolishing the toleration tax, allowing Jews unlimited settlement, enabling Jews to purchase group property, and permitting Christian employees. The Croatian Sabor still opposed granting these rights to Jews, however.[12] Nonetheless, in 1846 the toleration tax was eliminated in Croatia upon payment of a substantial lump sum.[13]

The struggle over the emancipation of Hungarian and, as a corollary, Croatian Jewry continued amid stormy debate. In 1849 the Hungarian National Assembly adopted a bill granting civil rights to Jews, but this had no practical effect, since shortly thereafter the Habsburgs crushed the Hungarian revolution and restored their old regime. Following the Ausgleich (or the Austro-Hungarian Compromise) of 1867, the Hungarian Diet the next year bestowed upon the Jews complete emancipation, that is, unconditional political and civil equality with non-Jewish subjects.[14] (This act paralleled a similar law promulgated the previous year by the Austrian Reichsrat for the Cisleithanian half of the Dual Monarchy.) The Jews of Croatia, however, had to wait five more years before they received the same rights, since according to the Nagodba of 1868, Croatia was autonomous with regard to religious affairs. Finally, on October 21, 1873, the Sabor adopted a law on civil equality for the Jews of Croatia, Slavonia, and Dalmatia, which stated the following:

Adherents of the Israelite faith are recognized both with regard to the free exercise of their religious laws and with regard to the enjoyment of political and civil rights as being on equal footing with the adherents of other faiths recognized by law in Croatia and Slavonia.

With regard to Israelite religious affairs, the state retains the right of highest supervision as pertaining to it, and also its legal control remains without restraint over Israelite educational affairs.[15]

At last, after having lived in Croatia with special residency permits for almost a hundred years, the Jews became eligible for full citizenship.

The granting of political equality to Jews as individuals did not necessarily signify complete religious equality for the Jews as a group, however. That official discrimination still persisted became apparent once again in the Law on Religious Relations, which the Sabor promulgated in 1905. This law promised, in Article 1, that "every legally recognized church or religious community is entitled to profess its own religion."[16] Subsequently, in Article 14, it stated that "conversion to whichever of the legally recognized religions is free according to one's own judgment for anyone who is eighteen years of age."[17] Nevertheless, according to the official explanatory note for this article which accompanied the text, this was not exactly the case. The addendum read as follows:

... Thus according to the proposed plan conversion from any Christian religion to a non-Christian [religion] is not possible. This single exception from the principle of legal equality is brought about due to the fact that a contrary ruling would be inconsistent with national conviction and feeling, and the demand for such a ruling has not manifested itself even on the part of the relatively small group of those with material interests themselves.[18]

On November 19, 1905, representatives from all the Jewish communities in Croatia-Slavonia met together in Zagreb to discuss this proposed law, which had recently been made public, and to protest against the restrictions regarding conversions.[19] Despite the lengthy petition which the Jewish leaders submitted to the authorities, the law passed in its original form and officially remained in effect for more than two decades.[20] Thus, although Croatian Jewry enjoyed many benefits due to their emancipated status, they never actually achieved complete acceptance as equals.

Shortly after the Croatian Sabor approved the Law on Religious Relations, it also issued a Law on the Organization of the Israelite Religious Community. This 1906 statute clarified and codified existing legislation but also revived controversy concerning the freedom of religious practice within the Jewish community itself. The new law brought to the fore once again the question of the status of the Orthodox minority, an issue which had constituted a problem within the Zagreb community for over sixty years.

The struggle between Orthodoxy and Reform had erupted for the first time in 1840. In that year the community hired as its preacher and religious instructor Moritz (Mavro) Goldman, a modern rabbi with a secular education who had studied under several famous rabbis in Prague and also under S. D. Luzzatto, the noted biblical and Hebraic scholar in Padua.[21] Goldman, with the consent of the communal leadership, introduced a number of reforms into the traditional service, such as sermons in German on the High Holy Days and every fourth Sabbath, decorum in the synagogue, choral singing, and the elimination of some of the *piyyutim* (religious poems).[22] As a result, in 1841 a schism occurred. Twelve of the more conservative members broke away and began to hold their own services under the bishop's auspices in Kaptol, thereby becoming known as the Vlaška

Street community, named after the main street in the clerical town. This split was based not on geography but on religious belief—the protest of the Orthodox against incipient Reform.

The Orthodox group, with the spiritual leadership of Aron Palotta, the official rabbi of Zagreb until his death in 1843, established a separate house of prayer and soon acquired their own cemetery.[23] The executive of the established Jewish community of Zagreb submitted a complaint against this secession to the authorities, claiming that the joint community, which comprised both Gradec and Kaptol, had by common consent recently built a new synagogue, hired a modern rabbi, and founded their own school. They accused the separatists of trying to destroy these institutions. The Orthodox, it was stated, refused to contribute to the rent for the synagogue or pay their communal or school taxes. Their children did not have proper religious instruction, their weddings were not conducted according to state law, and they did not record the birth of their children in the communal registry. In sum, the petition concluded, the secessionists were hindering the community from following progressive trends and were causing trouble and confusion. The Orthodox, of course, rebutted these charges.[24]

During the early years of the dispute, the Orthodox came under the jurisdiction of the bishop of Kaptol, who proved willing to protect them. After the merger of Gradec and Kaptol into a single municipality in 1850, however, the authorities refused to recognize the Orthodox as legally constituting a separate community. The Orthodox received permission to erect their own synagogue but were denied the right to maintain their own communal administration and hire their own rabbi and kosher slaughterers. According to a gubernatorial ordinance of 1852, all Jews must constitute a single community with one rabbi to keep the registry for all births, circumcisions, marriages, and burials. In 1856 a temporary reconciliation was effected between the two sides.[25]

The dispute broke out anew after the community constructed a synagogue with an organ in 1867 and introduced a modern prayerbook for the High Holy Days, the Mannheimer Machsor. The Orthodox faction once again petitioned the Sabor in 1870 to recognize them as a separate religious rite and thus free them from having to pay communal taxes which would help cover the expenses of the new building. Finally in 1873, despite considerable opposition from the established community, the Old Believers, as they were called in the official documents, gained the independent status for which they had fought for so many decades.[26]

The 1906 Law on the Organization of the Israelite Religious Community, however, once more eliminated the separate existence of the Orthodox community. Article 2 stated:

Each religious community has its own separate district within the borders of the Kingdom of Croatia and Slavonia.
Only one religious community may exist in the same district.
Every Israelite belongs to that religious community in the district in which he has a permanent residence.[27]

This regulation, apparently patterned after the 1892 Austrian law on Jewish communities rather than the Hungarian model, constituted a considerable victory for the established, Neologue community.[28]

The Orthodox, who had initially split with the main community over the hiring of a modern, secularly educated rabbi, felt further threatened by the requirements for a rabbinical appointment as stipulated in the new law. Articles 10 and 11 stated that all religious functionaries must be subjects of the land of the Crown of St. Stephen, that is, Hungary, and must command a working knowledge of the Croatian language. Moreover, a rabbi must possess both professional training and a general education, including at least a gymnasium, or high school, matriculation certificate. Without these qualifications one could not legally hold the title rabbi, perform marriages, or keep the communal registry.[29] While the citizenship and especially the linguistic provisions might seriously hamper the selection of any rabbi, the education clause specifically restricted the choice among Orthodox rabbis with traditional yeshiva training and thereby jeopardized the ability of the Orthodox to obtain proper religious leadership.

In Article 25 the new law nevertheless attempted to protect the rights of minority religious groups, specifically the Orthodox in Zagreb and the Sephardim in Zemun:

The Israelite religious community in Zagreb and in Zemun are obligated to maintain all those special religious institutions, which the Old Believers [Orthodox] in Zagreb and the Sephardim in Zemun, according to their own religious convictions, consider necessary for the carrying out of their religious creed especially with regard to ceremonies, taking as a basis today's generally pertinent regulations with respect to both actual and private needs.
But above all, the special property of the present "Old Believer Israelite Community in Zagreb" and the "Church-School Community of Sephardic Israelites in Zemun" and the revenues from the same institutions must be used for the maintenance of the religious institutions concerned.

> The members of the Israelite religious community, the Old Believers in Zagreb and the Sephardim in Zemun, shall themselves elect a special committee with complete autonomy in questions of belief and religious observances to administer these properties and these revenues, and at the same time to administer the religious institutions concerned.
>
> The chairman of that committee and his substitute must be members of the executive board of the religious community concerned.[30]

Thus, the Orthodox, no longer able to run their own affairs independently, now formed the Association of Old Believer Members of the Israelite Religious Community but continued to maintain their own institutions within the framework of the larger community, paying taxes to the central body and receiving sizable subventions from it.[31] So the situation remained until the interwar period.

Both in terms of numbers and power, the Neologues continued to dominate the Zagreb scene. The Orthodox never constituted a very large percentage of the local Jewish population. In 1925 the forty-nine families belonging to the Association of Old Believers comprised less than 2 percent of the communal taxpayers. By that same year a small Sephardic settlement of about ninety-five families had sprung up in Zagreb.[32] Nevertheless, the Jewish component in the Croatian capital remained overwhelmingly Ashkenazic and Neologue.

Just as the city of Zagreb experienced a period of rapid population expansion in the late nineteenth and early twentieth century, increasing from 29,218 in 1880 to 74,703 in 1910 and reaching 185,581 by 1931, so too the Jewish population doubled and redoubled from 1,285 in 1880 to 4,233 in 1910 to 8,702 in 1931. (See table 3.) On the eve of World War II the estimated number of Jewish residents in Zagreb was 9,467, including 8,712 Ashkenazim (Neologues), 625 Sephardim, and 130 Orthodox.[33]

Zagreb has always been a Catholic stronghold. At the turn of the century close to 90 percent of the city's inhabitants were Catholic, and in the interwar period the number was about 85 percent. The Jews, constituting approximately 5 percent of the populace, therefore comprised a significant proportion of the non-Catholic minority.

There does not appear to have been a clearly defined Jewish district in Zagreb at any time. Some Jews continued to live in Upper Town, the old Gradec, as well as in Kaptol, the former bishop's city; most of the later arrivals however established residence in the newer

Lower Town. No particular pattern of settlement can be traced from the evidence available. Like their Ashkenazic brethren elsewhere, but unlike the Sephardic poor in Sarajevo and Belgrade, the Ashkenazim of Zagreb felt no need to cluster together geographically. For the most part fairly recent newcomers to the city, they nevertheless managed to maintain a relatively high standard of living which allowed them to dwell where they chose.

Both by occupation and by wealth the Jews of Zagreb tended to belong to the middle class. Approximately a third of the communal taxpayers in 1934 classified themselves as merchants or commercial agents of various types, whereas almost an equal number were categorized as office workers or other kinds of salaried employees. Slightly more than 8 percent were physicians, lawyers, or engineers, and almost 3 percent were considered industrialists, whereas a similar 3 percent apparently qualified as artisans.[34]

The Zagreb community was undoubtedly the wealthiest in the country on an absolute, as well as a relative, scale. In 1939 the highest income bracket comprised 663 contributors (21 percent), paying over 1,000 dinars annually in communal taxes. Another 280 households (9 percent) fell into the middle tax category, paying 700 to 1,000 dinars; 2,275 (71 percent) formed the lowest group, paying 50 to 600 dinars.[35] As in the case of the Belgrade Ashkenazic community, given the high total number of taxpayers (3,218 out of 9,467 individuals), apparently relatively fewer families were tax-exempt than in the Sephardic communities.

Nevertheless, despite the larger segment of the affluent among Zagreb Jewry, real poverty, evidently, existed there simultaneously. In 1940 some assistance was given to 196 families from the Winter Campaign led by the Zagreb head rabbi, and to 128 persons by the Central Agency for Social Institutions.[36] Zagreb, then, like the other two cities, contained both the very rich and the very poor. The vast majority, however, fell between these two extremes, and by virtue of their income, their occupations, and their education, Zagreb Jewry may thus be considered as generally bourgeois.

Until World War II the Zagreb Jewish community maintained its own primary school. In the mid-nineteenth century the school's founders, none of whom had received a formal secular education themselves (although they were by no means illiterate), adopted the attitude that "here as elsewhere is felt an urgent need to establish a school for the purpose of the religious and scientific [secular] training of children, because the improvement of the political status of the Jews depends upon their intellectual advancement."[37] Under the direction of Rabbi Goldman this institution first opened its doors in 1841 as a three-year program with instruction in German. In 1852 the school closed temporarily for lack of funds due to the dispute between the Orthodox and the Neologues, but in 1858 it renewed its activity. After 1864 it became a standard four-year elementary school for seven- to ten-year-old boys and girls, with most of its subjects taught in Croatian.[38]

In the nineteenth century the school was supported by a combination of tuition fees, communal subsidies, and an annual subvention from the city of Zagreb.[39] During the interwar years, however, tuition was abolished, and although the institution might still theoretically have been eligible for state aid, the community accepted no outside help, but supported the school entirely out of its own resources.[40]

In the one hundred years of its existence over two-thirds of the Zagreb Jewish children of both sexes attended this Jewish day school, where they received instruction in both secular and religious subjects. The annual reports published by the school recorded an enrollment of 160 in 1869, which declined to 97 in 1889, climbed again to 192 in 1906, and then fell to 147 on the eve of World War I.[41] Attendance at the Jewish school increased substantially during the interwar period, hovering near the 300 mark in the mid- to late thirties.[42] Not all Jewish parents sent their offspring to this school, however. Between the wars some 100 to 125 Jewish boys and girls annually attended public primary schools; others went to private, generally Catholic, schools as well.[43]

After elementary school most Jewish children seem to have gone on to secondary schools of various kinds. During the academic year 1907/8, for example, 55 Jewish pupils attended the Zagreb gymnasium, making up 10 percent of the total enrollment, 154 were reported at the Realgymnasium (20 percent), and 61 at the commercial school (22 percent).[44] Of the 90 members in the graduating class of the Jewish school in 1934, only 3 girls did not continue their schooling, and 3 boys went into a trade, whereas 73 entered gymnasium and 11 enrolled in the municipal (or civic) school.[45] Three years later the total number of Jewish pupils within the middle school system, including both public and private institutions, reached a peak of close to 700.[46] Many students, upon graduation from high school, continued their education on the university level as well.

The Ashkenazim who came from elsewhere in the Habsburg Empire to live in Zagreb brought with them a variety of languages, especially German and Hungarian. While many of them, especially the earliest arrivals, were undoubtedly Yiddish speakers, the available sources and statistics persist in classifying them all as German speakers. There is, therefore, no way of knowing how many of them actually used Yiddish and for how long they did so. They continued to speak non-Slavic languages among themselves for some time, although they gradually acquired a knowledge of Croatian as well.

In the nineteenth century the community conducted its business in German, so that the 1859 statutes of the Zagreb Hevra Kaddisha (burial society) and the 1867 communal statutes were published in that language.[47] In 1885 Dr. Hosea Jacobi (1841–1925), the communal rabbi who had arrived in 1868, delivered his first sermon in Croatian,[48] but many of his congregants undoubtedly had considerable difficulty understanding it. *Židovska smotra,* a Zionist monthly, began publication in 1906 using German as its principal language. Although the 1912 communal statutes appeared in Croatian, the communal executive was apparently still conducting its meetings in German. In the same year a newly elected board member demanded that discussions be conducted in Croatian, but he was informed that many of the elected communal representatives did not know the language.[49]

The Jews were not the only inhabitants of Zagreb who used German as a medium for communication. According to one recent Yugoslav historian, one-fourth of the Zagreb population in 1890 were aliens, largely Germans, and "German was spoken in the better Zagreb homes even by those who were not of German origin."[50] The influence of German and, to a lesser extent, Hungarian culture upon the Jews thus remained strong, especially as long as Croatia continued to be under Habsburg rule.

With the creation of the new South Slav state, Jews became extremely vulnerable to the accusations of being "foreign." In September 1918 a news item appeared in several of the leading Croatian newspapers entitled "By any means, but not in Croatian, or How Zagreb Jews congratulate one another on the New Year." It reported that the Zagreb post office was flooded with postcards from Jews sending one another felicitations on the New Year. These cards, the article claimed, all contained three-fold good wishes, in Hebrew, Hungarian, and German, with no trace of Croatian whatsoever.[51] Under growing pressure it became more and more expedient for Jews to adopt the speech of their neighbors in public, if not in private life.

The Jewish school in Zagreb, which began with German as the language of instruction, changed to Croatian as early as 1864. Thereafter, all Jewish children born and educated in Zagreb learned the local language in school, if not beforehand. By 1880, according to the official census, 30 percent of the 13,488 Croatian Jews claimed Croatian as their mother tongue, whereas 56 percent reported German and 12 percent, Hungarian. Ten years later the percentage of Croatian speakers fell slightly, to 28 percent, as did that of the German speakers, to 52 percent, but the figure for Hungarian speakers increased to 17 percent. By 1900 the proportion of Croatian speakers had risen to 35 percent, and ten years later 46 percent claimed to be native speakers of that language. (See table 6.) Meanwhile, the percentage of reported German speakers declined dramatically, and the number of Hungarian speakers remained constant. Interestingly enough, a slightly higher percentage of men than women reported Croatian as their mother tongue, whereas the reverse held true for German. In the city of Zagreb itself, the adoption of the local language, for census purposes at least, proceeded at an even faster rate than in the province as a whole. At the turn of the century, 54 percent reported Croatian as their mother tongue; by 1910 the figure reached 60 percent.[52]

In addition, many Jews who claimed other languages as native reported a knowledge of Croatian as a second language. According to the 1900 reports, 41 percent of the Jews of Croatia knew the local language as well as their mother tongue, while 29 percent of the Zagreb Jewish community also acknowledged this skill.[53] These statistics would imply that by the beginning of the twentieth century, 83 percent of the Zagreb Jewish community and 76 percent of Croatian Jewry, taken as a whole, had a working knowledge of the Croatian language. The accuracy of these figures, especially regarding "mother tongue," is somewhat open to suspicion. Without denying the likelihood that some Jews actually spoke Croatian natively, a large part of the so-called native Croatian speakers probably spoke another language at home and among themselves. Thus technically they should have designated Croatian as their second language and not their first. Nevertheless, given the rapid rise of Croatian nationalism in the late nineteenth century, it is not too surprising that many Jews preferred to choose the local language as their own in theory, if not in practice. A majority of Croatian Jewry, however, undoubtedly could speak as well as understand the Croatian language before the outbreak of World War I.

During the interwar period, the trend toward linguistic acculturation continued. In the 1931 Yugoslav census 6,402 Zagreb Jews (nearly 75 percent of the total) reported Serbo-Croatian as their mother tongue; 1,059 (12 percent) acknowledged German and 653 (7 percent) chose Hungarian, with the remaining 7 percent identifying themselves as speakers of other languages.[54] By the mid-twentieth century the overwhelming majority of Zagreb Jewry, if perhaps not all actually native speakers of Serbo-Croatian as they claimed, certainly had a solid working knowledge of the language and were using it increasingly both in the street and even in their homes.

Although not much data on this subject exists, it would appear that the Ashkenazim of Zagreb were more likely than their fellow Jews elsewhere in the South Slav lands to change their family names radically and slavicize their first names. Hence such surnames as Marić, Brajković (formerly Breyer), Mačelski, or Rodanić, which are not very readily identifiable as Jewish, would occasionally occur in Zagreb, but were much less frequent in either Belgrade or Sarajevo. Similarly, such distinctively Yugoslav, or Croatian, personal names as Lavoslav, Slavko, Slavoljub, and Drago were more commonly found in Zagreb than elsewhere. Girls, however, were evidently given local Slavic names more rarely than boys. Most Zagreb Jews retained appellations similar to those of the Ashkenazim in other communities, that is, easily distinguishable as Jewish among the native nomenclature. Nevertheless, the Jews, especially in the twentieth century, seemed to be trying hard to gain acceptance on the Zagreb scene; hence there was a tendancy to adopt Croatian names as well as the Croatian language, so as not to be viewed as aliens.

The Jewish community of Zagreb was the most recently established of the three major Yugoslav Jewish communities under discussion. Its Ashkenazic-Neologue component constituted the largest and the wealthiest single Jewish community in the country. These Jews, whether merchants, white-collar workers, or professionals, belonged heavily to the middle class and, for the most part, were well educated, westernized, and secularized. By the twentieth century most of them were at least bilingual, if not trilingual, speaking Croatian, German, and often Hungarian as well. By culture and orientation, however, they tended to be more Austro-Hungarian than Yugoslav.

When World War I ended with the collapse of the Habsburg Empire, these Jews suddenly found themselves in a South Slav kingdom. They attempted to demonstrate their loyalty to the new state and, indeed, some had already, several decades earlier, become ardent Croatian supporters. But such efforts met with only limited success. The Croats in Zagreb appeared less willing than the Serbs in Belgrade, or even the Bosniaks in Sarajevo, to accept the idea of Jews as equals. Consequently, the Jews of Zagreb, well-off economically, for the most part lacked a deep-rooted sense of security and belonging.

4

BETWEEN TWO WORLD WARS

In the struggle for emancipation in western and central Europe, Jews were chiefly interested in gaining for themselves equal status as citizens, rather than special status as Jews as had existed in former times. Jewish liberals preferred to consider themselves members of the same nationality as their neighbors, differing only in religion. As a result, such notions as Germans of the Mosaic persuasion came into vogue. The Jewish nationalist movement began only at the end of the nineteenth century. In its early years especially, Zionism did not tend to concern itself greatly with national rights for Jews living in the Diaspora. The concept of Jews as a separate nationality gained much more popular support among the eastern Jewish masses than among western Jewry. In the Balkans before World War I, despite the growing nationalist consciousness of the local populace, the demand for recognition of Jews as a nationality simply never arose.[1]

By the late nineteenth century the Jews in the South Slav lands had achieved legal emancipation, and by 1918 they formally enjoyed full civil equality as individuals. With the creation of the Kingdom of Serbs, Croats, and Slovenes at the end of World War I, the Jews continued to be regarded officially as a religious rather than a national minority. The newly united state was compelled to sign a Minorities Treaty at the Peace Conference, whereby it guaranteed to all its inhabitants full protection of life and liberty "without distinction as to birth, nationality, language, race or religion."[2] Unlike the minorities treaties signed by Poland, Rumania, and Greece, the South Slav agreement did not include the so-called Jewish articles on education and the Sabbath. Such clauses were deemed superfluous for the new state, as well as Czechoslovakia and Bulgaria; in all three instances the Jews constituted a relatively small group and were considered unlikely to suffer any persecution.[3] The provisions on freedom of religion and full political and civil rights for all were reiterated in the constitutions of 1921 and 1931.[4] The Jews, thus, like all other minorities in the country, whether religious or national, theoretically had recourse to both national and international courts of law to present any grievances regarding infractions against their rights.

According to the 1921 census, out of a total population of approximately 12 million people, slightly more than 2 million (about 16 percent) belonged to the various linguistic minorities, meaning they were categorized as having a mother tongue other than Serbo-Croatian or Slovenian. Of these, 505,790 were classified as Germans, 467,658 as Hungarians, 231,068 as Rumanians, and 115,532 as Czechs or Slovaks, nearly all of whom lived in the Vojvodina, whereas 439,-637 were reported as Albanians and 150,322 as Turks, most of whom were to be found in Macedonia (or South Serbia, as it was then officially called). With respect to religious affiliation, 47 percent of the population were Serbian Orthodox, 39 percent Roman Catholic, 11 percent Muslim, and 2 percent Protestant, with less than 1 percent members of other religious groups or officially without religion.[5] Thus the Jews, numbering 64,746, or about a half a percent of the overall population, by no means constituted the largest or even the most significant minority in interwar Yugoslavia.

Like all the other minorities, the Jews were entitled by law to "an equal right to establish, manage, and control at their own expense charitable, religious, and social institutions, schools, and other educational establishments, with the right to use their own language and to exercise their religion freely therein."[6] In addition, the constitution granted religious minorities an annual state subsidy to support their clergy and religious institutions.[7] Indeed, the subvention to the Jewish community was, in comparison with the grants to other established denominations, by far the most generous. According to one contemporary source, in the 1930s the Serbian Orthodox church received 5.65 dinars per member; the Roman Catholic church, 6.05 dinars; the Protestants, 6.09 dinars; and the Muslims, 9.84 dinars. The Jews, however, were allocated 16.5 dinars per capita, two to three times the amount given to any other group.[8] This figure would seem to indicate that, according to their official designation as a religious minority, the Jews received fair treatment.

The Minorities Treaty accorded special concessions to national minorities with regard to use of their language in courts and public life, as well as education.[9] Such privileges were not fully extended to the Jewish minority. In fact, the right to instruction in one's own language in a public elementary school was restricted only to those territories that were transferred to Serbia after 1913, i.e., the former Austro-Hungarian lands, but not the Ottoman areas acquired after the Balkan Wars.[10] Hence, the Germans, Hungarians, and Rumanians in the Vojvodina benefited from minority educational provisions, whereas the Turks, the Albanians, and in effect the Jews did not.

The only specifically Jewish language spoken by any large number of the Jewish population was Ladino.[11] However, even before World War I, most Sephardim were becoming bilingual and chose to educate their children in schools where the language of instruction was Serbo-Croatian. Hence, in the interwar period there was little desire to create new Ladino schools, even if they had been allowed by law, and little need to fight for the use of Ladino in the courts as long as it might be spoken in private.

More problematic was the fact that many Ashkenazim, primarily in the Vojvodina, spoke Hungarian and had little or no knowledge of Serbo-Croatian. As Jews they were declared ineligible to be part of the Hungarian minority. They were not permitted to send their children to Hungarian-language schools but were forced instead to have their children educated in Serbo-Croatian, the language of their "official" nationality. The same policy applied to courts and communal records.[12] This dilemma, however, could not have been solved by the recognition of a Jewish nationality, which presumably would have allowed schools with Hebrew as the language of instruction, or else Ladino or Yiddish, but not Hungarian or German.[13]

Separate Jewish schools were not government supported, but the state did provide funds for public Jewish education because religion was a compulsory subject for all pupils at both elementary and secondary levels. The authorities allowed the existence of private Jewish kindergartens and primary schools, such as those in Zagreb, and permitted supplementary Hebrew courses as well.[14] In 1928 a Jewish theological seminary was created in Sarajevo to train religious officials and teachers; this institution received an annual government subvention. The language of Jewish religious instruction was, as a rule, Serbo-Croatian, although some Hebrew was used as well.

State law exempted Jews from appearing in court on the Sabbath and on Jewish holidays. In Sarajevo, where Jews made up over 10 percent of the population, Jewish holidays were legal holidays for all Jews;[15] elsewhere, this applied only to school children, civil servants, and members of the military.[16] In 1925, despite the protests of the local community and of the communal federation, the authorities prohibited Sarajevo Jews from keeping their shops open on Sunday even if they remained closed on Saturday.[17] On the whole, however, the religious minority status worked to the benefit of the Jews in their particular circumstances and little advantage would have accrued had the Jews officially constituted a separate nationality.

For the most part, the Jews themselves did not demand recognition as a national minority. Unlike the other minority groups, Jews were not concentrated in the border regions but were scattered in the various cities and towns throughout the country. (See table 7.) Geographical distribution and diversity of interests among the different Jewish factions made national minority status a somewhat impractical goal.

Yugoslav Jewry formed an almost exclusively urban element, in sharp contrast to the overwhelmingly rural character of the other peoples of the area. Yugoslavia was a country of peasants. In the interwar period, over three-quarters of the general population lived in villages and were engaged in agriculture and related occupations. By comparison, virtually the entire Jewish population was concentrated in urban centers, especially the bigger cities. Fewer than 5 percent of the Jews were to be found in rural areas or in localities without organized Jewish communities. Whereas less than 10 percent of the overall Yugoslav population were living in towns with more than 20,000 inhabitants in 1931, approximately 70 percent of the Jews were situated in such places. Indeed, about 40 percent of all Jews resided in Belgrade, Zagreb, and Sarajevo alone. Although the 68,405 Jews recorded in the 1931 census amounted to only .5 percent of the country's total inhabitants, they constituted more than 3 percent of the urban dwellers.[18] This tendancy toward urbanization, especially the gravitation to capitals or larger cities, reflects the general trend among European Jewry since the late nineteenth century.[19]

Yugoslavia had one of the highest rates of population growth in Europe during the interwar period; from 1921 to 1939 the number of its inhabitants increased 31 percent from 11,984,911 to an estimated 15,703,000.[20] By comparison, the Yugoslav Jews multiplied much more slowly: in 1938 there were some 71,342 Jewish residents of the kingdom, including 68,710 citizens and 2,632 resident foreigners (but not the several hundred refugees from German-occupied territories, who were considered merely as transients).[21] This figure reflects only a 10 percent increase over the 64,746 Jews reported in the 1921 census —slightly less than one-third the national growth rate. The Yugoslav population as a whole displayed a high death rate (19.8 per 1,000 in 1931) but an even higher birth rate (33.6 per 1,000); hence a large natural increase was ensured. The Jews, however, had a relatively low death rate (12.9 per 1,000 in 1931) but an even lower birth rate (12.3 per 1000), especially during the 1930s. As a result, their natural increase came to almost a complete standstill. Social factors obviously contributed to this biodemographic phenomenon: the predominantly middle class urban Jews simply had much smaller families than their agricultural and rural fellow Yugoslavs; as against the 3.6 children per family among the latter, the Jews produced only 1.6.[22]

In Yugoslavia the rate of population growth varied considerably from region to region. In the former Turkish areas, inhabited mainly by Orthodox and Muslims, the growth rate was much higher than in the former Habsburg districts.[23] Similarly, the Sephardim of Bosnia, Macedonia, and Serbia multiplied faster than the Ashkenazim of Croatia and the Vojvodina.[24] In Zagreb the Jewish community showed a moderate rate of natural growth prior to World War I with births considerably exceeding deaths. Thereafter, there was a general decline in number of births and a steady increase in annual deaths. Throughout the interwar period, the Zagreb Ashkenazic community witnessed a negative rate of natural growth, culminating in the 1930s with a constantly rising annual rate of deaths over births. This trend may be seen as typical among the Ashkenazim north of the Danube-Sava line. By contrast, in Sarajevo the annual birth rate always remained substantially above the annual death rate, although the former was declining rapidly, especially during the thirties. (See table 8.) A similar pattern was to be found among the Belgrade Sephardic population. The smaller Ashkenazic communities in Sarajevo and Belgrade also maintained a slight increase in births over deaths during these years.[25] In general, the economically weaker Sephardic communities produced a high natality rate, and the economically stronger Ashkenazic communities manifested a much lower one.

An annual excess of deaths over births in the thirties was not a situation unique to the Jews of Yugoslavia; it occurred among Jews elsewhere in Europe, especially in Germany but also in the countries bordering on Yugoslavia to the north and the west, Austria, Hungary, and Italy.[26] Such a natural decrease was undoubtedly intensified by the economic and political circumstances of the depression and the rise of nazism.

The changing population pattern within Jewish communities in Yugoslavia obviously did not depend solely on the rate of natural growth. Other factors also played a role. In spite of the relatively high fertility of the Sarajevo Jews, the size of the community did not expand very greatly during the interwar period. According to the 1921 census, there were 7,458 Jews living in Sarajevo; official estimates for 1939 report a total of 8,114 members of the combined Sephardic and Ashkenazic communities. This amounts to only a 9 percent increase, even less than the national Jewish average. This slow growth may be attributed to a considerable emigration from Sarajevo to other parts of the country, mainly Belgrade and Zagreb. By contrast, Zagreb, despite its very high mortality ratio, increased its Jewish population by 58 percent during the interim, growing from 5,970 to 9,467. Belgrade displayed an even greater population leap, more than doubling its 4,844 Jews in 1920 to 10,388 in 1939.[27] Such expansion was clearly not due to natural increase but rather to economic factors that led to the rapid growth of the country's two largest cities through general migrations from the provinces. This is but another illustration of the Jewish trend toward metropolitan centers in the twentieth century.

The urban nature of the Jewish community, as opposed to the general rural character of the country in which they lived, made the occupational stratification of Yugoslav Jewry totally different from that of the Yugoslav population as a whole. According to the 1931 census figures, 76 percent of the active Yugoslav working population were engaged in agriculture, forestry, and fishing; by contrast, only 111 Jews, or .6 percent of the Jewish working force, fell into this category. (See table 9). Even in large urban centers, the Jews did not parallel their fellow-city dwellers in occupational distribution. Proportionally more were engaged in commerce and credit and fewer in industry and crafts, more in the free professions and fewer in public service.[28] Much the same pattern could be found among Jews in Rumania, Hungary, and Czechoslovakia. Yugoslav Jews, however, seem to have demonstrated an even higher concentration in commercial fields as opposed to trades and industry than manifested by those Jews of neighboring lands.[29]

Within Yugoslav Jewry itself, considerable regional diversity in occupational distribution appears to have taken place. (See table 10.) In the former Habsburg territories to the north, and especially in those localities where few Jews lived, the proportion of Jews in commerce and the free professions, and often in white-collar employment as well, proved somewhat higher than in the south. But in the areas previously under Ottoman control, particularly Bosnia and Macedonia, the percentage of artisans was generally greater.

The old Sephardic synagogue Stari hram, Belgrade (destroyed)

The new Sephardic synagogue Bet Israel, Belgrade (destroyed)

The Jewish Street in Dorćol, Belgrade

The Sephardic cemetery, Sarajevo

The old Sephardic synagogue Il Kal Grandi, Sarajevo

The new Sephardic synagogue, Sarajevo (destroyed)

The Ashkenazic synagogue, Sarajevo

TOP LEFT:
The Ashkenazic synagogue, Zagreb (exterior) (destroyed)

BOTTOM LEFT:
The Ashkenazic synagogue, Zagreb (interior) (destroyed)

Schwarz Home, Jewish Home for the Aged, Zagreb

A Sephardic woman's dress costume

A Sephardic wedding, Sarajevo

When the occupational structure of the Zagreb and Belgrade Jewish communities (approximately equivalent to the Sava province and the Belgrade administrative district in table 10) are compared, however, amazing similarities immediately appear, which are surprising considering the Sephardic majority in Belgrade as against the overwhelmingly Ashkenazic predominance in Zagreb. True, Zagreb displayed a higher percentage of persons engaged in the free professions, and Belgrade revealed more artisans, but otherwise the distinctions between the two largest cities were minimal.[30] Local economic conditions probably provided the most significant factors in determining occupational stratification among Jews. Evidently, opportunities were available for the Sephardim in Belgrade, as well as for the Ashkenazim in Zagreb, to branch out from their traditional involvement in commerce and crafts into office work and the professions.

Such was not the case with Sarajevo as a comparison with either of the two larger and more rapidly expanding cities proves. Sarajevo, a more isolated center, was developing at a much slower pace and had a larger concentration of Jews relative to its general population. The Jewish occupational structure, especially among the Sephardim, most closely resembled the Belgrade Sephardic pattern, albeit in a much more intensified fashion, but was clearly different from that of Ashkenazic Zagreb. There was a much greater concentration of Sephardic artisans and workers, a comparable or higher proportion of merchants and fewer white-collar employees and professionals than either of the other cities.[31] (See table 10, comparing Drina Province with Sava Province and the Belgrade administrative district.) A provincial town experiencing economic stagnation in the interwar period, Sarajevo offered fewer outlets for occupational advancement than Belgrade, the national capital, or Zagreb, the major industrial and commercial hub. Traditional patterns of Jewish employment persisted and the poverty problem increased.

Despite basic similarities in the communal tax structures in all three cities, the Ashkenazic community of Zagreb was certainly economically much more comfortably situated than its Sephardic counterparts in Sarajevo and probably in Belgrade as well. Such a conclusion can be drawn by taking into account those who paid no taxes. Zagreb was clearly a wealthier and more progressive city than Sarajevo; Belgrade, in this as in most other respects, was median between the other two. Nonetheless, the fact remains that the Sephardim in both Belgrade and Sarajevo were, in general, relatively poorer than the local Ashkenazim. The Ashkenazim tended both by occupation and by income to belong to the middle class; the Sephardim appear to have been mixed among the lower, middle, and wealthier strata, with the concentration at the bottom rather than the middle or top. This state of affairs may be ascribed somewhat to geographic causes, but obviously social, cultural, and educational factors contributed as well.

During the nineteenth century the Jews living in the various South Slav lands were often familiar with the local language, but it is extremely unlikely that they ever used it regularly among themselves. The Sephardim spoke Ladino almost exclusively; the Ashkenazim communicated in Hungarian, German, and sometimes Yiddish. As long as the territories in which they lived belonged to Austria-Hungary and as long as the towns were predominantly under foreign influence, there was no real necessity for the Ashkenazim to acquire an extensive knowledge of any Slavic tongue. As long as the Sephardim lived in their own quarter and sent their children only to Jewish schools, they too were not required to speak a common language with their fellow burghers, except for commercial purposes.

But this situation was not to last. With growing slavization of the towns and burgeoning native nationalism, Jews became increasingly prone to adopt the speech of their neighbors in public, if not in private life. Also, by the twentieth century Jewish schools were on the decline; more and more Jewish parents were sending their children to public schools. Political and economic pressures on the outside, as well as developing secularism from within, led to the gradual linguistic acculturation of South Slav Jews to their environment.

The recently arrived Ashkenazim in Zagreb seemed to acclimatize themselves linguistically to their new surroundings at a more rapid rate than their Sephardic brethren in Belgrade or Sarajevo, who had been "natives" of the region for several centuries. (See tables 4, 5, and 6.) Indeed, according to the 1931 census, almost three-quarters (74 percent) of the Zagreb Ashkenazim considered Serbo-Croatian to be their mother tongue, whereas only about two-thirds (64 percent) of the Belgrade Sephardim and less than half (41 percent) of the Sarajevo Sephardim so determined.[32] In all probability, however, the extent of this phenomenon is more apparent than real. Census results often reflect a bias in favor of the dominant nationality and represent various other political and psychological factors quite unrelated to linguistic accuracy.[33] Undoubtedly, bilingualism, or often even trilingualism, was the rule rather than the exception among Jews in Yugoslavia in the twentieth century. Nevertheless, considerable differences in language usage did exist between Sephardim and Ashkenazim and even within these two groups in various parts of the country. (See table 11.)

While the question of language dominance remains largely unresolved, based on the 1931 census returns certain general observations can be made. On a national level, about 40 percent of the Yugoslav Jewish population—44 percent of the Ashkenazim and 34 percent of the Sephardim—identified themselves as native speakers of Serbo-Croatian. Half of the Ashkenazim still claimed either Hungarian (26 percent) or German (24 percent) as their mother tongue, while two-thirds of the Sephardim continued to speak Ladino as their first language.

Among the Ashkenazim extensive regional differentiation seems to have taken place. Those in Croatia adopted the Slavic local language much more readily than in the multiethnic Vojvodina. According to the 1931 census, 69 percent of the Jews in the Sava province (which was roughly equivalent to Croatia) claimed Serbo-Croatian as their mother tongue, whereas only 13 percent of the Jewish inhabitants of the Dunava province (the Vojvodina) did so. Of the remaining individuals in the Vojvodina, 43 percent identified themselves as native speakers of Hungarian and 29 percent, of German, while the rest chose other foreign languages, including some Yiddish (which was combined with Ladino under the label Jewish). In the Drina province (formerly Bosnia, including Sarajevo), almost 60 percent of the Ashkenazim chose Serbo-Croatian as their mother tongue, but strangely enough, in the Belgrade capital district, less than 10 percent of the Ashkenazim claimed the local vernacular, whereas 57 percent chose German and 28 percent, Hungarian. The Belgrade results would seem to indicate that the vast majority of these Ashkenazim were very recent arrivals, most of them coming from the Vojvodina.

Among the Sephardim, regional linguistic variations proved to be equally dramatic. In the Belgrade capital district 65 percent of the Sephardim identified themselves as native speakers of Serbo-Croatian, while the remaining 35 percent of the population reported Ladino as their mother tongue. In the Drina province (including Sarajevo) only 43 percent claimed Serbo-Croatian, whereas 57 percent of the Sephardim spoke Ladino natively. In the Vardar province (formerly Macedonia and encompassing the towns of Bitolj and Skoplje) 98 percent of the Sephardic inhabitants selected Ladino as their primary language; a mere 2 percent considered Serbo-Croatian as their native tongue. It would appear that Jews in border areas, such as Macedonia or the Vojvodina, which had only recently become part of an independent South Slav state, were less likely to acculturate linguistically to the local Slavic vernacular than Jews in the Yugoslav heartland, namely, Serbia, Croatia, or even Bosnia.

By 1939 the majority of Jewish citizens of Yugoslavia, certainly the entire younger generation, which had been educated in the language, undoubtedly had a working knowledge of Serbo-Croatian, and a relatively high percentage of both Ashkenazim and Sephardim considered it their mother tongue. All Jewish newspapers (except for a few in the Vojvodina which were in Hungarian or German) appeared in Serbo-Croatian. Almost nothing was published in Ladino. Most Jewish organizations conducted their affairs in the language of the land, although some meetings were held in Ladino, mainly in Sarajevo and Macedonia. In public life the Jewish community used Serbo-Croatian; in private, the acceptance of the language was not universal in all circles.

Yugoslav Jewry, like Jews elsewhere in the western world, placed great emphasis on the value of education. As a result they were proportionally over-represented in the institutions of higher learning in the country. At the elementary school level the number of Jewish pupils was somewhat below the percentage of Jews within the population as a whole, because elementary education was compulsory and because the age distribution among the Jews was older than the national equivalent, due to their lower birth rate.[34] According to statistics published by the Federation of Jewish Religious Communities in 1939, there were only 3,206 Jewish children attending elementary schools in 1938/39, that is, .2 percent of the total number of pupils in the country. (See table 12.) This represented only half the percentage of Yugoslav Jews on the national scale. In secondary schools the ratio of Jewish pupils to the total was nearly 2 percent, considerably higher than their national average would warrant. This does not come as any great surprise, especially considering that the Jews were concentrated in the larger cities where the majority of secondary schools were located. The Jewish pupils made up 2 percent of those attending academic high schools, 3 percent at the commercial academies and 2 percent at the technical high schools; they were not as well represented in normal schools or other specialized institutions. It followed naturally that many of the matriculants, especially from academic high schools, should have decided to continue with further study at university.

Before World War I nearly all Jewish students from South Slav lands received their degrees abroad, the majority from the University of Vienna. After 1918 a considerable number still attended universities outside the country, mainly in Vienna and Berlin in the twenties, but during the thirties more and more went to Prague and Paris. Exact figures are not available for the country as a whole or for Belgrade and Zagreb, but lists compiled by the regional government of the Drina province (formerly part of Bosnia) provide information concerning Jewish students from Sarajevo studying abroad in the early thirties. Of the 73 Sarajevo students studying abroad in 1930/31, there were 15 Jews: 14 Sephardic and 1 Ashkenazic, including 1 woman. Of these, 5 were studying in Vienna, 2 in Berlin, 4 in Prague, 1 in Brno, 1 elsewhere in Germany, and 2 in France. Half were enrolled at higher technical schools; the remainder in commerce or at the university. The following year, 1931/32, out of a total of 58, there were 16 Jews: 12 Sephardim and 4 Ashkenazim. Of these, 11 were in Prague, 3 in Vienna, and 2 in France; 9 were in technical fields, 2 in music, 1 in commerce, and the other 4 unspecified.[35] During the interwar period, however, there was a growing trend toward remaining in Yugoslavia for higher education rather than traveling farther afield.

Jewish students made up 4.5 percent of the Yugoslav university population in 1928/29. This corresponded to approximately nine times their percentage of the general population. In the fields of law, medicine, and business, they were particularly strongly represented. (See table 13.) The proportion of Jewish students rose to 5 percent in 1933/34, with 767 as a record enrollment, then it declined to 3 percent by 1938/39. By relative standards this remained a very high level of advanced education.

Belgrade, Zagreb, and Ljubljana were the major university centers in interwar Yugoslavia. Skoplje and Subotica both had branches of the University of Belgrade, the former in philosophy and the latter in law, but Sarajevo had no school of higher learning at all. In 1928 there were 405 Jewish students (71 percent) attending the University of Zagreb and 132 (23 percent), the University of Belgrade. By 1938 the two institutions were more evenly balanced: 263 (49 percent) were enrolled at Zagreb and 254 (47 percent) at Belgrade. Zagreb drew its Jewish students from Bosnia and the Vojvodina as well as Croatia. Belgrade received most of its students from the immediate vicinity in the earlier years but from a larger radius later on. In 1928 Jews made up 9 percent of the student body in Zagreb and .2 percent in Belgrade; ten years later, they amounted to only 4 percent in

Zagreb but 3 percent in Belgrade.[36] A handful of Jewish students were found studying in Subotica and Skoplje. Very few native Jews ever studied at the University of Ljubljana in Slovenia, although some Jewish foreign students did enroll in the medical faculty there after their attendance was restricted in Hungary and later Poland.[37] The Jews avoided Ljubljana, a very clerical Catholic town with almost no Jewish inhabitants, in large part due to its intolerant attitude toward them. Perhaps they were increasingly attracted to Belgrade because the atmosphere proved more sympathetic than Zagreb during the late thirties.

The fields in which Jewish students chose to specialize at Yugoslav universities throughout the interwar period showed a definite pattern away from law and philosophy, which formerly ranked first and second in popularity, toward medicine and engineering and other applied sciences. In 1928/29 of the Jewish students enrolled in the universities 38 percent were studying law, 25 percent philosophy, 16 percent medicine, and 10 percent engineering (technology), with 5 percent in business, and a mere 1 percent (8 students) in agriculture, 1 percent (9) in veterinary medicine, and the remaining few in music and teaching. Ten years later 17 percent were studying law, 15 percent philosophy, 26 percent medicine, and 27 percent engineering. By this time 4 percent (21) were studying agriculture, 3 percent (19) veterinary medicine, and 6 percent business administration.[38] Evidently, the depression, along with other factors such as the crowding of certain professions, exerted pressure on Jewish students to alter their course of study along more practical lines.

As might be expected, fewer Jewish women than men received a higher education in interwar Yugoslavia. In 1938/39 the numbers of Jewish boys and girls attending primary school and lower gymnasium in Yugoslavia were roughly equal, but girls made up only a third of the Jewish pupils at the higher gymnasium level (305 out of 919), although some 250 girls did attend other secondary schools, including trade academies and normal schools.[39] This would indicate that not as many girls were prepared to enter university, and in fact, not nearly as many did so. In 1923 only 14 percent (62 out of 436) of the Jewish student body at Yugoslav universities was composed of women; this percentage was slightly lower than the general female proportion of university students in that year, which amounted to 17 percent (1,874 out of 11,223). More and more Jewish women began attending university during the twenties, and by 1928 the number had doubled to 130, or 23 percent of the Jewish students, as compared to the overall 20 percent women within the university student body at that time. The number rose as high as 175 in 1933 but fell back to 131 by 1938. This, however, represented 24 percent of the Jews attending universities, since the total number had declined from 767 to 534 between those years.

The same trends in choice of fields could be seen among university women as among men—away from law and philosophy and toward medicine and engineering. In 1928 there were 38 women students studying law, 53 philosophy, 23 medicine and 2 engineering. Ten years later the picture had changed: there were only 19 women law students and 48 in philosophy, but 33 in medicine and 18 in engineering. With over a third of the Jewish women still in liberal arts and a sharp drop in the overall Jewish average, women now made up 60 percent of the Jews enrolled in philosophy.[40] Otherwise the women, like the men, responded to the practical demands of the hour; as their number in higher education increased from barely one-sixth to almost one-quarter, so did their practicality.

According to the calculations of Arthur Ruppin, the Zionist sociologist, among world Jewry the proportion of students was 15 per 1,000 in 1939.[41] Yugoslav Jewry probably fell slightly short of this mark. In the last interwar census, 1931, there were 677 Jewish students studying in Yugoslavia itself and an indefinite number abroad out of a total of 68,405 Jews; something over 10 per 1,000 in all. But the overall Yugoslav population was 13,934,038 in that year and the local university population 12,534, with some studying abroad. Thus the Yugoslav average on the whole was about 1 per 1,000.[42] By comparison with its milieu, Yugoslav Jewry's educational achievements were indeed impressive.

During the interwar years, Yugoslav Jewry was legally defined as a religious minority, but in actual fact these Jews demonstrated distinct socioeconomic traits which differentiated them from their fellow Yugoslav citizens in much more than religious affairs. While the Jews were by no means the only such minority in the country and were indeed among the smallest of these factions, they remained quite unlike all the other ethnic or religious groups. In contrast to the Germans, Hungarians, and Albanians on the one hand and the Lutherans, Calvinists, and Old Catholics on the other, the Jews were not concentrated in any one border area but were distributed somewhat unevenly throughout the country. Furthermore, in a predominantly rural and agricultural society, the Jews represented an overwhelmingly urbanized element, displaying many of the characteristics which go together with town living.

The rate of Jewish population growth was considerably lower than that of the general populace. Jewish families were, on the whole, smaller and the average age among Jews was higher than that of their neighbors. Jews were heavily concentrated in commerce, white-collar employment, and to a lesser extent, crafts and the free professions, as opposed to agriculture, mining, and forestry. Jews achieved a higher standard of education, both at the secondary school and the university level, than the surrounding peoples. All these factors distinguished the Jews from other national or religious groups in Yugoslavia and helped prevent their complete integration into general society.

The Jews, however, while retaining their distinctive socioeconomic traits, managed to adapt themselves quite successfully to their environment. They gradually acquired a knowledge of Serbo-Croatian, and by the interwar period many Jews considered that language to be their mother tongue. Most Jews in the country were undoubtedly bilingual, the Ashkenazim commonly speaking Hungarian or German and the Sephardim, Ladino, as well as the local vernacular. To varying degrees the Jews, in particular the Sephardic element among them and to a lesser extent the Ashkenazim, achieved acceptance as part of the urban scene in the South Slav lands. A considerable amount of local and regional variation took place as the Jews adjusted their lives, both as individuals and as communities, to the various milieus in which they found themselves.

The Jews thus formed a separate and distinct socioeconomic group within Yugoslav society in the three major centers where they resided. The Jewish community, on both local and national levels, formed the basic organizational unit in which Jewish activities of many types—religious, educational, cultural, and charitable—were formally concentrated. How this community functioned is discussed in the next section.

PART TWO

The Jewish Community

5

LOCAL STRUCTURE

On December 14, 1929, King Alexander signed the Law on the Religious Community of Jews in the Kingdom of Yugoslavia.[1] This legislation, modeled on the Croatian Law on the Organization of the Israelite Religious Community of 1906, was the first uniform regulation of Jewish communal activities for all of Yugoslavia. In the process of drafting the new law a controversy arose within Jewish circles as to the desirability of maintaining separate communities for different religious groups in the same district. A variety of possible alternatives presented themselves: (1) to continue to recognize all three rites, the Sephardic, the Ashkenazic, and the Orthodox; (2) to create one Jewish community in each district with different sections; (3) to acknowledge the status quo, but create no new Jewish communities where one already existed, or (4) any combination of the above.[2]

The first draft proposed by the Federation of Jewish Religious Communities in 1926 recognized all three rites. Two years later, however, the second version sanctioned only the Sephardic and the Ashkenazic branches with the decision between Orthodox and Neologue in any community to be decided by the majority. This attempt to dislodge the Orthodox met with strong opposition from the Union of Orthodox Jewish Religious Communities.[3] The final edition marked the success of the Orthodox in maintaining their distinct identity. The existence of separate Orthodox and Neologue communities and communal associations received endorsement, whereas only the status quo situation for the Ashkenazic and Sephardic communities was acknowledged. Thus, twenty Jews could form a new Orthodox or Neologue community where one did not already exist, but a Sephardic (Neologue) group could no longer break away from an Ashkenazic (Neologue) community or vice versa.[4] This constituted a substantial, if not a complete, victory for the forces for unity, since the vast majority of Yugoslav Jews were Neologue by affiliation. It would also seem to demonstrate an understanding between the Sephardim and Ashkenazim which was lacking between them and the Orthodox.

The Jewish community and its leaders warmly welcomed this law. Although it actually changed very little in the existing situation, it clarified and strengthened the legal position of the community as a whole. This enactment guaranteed to the Jewish community an annual state subsidy and municipal aid in districts which provided regular subventions for religious purposes in their budgets. All communal buildings were exempted from public taxes and official correspondence was freed from postage and related expenses.[5] The state also offered its executive arm to the Jewish community in collecting revenues when necessary.[6] Authority over the local Jewish communities was exercised legally by the state via the Federation of Jewish Religious Communities, which included both Sephardim and Ashkenazim, or the Orthodox Union, membership in one or the other of which was compulsory for all Yugoslav Jewish communities.[7] The institution of the chief rabbinate, as well as the two rabbinical synods, Neologue and Orthodox, also received official sanction for control over religious matters.[8] The law defined the duties of all these bodies and also attempted to standardize the statutes of the various communities. In addition, it specified the regulations for Jewish education in all public schools and legalized Jewish holidays for civil servants, the military, and students.[9] With the passage of this law, the government legally recognized the Jewish community and its organizational framework. Its intention was to protect the Jews as a religious minority and grant them all privileges enjoyed by other official religious groups.

The local community formed the basic organizational unit within Yugoslav Jewry. In general, a community consisted of all Jews living in a town and the surrounding district. On occasion, two or even three Jewish groups of different rites established themselves in the same locality; as a result, Sephardic, Ashkenazic, and Orthodox communities sometimes coexisted side by side, each claiming the affiliation of its own followers by birth or by conviction. Every Jewish community was a recognized legal body, which governed itself according to communal statutes ratified by the state.[10]

Membership in such a community was compulsory by law for all adherents of the Jewish faith residing in the country. Joining a community required no special admission fee. A membership fee had been required in the 1867 statutes of the Zagreb Jewish community, but it was rescinded in the 1912 and subsequent editions of the communal statutes. Withdrawal from the community was possible only by conversion to another religion or by moving elsewhere. A clause specifically covering this was included in the 1882 statutes of the Sarajevo Sephardic community; however, in all other cases it was taken for granted.[11] A member of a Jewish community was entitled to make use of communal facilities and participate in all communal activities and institutions. With few exceptions he also enjoyed the right to vote and be elected for communal office. In addition, all members were obligated to pay the community an annual religious tax, as well as various other fees for ritual purposes. Clauses on the rights and duties of the membership were included in virtually every extant statute of the Zagreb, Belgrade, and Sarajevo Jewish communities in the nineteenth and twentieth centuries. The nonvoluntary nature of association and taxation was by no means unique to the Jewish community in Yugoslavia, but reflected the prevalent situation among all accepted confessional groups in a country where religious affiliation was the general rule. In interwar Yugoslavia it was possible for an individual to declare himself a member of no religious group, but this occurred very infrequently. According to the 1921 census, 1,381 persons in all of Yugoslavia were officially "without religion," including 93 in Zagreb, 65 in Belgrade, and 16 in Sarajevo.[12]

The aim of the Jewish community, as defined by its statutes, was "to provide for the religious, educational, charitable and cultural needs of its members." To attain this goal, it "erected and maintained synagogues, schools and other educational, humanitarian, and cultural institutions." Almost the identical clause was to be found in the statutes of both the Sarajevo and the Belgrade communities in the twenties and thirties, while the Zagreb statutes differed slightly in wording but not in meaning. Although the Jewish community was intended by the state to concern itself primarily with religious matters, in actual practice, it had evolved a much broader sphere of activity for itself. In the twentieth century alongside religious services, ritual affairs, and standard Jewish education, communities branched out into such fields as social welfare, scholarships, summer camps, youth programs, kindergartens, sports and music, as well as modern Hebrew courses and support for Palestine. The synagogue did not serve as the exclusive focal point of Jewish existence; communal life grew up outside its walls as well. Indeed, the role of the Jewish community was gradually shifting from the maintenance of the Jewish tradition to the strengthening of Jewish identity.

The Jewish communities of Belgrade, Zagreb, and Sarajevo displayed remarkable similarities in their organizational structure both before and after the unification of Yugoslavia. Each community elected its own leaders. The board of directors, sometimes called the communal council, consisted of anywhere from eleven men in Belgrade to forty-five in Zagreb, including the president, two vice-presidents, a secretary, and a treasurer.[13] The official role of the president was to represent the community to the outside world. He and his officers on the board administered the day-to-day affairs of the community. Often the board or council was divided into a number of subcommittees, each headed by its own chairman. These committees were in charge of the diverse aspects of communal life: religious, educational, philanthropic, cultural, administrative, financial.[14] In addition, special committees took charge of elections and tax assessment. Some boards, such as those in Belgrade, also appointed men as tutors, whose function was the supervision of synagogues, schools, and various funds and communal institutions.[15]

The board of directors was responsible to the membership for its actions. The smaller communities, such as the Sarajevo Ashkenazic and the Zagreb Sephardic and Orthodox, retained the institution of the general meeting, which had been common in the nineteenth century and earlier, whereas the larger units, like the Zagreb Ashkenazic and the Belgrade Sephardic and Ashkenazic communities, found it expedient to replace this body with a separate communal council, varying in size from thirty-two to ninety persons, including the members of the board of directors.[16] The membership meeting or the representative council usually convened annually to discuss such matters as the budget, major expenses, the hiring and firing of the rabbi, and revision of statutes.

Elections took place every two to four years according to local regulations. With few exceptions all self-supporting male tax-paying members over twenty-one years of age received franchise. Members who were under guardianship, under surveillance for criminal activity, or behind in their tax payments were not allowed to vote. Communal functionaries and employees were sometimes denied voting privileges as well, as, for example, in the Belgrade Ashkenazic community in 1933 and the Sarajevo Sephardic community in 1922 and later. In the Sarajevo Sephardic community in the thirties, however, no tax requirement existed. In their revised 1929 statutes, the tax qualification was removed. This meant, in effect, the enfranchising of almost a third of the members of the community, since the poverty rate was extremely high. Subsequently, an effort was made to restore the requirements, but the move was defeated, hence the members paying no taxes were able to vote in all the communal elections in the thirties. During the interwar period, the tax-paying women members in Zagreb and Belgrade succeeded in gaining the right to vote in communal elections, and in Zagreb, university students over eighteen were also permitted to cast ballots.[17]

Eligibility for office was generally conditional upon citizenship, age, and wealth, rather than religious criteria, except in the case of the Orthodox. In the Zagreb Orthodox community, a member was denied the right to hold office if he did not "keep the Sabbath and holidays according to the *Shulhan Arukh*," "maintain ritual bathing practices as in the *Shulhan Arukh*," or if he "made use of non-Orthodox Jewish facilities, such as butchers, synagogue, etc." In addition, he could not enjoy the right to vote unless his wife "did not wear her own hair."[18] A candidate for election usually had to be a Yugoslav citizen, twenty-four or thirty years of age, depending upon the community, and a taxpayer above certain minimal limits. In the Zagreb and Sarajevo Ashkenazic communities the age limit was twenty-four, but elsewhere it was thirty. In Belgrade there was an additional restriction: a nepotism clause was written into the statutes so that fathers and sons, brothers, or other close relatives could not serve together on the communal administration.[19] Communal positions were always of an honorary nature and entailed no salary. They were not to be considered completely voluntary, however, since some communities levied a substantial fine upon members who refused to accept this honor or later were absent from meetings without proper excuse. Exceptions to this rule were usually made in the case of a man who had previously held the office, was over sixty, or in ill health. In Zagreb there was a 5,000 dinar fine for refusal to accept office unless exempted by other regulations.[20] Officers and councilmen could stand for reelection in most instances.

Within both Sephardic and Ashkenazic Neologue communities, power essentially lay in the hands of the elected leadership, with the authority of the rabbi almost entirely restricted to the religious sphere. According to their regulations, the rabbi could attend and vote at board meetings only when questions of religion or Jewish education were under discussion. In Orthodox communities, by contrast, the rabbi was a permanent member of the board by virtue of his position and played a much greater role in the conduct of communal affairs.[21] On the whole, however, it was the laymen rather than the rabbis who directed Jewish activities in interwar Yugoslavia.

A survey of the laws and statutes regulating communal life provides but a partial introduction to the mode of operations of these Jewish communities. For a more complete picture, it is necessary to investigate the practice as well as the theory and to analyse such factors as election results and budget allocations, as well as other aspects of the communities in action.

While most communal elections involved a single official list of candidates with very weak opposition if any, or a joint compromise list agreed upon in advance, strong alternative slates did present themselves during certain electoral campaigns. Voter participation fluctuated greatly, even within a single community, depending on the specific election. In the Belgrade Sephardic community, for example, in the uncontested single list elections of the 1920s, a mere one-third of the eligible voters bothered to cast their ballots, whereas in the hotly contested double list elections of 1932 and 1938, well over 90 percent of the electorate turned out to vote. In the joint list election of 1935, approximately 70 percent of the Belgrade Sephardic voters participated.[22] Similarly, in the case of Sarajevo's Sephardim, only 50 percent voted for a joint list in 1928, whereas 88 percent cast ballots in a fiercely fought election five years later.[23] Likewise in the Zagreb Ashkenazic community, during the interwar period, voter turnout fluctuated between 60 and 80 percent.[24]

Communal administration, as a rule, rested among a fairly small group of men who managed to keep themselves in office until a major crisis or shift in public opinion occurred. Important changes did take place nevertheless within the leadership of most Yugoslav Jewish communities during the interwar period. It is difficult to establish an actual pattern for all these developments, but definite parallels can be drawn between the various Ashkenazic and Sephardic communities.

In the Ashkenazic hierarchy the most striking common feature would seem to be the remarkable longevity of their presidents in office in the twentieth century. In Zagreb the record shows fifteen presidents in the century between 1840 and 1940; three of these served a combined term of nearly fifty years: Josip Siebenschein, a wealthy engineer, from 1873 to 1883 and again from 1891 to 1906; his son Dr. Robert Siebenschein (1864–1938), a prominent lawyer, from 1912 to 1920; and Dr. Hugo Kon, a lawyer, from 1920 to his retirement in 1935. In the Sarajevo Ashkenazic community, after a series of nine presidents from 1881 to 1898, Dr. Moritz Rothkopf, another lawyer, was elected and held office for thirty-five years until his death in 1933; in Belgrade, Dr. Friedrich Pops (1874–1948), also a lawyer, succeeded his father, a doctor, in 1910 and remained head of his community until it ceased to exist in 1941. The stability of the top leadership in these three communities perhaps was the result of the majority of the membership being completely satisfied with their administration throughout its years in office; but more probably they were somewhat indifferent to it.

No significant change took place within the top echelons of the Belgrade and Sarajevo Ashkenazic communities in the first half of the twentieth century. In Belgrade Dr. Pops was an active Zionist and very eminent Jewish leader on the national scale, who became president of the Federation of Jewish Religious Communities in 1933. His vice-presidents throughout most of his term of office were non-Zionists, like Bernard Robiček, one of the highest ranking Jewish civil servants as director of the tax division of the Ministry of Finance, who held communal office for some thirty-five years, and Geca Kon, a publisher and philanthropist, who paid the highest taxes of any member of the community. In 1940 a member of the new guard, Dr. Albert Vajs, who was a lawyer and a Zionist, joined the executive as third vice-president.[25] In Sarajevo Dr. Rothkopf belonged to the integrationist camp all his life; however, his vice-presidents, especially in his later years in office. were generally Zionists, for example, Oskar Grof, an engineer, and Iso Herman. It is evident that these men were not elected on any specific program, but as individuals. Their differences in ideology no doubt reflected to a great extent the diverse attitudes of their constituents, who belonged to neither school exclusively. Until near the end of the era, there were no real crises within either of these communities and hence no need or desire for radical change.

By way of contrast, the Zagreb community did undergo a sort of ideological conversion. In the 1920 communal elections, the voters expressed their dissatisfaction with their old leaders by turning them out of office. The shift from Robert Siebenschein to Hugo Kon represented a critical turning point in the history of Zagreb Jewry. The victory of a Zionist over an integrationist ushered in the era of Zionist predominance in Zagreb Jewish affairs. The Zionists ran on a specific electoral platform, such as their six-point program of 1930:

1. unity of the community;
2. the importance of the Jewish school and the Hebrew language;
3. the building of a Jewish center for the spread of cultural and

literary activities;

4. the strengthening of charitable and health institutions;
5. a united front of all Yugoslav Jewry; and
6. support for the Jewish Agency.[26]

The Kon administration faced some opposition over the years, at first from the anti-Zionist Narodni Rad (National Action) forces and later from a non-Zionist group around Otto Heinrich, a wealthy banker. In their efforts to maintain Jewish unity they joined coalition lists with the non-Zionists in the thirties so that their victory would be assured but other viewpoints could be represented in the administration as well. Zagreb was the main Zionist center for Yugoslavia, but all its inhabitants were by no means pro-Zionist. The Zionists maintained control over the communal institutions with the help of the moderate non-Zionists, while the extreme integrationists and anti-Zionists played a very small role in communal life.

In the Sephardic communities of Sarajevo and Belgrade, as in their Ashkenazic counterparts, Zionist affiliation did not constitute a major criterion in communal elections. In fact, of the four presidents of the Sarajevo Sephardic community from 1922 to 1941—Isidor Sumbul, an engineer; Avram Majer Altarac, a wealthy businessman; Mordehaj R. Atijas; and Dr. Samuel Pinto, a lawyer—not one was an active Zionist during the interwar period. There were almost no prominent Zionists on the Sarajevo board (except for Mihael Levi for a brief period beginning in 1933), but several staunch Sephardic movement supporters, such as Dr. Braco Poljokan and Dr. Vita Kajon (1888–1941), served in the thirties. In Belgrade the communal presidents in the twenties, Rafailo Finci (1870–1936) and Dr. Solomon Alkalaj (1878–1929), tended toward the Sephardic movement, but the last two presidents, Dr. Bukić Pijade (1879–1943) and Dr. David Albala (1886–1942), were both Zionist oriented. In between came the Serbs of the Mosaic faith, Šemaja Demajo (1877–1932) and Dr. Jakov Čelebonović. More Zionists were represented on the Belgrade board than in Sarajevo, but none of them was elected on a specifically Zionist platform.

A definite line of continuity in the composition of the Belgrade leadership can be traced through the twenties and most of the thirties with the exception of the three-year span between 1932 and 1935. In the 1932 elections an upset occurred when Dr. Jakov Čelebonović, an affluent lawyer of the older generation, defeated Dr. Bukić Pijade, the incumbent. Čelebonović ran on the non-Zionist slogan of "patriotism, brotherhood and faith" and claimed that "a Jew can be a good

Jew only if he is a good Yugoslav." His platform, which was essentially religious and somewhat reactionary in nature rather than nationalist or progressive, included planks on "strengthening religious feelings and maintaining our religious tradition," "attendence at God's temple," and "keeping religious ritual laws," as well as changing the voting and tax systems, education, social welfare, and most other aspects of communal life.[27] In the elections close to 100 percent of the eligible voters cast their ballots and the results were 444 for Čelebonović and 342 for Pijade.[28] According to the communal statutes of that time, all seats went to the winner. In all probability Čelebonović achieved his victory due to a large protest vote against the Establishment rather than on behalf of his particular program. Three years later Pijade was returned to office unanimously at the head of a coalition list. When in 1938 Čelebonović attempted a comeback, he was soundly trounced by a margin of almost 2 to 1.[29]

In Sarajevo a crisis occurred within the Sephardic community at around the same time as in Belgrade, but it arose out of somewhat different circumstances. Under the presidency of Avram Majer Altarac, the community had built a magnificent new synagogue, which was dedicated in 1930. This impressive structure created a staggering debt that the community was unable to repay on schedule. As a result of this state of financial chaos Altarac lost the election of 1933 to one of his former vice-presidents, Mordehaj Atijas, who, along with a group of reformers, set about to improve the monetary situation as well as introduce other necessary changes, such as a progressive tax system and proportional elections. The election results were 920 to 820 against Altarac.[30] Atijas remained in power until 1938, when another member of the same faction, Dr. Samuel Pinto, took office. Hence, the change in leadership in Sarajevo in the early thirties was more lasting than in Belgrade.

The major communities all inaugurated various electoral reforms in the interwar period. In Zagreb the Kon administration abolished the curial system, which weighted the votes of the wealthy, and replaced it with equal suffrage for all taxpayers in 1923. After the opposition victories in Sarajevo and Belgrade, both communities saw fit to devise a more equitable proportional distribution of seats among various lists, so that one candidate list did not win all positions to the exclusion of any others.[31] Both these reforms were important steps in the democratization of communal administrations.

The boards of directors drew their members chiefly from the wealthier strata of the Jewish community. In the Belgrade Ashkenazic community in 1940, for example, out of the twenty-five men elected, fourteen (56 percent) belonged to the upper tax bracket, nine (36 percent) were in the middle category, whereas only two (8 percent) were in the lowest range.[32] Hence, in a community that was relatively well-to-do by Yugoslav standards, within the leadership ranks on the eve of World War II the most affluent were overrepresented at a rate of roughly seven times their percentage of the population, whereas the middle class element was doubly represented and the lower class held only 10 percent of its proportional weight in seats. This skewed distribution would undoubtedly be even more dramatic for other communities, especially among Sephardim.

Professionals held a disproportional number of seats in comparison with their actual representation within the population. Lawyers seem to have had almost a monopoly over the office of president of Ashkenazic communities, but they did not control the office quite so exclusively among the Sephardim, especially in Sarajevo. In Belgrade Sephardic circles three lawyers, as well as three physicians and two businessmen, served as president during the interwar period, while in Sarajevo, one engineer and two businessmen, but only one lawyer, were elected to that office.

A survey of the members of the Belgrade Sephardic board of directors by occupation from 1922 to 1939 shows a fairly constant composition. About one-third of the eleven-man board were professionals—either two lawyers and two doctors or three lawyers and one doctor. The remainder were predominantly businessmen, with an occasional banker or industrialist. It is striking to note that this pattern holds true for both candidate lists during competitive elections such as in 1932 or 1938 between Pijade or Albala and Čelebonović. Lower class occupations were not represented at all on the governing board. The communal council membership, however, was slightly more in line with the general occupational distribution. Among both sets of candidates for the twenty-five member body during the 1930s, about half were businessmen; several were professionals, including doctors, lawyers, and an engineer; and there were a handful of bank clerks, civil servants, and the occasional artisan.[33]

Exactly the same picture was apparent on the Zagreb communal scene, where in 1930 the Zionist list included, out of forty-five candidates for the executive board: sixteen lawyers (36 percent); thirteen businessmen (29 percent); six industrialists; two doctors and two dentists; plus six others. Among the forty-five nominees for communal council were: eight lawyers (18 percent); twenty-one businessmen (46 percent); one industrialist; four doctors; one dentist; one engineer and eight others.[34] Similar evidence could also be provided for the Belgrade and Sarajevo Ashkenazic leadership.[35] Although no accurate data is available for the occupational distribution of the Sarajevo Sephardic communal council, it can be demonstrated that its university-educated segment increased considerably in those two decades. In 1924 only two members held the title doctor, but in 1938 their number tripled to six.[36]

Communal administration was thus concentrated in the hands of a relatively small, affluent and well-educated elite. Presumably, this class had more time and more inclination to devote itself to Jewish public service. It also possessed the necessary skills and contacts to provide effective leadership. Those men who were active in running the Jewish community tended to be prominent in other branches of Jewish life as well.

The annual budget, which the executive proposed and the communal council approved, determined the course of communal affairs for the coming year. The expenses of the Jewish community were extensive and varied. The budget had to cover maintenance of the synagogues, schools, and other communal institutions, the costs of the rabbinate and *beth din* (Jewish court), if it existed, the salaries of all functionaries and employees, administrative expenses, as well as contributions, subventions, and charitable donations to many local and national Jewish causes.[37] In addition, some communities had special expenses and outstanding debts arising out of the construction of a new synagogue, as in Sarajevo, or a Jewish communal center, as in Belgrade and Zagreb.

The Zagreb community, being the largest in size, also generally revealed the highest budgetary allowance, which ranged from about two to two and a half million dinars (between $35,720 and $44,640) annually during the late twenties and the thirties. While the total amount allocated for administrative costs remained fairly constant, the percentage distribution of allotments tended to shift gradually away from the religious sphere toward education and especially the social fields. In 1926 over half the budget went for religious purposes, whereas eleven years later less than a third was devoted to those ends, and much of the rest went to support the German refugees and related projects.[38] The budget of the Belgrade Sephardic community rose from about one million dinars in 1924 to two and a half million five years later and then fell to two million by 1940.[39] The Sarajevo Sephardic community followed a similar pattern, increasing from one million dinars in 1925 to one and a half in 1930 and then to almost two million in 1940.[40] The cost of maintaining such a community continually increased, but the means available to meet such expenses were limited. Costs frequently far exceeded actual revenues. Often considerable portions of the annual budget were spent paying off accumulated debts which were almost impossible to liquidate given the financial circumstances of the thirties.

The community derived its revenue primarily from direct and indirect taxation, plus income from property and special contributions. Among the various types of income, the most common included: the main communal tax; the sale of seats and honors in the synagogue; taxation on engagements, weddings, dowries, divorce and *halitzah* (release from a levirate marriage); charges for burial and cemetery plots, as well as certificates from the communal registry. The community also received profits from the sale of kosher meat and matzoth and flour for Passover.[41] About half the revenues in both Belgrade and Sarajevo were derived from the main communal tax, with from 10 to 15 percent from selling pews and equal amounts each from kosher products and other taxes. A token sum was received from the municipality, and the state contributed mainly to the support of rabbis and religious teachers.[42]

Communal taxation was based on a graduated system of classes according to wealth. The principal tax was proportionate to the amount of state tax paid by the individual and was standardly assessed at around 20 percent of this value. All other forms of taxation were derived from these set tax categories. For example, according to the Belgrade Sephardic statutes of 1926, there were nineteen regular tax brackets ranging from 50 dinars annually to 5,000, plus several special categories up to 10,000 dinars. Weddings fell into seven categories, from 100 to 2,000 dinars, with an additional 2 percent of the dowry added on, and divorces ranged from 600 to 1500 dinars.[43] The community looked after all one's religious and ritual needs on the journey from birth to death and one paid along the way. The very poor were exempted from communal taxation and many received welfare payments instead.

During the thirties it became necessary to revise the tax structure to meet new emergency situations. In 1933 the recently elected executive of the Sarajevo Sephardic community proposed a progressive tax from 10 to 60 percent of the state tax in order to remedy the community's disastrous financial state in an equitable fashion. This scheme met with fierce opposition from some of the wealthier members of the community, including a few former members of the board of directors, since it placed a much greater tax burden on the affluent elite, while easing the lot of the poorer classes. A heated controversy raged for several years, since the state at first refused to approve a tax rate of more than 30 percent of the state income tax, although of 1,073 taxpayers, only 158 would have been affected by this measure. Even after the new plan was introduced, the community could still not meet all its current expenses due to its heavy debt payments.[44] In 1940 the communal tax was raised another 5 percent within the 60 percent limit in order to contribute more money to the refugee fund.[45] Similarly, a 50 percent surcharge was added to the Belgrade Ashkenazic and Sephardic communal tax assessment in 1940 to support the efforts of the Federation of Jewish Religious Communities on behalf of the refugees.[46]

Despite the difficulties that the communities faced in attempting to balance their accounts and despite the opposition that they sometimes encountered in collecting or raising taxes, the record shows positive results in the expansion of communal activities and increased concern for the growing needs of modern Jewish society. Annually the Jewish community of Zagreb made sizable contributions to charity, the Jewish home for the aged, scholarships and support for Jewish academic associations, Hebrew education, women's organizations, sports and summer camps and cultural programs, as well as the Jewish National Fund and Keren Hayesod (Palestine Foundation Fund).[47] The communities in Belgrade and Sarajevo did the same but on a more modest scale. The Yugoslav Jewish communities did much more than merely take care of local necessities. They offered their staunch support in trying to solve world Jewish problems, participating actively in appeals for Palestine as well as the refugee cause.

Religious concerns continued to occupy an important place in the twentieth-century Yugoslav Jewish community. Authority in matters of religion rested in the hands of the local rabbi, who was generally elected by the community at large. To qualify for the office of rabbi in any Yugoslav town a candidate had to possess a university degree as well as the prerequisite Jewish training and ordination from a recognized institution or three famous rabbis.[48] In addition, the state required that any permanent Jewish religious official be a Yugoslav citizen and fluent in the local language.[49] Difficulties frequently arose in attempting to comply with the citizenship stipulation, since Yugoslavia produced very few rabbinical students and had no facilities for their training.

The three largest cities could boast of some of the finest rabbis in the land and even managed to recruit several of their own natives for the position. The two leading Sephardic rabbis were Dr. Isaac Alcalay and Dr. Moric Levi [Moritz Levy]. Rabbi Alcalay (1881–1978) was born in Sofia, but grew up in Belgrade from an early age. He received a scholarship from the Belgrade Sephardic community to study at the university and the rabbinical seminary in Vienna. Upon his return he became the communal rabbi and shortly before World War I erupted, he was appointed chief rabbi of Serbia. In 1923 he accepted the post of the first chief rabbi of the Kingdom of Serbs, Croats, and Slovenes, an office which he filled until World War II.[50] His contemporary, Rabbi Levi (1879–1942), a native of Sarajevo, also completed his higher education in Vienna, where he wrote a doctoral dissertation entitled "Die Sephardim in Bosnien."[51] After serving as rabbi in Sarajevo for ten years, Moric Levi was unanimously elected head rabbi of the Sephardic community in 1917, and he functioned in that capacity throughout the interwar period.[52] Rabbi Levi also directed the Jewish Middle Theological Seminary, which was founded in Sarajevo in 1928 to train religious officials and teachers. As university-educated rabbis, Alcalay and Levi represented a new generation of Sephardic intellectuals in their respective communities. They lectured to their congregations in both Ladino and Serbo-Croatian. Rabbi Levi was a leading activist in the Yugoslav Zionist movement; Chief Rabbi Alcalay was a Zionist sympathizer but also an ardent Yugoslav patriot and monarchist. Both men enjoyed the love and respect of their communities as well as considerable prestige in Yugoslav Jewish life.

The dean of the Ashkenazic rabbis in the South Slav lands until his death in 1925 was Dr. Hosea Jacobi, the head rabbi of Zagreb. Born in Prussia in 1841, Rabbi Jacobi received his doctorate from Halle with a thesis on "Die Stellung des Weibs in Judentum." He came to Zagreb in 1867 and subsequently played a very prominent role in the development of nearly all aspects of Zagreb Jewish life. In his youth he was considered a liberal, but in his old age he became rather conservative in outlook.[53] His successor, Dr. Gavro Schwarz, was born in Hungary in 1872, raised in Slavonia, and educated in Budapest and Vienna. Rabbi Schwarz spent most of his career as a religion teacher in Zagreb high schools. He was elected communal rabbi in 1923 and head rabbi five years later. Schwarz was a prolific writer all his life. In 1902 he edited a Hebrew prayerbook with the first Croatian translation, and he later published textbooks for use in religious instruction for Jewish students in public schools.[54] In addition to writing numerous articles, he was the author of a history of the Zagreb Jewish community to the mid-nineteenth century.[55]

While Dr. Schwarz still belonged to the older group of Yugoslav rabbis, Dr. Miroslav (Šalom) Freiberger, his junior colleague, represented the younger generation. Born in Zagreb in 1904, Freiberger received his elementary and secondary schooling in his hometown and then studied rabbinical and secular subjects in Berlin on a communal scholarship. Upon his return to Yugoslavia, he taught religious instruction and was rabbi in Osijek for a number of years and in 1936 was elected rabbi of the Zagreb Jewish community. Rabbi Freiberger modernized the earlier Serbo-Croatian translation of the prayerbook, publishing his edition shortly before the outbreak of World War II. Šalom Freiberger was an active Zionist youth leader and somewhat of a radical, but at the same time he tried to preserve what he could of traditional Jewish values and customs.[56]

The Ashkenazic rabbis of Belgrade and Sarajevo were also men of considerable standing among Yugoslav Jewry. Ignjat Schlang was the rabbi of the Belgrade Ashkenazic community from the turn of the century. In 1926 he published a historical work on the Jews of Belgrade.[57] Dr. Samuel Weszel (1871–1928) was the much beloved head rabbi of the Sarajevo Ashkenazic community from 1898 to his death.[58] His successor, Dr. Hinko Urbach, had previously served in several other Yugoslav Jewish communities and was an active Zionist.[59]

The duties of the rabbi were defined by the communal statutes. In the Belgrade Sephardic community in the thirties, for example, the head rabbi had the following spheres of activity:

1. he was to see to the observance of religious regulations and kashrut, as well as all other questions of religious-ritual and cultural character;
2. he was to set the time for holding regular and special religious services in agreement with the communal president, prescribe the order of the liturgy and of choral prayers in the synagogue and outside it and supervise the correct conduct of the religious service;
3. he was to perform marriages, attend funerals . . . and conduct all other religious functions in the public and private life of the Jews of the Sephardic rite;
4. he was to direct the communal yeshiva and hold lectures there;
5. he was to decide on religious and ritual questions put to him by the communal board and give his opinion;

6. he was to give sermons and appropriate speeches in the synagogue and outside it, according to the custom which prevails among the Sephardim in Belgrade, and upon the decision of the communal board participate in all holy services in the synagogue and outside;

7. he was to maintain supervision in the capacity of school director over the correct implementation of instruction of religious knowledge in the schools and insofar as there were not enough qualified persons for the task, give these lectures himself;

8. he was to give a professional opinion on candidates for religious functionaries of this community;

9. he was to participate upon the invitation of the communal board among delegations and representatives of the community before the authorities or individual spokesmen, as the highest religious organ of this community;

10. he was to conduct all other usual religious functions in the community which the communal board delegated to him;

11. he was to maintain supervision over all the communal religious functionaries with regard to the correct conduct of their duties;

12. he was to keep the archives of the central communal rabbinate.[60]

The rabbis of other communities had responsibilities roughly equivalent to those of the Belgrade head rabbi. Although the framework within which he operated was relatively limited, the rabbi's powers were extensive in the religious field and he occupied the highest communal office.

The rights and duties of the other communal functionaries—the *hazan, shammash* (beadle), *shohet* (ritual slaughterer), *mohel* (circumciser), and so forth—were spelled out in similar detail in the statutes. These employees were appointed and dismissed by the board of directors according to specified regulations. In their case, too, a permanent appointment was conditional upon Yugoslav citizenship, and the hiring of foreigners on a temporary basis required governmental permission for each individual. All communal employees were subject to prescribed disciplinary action if they committed any infractions in the way of duty, and they (or their widows) were also eligible for pensions upon retirement (or death).[61] Communal functionaries fell into much the same category as civil servants. They were not very well paid, but they enjoyed the security of tenure. In performing their various functions, the communal officials enabled the members of the Jewish community to fulfill their religious obligations.

The center of Jewish religious life was, of course, the synagogue.

Each community had one or more public houses of worship, according to need. Private chapels were allowed in Zagreb but forbidden by statute elsewhere. In Sarajevo and Belgrade regular services were held in a number of smaller synagogues in the Jewish neighborhoods until into the twentieth century. The oldest synagogue in Sarajevo, Il Kal Grandi, was built in 1581 into the walls of the original Jewish quarter. Nearby was located Il Kal Nuevo (Ladino for "the new synagogue"), constructed later to accommodate the overflow. When Jews began to move out of the Čaršija district and into Bjelave, they set up houses of prayer near their new homes, such as Bet Tefila, or Il Kal di la Bjelave (the Bjelave Synagogue), and the smaller Il Kal di Machoro, named after its leader.[62] A similar situation prevailed in Belgrade's Jewish quarter, Dorćol: the oldest synagogue still standing in the interwar period was Il Kal Viežo, or Stari hram (the Old Synagogue). Across the street had been situated Il Kaliziko (the Little Synagogue) and not far away, Il Kal Nuevo, with the communal *mikvah* (ritual bath) nearby, but both these prayerhouses were destroyed when Dorćol was bombed during the First World War.

The twentieth century introduced the first modern trends into these very traditional Sephardic communities. In 1903 Abraham Kapon, a reformer from Bulgaria, began to hold "modern services" in the new Jewish school building in Sarajevo, and for the first time women were no longer relegated to sitting behind a thick grating. Another of Kapon's innovations was a synagogue choir, which led the singing, while the rest of the congregation prayed silently. As a result, this synagogue was nicknamed Il Kal di los Mudos (the Synagogue of the Mute) or else Il Kal di Kapon.[63] Most of its members belonged to Sarajevo's young intellectual generation, which began to emerge around the turn of the century. It is not certain, however, how long this synagogue remained in existence; Kapon, its hazan-rabbi, died in 1930.

A more typical trend among the Serbian and Bosnian Sephardim was the modernization of synagogue buildings, rather than reform in religious services and rituals. An actual reform movement as such never developed among the Sephardim. The older generation remained entirely traditional in their religious observances, while many of the youth in the twentieth century turned away from religion entirely. There does not appear to have been much middle ground in the religious sphere between the two extremes. Meanwhile, as the communities were growing and expanding outside the boundaries of the old Jewish sections, they began to feel the need for religious facilities in the newer areas of Jewish settlement.

In the early years of the twentieth century, a dispute arose in Belgrade between the incumbent communal leadership and a group of younger activists over the construction of a synagogue outside Dorćol. The older leaders felt that a modern temple was necessary to meet the needs of a modern community. They succeeded in erecting the large, up-to-date Bet Israel synagogue, which was located on Cara Uroša Street in Zerek, the newer Jewish business section. Opening ceremonies took place on September 7, 1908. The younger generation, however, protested against the cost of the building and the methods of raising and disbursing funds. In 1909 these Young Turks, as they were called, took over leadership in the Sephardic community.[64]

During the interwar period, a demand grew up for synagogue facilities away from the downtown area in Fišeklija, a recently developed district where many of the more well-to-do families were now living. As a result, a temporary chapel was established on Kralja Aleksandra Boulevard, where services and religious instruction were held.[65]

In Sarajevo a similar situation prevailed. There was not enough room in the existing synagogues to accommodate comfortably all the members of the growing community, especially women and children. In 1909 Il Kal Grandi was enlarged and renovated, but this limited expansion did not solve the problem. In the early twenties the communal council, under the leadership of Avram Majer Altarac, decided to raise money and buy land for the construction of a new edifice. The supporters of the new synagogue building argued their case along the following lines:

Jewish spirit and Jewish feeling are weakening in our homes and families from day to day. We must stem this evil tide; we must strengthen Jewish consciousness by all possible means, and we shall achieve this by erecting a synagogue which will be in keeping with the spirit of our times. The new Sephardic temple will be modern and attractive, and it will be that [force] which will firmly bind us one to another. In it we shall not only cultivate our religious feeling, but also elevate our cultural level.[66]

By 1930 the magnificent structure was completed.

Built in Moorish style along the banks of the Miljačka River, the Sarajevo temple was praised as being unique in the Balkans for its beauty. Its sanctuary could seat 682 with space for a choir and an organ, which did not yet exist, while the women's gallery held 300.

In addition, there was a daily chapel with room for 190 men (and 20 women) and a special hall for weddings.[67] Again, it was the younger generation who objected to the idea of the new synagogue, feeling that such lavish expenditure was not warranted at that time. Indeed, although the Sephardic community was immensely proud of their elegant temple, they never managed to pay off the debt incurred in building it.

After the new synagogue was inaugurated, the communal leaders attempted to close all the other Sephardic synagogues in town, especially the popular Bet Tefila in Bjelave, since theoretically the new temple should have been large enough to accommodate the entire community, at least for regular services. This proposal failed, however, since the old-timers in Bjelave preferred to pray among their own circle, close to home.[68] Thus, the old and the new prayerhouses continued to function side by side in Sarajevo.

The Ashkenazic communities in Sarajevo and Belgrade each had their own ample-sized and tastefully decorated synagogue. The Sarajevo synagogue, also built in Moorish style, was located on the opposite bank of the Miljačka from the Sephardic houses of worship; it opened its doors in 1902. Its Belgrade counterpart, finished in 1925, was situated on Kosmajska Street, not far from the main business section.[69]

In Zagreb, as in Belgrade and Sarajevo, the Ashkenazic-Neologue community had one large synagogue, which was located in the Lower Town. This building was repaired and enlarged several times, but still only had a seating capacity of about three hundred in the thirties. This figure seems amazingly low, considering that it served a community of some ten thousand Jews, but perhaps this fact is indicative of the nonobservant nature of this Jewish society. When the temple was constructed in 1867, an organ was included in the original architecture. This was the feature which helped perpetuate the rift between Neologue and Orthodox in Zagreb. Even more radical reforms were later introduced.

Shortly after World War I, an article appeared in the Zagreb Jewish press condemning recent changes in the main local synagogue as "sinful." The author described the contemporary situation as follows:

Last Saturday there was a religious service in our synagogue with a completely new face: for minutes a man could think that he was in some parish church, and not in a Jewish synagogue. The haftorah [prophetic portion] was read silently and not recited aloud, and at that time—they played the organ, either to increase the impression that one was in church or to amuse the congregation which was bored. Tefila [the standing prayer] was not repeated, but the cantor also read silently—or didn't read, who would know? And then most important: the reading of the Torah [Bible] was cut in half. . . .[70]

Several years later, another critic attacked the mixed Jewish and non-Jewish choir and the recent innovation of confirmation for girls.[71] Clearly, this brand of Judaism was much too left-wing for the Orthodox, or even the Sephardim, to tolerate.

In 1925 a small group of Orthodox again seceded from the larger community and received permission from the Yugoslav government to function as a separate entity. The Association of Old Believer Members of the Israelite Religious Community continued to exist within the framework of the established Zagreb Jewish community, however, and a considerable number of Orthodox remained affiliated with this body; only a minority broke away to form their own community.[72] The ultra-Orthodox element refused to share any kind of religious facilities with the Neologues and the two factions associated with one another as little as possible. At the same time that the Orthodox left the larger group, the recently arrived Zagreb Sephardim also decided to part ways with the parent community. Although both the Orthodox and the Sephardim had received rather generous treatment at the hands of the Ashkenazic-Neologue community over the years, the two branches evidently felt that the role of poor but independent equals better suited their interests than that of pampered stepchildren.[73]

The small Orthodox community could not afford to build a proper synagogue of their own, so they continued to hold daily services in rented rooms and halls. In 1930 they petitioned the city of Zagreb for a donation of land in the center of town for the purpose of erecting a permanent shul, but their wishes were never fulfilled.[74] The Sephardim, too, had the problem of lack of funds for their own building and they adopted a similar solution, renting quarters which were suitable for their needs.[75]

A synagogue was not the only prerequisite for a Jewish community. In fact, a community might operate indefinitely without a permanent house of prayer, but it could not exist long without its own cemetery. When a group of Jews combined forces to form their own community, one of their first tasks was to purchase a plot of land to serve as a Jewish cemetery. Often the earliest communal body organized turned out to be the Hevra Kaddisha.

Sarajevo and Belgrade both had Sephardic cemeteries dating

back to the sixteenth century when the communities were originally founded. The Sarajevo cemetery exists to this day, with its characteristic low, rounded tombstones, engraved in faded Hebrew script, whereas the old Belgrade cemetery was leveled and some of its remains transferred to the new Jewish cemetery in 1928 in order to make way for a city development project and park.[76] The Ashkenazic communities in Sarajevo and Belgrade had their own cemeteries, separate from those of their Sephardic brethren.

By 1811, barely five years after they organized as a community, the twenty Jewish families in Zagreb bought land for a cemetery, which was used until the 1860s, when new burial grounds were purchased. The early Orthodox community had their own cemetery, but later they evidently joined their non-Orthodox coreligionists.[77] This arrangement did not satisfy the twentieth-century Orthodox, who insisted on burying their dead in the nearest Orthodox cemetery, which was in Ilok, some distance away. In 1933, with the support of the Orthodox Union, they appealed to the municipal authorities for permission to acquire a piece of land for their own cemetery in Zagreb.[78] Hence, each of the Jewish communities in Belgrade, Sarajevo, and Zagreb, except for the Zagreb Sephardim, owned and administered their own burial grounds, which were often adjacent to the main local cemetery.

Similarly, all seven communities had separate burial societies.[79] The activities of the Hevra Kaddisha were not strictly limited to actual burial services, but as spelled out by the statutes of the Zagreb Hevra Kaddisha of 1924, its tasks included:

1. caring for the sick poor,
2. supporting the indigent,
3. visiting the sick,
4. carrying out ritual functions in case of death,
5. burying the dead,
6. reciting prayers in memory of the deceased, and
7. administering legacies and endowments.[80]

Membership in this society was open to all who paid annual dues. In some cases payment of such fees was compulsory for all communal members, but ordinarily it was a voluntary matter.[81] Historically, the Hevra Kaddisha had often been a rather elite society of the more important communal leaders, and had served as a powerful charitable organization in addition to fulfilling its burial functions. By the twentieth century, however, some of this prestige had been lost, and its nonburial activities were shared with other organizations within the community.

For the most part, the same men who provided the leadership within the Hevra Kaddisha also were prominent in general communal administration. This type of service tended to appeal to the older generation and wealthy philanthropists rather than younger activists, or else to the more traditional and devout segment of Jewish society rather than the secular Zionists.

Among the Sephardim in Sarajevo, a separate burial fund, originally known as Poale Cijon (Workers of Zion), sprang up alongside the Hevra Kaddisha in the mid-twenties. It was a considerably larger and more popularly based organization that concerned itself only with taking care of the funeral expenses of its dues-paying members. In 1931 it reached an agreement with the older and more established Hevra Kaddisha, enabling the subsidiary burial society to continue to function on a more limited basis.[82]

Among the numerous functions of the Jewish communal administration, one of its most crucial responsibilities lay in the field of Jewish education. Within the board of directors a special school committee was appointed to supervise religious instruction, with regard to both teachers and programs, whether in Jewish or public schools. The future of the community depended upon the adequate transmission of Jewish traditions and values from one generation to the next, for in order to combat the threat of complete assimilation, it was essential that Jewish awareness be increased and a sense of Jewish identity be instilled among the youth.

Throughout much of the nineteenth century, education in the South Slav lands tended to be strictly confessional in character. Consequently, as previously noted, Jewish children attended Jewish schools almost exclusively. Such institutions displayed a strong religious emphasis, and secular subjects, including the local language, usually received little or no attention. This trend was particularly evident in Sephardic centers, such as Belgrade and Sarajevo, where relatively few Jewish children learned Serbo-Croatian in school before the latter part of the century.

The typical *meldar* shared many similarities with the traditional *heder* of northeastern Europe. Little boys, from the age of six or even younger, spent the entire day in a small, badly lit room learning to read and recite by rote, and often translating into Ladino, excerpts from the prayerbook and the Bible. The teachers, who were communal functionaries, had no pedagogical training whatsoever and taught with the aid of a stick. Girls rarely received any formal education at all.[83]

In Belgrade the community erected a new school building on Solunska Street in the heart of Dorćol in 1847; several decades later Jewish children began attending on a part-time basis the public school in the area.[84] In 1894 Serbian was introduced into the curriculum of the Jewish school in Sarajevo so that Jewish children could study secular subjects within their own educational framework. This school on Suljemanska Street in the Čaršija district could boast in 1903 of airy, new quarters, which housed three classes totalling some 247 pupils. The community could not afford to run this school on its own, however, and in 1910 they gave the building to the city as a public school. Most of the pupils and the teachers there continued to be Jewish.[85]

The Zagreb Jewish community proved much more successful in its educational enterprises. The Jewish elementary school lasted from 1841 until World War II. The majority of Zagreb Jewish children of both sexes attended this four-year day school, which taught secular as well as religious subjects. The community maintained the school entirely out of its own resources, and both the older liberals and the younger Zionists gave it their support. As pointed out in a 1921 editorial in *Židov,*

in places like Zagreb, where until recently aggressive assimilation ruled in the community, the school was nevertheless preserved as the pet of the community. Much was sacrificed for it and there were few who thought about closing it. Unconsciously at least, an attachment to Judaism was traditionally rooted in such a way that it was felt that the synagogue, which was becoming increasingly empty, would lose even a *minyan* [quorum of ten men] if there were no Jewish school. Here it was not a question of the struggle of "religious reactionaries" against progress. . . .[86]

As the communal executive came under Zionist control, so too did the curriculum of the local Jewish school. Modern Hebrew with Sephardic pronunciation was added to the program, although the prayers were still taught with the traditional Ashkenazic accent. In order that Jewish education of this caliber be accessible to every member of the community, tuition fees were abolished in 1924. The school accepted all Jewish pupils on an equal basis regardless of the affiliation of their parents. Thus, Sephardic and Orthodox children were also enrolled there. The school enjoyed high academic standards and ranked among the best in the city in competitive high school entrance examinations.[87]

Sporadic opposition to the idea of a Jewish school developed among the extreme integrationists, and in the fall of 1922 their Narodni Rad association issued a circular letter to all Jewish parents, which read as follows:

The Israelite confessional school of Zagreb was in its time considered a seedbed for religious education. It has grown under the direction of Jewish nationalist communal leadership into a seedbed of Jewish nationalism. In the minds of children then is planted a seed, which with its later effects will lead to difficult fates, struggles and break-downs.

Parents! Don't allow that your children be ruined. . . .

Parents! The religious education of your children is not con-nected to the confessional school. According to state laws on educa-tion, the Israelite religious education of your children is safeguarded even if they attend general public schools.

Therefore: Parents! Rescue yourselves from the false and disas-terous deceit of Jewish nationalism, and do not send your children to the confessional school! Send your children to general public schools![88]

Indeed, many Jewish parents, whether due to ideological or other considerations, preferred not to send their children to a special Jewish school. Their numbers, however, were declining by the thirties: in 1933 there were 144 Jewish pupils attending public elementary schools, but by 1940 there were only 79 such pupils enrolled.[89] Reli-gious instruction was compulsory for all Jewish children in public or private elementary, secondary, and vocational schools. Usually the local rabbi or another qualified religious teacher visited the various schools in the area weekly to offer the required classes.

In other centers where Jewish day schools no longer existed in the interwar period, instruction in religious subjects was supplied either after regular school hours in a Jewish school building, as was generally the case in Belgrade, or during the school day by special instructors, as in Sarajevo. The curriculum, which was set by the Federation of Jewish Religious Communities in conjunction with the Ministry of Education, included the Bible, liturgy, customs and cere-monies, Jewish history, and basic Hebrew. On the whole this system was not very effective and presented many difficulties in its opera-tion. In elementary and secondary schools with large Jewish enroll-ments, which generally meant those situated in old Jewish neighbor-hoods, like the Čaršija district in Sarajevo or Dorćol in Belgrade, pupils received regular weekly instruction during school hours and managed to cover the prescribed course of study. In less central regions, where there were fewer Jewish pupils attending schools or where Jewish children had to travel considerable distances to special afternoon or Sunday schools, instruction was usually inadequate and attendance irregular.

When the communal executive attempted to cope with these problems, they discovered that proposed improvements tended to be unfeasible, since trained personnel and additional facilities were unavailable and parents were generally uncooperative. The various school boards set up Home and School associations, hoping to gain needed support for their efforts.[90] The quest on the part of Jewish leaders for high-quality Jewish education suited to time and place never found a solution before the outbreak of World War II.

Auxiliary facilities to supplement the standard Jewish education were established in all three cities with full communal support. In 1923 a Jewish kindergarten was organized in Zagreb. Using Montessori methods, Mirjam Weiller taught Yugoslav and Jewish songs, as well as beginning Hebrew, to almost 60 little children in morning and afternoon sessions. Similar institutions also grew up in Belgrade and Sarajevo.[91] Special Hebrew courses were also introduced, often by the Zionist youth groups as in Zagreb. The most successful of these programs developed in Sarajevo under the name Safa Berura. This private school offered courses in such subjects as elementary and advanced modern Hebrew, Hebrew literature, and the Bible. It served pupils of all ages, but the majority of its students were in the upper two grades of middle school and belonged economically to the poorer strata. In the academic year 1924/25 a total of 110 pupils enrolled. Safa Berura achieved a considerable degree of popularity in Sarajevo and received the financial backing of both the Sephardic and the Ashkenazic communities, as well as the local Zionist and other Jewish organizations.[92]

In the realm of education, the various Jewish communities in Yugoslavia maintained reasonably satisfactory instruction in basic religious knowledge on the elementary level, but achieved barely adequate results on any higher plane, except for the Jewish Theological Seminary in Sarajevo (which will be discussed subsequently as a national rather than a local institution). With the help of the Zionist Federation and its local affiliates, supplementary courses became available for teaching Hebrew and awakening Jewish national consciousness, but traditional Jewish religious education was definitely not in vogue in the interwar period.

Jewish secondary schools developed out of necessity, when a numerus clausus was introduced on higher education for Jewish pupils in the fall of 1940.[93] In Belgrade and in Sarajevo, Jewish and non-Jewish teachers immediately volunteered to instruct in these hastily improvised institutions. These efforts met with complete approval and support on the part of the community at large. These middle schools taught much the same curriculum as regular gymnasia but included extra Jewish content as well.[94] The special schools were created to meet an emergency situation and survived for only a brief time and under unusual circumstances, but their mere existence attests to the vitality of the Jewish community itself and its determination to respond to discrimination in as positive a fashion as possible. Education, both Jewish and secular, remained a prime consideration for a community which could not visualize a life without it.

The Yugoslav Jewish community in the interwar period thus formally constituted a state-recognized religious body, patterned on the Central European model. Membership was compulsory for every Jew and all those who could afford it paid communal taxes. While franchise was becoming increasingly democratic, communal leadership remained in the hands of a fairly small, elite group of relatively wealthy lawyers, doctors, and businessmen, who were consistently re-elected to office. Lay volunteers predominated over professional leadership, such as rabbis and other paid communal officials.

The various local communities, whether Sephardic or Ashkenazic, shared the same basic organizational structure, but each community governed itself according to its own statutes and set its own priorities according to its particular needs and circumstances. Nevertheless, despite the continued importance of maintaining religious institutions, such as synagogues and cemeteries, and supervising basic Jewish education, the trend within Yugoslav Jewry was a gradual moving away from preserving traditional values to developing new responses to the demands of postemancipation Jewish society.

In addition to local communal institutions, which remained the basis for Jewish activity during the interwar years, Yugoslav Jewry also developed a strong supracommunal organization which coordinated its communal affairs and represented it to the outside world.

6

NATIONAL INSTITUTIONS

The unification of the South Slav lands after World War I brought together within one political unit the extremely diverse Jewish inhabitants of this region. For the first time the deep-rooted, traditional Sephardic communities of Serbia, Bosnia, and Macedonia came into direct contact with the large and fairly recent integrationist-oriented Ashkenazic communities of Croatia and the Vojvodina. Patriotic Serbian citizens confronted staunch Magyar nationalists, as Serbo-Croatian became the vehicle of communication between native speakers of Ladino and Hungarian. At the outset Jewish life was fragmented into a large number of independent, self-governing communities, both big and small, with no official ties between them. This newly created Yugoslav Jewry lacked organization and structure and possessed neither a recognized spokesman nor a representative body. After the hardships of the long war years the state of existing Jewish institutions approached chaos and degeneration, and strong measures were urgently needed to unify Yugoslav Jewry and revive Jewish spirit among them.

The idea of a communal federation among South Slav Jews was by no means a new one; it had appeared on the scene considerably before the outbreak of World War I. In 1897 Dr. Hugo Spitzer (1858–1934), president of the Osijek Jewish community in Slavonia, proposed the formation of a central organization for all the communities of Croatia-Slavonia. This suggestion met with opposition from the Zagreb community, which wanted complete control over any such body and at the same time feared interference with its own autonomy. As a result of these preliminary objections, the project was shelved for a number of years. However, in 1905, when the Croatian

Sabor introduced a law governing relations among religious groups without first consulting any Jewish authorities, Jewish communal leaders decided that they must act quickly to prevent the repetition of such an occurrence. Despite the agreement of the Zagreb executive to cooperate in the renewed efforts, nothing was done until June 1908 when a group of communal representatives and rabbis met in Zagreb to discuss the organization and its proposed statutes. The following spring a federation of Jewish communities of Croatia-Slavonia was created, on paper at least, with Dr. Dragutin Goldmann, president of the Zagreb Jewish community, at its head. But this institution never actually went into operation due to continued obstructionism on the part of the Zagreb community. Thus, by the time World War I broke out, Croatian Jewry had laid the foundations for a central communal organization, but the labors of Dr. Hugo Spitzer had not yet borne fruit.[1]

In Serbia, too, the concept of an association of Jewish communities had been considered before the war, but no concrete action had been taken in that direction. As he later recalled in reminiscences on this subject, Dr. Friedrich Pops, the president of the Belgrade Ashkenazic community, reached the conclusion even before the end of the fighting that some type of communal federation would be essential in the future state in order to unite all the Jewish inhabitants with their different backgrounds and attitudes. He foresaw the difficulties that would face the former Hungarian Jews in particular in their new country and stressed the need to establish Belgrade, the capital, as the focal point for Yugoslav Jewish activities. While still an emigré in Switzerland during the final years of the war, Pops approached a number of prominent Belgrade Jews, both Sephardim and Ashkenazim, who were also abroad, and received their support for his proposal. Following the declaration of peace, he and his colleagues returned home and began the complex arrangements for creating a central Jewish intercommunal organization.[2]

The Federation of Jewish Religious Communities was organized as a result of the combined efforts of Dr. Hugo Spitzer and Dr. Friedrich Pops, who continued to play a crucial role in its operations and devoted their lives to achieving its success. In their careers and outlook these two Jewish leaders were remarkably similar. Both men were lawyers and served for long terms on their local municipal councils. Each was president of his respective Jewish community for many years and an active Zionist. Spitzer, whose father had been head rabbi of Osijek, was the first president of the Federation of Zionists of Yugoslavia from 1918 to 1922 and the first president of the Federation of Jewish Religious Communities, an office he held from 1921 to 1933.[3] Pops, whose father had also been president of the Belgrade Ashkenazic community, was vice-president of the Zionist Federation for a long period of time, as well as acting president and eventually president of the communal federation from 1933 until his death in 1948.[4] It was these men who set the tone for Jewish life in Yugoslavia on a national scale and largely determined the course that the Federation of Jewish Religious Communities was to take during the interwar years.

In April 1919 the Belgrade Jewish leaders summoned representatives from the larger Jewish communities, as well as the Zionist Federation and the Political Committee of Jews of Bosnia-Hercegovina, to a conference to discuss the idea of a federation. The integrationist-dominated Zagreb communal executive, however, rejected the invitation vehemently, declaring it to be Zionist inspired and hence unpatriotic. The Novi Sad Jewish community also declined to attend. As a result, the Belgrade planning conference consisted of the delegates from six communities, two each from Belgrade, Sarajevo, and Osijek. This meeting resolved that it was an absolute necessity to form an organization or association of all Jewish communities in Yugoslavia, which would concern itself with religious, cultural, political, and humanitarian needs and serve as the legitimate representative of all the Jews of the kingdom. With this goal in mind, they called a congress of all communal presidents to be held in Osijek.[5]

The founding congress convened on July 1, 1919, with fifty-one communities, including Zagreb, participating in its deliberations. The delegates voted unanimously to create a federation, but a dispute ensued as to its name and its nature. Integrationist circles favored the word *Israelite* rather than *Jewish* as part of the official title, whereas the Orthodox members proved particularly intransigent on the question of communal autonomy and the protection of their rite. Eventually, a compromise was reached and the final vote overwhelmingly supported the following formula:

The Federation of Jewish (Israelite) Religious Communities is the central organ and representative of all Jewish (Israelite) religious communities in the Kingdom of Serbs, Croats and Slovenes, and has as its task to look after [the interests of] individual communities, mediate in official communication between [them and] state authorities, as well as represent them before state authorities if requested, and offer opinions on all legal projects, decrees and regulations which concern the Jewish (Israelite) Religious Communities.[6]

This end product appeared to be a defeat for the Zionist forces, who had proposed a much broader program for the future federation based on nationalist rather than religious grounds. It was still too early for such hopes to be realized, however. The Osijek conference had achieved temporary unity among all factions of Yugoslav Jewry —Sephardim and Ashkenazim, Orthodox and Neologues, Integrationists and Zionists—but in order to do so, it had left the newly born supracommunal organization a somewhat weak institution, limited in scope and opportunities.

At first all Yugoslav Jewish communities belonged to the one federation, but the Orthodox, fearing for their own autonomy and special interests, soon seceded. In 1924 they set up their own equivalent institution called the Union of Orthodox Jewish Religious Communities with its seat in Senta (later Subotica) in the Vojvodina.[7] This split received sanction in the Law on the Religious Community of Jews in 1929, amid considerable opposition on the part of the majority of the members of the Federation of Jewish Religious Communities. Unity of all Yugoslav Jewry had been one of the principal planks in the original project and this ideal was destroyed, at least partially, by the existence of a rival Orthodox organization.

The statutes of the federation received formal ratification from the Ministry of Religions in August 1921, at which time the adjective *Israelite* was deleted from its official title. According to this document the goals and areas of concern of the Federation of Jewish Religious Communities were

1. striving towards uniform organization of religious, administrative, educational, and charitable institutions of all religious communities through the adoption of uniform statutes;
2. organizing and directing Jewish religious instruction and supervising Jewish schools already existing or to be founded henceforth;
3. building and maintaining schools for the training of rabbis, teachers, and cantors and giving monetary aid to candidates in these fields;
4. creating, maintaining, and making nationwide the administration of the following:
    a. caring for communal officials in case of incapacity and for their families in case of death of their guardian, insofar as the means of the respective community does not suffice;
    b. caring for the sick, the education of orphans, and charity for the poor, as well as professional assistance;
    c. improving general and vocational education among Jews;

5. helping individual communities to fulfill their tasks;
6. mediating in communications between state authorities and individual communities;
7. resolving quarrels which arise between individual communities, upon the complaint of one side, and quarrels which arise between members and the executive of individual communities, as well as between rabbis or other functionaries and the executive of a community;
8. debating and deciding on questions which pertain to the religious life of Jews in the Kingdom of Serbs, Croats, and Slovenes, which do not touch on the practices of a particular community.[8]

For the most part these functions closely paralleled the duties of the member communities and were restricted to the traditional fields of religion, education, and charity. In addition, however, the federation was empowered to settle disputes within communities and represent them to the outside world.

The headquarters of the communal federation was located in Belgrade, and from the outset Belgrade Jewish leaders dominated the organization. The federation conducted its activities through local communal administrations, a central committee, and a triennial congress. Each community appointed delegates to the congress, which in turn elected the members of the central committee. This body originally consisted of thirty members: six rabbis and twenty-four laymen, with six substitutes. The rabbinical members generally included both Belgrade and Sarajevo rabbis, as well as one each from Zagreb and Novi Sad. Of the laymen, at least six had to be from Belgrade according to statute. The Belgrade representatives, who also encompassed either the president or one or more of the three vice-presidents plus the secretary and the treasurer, formed the executive board which took care of the day-to-day affairs of the central administration.[9] Thus, by definition, a minimum of one-third of the central committee of the federation originated in or around the nation's capital, and this third virtually controlled the management of all business.

The theory of Belgrade supremacy within the federation was borne out in practice as well. A survey of attendance at board meetings during the twelve years of the presidency of Dr. Hugo Spitzer, from 1921 to 1933, shows that the president himself, as well as his Zagreb vice-president, Dr. Hugo Kon, barely attended one such gathering per year, whereas the two Belgrade vice-presidents, Dr. Friedrich Pops, who was acting chairman in Spitzer's absence, and Šemaja Demajo, were present at virtually all of the eight sessions held annually. Similarly, the same small group of gentlemen from Belgrade—

Rafailo Finci, Lazar Avramović, Bukić Pijade, David Hochner, as well as Lavoslav Brandajs from nearby Zemun, and later David Albala and Bernard Robiček (all of whom were active participants in Jewish communal life)—appeared at practically all meetings held during these years, while the other dozen and a half members from elsewhere were usually conspicuous in their absence.[10] The non-Belgraders, also men prominent in local Jewish affairs, were in evidence every three years at the congresses, where they were consistently re-elected, but during the interim everything was left in the hands of the Belgrade clique. The situation continued in much the same fashion throughout the thirties.

It would seem that with respect to national Jewish life, Belgrade played much the same role as capital cities elsewhere in Europe, such as London, Paris, and Berlin in the west and Budapest, Prague, and Sofia in the east. This evaluation holds true only partially, however, since Belgrade, unlike the other examples, was not considered the only major Jewish center in Yugoslavia but had to compete with Zagreb and at times Sarajevo in this respect. It was natural that Belgrade should have become the home of the Federation of Jewish Religious Communities, since it was indeed the administrative heart of the country. Zagreb, however, became the seat of Zionist headquarters and thereby acted in an almost parallel capacity in directing Jewish affairs. Sarajevo clearly resented such outside domination for traditional and personal reasons and sporadically rebelled against both rivals. In the internal politics of the communal federation, as well as in the rivalry among the various cities, can be seen a miniature replica of interwar Yugoslavia: a centralized bureaucracy in Belgrade, dominated by Serbs, in this case Serbian Jews, was resented by the Croats, that is, the Jews of Zagreb, who were jealous of their own special prerogatives, as well as by the "deprived" or "underprivileged" provincials, the Sarajevo Sephardim.

During the first decade of its existence the communal federation did not prove to be a very powerful institution and hence did not command a great deal of respect from its affiliated members. In January 1922 the central bureau began operating on the premises of the local Jewish Nationalist Society. Several years later the head office moved to its own quarters on Kralja Petra Street.[11] The first secretary-general appointed was Ivan Kohn, a school director from Zemun, who held this responsible position until 1936. This office administered all business of the federation and annually conducted up to seven thousand transactions by correspondence. In the beginning many communities, especially the smaller ones, were fearful for their autonomous status and distrusted this central authority. They frequently tried to circumvent the federation by appealing directly to the Ministry of Religions to solve any difficulties. This practice undermined the prestige of the new body and decreased its efficiency in running Jewish affairs. As a result of strong objections on the part of the federation, the ministry issued a decree stipulating that all questions concerning members of the Jewish faith must first be referred to the federation before a final decision could be reached.[12] Over the years, however, the institution became more firmly established and gained greater confidence among its membership forcing the central office to expand its services to meet the ever-rising demands of its affiliated communities.

The Federation of Jewish Religious Communities levied annual dues upon its member communities to finance its many projects. From the original 2 dinars per communal taxpayer, the federation raised its fees to 10 dinars in 1921 and eventually to 25 dinars per year in 1927.[13] Communities were often reluctant to pay this amount, however, especially in the early days; hence the central institution sometimes found that it could not meet its proposed budget, which had increased from 100,000 dinars in the early 1920s to around five times that amount by the mid-1930s.[14] Despite complaints of lack of funds and frequent appeals to recalcitrant communities to pay their back debts, the federation nevertheless generally succeeded in remaining solvent and expanding its resources.

The ideological orientation of the communal federation and its leaders became increasingly Zionist over the years. The Fifth Congress of the Federation of Jewish Communities, held in Belgrade in April 1933, shortly after Hitler came to power in Germany, was a landmark in the institution's development. For the first time a majority of the delegates supported a Zionist platform based on Jewish nationality, the primacy of Palestine, and solidarity with all Jewry. They passed a series of resolutions advocating the Jewish Agency, the future World Jewish Congress, and the financing of extensive work programs, including *hakhsharah* (preparation for emigration to Palestine).[15] Henceforth, the Zionists maintained almost complete control over the organization. This situation did not fail to arouse opposition from some of the anti- or non-Zionist integrationists on the one hand and from the Zionist Revisionists on the other, as well as from a part of the Sephardic Establishment.

In 1934 a small group of Belgrade Sephardic integrationists, led by Avram Lević and Dr. Jakov Čelebonović, published a declaration in a local paper, *Štampa,* condemning the majority of Yugoslav Jews for being opposed to assimilation and claiming for themselves a monopoly on Yugoslav patriotism. The executive board of the federation called an emergency conference of Jewish public workers in Belgrade on July 15 to reply to these accusations. This gathering issued a statement declaring that only the Zionist Federation represented Zionist or Jewish nationalist endeavors, whereas the Federation of Jewish Religious Communities was the sole legitimate organ representing the whole of Yugoslav Jewry; therefore, they considered it harmful for individuals or other groups to attempt to assert exclusive rights over civic duty and pride.[16]

Two years later another dispute arose over the election of a new secretary-general to replace Ivan Kohn. The central committee chose Šime Spitzer of Zagreb, the candidate recommended by the Zionist Federation, over Mihael Levi of Sarajevo, also an ardent Zionist. Rejecting this appointment because of a minor scandal in which Spitzer had been involved some years previously, all the Sarajevo members, both Ashkenazim and Sephardim, as well as some of the Belgrade Sephardim (including Dr. Bukić Pijade), resigned temporarily at least from the central committee.[17] The resentment over this issue remained fierce and some of the Sarajevo Sephardim never returned to their seats on this body, boycotting the final congress of 1939.[18] The Sarajevo Jewish paper, *Jevrejski glas,* complained that Sephardim were being eliminated from leading positions in national Jewish life.[19] Sarajevo still retained unpleasant recollections of a long and bitter feud in the previous decade with the Zionist Federation in Zagreb, and this memory undoubtedly exacerbated its relations with the Zionist-dominated communal federation in the thirties.

Meanwhile, the Zionist Revisionists, who were staunch enemies of the Zionist Federation, exploited this misunderstanding by constantly publishing attacks on the communal federation and its "crisis" in their newspapers. They charged, in a somewhat exaggerated fashion, that the two federations, Zionist and communal, were in fact one and the same.[20]

The Federation of Jewish Religious Communities continued to gain strength and broaden its program, but as it grew older internal as well as external difficulties evolved. When World War II broke out, Yugoslav Jewry, which could not solve its own minor squabbles, certainly was not equipped to handle the major new problems which now confronted it.

The communal federation began as a fairly traditional institution, modeled somewhat along the lines of earlier Jewish supracommunal bodies, such as the former Council of the Four Lands in Poland. Despite the fact that it received official state recognition and eventually derived its legal status from the Law on the Religious Community of Jews of 1929, it would be a mistake to consider it a government agency. Unlike the French consistorial system, it was created entirely upon the initiative of the Jews themselves and not by the state, and it was intended primarily to serve Jewish interests. South Slav Jewish leaders, especially the Zionists among them, wanted to unite all communities into one body that could represent their views to the central and local authorities; it was totally a voluntary union and did not originate through state pressure. Thus, it was an organization of Jews, run by Jews and for Jews, and not a product of authoritarian government, as implied by such scholars as Salo Baron.[21]

The Jewish community, like all other recognized confessional groups, received an annual state subsidy to support its clergy and other religious institutions. According to the Decree on Permanent Annual Aid to the Religious Community of Jews in the Kingdom of Yugoslavia of March 3, 1930, the sum regularly allotted to the "Israelites" amounted to 1,131,220 dinars ($20,000), which was divided proportionally among the chief rabbinate (228,400 dinars), the Federation of Jewish Religious Communities (837,304 dinars), and the Union of Orthodox Jewish Religious Communities (65,516 dinars).[22] In comparison with the grants to other established denominations, the subvention to the Jewish religious minority was by far the most generous. According to one contemporary source, the Serbian Orthodox church received 38,326,630 dinars, or 5.65 dinars per member; the Roman Catholic church 26,626,219 dinars, or 6.05 per person; the Protestants 1,444,000 dinars, or 6.09; and the Muslims 15,377,200 dinars, or 9.84. The Jewish community, however, was given 16.5 dinars per capita, or two to three times the amount given to any other group.[23] This situation should not be interpreted as deliberate favoritism of the government toward the Jews, rather it indicates the high maintenance costs of the many small Jewish communities scattered throughout the country, each of which needed to support the required religious functionaries and teachers. Nevertheless, this fact is indeed significant and reflects positively on the relations between the state and the Jewish community.

This state aid provided about two-thirds of the revenues of the communal federation and an even larger percentage of the income of the Orthodox Union.[24] It could, however, only be used for specific purposes stipulated by the state, such as salaries of rabbis, cantors, and other religious officials, pensions for them and for their families, aid to poor communities, support for the theological seminary, scholarships for students studying abroad, inspection of Jewish communities, and travel expenses for rabbis.[25] Since the amount granted by no means covered all costs in the outlined categories, this money was distributed only among the smaller and less affluent communities, those which could not afford to pay for all the necessary facilities of Jewish life on their own.[26] The two communal associations submitted frequent petitions for a raise in the subvention to subsidize rising costs and increasing numbers of religious officials, but the grant remained constant throughout the thirties.

Although the Federation of Jewish Religious Communities actively engaged in defense activities on behalf of native- and foreign-born Jews,[27] its major concerns were within the internal Jewish communal sphere, dealing with religious matters such as education, functionaries, and applications of Jewish law. The federation shared jurisdiction over religious affairs with the chief rabbinate and the rabbinical synod.

The spiritual leader of Yugoslav Jewry was the chief rabbi, whose office was established in 1923 with the appointment of Dr. Isaac Alcalay, rabbi of the Belgrade Sephardic community, to this position. The chief rabbinate became the sole institution to represent the entire Jewish population, both Neologues and Orthodox, Ashkenazim and Sephardim. Theoretically, according to the Law on the Religious Community of Jews of 1929, the chief rabbi was to be chosen by royal decree, upon the suggestion of the Ministry of Justice, from three candidates elected jointly by the central committees of both communal associations; the presidents of the Jewish communities of all rites in Belgrade, Zagreb, Skoplje, Sarajevo, Novi Sad, Subotica, and Osijek; and all rabbis serving in Jewish religious establishments in the kingdom.[28] In practice, the stipulation that the seat of the chief rabbinate be in Belgrade restricted the selection to the two rabbis of the capital, and in actual fact, Rabbi Alcalay was the only individual ever to occupy this position.

The chief rabbi generally performed ceremonial functions as official religious representative of the Jewish community, somewhat along the lines of the Serbian Orthodox patriarch or the Catholic archbishop. He received a generous annual state subsidy amounting to 228,400 dinars ($5,000), which covered all personal and administrative expenses. By virtue of his formal status, the chief rabbi enjoyed a considerable degree of prestige and respect.

Within the Federation of Jewish Religious Communities, a rabbinical synod was formed, consisting of five members plus the chief rabbi as its head, which arbitrated all questions of a religious character.[29] This body exercised the right to examine and advise the federation concerning qualifications of rabbis, religious teachers, cantors, and other religious officials, and it could also take disciplinary action against rabbis and other functionaries. The clerics alone were not always the final authority on religious matters, however. If the central committee of the communal federation disagreed with the opinion of its synod, a special committee, including the six members of the synod and six lay members of the central committee with the chief rabbi presiding, reached a final verdict by majority vote.[30] The federation, like its member communities, was concerned with preserving lay predominance and feared excessive clerical power, even in the religious field.

Within the sphere of influence of the rabbinical synod lay the supervision of Jewish education throughout the country. The synod was responsible for providing suitable textbooks for religious instruction in public schools. The most urgent concern was the lack of appropriate Jewish history books in Serbo-Croatian. To fill this need the federation sponsored the writing and publication of a two-volume biblical history by Jakov Maestro of Sarajevo, which appeared in 1933, and a two-volume history of the Jewish people from the destruction of the First Temple to the present by Solomon Kalderon of Belgrade, which was completed two years later. These works were issued in both Cyrillic and Latin alphabets for use in all elementary and middle schools.[31] In addition, by 1937, the synod organized a system of inspections of all Jewish communities, their educational facilities, and personnel. This program, combined with the districting of the entire country into communities with clearly defined boundaries, substantially increased the efficiency of communal administration and religious knowledge instruction.[32]

Undoubtedly the most ambitious project launched by the Federation of Jewish Religious Communities in the first decade of its existence was the founding of a Jewish theological seminary in Sarajevo. The need for such an institution was keenly felt in all parts of the country because very few qualified native-born religious officials were to be found in the South Slav lands and foreign-born functionaries could only be hired on a temporary basis. The original planners never intended to train rabbis within the country, since facilities for a proper rabbinical seminary could not be maintained for so limited a supply of candidates as Yugoslavia produced. Instead, the project covered only advanced Jewish education on the secondary school level to provide the requisite number of religious teachers, cantors, assistant rabbis, and other minor Jewish functionaries, to meet especially the demands of the smaller Jewish communities. The proposal to found the seminary appeared in the debates of the first few congresses of the federation in the early twenties, but the idea became reality only in September 1928, when the Jewish Middle Theological Seminary opened its doors for the first time.[33] Because Sarajevo preserved the most traditional Jewish atmosphere and possessed the necessary facilities and instructors, it was chosen as the site for the new school. Dr. Moric Levi, the head rabbi of the Sephardic community, became rector of the seminary and also taught several courses. He was assisted by Rabbi Urbach of the Ashkenazic community and Jakov Maestro, the local religious teacher, in the conduct of the Jewish curriculum. Lectures on standard high school subjects were given by a number of other instructors, mainly non-Jews.[34] Included in the program of study were Bible, Talmud, Jewish history, *Shulhan Arukh,* Midrash, Hebrew, and Jewish music, and such regular secular normal school subjects as pedagogy, Serbo-Croatian, German, and general history.[35]

Because it was considered a national body rather than a local Sarajevo school, money to support the seminary came from the annual state subsidy and the budget of the federation.[36] The communal federation administered this institution through a curatorium of ten persons, two rabbis and eight laymen, elected by the central committee, which always counted among its ranks several prominent representatives of both Sarajevo communities.[37]

Although the school was designed to accommodate both Sephardic and Ashkenazic students, the first class of sixteen included only four Ashkenazim, all from the Vojvodina. Of the Sephardim, five came from Sarajevo itself, three from Bitolj, two from Belgrade, and one each from Travnik and Split.[38] Much the same pattern prevailed throughout the thirties. The seminary began with a four-year program, but in 1934 this was extended an extra year.[39] By 1939 twenty-five graduates of the first two classes had left the institution to take positions in all parts of Yugoslavia, and sixteen more students were enrolled in the third class. Still there were not enough candidates to fill all the available jobs, especially among the Ashkenazic congregations, and religious personnel continued to be imported from the outside.[40] In addition, during the thirties an average of four to six rabbinical students from Yugoslavia, many of them from the seminary, received scholarships every year to study advanced theology abroad. Hence the South Slav lands managed to produce and hire some of their own rabbis, even though the supply was never enough to meet the demand. Among the graduates of the seminary were a number of men who later became prominent rabbis, such as Dr. Solomon Gaon, Haham of the Spanish and Portuguese Congregation of the British Commonwealth, Grand Rabbi Dr. Georges Vadnai of Lausanne, Switzerland, and Grand Rabbi Emmanuel Bulz of Luxembourg.[41] The seminary thus fulfilled a very important goal in the Yugoslav Jewish community by providing qualified persons of the younger generation who helped perpetuate both the religious and other aspects of organized Jewish life.

Under the aegis of the federation and particularly the rabbinical synod also fell the issue of the validity of the *beth din,* specifically in Serbia. Legislation on marital law and divorce in Yugoslavia varied extensively according to region. In the Vojvodina, for example, only civil marriage and divorce existed and no question of religious jurisdiction arose. In Croatia provisions were incorporated into the statutes so that all divorce cases passed through civil courts but were supposedly resolved according to religious law. In Bosnia, by contrast, only religious courts had the power to decide marital disputes, hence the authority of the *beth din* never came into question. In Serbia the practice had followed along the lines of Bosnia. The *beth din* functioned according to its traditional role, and its rights were never disputed until after World War I.[42] In 1921 an appeal of a Jewish divorce case came before the Belgrade Cassation Court, the highest court in Serbia. In this instance, it was ruled that civil courts could not decide such a matter since it fell under the competence of the religious court. Ten years later, however, in another case this verdict was reversed, repealing the authority of the *beth din.* (The underlying cause for this change of policy probably can be traced to the Minister of Justice at that time, Dimitrije Ljotić, an anti-Semite who later became head of a tiny Fascist party.) The Federation of Jewish Religious Communities and the Belgrade Sephardic community, whose powers were being usurped, loudly protested this second ruling, claiming that it encroached upon traditional religious rights and privileges. After a lengthy dispute, the federation gained a victory and both the Belgrade Sephardic and Ashkenazic communities were able to restore to their statutes the institution of the *beth din.*[43] Attempts at unifying Jewish marital regulations for all of Yugoslavia failed completely, however, due to the chaos reigning in the Yugoslav legal system.

Another religious-legal problem which confronted the federation involved the question of conversions to and from Judaism. Initially, the question arose in Croatia, where, according to the interconfessional law of 1905, persons could not convert to any non-Christian faith.[44] The Jewish community considered this provision discriminatory since it infringed upon the equal status of their religion.[45] The authorities evidently did not always enforce this law; according to the statistics of the Zagreb rabbinate, 125 individuals converted to Judaism between 1911 and 1930.[46] However, the issue of whether or not outsiders could join the Jewish community arose again in 1930, when a number of attempts were made to apply the old restrictions. The Zagreb communal executive in particular became very upset by these incidents and introduced the matter before the Fourth Congress of the federation in 1930, which passed a resolution against such interference with religious rights.[47]

As the 1930s progressed, the communal federation became more concerned with converts from rather than to Judaism, however. In 1938 a virtual epidemic of conversions broke out, especially in Zagreb. The total number of converts reported in Yugoslavia for 1938 was 821, of whom 580 were Yugoslav citizens and 241 foreign nationals. The vast majority of these converts were undoubtedly Ashkenazim, since 624 of them came from Savska province, formerly Croatia-Slavonia, (431 from Zagreb alone) and 96 from Dunavska province (the Vojvodina). The other 100 or so individuals, including 35 from Belgrade and 39 from Drina province (Bosnia),probably were also predominantly Ashkenazic, although living in heavily Sephardic areas—there were 23 converts in the Sarajevo Ashkenazic community alone.[48] In December of that year the Jewish press published the names of 205 individuals from Zagreb and 82 from elsewhere who had recently left Judaism in an attempt to escape the deteriorating situation of European Jewry. Among these persons were many wealthy and prominent Jewish integrationists, including one non-Zionist member of the Jewish Agency and the board of the Zagreb Jewish community, Dr. Milan Marić, an industrialist and the Turkish consul in Zagreb.[49] Not only did this development have an unfortunate psychological effect on the Jewish community, but it also caused extensive monetary damage, since Zagreb alone lost some 200,000 dinars in communal tax payments.[50] The Jewish press immediately denounced these people as traitors, cowards, and worse, and the federation took what few steps it could to counter the movement.[51] Most of these individuals converted to Catholicism, which was not too surprising since the majority came from Zagreb. An additional factor, which to a certain extent must have influenced their choice of a new religion, was the hesitancy of the Serbian Orthodox church to perform such rapid conversions on a large scale.[52] Even the Catholic Church expressed some suspicion as to the sincerity of the motivation of these Jews for seeking religious salvation. The conversion plague was of short duration, however. Its impact proved serious only in Zagreb; elsewhere it occurred only on a relatively small scale, affecting fewer people. The vast majority of Yugoslav Jewry chose to retain their Jewish identity, despite the ever-increasing Fascist menace from abroad.

The Federation of Jewish Religious Communities, the chief rabbinate, and the rabbinical synod were not the only national institutions that dealt with the religious concerns of the Jewish community. The religious functionaries themselves felt the need to create their own associations that would present their particular viewpoints. The first actually to found such an organization were the Yugoslav rabbis. Following a preliminary planning conference held in Vinkovci (Croatia) in July 1923, a constituent assembly met in Zagreb in October of the same year to organize a rabbinical federation with Rabbi Isaac Alcalay as president. Its purpose was to elevate Jewish religious and cultural life in the country, spread Jewish education, and represent professional group interests.[53]

At meetings of the rabbinical association, as well as within the communal federation, lively debates occurred on the subject of the rights and duties of the rabbi in Jewish communal life. The rabbis insisted that they have exclusive and independent authority in deciding all matters of religious ritual. They felt that the communal rabbi should be entitled to complete control over marriage, *get* (divorce certificates), and *halitzah* according to religious law through the vehicle of the *beth din,* wherever one existed. They also fought for permanent appointments and the maintenance of supervision over registry books.[54] Eventually, the rabbis managed to win many of their demands, but they never succeeded in freeing themselves totally from lay surveillance.

Among the Jewish religious officials, not only the rabbis but also the cantors and later teachers and other communal employees decided to organize. In January 1922 even before the Association of Rabbis had crystalized into existence, a congress of Yugoslav cantors convened in Subotica to discuss the founding of an Association of Israelite Cantors in the Kingdom of Serbs, Croats, and Slovenes.[55]

The aims of this organization, as expounded in its statutes of 1924, were multifold in nature:

1. that cantors receive from the community the proper respect which should be accorded to them as *shelihei zibbur,* that is, as religious representatives of the community in public prayer;
2. that as a condition for hiring, Jewish communities demand of cantors such a degree of theological and musical training as befits the honor of a *sheliah zibbur;*
3. to assure Jewish communities in the kingdom worthy cantorial candidates;
4. to purify synagogue singing, especially recitations, of all traits which do not correspond to synagogue style so that all singing will bring honor to Yugoslav Jewry;
5. to encourage excellent composers to write new synagogue music of highest quality;
6. to defend and represent the class interests of Jewish cantors in the kingdom;
7. to advance the artistic spirit by periodic meetings and discussions of professional questions; and
8. to provide insurance benefits for cantors in their old age or for their widows.

To meet these goals, the association sought proper recognition for its members in communal statutes as well as within the communal federation. It also demanded a seat on the central committee of the Federation of Jewish Religious Communities. In addition, the cantors pressed for the creation of special schools within the country to train future professional cantors and for scholarships to support such students.[56] The cantors clearly resented what they considered to be the neglect and ill-treatment of their position on the part of the Jewish community at large. They strove to improve their status, morally, materially, and artistically.

The cantorial association had its base in Zagreb. From 1924 to 1927 Josip Rendi, the head cantor of Zagreb, held the presidency, while David Meisel, head cantor of Karlovac (Croatia), served as vice-president and later as Rendi's successor. The membership was almost exclusively Ashkenazic, mainly drawn from Croatia and the Vojvodina; Bosnian or Serbian cantors participated only rarely in its activities.[57] For a brief period of time, in 1928 and 1929, the cantors enjoyed their own monthly magazine, containing news in the field, with most articles written in German. During the thirties, however, this organization all but disappeared from public view.

On occasion, the idea had arisen of creating a Jewish teachers' association to improve the quality of religious instruction, but this particular project was never realized.[58] In 1938, however, an Association of Education and Administrative Employees of Jewish Institutions in the Kingdom of Yugoslavia was organized instead. This body was intended to represent the common interests of its members, improve working conditions and pay, provide pensions and insurance, supply legal service (especially to foreigners), help members find jobs, and publish an information organ. A representative also sat on the central committee of the Federation of Jewish Religious Communities.[59] The communal employees joined with the rabbis and the cantors to approve a plan for a central pension fund, which went into effect in 1938 after many years of deliberation.[60] By the outbreak of World War II, the various functionaries of the Yugoslav Jewish communities had effectively organized themselves, thus strengthening their position considerably. Group consciousness had developed to such an extent that it became possible for all to unite to improve their combined status and safeguard their individual futures.

Considering the wide diversity in historical tradition and outlook among the various Jewish communities in the South Slav lands, it is indeed impressive that in such a short time Yugoslav Jewry managed to create a strong, centralized supracommunal association. The Federation of Jewish Religious Communities succeeded in bringing together its Sephardic and Ashkenazic components, revealing relatively little friction among either the rabbinical or lay leadership within this national body. The Neologues and the Orthodox, however, were unable to reach a similar rapprochement and a separate Union of Orthodox Jewish Religious Communities existed alongside the federation, with minimal contact between the two institutions over the years.

While the federation served as a defense agency and as a representative body to the outside world, it directed a great deal of its attention toward religious affairs. In addition to the chief rabbinate and the rabbinical synod, which operated within the framework of the communal federation, however, several professional associations of religious officials developed outside its aegis to protect the interests of rabbis, cantors, teachers, and other communal functionaries. The Yugoslav Jewish community was thus highly organized on a national level for both internal and external purposes, and the community was reasonably united and sufficiently well equipped to deal efficiently with its day-to-day concerns under normal circumstances.

With these central institutions providing countrywide coordination and direction, the Jewish community continued to derive its greatest strength from the local organizations, which supplied the support and the leadership necessary to ensure a vibrant and active Jewish society in Yugoslavia.

7

SOCIAL AND CULTURAL ORGANIZATIONS

Jewish life in Yugoslavia revolved around an extensive network of local organizations with various functions. Each of the three majors centers had over a dozen such institutions, including charitable and benevolent associations, cultural societies, sports clubs, and social groups. These organizations fell into a number of categories according to the sex, age, wealth, religious affiliation, or ideology of their membership: men or women, youth or adult, rich or poor, Sephardic or Ashkenazic, Zionist or non-Zionist.[1] Many of these entities developed around the turn of the century; during the interwar period a few disappeared, and others were created to fill the new needs of the times. Although the activities of the different societies often overlapped, as did their leadership and membership, nevertheless, all these organizations performed the vital task of strengthening the community and involving its members in a full panoply of useful and positive joint enterprises.

Within the realm of social welfare were numerous societies devoted to aiding the poor, caring for the sick, the orphans, and the aged, providing interest-free loans, granting scholarships to needy students and apprentices, or any combination of these functions. In Sarajevo, for example, during the interwar period, roughly a dozen charitable associations operated side by side. In the Sephardic community, along with the Hevra Kaddisha, there existed La Benevolencia (Ladino for "benevolence") to aid students and apprentices and La Humanidad (Ladino for "humanity"), which concerned itself primarily with poor women and children. Kanfe Jona-Bikur Holim (Hebrew meaning "the wings of doves" and "visit the sick") looked after sick men, and Sociedad de vizitar dolientes (Ladino for "society for visiting the sick") gave similar aid to women. Ezrat Jetomim (Hebrew for "aid to orphans") cared for orphans, and Mizgav Ladah (Hebrew for "help for the oppressed") clothed poor children, while La Gloria (Ladino for "glory") provided dowries for brides. In addition, among the poorer classes, mutual interest groups arose, such as the burial fund, Poale Cijon (Hebrew for "workers of Zion"), the credit unions, Melaha (Hebrew for "work") and Geula (Hebrew for "redemption"), and the loan society, Ezra Becarot (Hebrew for "aid in difficulties"). All of these helped to ease the difficult economic situation, especially in the thirties.[2]

Within the Sarajevo Ashkenazic community, alongside the Hevra Kaddisha, functioned the Ashkenazic Women's Society, which took care of needy women and children, Hahnusas Hakala (Hebrew for "dowry for the bride"), which gave assistance to poor brides, and Ahdus (Hebrew for "unity"), which acted as a general aid society. Actually, Ahdus was more than a charitable organization; it also served religious, social, and cultural ends. Especially during the early years of its existence, beginning in 1906, its members comprised the lower echelons of the Ashkenazic ranks, the small merchants, artisans, employees, and clerks, most of whom had recently emigrated from small towns in Galicia, Bukovina, Silesia, and Moravia. They formed their own circle of Yiddish speakers, providing entertainment, such as plays, in their native tongue. Until 1926 they also held their own religious services, according to the Orthodox rite, for the High Holy Days. After World War I, the membership of Ahdus expanded, losing its specifically East European character and becoming more closely associated with the larger Ashkenazic (Neologue) community, whose service club it then became.[3]

The most important humanitarian and educational association in Sarajevo, however, was La Benevolencia. A study of the growth of this organization and its activities sheds considerable light on the development of the community and its institutions. In 1892 a small group of wealthy Sarajevo Sephardim decided to form a society that would provide organized and constructive assistance to the many impoverished Jews of the city and thereby alleviate the need for the poor to beg for money weekly on every doorstep. Among the founding members were Izahar Z. Danon, its first president; Ješua D. Salom, for many years president of the Sephardic community and also of La Benevolencia; Ašer Alkalaj; Avram Levi-Sadić and Bernardo Pinto, all very prominent men in Sarajevo Sephardic circles.

The early program consisted of regular monthly aid to the poor, free medical care for the sick, and assistance to needy pupils and apprentices. By the end of the century, however, the society began to shift its emphasis away from charity and toward support for education. At that time the Sarajevo Sephardic community completely lacked an intellectual class, since virtually none of the native Jews had received a higher education. To fill this gap La Benevolencia initiated a policy of granting annual scholarships to high school and university students to encourage them to continue their academic work. Its contributions to charitable causes gradually declined before World War I, while its donations toward schooling dramatically escalated. La Benevolencia issued a proclamation which read: "Everyone who desires to learn a trade or attend school—and that surely means everyone who wants to secure himself a future—but does not have the means to do so, let him apply to La Benevolencia and it will help all in safeguarding their existence."[4]

Begun as a local organization for the benefit of the Sarajevo Sephardic poor, by 1908 La Benevolencia had expanded its activities to include all the Sephardim of Bosnia-Hercegovina, and in 1923 it opened its ranks and its pocketbook to Ashkenazim as well.[5] Branches of the organization sprang up in many small towns in the province, as well as in larger centers outside Bosnia. From 1899 to 1923 La Benevolencia supplied scholarship aid to a total of 148 candidates—62 in secondary schools, 9 in preparatory schools and 32 at university (mainly abroad)—in the amount of 572,000 crowns.[6] In the next decade, it supported 83 university students (almost 70 percent of whom studied within Yugoslavia) and 280 high school pupils, as well as 282 apprentices in various trades, spending a total of 1,526,240 dinars ($27,250) on academic education and 604,482 ($10,-800) on apprenticeships.[7] During the twenties, the society continued its general policy of generous aid to encourage advanced studies, but by the thirties, it had begun to re-evaluate and revise its basic program.

No longer did it give liberal aid unquestioningly to aspirants for the free professions attending universities abroad or even in Zagreb and Belgrade. Instead, it reduced its academic support to a minimum and concentrated its attention on training apprentices for various practical trades. Gone were the days when the Sarajevo Jewish community desperately needed intellectuals and professionals. No jobs existed for qualified graduates in the thirties, hence La Benevolencia diverted its funds to the "productivization" of the Jewish labor force, as the jargon of the day termed it. In its campaign to attract greater numbers of apprentices, La Benevolencia offered job counseling and an employment service, as well as monthly monetary aid, medical care, and clothing. It also began to develop an interest in helping girls secure their own economic future through training in vocations and household skills, as well as teaching.[8]

Aside from these scholarship programs, La Benevolencia branched out into other cultural projects within the Jewish community, such as popular lecture series, the collection of Sephardic folklore, the establishment of a library, and the amassing of historical material on Jews in the Dubrovnik state archives. The society published a commemorative volume on its thirtieth anniversary in 1924 and a special edition in collaboration with the Belgrade charitable organization Potpora (Serbian for "aid") ten years later. It also brought into print Jorjo Tadić's scholarly work on the Jews in Dubrovnik in the Middle Ages, a collection of short stories by the noted Yugoslav Jewish writer from Sarajevo, Isak Samokovlija, and a memorial to Maimonides.[9] In addition, La Benevolencia organized night courses for working youths, offering instruction in Serbo-Croatian, accounting, commercial law, and hygiene, as well as Jewish history.[10] It gave regular subventions in generous amounts to other Jewish institutions in Sarajevo, such as the choral society, La Lira, the local Jewish paper, *Jevrejski glas,* and the Hebrew school Safa Berura, and contributed 62,500 dinars to the building of the new Sephardic synagogue. It also supported campaigns to collect money for the Jews in Bitolj and the refugees from Nazi Europe. Not only did it cooperate with Jewish organizations, but it also came to the assistance of its non-Jewish counterparts, the Serbian society Prosvjet (meaning "education"), the Croatian Napredak (literally "progress"), and the Muslim Gajret.[11]

The association derived its income from membership dues and other donations, and loans from local banks. In the 1930s it could boast of about five hundred members in Sarajevo itself and another three hundred outside.[12] The leading figures in La Benevolencia during the interwar period included Dr. Jakov Kajon, its president for many years, Dr. Vita Kajon, Dr. Samuel Pinto, Dr. Kalmi Baruch, and Dr. Braco Poljokan, Sephardic intellectuals who were very active in communal affairs. La Benevolencia was thus the most powerful Jewish humanitarian and cultural organization in Sarajevo, and it tried repeatedly to incorporate some of the smaller societies into its ranks in order to increase efficiency in looking after the city's poor Jewish masses, as well as its cultural and educational needs.

The Belgrade scene looked much the same. Potpora was the local equivalent to La Benevolencia. A group of younger communal leaders established the association in 1897 to provide scholarships for needy students who wished to attend university either at home or outside the country. The founding members were Solomon Azriel, Dr. David Alkalaj, Benko Davičo, and Dr. Jakov Čelebonović. Dr. Bukić Pijade served as president of the organization from 1920 to 1931; he was followed in office by Leon de Leon. The first individual to benefit from its support was Isaac Alcalay, the future chief rabbi. After World War I, the society broadened its program to include care for war orphans. Between 1919 and 1931 it gave aid to 68 students and 98 orphans. Potpora, with a membership of around 400 in the thirties, operated on a somewhat smaller scale than La Benevolencia, and work with apprentices in Belgrade was not nearly as successful as in Sarajevo.[13]

In addition, within the Belgrade Sephardic community a number of other charitable societies continued to function during the interwar period, such as Bikur Holim, the sick fund; Anije Air (Sephardic Hebrew for "poor of the city"), the poor fund; Milosrdje (Serbo-Croatian for "mercy"), which also provided money and other necessities for the poor; Hesed šel emet (Hebrew meaning "righteousness of truth"), which erected gravestones for the dead; and Oneg Šabat-Gemilut Hasadim (Hebrew for "enjoyment of the Sabbath" and "good deeds of the righteous"), which among other tasks recited *limudim,* or prayers in memory of its deceased members. Alongside, several new institutions grew up, including the Home for Old Mosaic Men and Women, which supplied free room, board, and medicine for a few elderly poor, and the cultural and humanitarian society Šemaja Demajo, named after the Jewish member of parliament. Among the women, the Jewish Women's Society flourished in the Sephardic sector, while Dobrotvor (Serbo-Croatian for "charity") operated within the Ashkenazic circle.[14] Interestingly enough, aside from the women's club and the Hevra Kaddisha, the Belgrade Ashkenazic community never created any other charitable or benevolent associations to take care of their own poor and sick and hence had no equivalent of Sarajevo's Ahdus. This situation can probably be attributed to the relatively high standard of living among the Ashkenazim in Belgrade and their lack of local traditions due to their recent arrival, compounded by growing integrationist tendencies.[15]

The most important welfare activity of the Belgrade Sephardic community proved to be the annual Winter Campaign, which the communal executive helped organize with the various service agencies, such as Milosrdje and Šemaja Demajo. Under this project, every year around Hanukkah, a general collection of used clothing and goods, as well as money, took place, followed by free distribution of food, wood, and clothes among the needy poor, sick, and elderly of the community. In December 1939, for example, in response to this appeal the campaign was able to amass over 100,000 dinars worth of wares and money, which were then used to cover the humanitarian exigencies of the winter and the coming year.[16]

Unlike Sarajevo and Belgrade, Zagreb was not known for its multiplicity of Jewish organizations serving similar social needs. Jewish leaders made a much greater effort to achieve efficiency and uniformity in the distribution of welfare aid through centralization. Thus, in 1927 representatives of the communal executive, the Hevra Kaddisha, the Israelite Women's Society and their affiliates, and the head rabbi formed a special committee to handle all necessary services, such as regular monthly aid to disabled and elderly men and women; emergency aid to poor families; temporary aid to the needy for three to six months; care for the ill in hospitals and clinics; aid to the blind, deaf, and otherwise disabled; and care for orphans. This body also gave help to youths learning a trade or business and scholarships to students in secondary or higher schools and to girls interested in earning a living. In addition, it provided interest-free loans or guarantees to poor businessmen and artisans. In 1929 these contributions totaled over one million dinars.[17]

This type of aid, although essential, was not enough in itself to solve the poverty problem, especially in the thirties. The Jewish community began to recognize the need for what was termed productive social work to help people to help themselves. To this end, the Central Jewish Bureau for Productive Social Aid came into existence in Zagreb in 1933, starting as a regional institution but gradually extending its program to all Yugoslav Jews. By 1935 it had 284 patrons, mainly from Zagreb. Its purpose was to train Jewish youth in practical fields, such as trades and manual labor, stressing the importance of *hakhsharah.* One of the major projects of the Central Bureau was a Home for Apprentices, which opened in 1934 with a capacity of 20 trainees per year. These apprentices came from all over Yugoslavia to learn a variety of trades, becoming electricians, plumbers, watchmakers, machinists, opticians, tailors, and bookbinders. The bureau also supported a Home for Girls, which annually housed 9 young women who were learning to be seamstresses, hairdressers, mothers' helpers, dental technicians, and kindergarten teachers. These young people also received such services as vocational counseling, employment placement, evening courses and lectures, medical care from the central institution. The task of popularizing artisanry and manual labor among Jewish youth was by no means easy in interwar Yugoslavia, and the success of this agency in training 60 boys and 20 girls in five years constituted a considerable achievement on its part.[18]

Another important enterprise of the Central Bureau and other Jewish service agencies was the Campaign to Help Bitolj Jews. The Jewish community in the town of Bitolj in Macedonia faced a desperate situation of extreme poverty, helplessness, and hunger. Over half of its 3,000 Jews were in urgent need of assistance. Previously various commissions had attempted to deal with the problem, but none succeeded until the Central Bureau in Zagreb took over control and organized a special committee of its own. One of its first projects was to found a home for orphans in Bitolj, which housed 80 children from two to seven years old. Another project enabled many youths to learn useful trades; another arranged for the emigration of a considerable number of Bitolj Jews to Palestine as manual laborers.[19] Thus the bureau developed some constructive solutions to a most difficult dilemma for which all Yugoslav Jews shared at least moral responsibility.

Zagreb could boast of Yugoslavia's largest and finest Jewish home for the aged. In 1906 Lavoslav Schwarz, a wealthy local philanthropist, bequeathed a legacy of 400,000 crowns for the founding of an old-age home to be named after him. In 1911 the Schwarz Home began operation with 8 residents; from that time to 1940, 293 elderly people took advantage of its facilities. In the interwar period, a number of university students and apprentices also lived there. A new wing was added in 1932 to the already existing structure, which now included hospital rooms, a library, and a chapel where daily services took place. By 1939 the Schwarz Home could accommodate close to 100 persons. Maintenance of the home depended upon substantial annual contributions from the Zagreb Jewish communal executive, the Hevra Kaddisha, the Israelite Women's Society, and the Zagreb B'nai B'rith Lodge, as well as money collected by the Society of Friends of the Schwarz Home, to which 262 members belonged. The head rabbi conducted an annual campaign to raise funds for its support, and the residents and their families paid according to their ability.[20] The Zagreb Jewish community attempted to establish a Jewish hospital in the city but these efforts never bore fruit.[21] Thus, social institutions were distributed among the three largest and wealthiest Ashkenazic centers: the only sizable Jewish home for the aged was in Zagreb, the one Jewish hospital was in Subotica in the Vojvodina, and the main orphanage for children over seven was located in Novi Sad, also in the Vojvodina. Neither Belgrade nor Sarajevo, both predominantly Sephardic with relatively lower economic status, managed to operate any welfare facilities on a similar scale.

Along with the rather traditional humanitarian societies which distributed charity to specific categories of the needy, such as were found in Sarajevo and Belgrade, and the somewhat more modern welfare institutions of Zagreb, Yugoslav Jewry also supported another special type of service club in the form of B'nai B'rith. Lodges affiliated with the international Independent Order of B'nai B'rith and bearing the motto Philanthropy, Brotherly Love, and Harmony, developed first in Belgrade and later in Zagreb, Sarajevo, Osijek, Subotica, Novi Sad, and Skoplje. Membership within their ranks proved to be highly selective, including only the wealthiest and best-educated elements of both the Ashkenazic and Sephardic community. In 1933 Lodge Serbia in Belgrade had the largest membership of 124, including 16 lawyers, 19 physicians, 12 bankers, with the remainder mainly wholesalers or manufacturers; Lodge Zagreb, which consisted of 67 members, had 8 lawyers, 14 physicians, 6 bankers, and the rest predominantly owners of industrial or business establishments; and Lodge Sarajevo with 40 brethren comprised 5 lawyers, 9 physicians, 2 bankers and other well-to-do Jewish citizens. Indeed, lists of members read like an official *Who's Who* of the Jewish community, with rabbis and communal and organizational leaders strongly represented.[22] In Yugoslavia the general public seems to have considered B'nai B'rith to be a Jewish branch of Freemasonry, despite the fact that the lodges maintained no contact at all with the Masons. There was, however, a superficial resemblance between the two groups with their use of rituals, secrecy, and selectivity.[23]

The first B'nai B'rith lodge on South Slav soil was established in Belgrade in 1911. Named Lodge Serbia, it belonged to District 11 of the Independent Order of B'nai B'rith based in Istanbul. Its founders were twenty of the leading Belgrade Jews of both religious rites, including Rabbi Isaac Alcalay, Rabbi Ignjat Schlang, Dr. Bukić Pijade, Dr. Friedrich Pops, Šemaja Demajo, Rafailo Finci, Dr. Solomon Alkalaj, Dr. David Alkalaj, and Adolf Rešovski, who served as president of the organization from 1911 to 1920.[24] One of its principal achievements in the early years was the introduction of a certain degree of harmony and understanding into the relationship between Belgrade's Sephardim and Ashkenazim; for the first time, the two groups began to work together in a constructive fashion.

B'nai B'rith engaged in a variety of activities. In Belgrade the lodge sponsored public lectures, donated money to local, national, and foreign Jewish institutions, and initiated the project of a Jewish museum. One of its goals was to improve relations between Jews and their environment. Most important, however, were the talks and discussions on contemporary Jewish problems conducted among the brethren themselves at their regular meetings.[25] Undoubtedly, a fairly large percentage of the important decisions affecting the internal developments of Yugoslav Jewish life evolved from debates within this closed circle.

Lodge Zagreb followed much the same pattern as its Belgrade equivalent but entered the picture some sixteen years later in 1927. It divided its endeavors into three spheres: charitable-social, pro-Palestine, and Jewish cultural-artistic. Among its members were the prime movers for such projects as raising money for the Schwarz Home and the creation of the Central Jewish Bureau of Productive Social Aid. They contributed substantial sums to these causes, as well as for general charitable purposes, scholarships and subventions for Jewish education and literature. B'nai B'rith gave its support to Jewish theater groups abroad, including Habima and a Vilna troup, and to Jewish artists in Yugoslavia. The Zagreb lodge was strongly Zionist in sentiment, and during the first five years of its existence, it contributed some 250,000 dinars for Palestine purposes, to such groups as Keren Hayesod, Jewish National Fund, and the Emergency Fund of 1929.[26]

The creation of the Sarajevo lodge was delayed until 1933 due to a large extent to complex problems within the Jewish community of that town. In its ranks were most of the Zionist faction in the Sarajevo dispute of the 1920s, but at its head sat Dr. Vita Kajon, one of the leaders of the Sephardic opposition.[27]

In 1935 the Yugoslav lodges succeeded in breaking away from B'nai B'rith District 11 and forming District 18 with their own Grand Lodge for the Yugoslav Kingdom as a whole. The Grand Lodge met annually to discuss general Jewish and B'nai B'rith questions and programs. Dr. Bukić Pijade of Belgrade filled the office of Grand Master, and among the members were to be found the various presidents and past presidents of all the Yugoslav lodges, including Aron Alkalaj, Rabbi Isaac Alcalay, Rabbi Ignjat Schlang, Ivan Kohn, Heinrich Fleischer, Dr. Cesar Kajon, Dr. Rafailo Margulis, Pavle Winterstein, and Josef Hollander from Belgrade; Dr. Gavro Schwarz, Dr. Milan Schwarz, Dr. Oskar Spiegler, Mavro Kandel, Dr. Beno Stein, Dr. Marko Bauer, Dr. Marko Horn, Dr. Pavao Neuberger, Lav Stern, and Julije Fischer of Zagreb; and Dr. Vita Kajon, Mihael Levi,

Dr. Leon Perić, Dr. Jakov Kajon, and Dr. Adolf Benau in Sarajevo.[28] The correspondence carried on under B'nai B'rith auspices stretched around the world from nearby Sofia and Bucharest to Cincinnati, London, Berlin, Prague, Jerusalem, and even to Cairo, Johannesburg, and Buenos Aires. B'nai B'rith leaders concerned themselves with a wide spectrum of Jewish matters both at home and abroad.[29] Through its involvement in B'nai B'rith, Yugoslav Jewry established yet one more contact with the outside world and was able to play a more active role in international Jewish affairs.

Since practically all the top leadership of both local and national Jewish institutions belonged to B'nai B'rith, it was inevitable that the lodges became involved in the quarrels between various communities or within the Federation of Jewish Religious Communities or the Zionist Federation. The question of B'nai B'rith solidarity became a major issue in the conflict over the results of the election of the general secretary of the communal federation in 1936. A special conference met in Slavonski Brod (Croatia) to discuss the action of Dr. Bukić Pijade, who resigned from the central committee of the federation in protest against the selection of Šime Spitzer of Zagreb over Mihael Levi of Sarajevo. Should all members of B'nai B'rith have followed the example of their grand master? No final decision on this subject was possible, since the Zagreb brethren found themselves on one side of the fence and their Sarajevo colleagues on the other.[30] In short then, B'nai B'rith acted as more than merely a service organization supporting Jewish charities; it also functioned as a forum for Jewish leaders in different parts of the country to express their opinions on important topics of the day. Quite predictably, the Zagreb lodge represented the Zionist viewpoint, Sarajevo, the Sephardic position, and Lodge Serbia perhaps the Yugoslav stand.

Jewish women also played an active role in charitable and related work in Yugoslavia. Generally, they belonged to separate women's associations organized along lines roughly equivalent to the men's counterparts. Twenty-four women's clubs from various parts of the country held a congress in Belgrade in 1924 to form an Association of Jewish Women's Societies for the entire kingdom; ten years later this body, which coordinated much of the charitable, educational, and cultural activities of Jewish women in Yugoslavia, had grown to forty member-clubs. At the forefront of this association sat Jelena Demajo, the president of the Jewish Women's Society in Belgrade; Eliza Feldman, president of the Belgrade Ashkenazic women's society, Dobrotvor, and Ilka Böhm, president of Sarajevo's La Humanidad, served as its vice-presidents. In its leadership, at any rate, this organization seemed to represent primarily Sephardic interests, especially in Belgrade and Sarajevo.[31] On the other hand, a Federation of Zionist Women (WIZO), which appears to have been heavily Ashkenazic, was organized in Zagreb in 1928. By 1940 this federation, headed by Julia König of Zagreb and Reza Steindler of Belgrade, consisted of sixty-seven local groups in nearly all major Jewish centers with approximately five thousand members.[32] The WIZO affiliates participated in all Zionist activities in the country, whereas the members of the Association of Jewish Women's Societies took part in the many welfare projects launched by the Jewish communities, particularly those affecting women and children.

Sephardic women lived an extremely sheltered existence in the South Slav lands until the late nineteenth century. They received very little formal education and spent most of their days, both before and after marriage, working in the home. In the 1860s, however, gradual changes started to take place, especially in Belgrade. Women were no longer wearing traditional Jewish dress and keeping their heads covered. Girls began to attend elementary schools, where they learned Serbian and other subjects; those from wealthy families sometimes went to private schools, where they acquired a knowledge of music, foreign languages, and handicrafts. Poorer girls, who in the past had generally been compelled to seek employment in the households of the rich, were now increasingly being taught sewing and other useful trades.[33] A new way of life was developing in the old Jewish quarter and Jewish women were becoming more aware of the world around them.

Jelena Demajo represents an excellent example of this new breed of Sephardic women. Born in Dorćol in 1876, she grew up in a home in which Ladino was spoken exclusively, but unlike most girls of her generation, she not only completed elementary school but also graduated from Girls' High School. Until her marriage, she taught in the public school in the old Jewish quarter. Thereafter she became actively involved in Jewish women's activities in Belgrade.[34]

In 1874 a handful of Sephardic women formed the first women's club in Serbia, the Jewish Women's Society. In the beginning this philanthropic organization, which aimed at helping young mothers and poor widows, had no executive board and no statutes and held no formal meetings; it recruited young wives as members, collected money from friends, and distributed it to needy women. By the end of the century, however, this association had begun to keep accounts (in Ladino), and in 1905 Jelena Demajo, its first secretary, started to take minutes of meetings in Serbo-Croatian.[35]

The members of the Jewish Women's Society contributed to the Serbian war effort during the Balkan Wars and World War I, demonstrating their patriotism by helping the Red Cross to prepare bandages and working as nurses in hospitals. One of their leading members, Neti Munk, received a royal decoration for her years of service as a nurse at the front. The Women's Society took upon itself the responsibility of looking after war widows and orphans, as well as helping refugees and families in distress with food and shelter.[36]

After World War I the Jewish Women's Society underwent extensive reorganization and, with Jelena Demajo as its president, greatly expanded its membership and programs. In 1924 when this society celebrated its fiftieth anniversary, 470 Sephardic women were counted among its ranks. One of its major projects was the creation of a School for Working Girls, which began operation in 1920 to train girls as seamstresses. The school started with 14 students, but by 1924 enrollment had reached 54. After ten years, having educated some 200 young women of all religious confessions, the school passed into state hands. In 1923 a special Vacation Committee emerged to arrange for poor and sickly children to spend their holidays on the coast. In the same year, the society inaugurated a series of popular lectures on medical subjects for women delivered by several of the local Jewish doctors. Among its later enterprises, the society erected its own building with a day-care center, which fed and looked after 80 children from seven o'clock in the morning until six in the evening.[37] In addition, the Jewish Women's Society cooperated with various other Jewish and non-Jewish institutions in Belgrade in their programs and campaigns and offered regular and emergency aid to needy families and individuals. It was one of the most active Jewish organizations in Belgrade and served a very important social function within the Sephardic community.

Similarly, the Ashkenazic women's society, Dobrotvor, played a parallel role within the sister community. It operated in much the same fields but on a somewhat smaller scale. Founded in 1895, Dobrotvor had as its principal aim helping the poor, especially the sick and disabled, poor widows and their families, and impoverished girls preparing for marriage. It offered monthly as well as emergency aid and twice a year, before Passover and before Rosh Hashanah, it distributed food; around Hanukkah it provided winter supplies in the form of fuel and warm clothing. Dobrotvor, like all similar associations, derived its revenue from membership dues, teas, entertainments, and gifts donated in the synagogue, as well as special contributions from benefactors and philanthropists.[38]

In Sarajevo during the interwar period, the Sephardic women's society, La Humanidad, which had been founded in 1894, operated a day-care center as well as a holiday camp for poor children, in addition to the usual welfare contributions to new mothers, poor brides, orphans, invalids, and girls learning trades; the Sociedad de vizitar dolientes specialized in looking after the elderly and the sick.[39] The Ashkenazic Women's Society, which began work in 1901, also fulfilled a similar role among Sarajevo's Ashkenazic poor, widows, and orphans.[40] In Zagreb, too, the Israelite Women's Society Jelena Prister, organized in 1887, conducted its operations in much the same fashion.[41]

The most ambitious undertaking of the Zagreb Jewish women was the project of the Israelite Vacation Colony. This institution started on a rather uncertain basis as early as 1906, when a committee of women began arranging to send sickly children to the seaside to recover their health. It took on its permanent form in 1913, however, with the formal founding of an independent association called the Israelite Vacation Colony. Between 1906 and World War I, this group of women sponsored the visits of 250 children to the sea and 63 to the mountains; between 1915 and 1922, it helped an additional 300 enjoy similar vacations. In 1923, thanks to a generous endowment from Mathilda Deutsch-Mačelski, its wealthy president, the Israelite Vacation Colony was able to purchase Villa Antonia, a large home in Crkvenica on the Dalmatian coast. This building, with supplementary athletic and hospital facilities, could accommodate 50 children at a time, or 100 to 150 per summer. From 1923 to 1939 some 2,500 poor children, mainly from Zagreb but also some from other parts of the country, took advantage of the Israelite Vacation Colony's sponsorship and spent one month or more on the sunny Adriatic. In addition, in 1940 a new mountain home at Ravna Gora in northern Croatia opened its doors to these children. This organization not only gave its services during summer holidays; during the school year it supplied milk and bread to needy children attending the Jewish school and occasional help to their parents as well.[42]

The Belgrade and Sarajevo endeavors in the realm of holiday camps for poor children were modeled after the Zagreb example; operating on a much more limited basis, they never managed to attain the excellent facilities and high standards of the Israelite Vacation Colony in Zagreb. Nevertheless, the women's organizations in all three cities made worthwhile contributions to the well-being of their respective communities, particularly with regard to child care, but also in the field of general social service.

Alongside the many charitable associations, within the Yugoslav Jewish community there also functioned a number of cultural organizations, including choral societies, drama groups, and literary clubs. These groups drew their membership mainly from the ranks of the young intellectuals who began to appear on the local scene in the early twentieth century. They devoted their efforts to raising the cultural level of their environment, as well as increasing the awareness of Jewish contributions in the various artistic fields.

Founded in 1879 in Belgrade, the Serbian-Jewish Choral Society became the first Jewish cultural association in the South Slav lands. It began as an all-male Jewish choir, but by the 1890s it allowed girls to join as well, thus representing the earliest attempt at forming a mixed social group in Belgrade Jewish circles. (A special committee from the Jewish Women's Society volunteered to act as chaperons, so that girls might be permitted to participate in this collective activity.) The society presented frequent public performances, including the first Belgrade production of Smetana's opera *The Bartered Bride.* It also made a number of singing tours through Serbia, Bosnia, Croatia, and Bulgaria. Its visit to Sarajevo in 1912 marked an important moment in the growth of relations between the Jewish communities of the two cities. The mixed choir cultivated a repertoire of both Yugoslav and Jewish music, including secular and religious compositions. The Serbian-Jewish Choral Society was a very popular Belgrade institution up until World War II; many prominent communal leaders took an active part in the organization, which served not only to strengthen Jewish consciousness but also to develop closer ties between Jews and Serbs.[43]

The Sarajevo equivalent in the musical sphere was La Lira (Ladino meaning "lyre"), which started as a Jewish instrumental group around the turn of the century but gradually developed into a choir. La Lira, which was also primarily Sephardic, adopted a pro-Zionist position as early as 1902. It too sang Slavic as well as Ladino and Hebrew selections, performing in synagogue concerts and at public events. Its repertoire included Verdi and Wagner along with local Yugoslav composers and a variety of Jewish music. The choir sang at Jewish weddings and occasionally at other ceremonies, although the traditional character of the Sephardic community caused it to frown upon the participation of a mixed choir in religious services. In 1928 La Lira toured South Serbia (Macedonia), offering concerts primarily to Jewish audiences in Niš, Skoplje, and then in Salonika. Three years later the choir visited Belgrade and the Vojvodina, and in 1934 they traveled to Palestine with 101 members, giving performances in various parts of the country.[44] La Lira provided a valuable cultural outlet for Sarajevo Jews of all ages. It was not the only Jewish musical group in Sarajevo, however, since Matatja, the organization of Jewish working youth, also had a choral and instrumental section within its framework.

The Zagreb Jewish community did not produce a similar musical association until considerably later. The Jewish choral society Ahdut did not come into existence until 1933. Its aim was to cultivate general secular and Jewish synagogue vocal music. Ahdut gave concerts of Jewish music of the eighteenth to the twentieth centuries, which included the works of local Jewish composers such as Eliša E. Samlaić and Marko Rothmüller. This mixed choir of about thirty singers and several soloists performed its selections mainly in Hebrew.[45] Ahdut apparently was more exclusively Jewish in its orientation than either the Serbian-Jewish Choral Society or La Lira.

Omanut (Hebrew for "art"), a society for the promotion of the Jewish arts, also made its appearance in Zagreb in the 1930s. Its program included publishing musical works by Jewish and Yugoslav composers and developing public interest in Jewish arts by all possible means. It too sponsored concerts and musical evenings, as well as special entertainments and lectures. The most valuable contribution of this society was its monthly literary journal, *Omanut,* published from 1936 to 1941 under the editorship of Dr. Hinko Gottlieb (1886–1954), Eliša Samlaić, and Dr. Lavoslav Glesinger. This periodical contained articles on Jewish themes submitted by local and foreign authors. Omanut also issued a series of twenty-four works, including a collection of five Sephardic songs from the sixteenth century and a translation of Cecil Roth's *The Jewish Contribution to Civilization.*[46] Both Omanut and Ahdut worked to develop increased appreciation for Jewish music and literature and to support the efforts of young Jewish artists.

Belgrade and Sarajevo also encompassed several amateur drama groups, which proved immensely popular among the Jewish public. In Belgrade the Max Nordau Society began presenting Jewish theater, mainly in Serbo-Croatian translation, shortly after World War I; its performances were generally well received by the Jewish community as a whole.[47] In Sarajevo the drama section of the working youth association Matatja presented numerous productions in Ladino, among them the social plays of the local writer Laura Papo Bohoreta, while Ahdus, the Ashkenazic club, introduced several successful Yiddish theater productions.[48] Although the actors were probably not at the highest professional level, nevertheless these groups added to the Jewish spirit of their respective communities during the interwar period. Zagreb never developed any Jewish theater of its own, but welcomed visiting troups from abroad.[49]

Communal leadership felt a great need to expand Jewish knowledge and popularize Jewish culture among youth and adults alike. With this in mind, they encouraged the establishment of literary societies, public lecture series, libraries, and reading rooms in all the major Jewish centers. In Belgrade the first such enterprise, the Serbian-Jewish Youth Group, originated around the turn of the century upon the initiative of a handful of young Jewish workers and intellectuals. They started a library, organized concerts and plays among themselves, and even attempted to publish their own paper. This pioneer effort, in the beginning more Serb than Jewish in orientation, gradually declined in its activities and disappeared during World War I.[50] In Zagreb an association called Literary Meetings of Jewish Youth was formed in 1898 among high school pupils under the supervision of Dr. Hosea Jacobi, the head rabbi, and later Dr. Gavro Schwarz. The group began with 38 members and grew to 100 by the 1920s. It held regular weekly meetings with lectures, discussions, and readings pertaining to Jewish, and later Zionist, themes and developed its own library of several thousand volumes.[51] Among the older generation the Israelite-Croatian Literary Society developed in the early years of the twentieth century with a membership of over 100 prominent Zagreb Jews, both integrationists and Zionists. This adult literary society saw as its task the spreading of knowledge of Jewish religion, history, and literature in order to arouse interest in the community and its institutions. It also held talks and debates on a variety of Jewish topics and founded its own library and reading room. After the war, however, it ceased to be very popular and eventually went out of existence.[52] To fill the cultural void B'nai B'rith in Belgrade and later Omanut in Zagreb offered public lectures; in Sarajevo La Benevolencia, La Gloria, and a short-lived organization called Tarbut (Hebrew for "culture") tried to do the same but with little apparent success.

Unlike many of these earlier ventures, the Belgrade Jewish Reading Room, which opened in 1929 in the newly constructed Jewish communal building, proved to be a viable institution. As was typical for Belgrade, its Reading Room stressed a dual purpose: expanding Jewish knowledge and awareness, and increasing intellectual contacts and improving relations between Jews and Serbs. The greatest achievement of the Reading Room was its annual popular lecture series covering a wide range of subjects and delivered by well-known local Jewish and non-Jewish scholars and public figures. A random selection of topics from 1939 included: "The Jews in the Roman Empire," "Jews and Their World Mission," "The Philosophy of Herman Cohen," "Travels in the Polar Regions," "Neurosis, Its Causes and Cures," "Roosevelt's America," "The Social Mission of Upton Sinclair," and "The Organization of the Balkans." In addition, it conducted special lectures for Jewish youth. The Reading Room provided a library of approximately 3,500 books and 700 newspapers and periodicals from Yugoslavia and abroad of relevance to Jewish readers. This society, whose president from 1929 to 1941 was Aron Alkalaj, had a dues-paying membership of 330.[53]

Cultural activity among Yugoslav Jews was not confined within the limits of formal organizations such as those described above. On the contrary, a significant number of Jewish intellectuals made noteworthy contributions to Jewish culture and to arts and letters in Yugoslavia. The earliest secular writer of any importance to emerge from the Serbian-Jewish milieu was Hajim S. Davičo. Born in 1854 in Dorćol, he spent part of his early childhood years in the provincial town of Šabac, but received most of his education in Belgrade, where he, unlike other Jewish boys of his generation, attended both gymnasium and university. A career civil servant and diplomat, he served as consul in Budapest and Trieste in the late nineteenth century and also as chief of the Ministry of National Economy. After his retirement from government service in 1901, he headed a Serbian commercial agency in Munich until the war, when he moved to Geneva, where he died in 1918.

Davičo began writing in high school and published articles in virtually all the leading Serbian newspapers in the 1880s and 1890s. He wrote literary criticism, political works, travelogues, folk tales and novels. He was best known, however, for his stories about life in the old Belgrade Jewish quarter, describing its patriarchal structure and religious and spiritual conservatism.[54]

Three of his novellas, all named after girls, "Naomi," "Luna," and "Linda," were published in 1898 in a book entitled *Sa Jalije* (from Jalija, the Jewish quarter), while a fourth, "Buena," appeared in 1913. "Naomi" unfolds the tale of the unhappy love of a beautiful Jewish maiden and a silent but intelligent youth from Jalija, named David. Naomi is despondent because her father, against her will, has married her off to another man, a stranger, and has ruined her life and her happiness. Later, both David and her husband express their love for her at her graveside. "Buena," perhaps this writer's finest work on a Jewish theme, portrays the conflict between the traditional, oriental way of life in the Jewish quarter and the encroaching European influence. Davičo depicts the Jewish experience, with the special flavor of its holidays and religious ceremonies, such as Tisha B'Av in the synagogue, Shavuot in the women's gallery, Lag Ba-Omer with its children's outings, and Purim celebrated in the streets.[55] Thus, in these stories, all of which he wrote in Serbo-Croatian, Davičo helped preserve the spirit of the Jewish past in Belgrade.

In Sarajevo, one of the most popular literary figures during the interwar period was Laura Papo (née Levi, 1891–1941), who may well be considered the first educated woman in the Bosnian Sephardic community. She did not attend school in her native Sarajevo, but in Istanbul, where she lived with her family from 1900 to 1908, and later in Paris, where she studied French literature. An extremely intelligent woman, she spoke Spanish, French, and German fluently and also knew some Turkish, Greek, and English. In addition to writing and teaching languages, she played the piano and composed music. Using Ladino with Latin orthography, "La Bohoreta" (the eldest girl), as she was nicknamed, wrote poetry, short stories, and dramas dealing with the social problems of the era, many of which were performed by Matatja. She vividly described the process of pauperization of the Sephardic lower class, the petty shopkeepers, the artisans and the workers of Sarajevo in the thirties. She also collected Sephardic folklore and composed an essay entitled "La mužer sefardi de Bosna" (the Sephardic Woman of Bosnia). Laura Papo Bohoreta was one of the few Jewish women intellectuals and the only Yugoslav writer in her day to produce a significant volume of work in Ladino. Her writings therefore have special value both as linguistic evidence and contemporary commentary.[56]

The most important Jewish author, however, was Dr. Isak Samokovlija, who gained national recognition both before and after World War II and became one of the most popular Yugoslav writers of the twentieth century. A physician by profession and a man with a deep social conscience, he began writing stories in the mid-1920s, portraying the existence of the poor Jews of Bjelave in a most vivid fashion. He introduced the milieu of Bosnian Sephardic Jewry into Yugoslav literature in a series of six volumes of short stories published from 1929 to 1953, as well as four dramas written in the thirties. Among his better known works are the tales named "Samuel the Porter,"

"From Spring to Spring," and "The Jew Who Did Not Pray on the Sabbath." Samokovlija was a vocal social critic and an active member of the Sarajevo Jewish community.[57]

Other Yugoslav Jewish litterateurs of note include Dr. Hinko Gottlieb, a Zagreb Zionist poet, essayist, and translater of Jewish works from Yiddish and German,[58] Dr. Žak Konfino (1892–), a Belgrade short-story writer, and Oskar DaviČo, a member of the younger literary generation, also from Belgrade. In the field of Jewish scholarship was Dr. Kalmi Baruch (1896–1945), a Hispanicist and Ladino specialist in Sarajevo.[59]

Not only did Yugoslav Jewry produce a group of writers who dealt with Jewish themes, it also spawned several competent Jewish artists. From Belgrade came Leon Koen (1859–1934), Marko Čelebonović, Bora Baruch (1911–1942), and Moše Pijade (1883–1955); from Sarajevo emerged Danijel Ozmo (1912–1942) and Danijel Kabiljo-Danilus (1894–1944), and from Zagreb, Slavko Brill. These men produced paintings, lithographs, and sculptures of considerable local and sometimes international repute, treating in part at least Jewish subjects, such as "Joseph's Dream" by Koen or the bust of Moses by Brill.[60] While none of these artists ever actually achieved world fame, they did add to the prestige of the Jewish community within Yugoslavia, and their works demonstrated a respectable level of cultural development whether taken in a Jewish or a general perspective.

Before the turn of the century, local Jewish newspapers rarely appeared in the South Slav lands, except for a Belgrade popular monthly in Ladino *El amigo del pueblo* (The Friend of the People), which was published in the 1880s and 1890s. In 1900 Abraham Kapon, the Sephardic reformer from Bulgaria, founded a Ladino weekly in Sarajevo called *La alborada* (The Dawn). This paper contained articles on the situation of world Jewry and Zionism, the Bible and Jewish holidays, folklore, and essays on the history of the Jews in Bosnia. It received its support from the young intellectual group but lasted only eight months, from December 1900 to August 1901, due to the opposition of the communal executive.[61] This represented the last serious attempt to create a Ladino publication within Yugoslavia. Not until after World War I did Jewish papers spring up again in either Sarajevo or Belgrade, but when they reappeared, they used Serbo-Croatian as their vehicle of communication.

In Zagreb, the earliest product of the Jewish press was the Zionist paper *Židovska smotra* (Jewish Review), which was published for the first time in November 1906. Originated by the brothers Alexander and Herman Licht, it began as a monthly in German but eventually switched to being a Serbo-Croatian biweekly, which included ideological articles, cultural information, short stories and poems in the original and in translation, and news from the Zionist movement, the general Jewish scene, and the various South Slav lands. *Židovska smotra,* which had approximately twelve hundred subscribers, became the organ of the national Zionist Association and continued publication until the outbreak of World War I.[62]

In 1917 its successor *Židov-Hajehudi* (The Jew) first appeared in print and it soon became the official voice of the Zionist Federation. Operating as a weekly, which published every Friday, *Židov* derived its income from some three thousand regular subscriptions, advertising, and a sizable subvention from the Zionist Federation. De facto, it became the national Jewish newspaper, containing news from all over the country and all over the world. Although it was the spokesman for the views of the Zagreb Jewish leadership and strongly Zionist in orientation, it kept the Jewish reading public in Yugoslavia well informed on contemporary Jewish issues both at home and abroad.[63] *Židov* was the only Jewish paper to bridge the entire interwar period in Yugoslavia.

Within the Sarajevo Jewish sphere, a number of newspapers began publishing in the decade following World War I. They were all informative in character, but each had a particular sociopolitical, cultural, or ideological bent. They reported on the activities of the Jewish community in Yugoslavia as a whole, but especially those of the city of Sarajevo, acquainting their readers with current events and meetings. The first to appear was *Židovska svijest* (Jewish Conscience), a Zionist weekly edited by Mair Musafija and David Levi-Dale, which lasted from 1919 to 1924, when the so-called Sarajevo dispute between the Zionists and the Sephardists forced it to dissolve. It resurfaced from 1924 to 1928, however, using the name *Narodna židovska svijest* (Nationalist Jewish Conscience), under the ownership of Dr. Žiga Bauer, a leading Zionist. An opposition paper, *Jevrejski život* (Jewish Life), which presented the opinions of the supporters of the Sephardic movement, entered competition during the same five years. Run by Albert Koen, Dr. Braco Poljokan, Dr. Kalmi Baruch, and Benjamin Pinto, it was also a weekly and printed articles on cultural, political, and economic issues that were mainly of local interest. When the feud between the two rival factions finally reached a settlement in 1928, both papers were disbanded and in their place *Jevrejski glas* (Jewish Voice) was established. This new entity, which had some fifteen hundred subscribers, effected a more or less satisfactory blend of Sephardic and Zionist ideas, since its original owner was Dr. Žiga Bauer, but its editor in chief and later owner until 1941 was Dr. Braco Poljokan.[64] *Jevrejski glas* was less international in content than *Židov* and tended to concern itself primarily with Sarajevo or Yugoslav Jewish problems. To a considerable extent, these newspapers reflected the communities which they served; hence, it was natural that Zagreb's *Židov* should have been more Zionist and yet at the same time more cosmopolitan in nature, while Sarajevo's *Jevrejski glas* was Sephardic in orientation and somewhat provincial.

Similarly, Belgrade's lack of its own regular Jewish paper, despite repeated attempts to establish one, was perhaps indicative of its character too. Neither outspokenly Zionist nor fanatically Sephardic, the Belgrade Jewish community apparently was composed of middle-of-the-road serbianized Jews who could not support their own paper for very long. Before the Balkan Wars, the Zionists made their first attempt to publish the *Jevrejski glasnik* (Jewish Spokesman) under the guidance of Dr. David M. Alkalaj (1862–1933) but they only succeeded in producing about ten editions. In 1920 Dr. David Albala made a fresh effort which also lasted for only a very limited time. The next try, by David Azriel in 1924, ended in failure as well. In 1933 the Federation of Jewish Religious Communities issued three editions of their own *Glasnik,* under the editorship of Dr. David Albala, and in 1936 it began to print a monthly called *Službeni list* (Official Paper), which was edited by Šime Spitzer and contained official news of the federation and its activities; this paper appeared for several years. Finally, in 1939 the Belgrade Sephardic community started to publish its own monthly called *Vesnik* (Courier), with Dr. David Albala and David Levi-Dale in charge. In 1941 the Ashkenazic community also managed to distribute several numbers of its own *Glasnik.*[65] As the home of the communal federation, the national capital, and Yugoslavia's second largest Jewish community, Belgrade should have been able to maintain at least a permanent local news sheet during the interwar years, if not a newspaper with a broader scope; its failure to do so would seem to disqualify the city from any claim to a position of absolute supremacy in Yugoslav Jewish life.

This survey has by no means exhausted the supply of Jewish papers, periodicals, and other publications produced in Yugoslavia between the wars. A number of Zionist periodicals for young people regularly emanated from Zagreb, such as *Haaviv* (Hebrew, meaning "the spring") for children and *Gideon* and its successor *Hanoar* (Hebrew for "the youth") for older youths.[66] Several more Zionist papers emerged from the Vojvodina, including *Jüdisches Volksblatt* and *Israel* (both in German) and *Malchut Jisrael* (Hebrew for "kingdom of Israel" —the Zionist Revisionist paper which later moved to Zagreb and adopted the name *Jevrejska tribuna,* or Jewish Tribune).[67] Quite a few other journalistic ventures also made brief appearances on the Yugoslav scene. However, the vast majority of the output of the Jewish press in interwar Yugoslavia was clearly Zionist inspired. That there were plenty of non-Zionists in Yugoslavia at the time (excluding the supporters of the Sephardic movement), there can be no doubt; these people, however, put their opinions on paper only on rare occasions. Three independent, that is non-Zionist, papers appeared for brief periods, one in each of the three cities: *Jevrejska tribuna* in Sarajevo in 1921, *Jevrejski list* in Zagreb in 1934, and *Beogradske jevrejske novine* in Belgrade in 1936–37. The Zionists, however, succeeded in monopolizing the greatest share of the national Jewish press.

The Yugoslav Jewish community contained within it a wide range of local organizations, most of which were primarily charitable or cultural in orientation. The level of participation in such activities was relatively high, especially in Sephardic centers such as Sarajevo and Belgrade where Jewish involvement tended to be greatest. While undoubtedly the same small group who ran the Jewish communal administration supplied much of the leadership for the other organizations as well, nevertheless, the many societies provided a variety of outlets for special interests and skills and served useful social and humanitarian functions as well. The Jewish community not only took care of its own needy but also contributed both talented individuals and groups to the general cultural scene. Through the Jewish press the community was able to maintain contacts with its members both locally and nationally as well as keep in touch with current developments in the Jewish world as a whole.

These various organizations did not demonstrate strong ideological positions, but rather were broadly "Jewish" in nature, given their membership, the people they served, or the general content of their programs. Other organizations adopted specific ideologies. These groups, as well as the complex question of Jewish identity in a multinational state such as Yugoslavia, are considered in the following chapter.

PART THREE

The State and the Jews

8

CRISIS OF IDENTITY

National identity has been a problematic issue for Jews in the modern era. In traditional Jewish society being a Jew tended to constitute one's complete self-identification; however, Jewish national awareness did not develop into an active political force until the advent of modern Jewish nationalism in the late nineteenth century. Meanwhile, in the struggle for emancipation and in the subsequent effort to consolidate citizenship rights, many Jews, especially in western and central Europe, began to adopt the nationality of the country in which they resided, thereby considering themselves, for example, Frenchmen, Germans, or Hungarians of the Jewish faith. Thus, the concept of a Jewish nationality constituted a serious threat to these integrationists who maintained that Jews were adherents of a different religion but not members of a separate nation.

In Yugoslavia the multinational complexion of the region complicated the advocacy of integrationism as a satisfactory solution to the Jewish identity problem. The opponents of Jewish nationalism, who saw themselves as Serbs or Croats of the Mosaic persuasion, faced serious obstacles in supporting their position. A Jew from Belgrade might consider himself a Serb, and a Jew from Zagreb a Croat, but for a Jew from multiethnic Sarajevo, Bitolj, or Novi Sad the answer was not quite so simple. A Hungarian-speaking Jew from the Vojvodina, for instance, who regarded himself as a Magyar found himself doubly outcast in the newly created Slavic state.[1] In the South Slav lands, moreover, national identity tended to be closely tied to religious denomination. As a general rule, being Croat also meant being Roman Catholic, while Serb affiliation was linked with Eastern Orthodoxy. It was thus difficult to associate oneself with a nationality while not at the same time sharing its religion. The term *Yugoslav* merely denoted citizenship rather than nationality, hence the designation Yugoslav of the Jewish faith could never become a viable reality. Indeed, had the notion of Yugoslavism, as opposed to Serb or Croat nationalism, achieved greater success over the years, undoubtedly it would have attracted strong support from the Jewish population, since its neutral stand on the issue of religion would have rendered it more applicable to Jewish citizens.[2]

Jewish identification with any of the South Slav nationalities did not begin to develop until toward the end of the nineteenth century and even then its intensity varied greatly from region to region. The Ashkenazim to the north and west belonged for the most part to the Hungarian or German sphere of influence. They represented the emancipated, fairly assimilated type of Jews common in western and central Europe at that time, but they had acculturated themselves linguistically and socially to the "master nations" of the Habsburg Monarchy, rather than the surrounding nationalities. In the Vojvodina the Jews clung to their Hungarian speech and loyalties, whereas in Croatia they gradually acquired a knowledge of the local language and associated more with their Slavic neighbors.

Around the turn of the century, integrationist ideas managed to gain considerable popularity; indeed, some individuals propounded extreme views on this subject. Imbued with strong feelings of romantic nationalism, Vladimir Sachs, a native of Zagreb, delivered a lecture in 1910 entitled "Israelites and the Christian-Socialist Cultural Program," in which he stated the following:

We are Croats of the Jewish faith.
   In Croatia there are many faiths, but all adherents of these faiths may be and must be only Croats. Today there no longer is a Jewish nation. That which existed several thousand years ago has ceased to exist. A nation without a language is not a nation. Jews are members of different nations like Catholics, and just as there is no separate Catholic nation, there is also no Jewish nation. Believe me, we Jews are by and large loyal Croats. . . .

Sachs further advocated Jewish support for the Christian Socialist electoral program on the basis of common interests and goals.[3] In exceptional cases Jews played an active role in the Croatian nationalist revival in the late nineteenth and early twentieth centuries. Vid Morpurgo of Split became a prominent publicist and benefactor of the Illyrian movement.[4] Two baptized Jews, Dr. Hinko Hinković[5] and Josip Frank, were important prewar parliamentary figures, the former involved in the Serb-Croat coalition of 1905 and the latter as the right-wing anti-Semitic leader. These examples, however, were scarcely typical of the general pattern of Croatian Jewry as a whole.

For the most part, Croatian Jews spoke Hungarian and German among themselves and Croatian in the streets. Their social life remained primarily within their own circle, since they were not as a rule fully accepted into Croatian society. Although they occupied important economic positions, few Jews held high office or were prominent in public life. Jews also did not participate to any significant extent in Croatian intellectual or cultural life nor were they well represented in journalism. Anti-Semitism, while rarely overt, never seemed too far from the surface and such outbursts could never be eliminated from possibility. Croatian Jews enjoyed a feeling of relative security; they were partially assimilated in their environment, and yet few really achieved a true sense of belonging.[6]

While outright support for radical Croatian nationalism was extremely rare among Jews, many of the more moderate liberals who dominated the Zagreb Jewish scene in the early twentieth century were in staunch opposition to Jewish nationalism. Indeed, Zionism was an anathema to the influential group of wealthy integrationists who controlled Jewish communal politics in Zagreb prior to the creation of the Yugoslav state.

In 1918 the executive board of the Zagreb Jewish community, headed by Dr. Robert Siebenschein, refused to approve any action on the part of the community in support of Palestine.[7] The following year this same faction presented a resolution to the *ban* of Croatia vehemently opposing a petition by the Zionist Federation for the recognition of the Jews as a national minority in the new kingdom. Their statement read as follows:

1. The executive most definitively rejects any endeavor which has as its aim that the Jewry of Yugoslavia be proclaimed as a separate nation or a separate nationality in this its homeland. Yugoslav Jewry is an organic part of this nation as a whole, and Yugoslav Jews are children of the Yugoslav nation.
2. The executive solemnly declares that along with its religioethical and humanitarian tasks it considers it as its holy duty to nurture and strengthen among its cofaithful a steadfast loyalty towards the Croatian national ideals and also towards our young Kingdom of Serbs, Croats, and Slovenes.
3. The executive therefore rejects the stand of the Zionist Organization that the question of a Jewish nationality be taken up on the

agenda of the National Council of Serbs, Croats, and Slovenes in
Zagreb. . . .[8]

The Zagreb executive at the same time attempted to sabotage the
initial efforts to form a federation of Jewish communities by not
participating in its organizational stages, since it considered the project to be Zionist inspired.[9] Nevertheless, in the long run, the integrationists failed to maintain their position of power in the community,
being decisively defeated by the Zionists in the first postwar communal elections, which took place in 1920.

By 1922 the Zagreb integrationists had organized themselves
into a group called Narodni Rad. While advertising for new members
to join their ranks, they presented this program:

The association Narodni Rad accepts [as members] Croats, or other
Yugoslavs, adherents of the Jewish confession, regardless of their
political party views.
   It rejects decisively the Jewish nationalist trend, Zionism, which
separates us more and more from our national milieu by its propaganda and its organizational work.
   We feel ourselves to be a living part of this [Croatian] nation and
maintain that we should be called fellow nationals along with all
other confessions and work for its progress. We deny any separation
from other confessions and we especially do not want to proclaim
ourselves as a separate nation, concerned only with our own interests
and calling "home" a land outside these borders.
   We do not want our children educated in the spirit of Jewish
nationalism, but of Croatian, particularly Yugoslav [nationalism].
   We have decided at last to rise out of our passivity and declare
ourselves for what we really are; we have decided to resolve with
regard to nationality the question of our homeland and to work for
our national ideal.[10]

This declaration ended with the signatures of Mirko Breyer, the
antiquarian book dealer, who was president of the organization, as
well as some thirty committee members, including seven lawyers,
seven merchants, three industrialists, four engineers. The rest were
mainly white-collar workers. Soon after this appeal, an article by
Mirko Breyer, entitled "The Voice of Heart and Conscience," appeared in an edition of the journal *Nova Evropa* that dealt with Yugoslav Jews. Here Breyer elaborated his position further with renewed
attacks against the Zionists.[11] Narodni Rad never really confronted
the issue or made a clear choice between Croatian and Yugoslav
nationalism. Probably they came closer to the Yugoslav standpoint
than most Croatian nationalists of the interwar period, but they
dared not abandon Croatian loyalties completely for fear of alienat-
ing their neighbors.

Hugo Spitzer (1858–1934), first president of Federation of Jewish Religious Communities

Friedrich Pops (1874–1948), second president of Federation of Jewish Religious Communities

Hugo Kon, president of the Zagreb Ashkenazic community, 1920–35

David Albala (1886–1942), Belgrade Jewish communal activist

Hosea Jacobi (1841–1925), head rabbi of Zagreb Ashkenazic community

Alexander Licht (1884–1948), Zionist leader

The girls' sporting club Makabi, Sarajevo, 1923

David M. Alkalaj (1862–1933), Zionist leader

The Ashkenazic women's society Dobrotvor, Belgrade, 1920

The Jewish choral society La Lira, Sarajevo

Leaders of the cultural section of Matatja, Sarajevo, 1935

Laura Papo Bohoreta (1891–1941), dramatist, Sarajevo

The Sephardic student association Esperanza, Zagreb

The first members of the *hakhsharah* farm of Hashomer Hatzair, Sarajevo

Despite its efforts, Narodni Rad never attracted the support of any significant number of Zagreb Jews. It consisted of a small circle of affluent and successful entrepreneurs and professionals, generally from well-established Zagreb Jewish families, who despised the mere idea of Jewish nationalism and felt personally threatened by it. Associated with this group were such individuals as Dr. Robert Siebenschein, a prominent lawyer and president of the Zagreb Jewish community from 1912 to 1920; Sandor A. Alexander (1866–1929) and Samuel D. Alexander (1862–?), both wealthy industrialists, the former, among other offices, honorary president of the Zagreb Chamber of Commerce, and the latter president of the Federation of Industrialists and vice-president of the Zagreb Stock Exchange.[12] This organization seems to have disappeared by the 1930s and ceased to have any effect on Jewish communal life in Zagreb. Some of its members continued to play active roles in public life throughout the interwar period, but the integrationists on the whole lacked effective spokesmen and organization.

Among the younger generation of Ashkenazim there were few, if any, vocal integrationists, but the fact that they did not preach integrationism as a doctrine does not mean that some did not practice it. Many of the youth considered themselves anational or even apolitical, while others, especially the sons or daughters of the wealthy, turned to communism. Unlike the Zionists, the integrationist youth did not tend to form official groups and did not publish journals and propaganda for their cause. Hence it is difficult to follow their activities or even to estimate their numerical strength.

One clear indication of their presence, however, is to be found in the intermarriage and conversion statistics compiled by the Zagreb rabbinate. From 1928 to 1932, for example, 42 intermarriages between Jews and non-Jews (primarily Catholics) were reported in Zagreb, an average of 8 per year, as opposed to 310 Jewish marital unions, or roughly 62 per year. According to these estimates, then, 620 Jews chose Jewish mates, while 42 married outside the fold. As for conversion to Christianity (for the most part undergone for purpose of marriage), 396 Jews received baptism in Zagreb, or approximately 20 per year, from 1912 to 1932. During the same period, there were 129 converts to Judaism, about 6 per year.[13] Although these figures are fragmentary at best, since undoubtedly not all mixed marriages or even conversions from Judaism were entered in the communal registry, they do point to a steadily growing contact between Jews and their Christian neighbors. Nevertheless, intermarriage does not appear to have been considered a particularly serious problem in Zagreb, or by implication, in interwar Yugoslavia. This can to a certain extent be inferred from the general silence of rabbis and communal leaders on this issue. Intermarriage was on the increase toward the end of the thirties, but Jewish marriages were climbing too. Between 1936 and 1938, there were 277 Jewish marriages in Zagreb, or about 92 per year, while in the same time span, 46 intermarriages were reported, or about 15 per year. Thus, out of 600 Jews, 92 percent married fellow Jews and 8 percent non-Jews.[14] Assimilation had succeeded to a point, but it did not yet seem critical to the future of the Jewish community.

In Serbia integrationism never appeared to be as strong as in Croatia. Indeed, especially among the Sephardim, it took on quite another form. In Belgrade the concept of Serbs of the Mosaic faith developed around the turn of the century. Among its first proponents were the members of the Serbian-Jewish Youth Group. Their ideology, however, had a somewhat different ring from that of their Zagreb Ashkenazic counterparts. In 1897 one of their spokesmen, Leon Koen, published an "Address to Serbian Youth of the Mosaic Faith," in which he proclaimed:

Yes, I feel, I am, and indeed I want to and I must be a true Serb, a Serb Mosaic. Because I am confident in my soul that my dear and fully tolerant fatherland Serbia will not, or even cannot, interfere in the least with . . . the practice of that holy faith of my ancestors who as prophets of the world proclaimed for the first time the recognition of monotheism to humanity.
. . . we [must] openly state our patriotism and all our coreligionists who are in this land [must] solemnly declare themselves Serbs of the Mosaic faith, Mosaic Serbs, and as such they must belong to the Serbian nation. . . .[15]

Such a statement is indicative of the patriotic spirit felt by many Serbian Jews for their native land, but it does not actually constitute a denial of the existence of a Jewish nation.

A prominent Sephardic integrationist, Dr. Jakov Čelebonović, became president of the Belgrade Sephardic community in a very hotly contested election in 1932. He ran on the slogan of Patriotism, Brotherhood and Faith, claiming "a Jew can be a good Jew only if he is a good Yugoslav." Once in office he asserted:

We feel ourselves fortunate as Yugoslavs of the Mosaic faith and we may be thankful that in our state we enjoy full freedom, equality and brotherhood, as all other Yugoslavs of different faiths in this nation: "he is my brother whatever his religion" [a Serbian saying]. As it is by law, so it is in fact. . . .[16]

Čelebonović, together with Avram Lević, a high-ranking civil servant, later attempted to organize a committee to foster Yugoslav nationalism among Jews. In a statement published in 1934, Lević condemned "those Jews from across the Sava" (i.e. the Ashkenazim) who allegedly did not exhibit sufficient patriotism and who educated their children in the paths of Zionism. He stated further, "One may sympathize with Palestine, but one must love Yugoslavia. I doubt that one can love one and the other country with equal love. A son has only one mother. Love cannot be divided if it is true. . . ."[17] The integrationist stance of Čelebonović and Lević represents a minority viewpoint among Belgrade Sephardim, however. Most Serbian Jews tended to disagree with the contention that one could not be a loyal Serb and a Jewish nationalist, or even a Zionist, simultaneously.

An excellent example of a so-called Serbo-Zionist was Dr. David Albala, the last president of the Belgrade Sephardic community before World War II. David Albala was born into a poor Sephardic family in Dorćol in 1886 and attended elementary and secondary school in Belgrade, where he was imbued with an intense patriotic feeling for his native Serbia. While studying medicine in Vienna from 1905 to 1910, he came into contact with modern Jewish nationalism for the first time and joined Bar Giora, a Zionist organization of Jewish students from the Balkans. Upon his return to his hometown, he helped organize local Zionist youth clubs and later became very prominent in the Belgrade Jewish Nationalist Society and in the Yugoslav Zionist Federation. He was also a leading member of the Belgrade Jewish community in the thirties, holding office as vice-president and then president after 1938, and also serving on the executive board of the Federation of Jewish Religious Communities.

Albala remained an active Jewish worker all his life, but he also continued to espouse Serbian patriotism. During the Balkan Wars and World War I, he served as a medical captain in the Serbian army. After the war, as a lieutenant-colonel in the reserve corps, he enjoyed wearing his uniform whenever possible, including at his own wedding in 1920. According to his wife, who later became his biographer, "no national holiday or any other formal occasion went by that he did not deck himself out in military attire. . . ."[18] The best illustration of Dr. Albala's joint Serbian-Jewish efforts is his visit to the United States during World War I. Representing the Serbian government-in-exile, he embarked on a speaking tour of American Jewish communities to raise money for war bonds and to gain support for Serbia at the Paris Peace Conference. It was Dr. David Albala to whom an official letter, dated December 27, 1917, was addressed, expressing the sympathy of the Serbian government for the Balfour Declaration. Having maintained contact with the Yugoslav royal family during the interwar years, Albala was sent in 1939 as a personal envoy of the Regent, Prince Paul, on a second mission to the United States, where he died in 1942.[19] Serbian Sephardim, such as Albala, did not feel they had to abandon their Jewish national identity in order to be patriotic Yugoslav citizens.

National identification for Jews in Yugoslavia was not limited, however, to a choice between integrationism, adoption of Serb, Croat, or Hungarian nationality, or Zionism. Another alternative presented itself, especially among the Sephardim, namely Diaspora nationalism. For the majority of Sephardim the concept that the Jews constituted a separate nationality was not alien to their way of thinking. It would be difficult to conceive of the Sephardim of Sarajevo, for example, as belonging to the integrationist camp. Retaining the heritage of the Ottoman millet system and growing up in a multiethnic society among Muslim Bosniaks, Catholic Croats, and Eastern Orthodox Serbs, they had always considered themselves, consciously or unconsciously, Jews by nationality. The Sephardic community had only recently begun to break away from its traditional patriarchal way of life, and although these Jews had become very much acculturated to their Bosnian milieu, they remained a separate and distinct entity which had little prospect of merging with any other group. Nevertheless, having lived in the city for over three centuries, these Sephardim felt themselves to be an integral part of Sarajevo society. Immediately after the establishment of the Yugoslav state, the Political Committee of Jews of Bosnia-Hercegovina, a predominantly Sephardic body, issued the following declaration:

We Jews of Bosnia-Hercegovina, who have always lived in brotherly communication with the people of this land and have shared with them all fates in joy and misfortune following with best wishes the political aspirations of the Yugoslav peoples, feel it our duty to make the following statement:

As conscious and nationalist Jews, who always value highly the great idea of self-determination of nations and democracy, we join the program of the National Council of Serbs, Croats, and Slovenes contained in the proclamation of October 19, 1918, and as sons of this land we see guaranteed in this proclamation the free development of the Jews of Bosnia-Hercegovina.[20]

The idea that while preserving their Jewish identity, Jews should also be "good Yugoslavs" and participate actively in the political life of their country was elaborated in a brochure written in 1920 by Dr. Sumbul Atijas, a Sarajevo Sephardic lawyer:

> . . . the position of the Jews demands cultural-political work along parallel lines in the direction of reawakening Jewish national consciousness and in the direction of awakening consciousness and love towards that nation in whose midst we live. . . .
>
> To be a Jew does not mean to withdraw oneself from that nation of which one has grown to be an organic part after a long period of joint activity. We are Jews, but we are at the same time also Yugoslavs. Our origins, faith, many ethnological elements and Ladino or other such jargons link us to Jewry, while the Serbo-Croatian language, a great part of the culture, our native hearth, long lines of ancestors and last but not least our present existence tie us to Yugoslavism. . . . Our duty as Yugoslav Jews is that we work along parallel lines to awaken Jewish and Yugoslav consciousness in our masses. We must educate our Jews to be good Yugoslavs as well as good Jews and [we must] create harmony between the past and the present. . . .[21]

What these Sephardim seem to have been advocating was a form of Diaspora nationalism, that is, the recognition of Jews as a separate national entity within multinational Yugoslavia. Thus, for them Jewish nationalism was in no way inconsistent with Yugoslav nationalism. The Sephardim for the most part did not appear to feel threatened by the accusation of dual loyalties.

But some Sephardim went one step further in defining their Jewish identity in a specifically Sephardic context. While the Zionists advocated the theory of one Jewish people united in the building of their national homeland in Palestine, the Sephardists did not share this doctrine. They considered themselves more deeply Zionist than the Ashkenazim, since they had been raised in that tradition and had not merely adopted it later in life; but they felt that they had particular interests and needs which the Ashkenazim did not understand. The Sephardists tended to favor both work in Palestine and work in the *galut* (Diaspora), not exclusive concentration on the former with consequent neglect of the latter. They advocated raising the economic and cultural level of their Sephardic brethren wherever they might be found. The Zionist leadership in Zagreb, however, regarded this outlook as separatistic and generally opposed the idea that Sephardim should receive special treatment or form a distinct group within the broader Zionist movement.[22]

Initially, Zionism had acted as a force to draw the local Ashkenazim and Sephardim in Sarajevo closer together. Since before World War I, the two groups had belonged to the Jewish Nationalist Society, which later became the Sarajevo branch of the Yugoslav Zionist Federation. Conflict between the Sephardists and the Zionists erupted in 1924. In that year, a protest movement arose, led by a group of Sephardic intellectuals who opposed the unitary philosophy of the Zionists. They wanted stronger Sephardic representation on the national level and in their local organization and its newspaper, *Židovska svijest*. When the Jewish Nationalist Society refused to accept a list submitted by Dr. Sumbul Atijas of some three hundred Sephardim for membership, the Sephardist leaders had the association's property and paper confiscated by police decree.[23] Then the Sephardists, headed by Dr. Vita Kajon, Dr. Braco Poljokan, Dr. Kalmi Baruch, Dr. Josip (Pepi) Baruch, and other prominent figures, took over the society, renaming it the Sarajevo Local Zionist Organization, and began their own newspaper, *Jevrejski život*.[24] Meanwhile, the old guard Zionists, including Oskar Grof, Dr. Žiga Bauer, and Dr. Adolf Benau among the Ashkenazim, and Mihael Levi, Silvio M. Alkalaj, and David Levi-Dale among the Sephardim, renamed their paper *Narodna židovska svijest* and reorganized themselves into the Jewish Club to continue their former operations.[25]

For the next five years there was much confusion in Sarajevo Jewish circles. The two factions published vicious attacks against one another in their respective organs and both sides refused to compromise. Zionist activity came to a virtual standstill in Sarajevo during this period since neither organization gained official sanction. At Zionist headquarters in Zagreb, opinion tended to favor the old leadership, but it proved impossible to ignore the Sephardic opposition, whose position was supported by a large part of the Sarajevo community.

At each annual conference of the Federation of Zionists of Yugoslavia, the Sephardic question came under heated debate and numerous resolutions were passed in an attempt to solve the so-called Sarajevo dispute.[26] At the 1924 meeting of the Federation Executive, a spokesman for the Sephardists, Dr. Vita Kajon, tried to explain the reasons behind this split:

This movement has emerged in the first place because most of us [Sephardim] think differently not only about the methods of Zionist work but, if you will, about Zionism itself. We conceive of Zionism very broadly. Our life differs from Jewish life in other countries. We do not see in Jewry only two poles, nor do we recognize on the one side Zionism and on the other side assimilation. Our life is full-blooded. For us, the center and pivot of Jewish life is not to be found within the Zionist organization. Also outside of it there is a Jewish nationalist life . . .[27]

The Zionist leadership in Zagreb, however, replied by merely reiterating its basic policy, namely, the necessity for "absolute unity of Sephardim and Ashkenazim" in order to help achieve the Zionist goal of the creation of a Jewish homeland in Palestine.[28]

Finally, in 1928 the two opposing sides reached an agreement whereby both would participate in the same body, under the presidency of the Sephardic head rabbi, Dr. Moric Levi, who was himself a staunch Zionist. A new joint Zionist-Sephardist paper, *Jevrejski glas,* also began publication that year.[29] Despite this settlement, however, the Sarajevo Sephardim never became particularly ardent Zionists, preferring a more Sephardic approach to Jewish nationalism.

The Yugoslav Sephardim played a very active role in the Universal Confederation of Sephardic Jews, which was organized at the second Sephardic World Conference held in Vienna in 1925. This organization aimed at raising the intellectual, national, and religious standards of Sephardic Jewry and increasing their efforts to help in the rebirth of Palestine. While willing to cooperate with the World Zionist Organization, these Sephardim also stressed their concern for the Sephardic element in Palestine and demanded fair and equal treatment. In addition, they wished to preserve their own special traits, rites, and traditions in contradistinction to the customs of their more numerous, wealthier, and more cultured Ashkenazic brethren.[30]

In 1925, shortly after the creation of the confederation, the Belgrade Sephardim founded their own local branch association, the Belgrade Organization of Sephardic Jews, in order to try to achieve these goals.[31] Dr. Solomon Alkalaj, president of the Belgrade Sephardic community and B'nai B'rith Lodge Serbia, as well as a member of the steering committee of the Yugoslav Zionist Federation, served as the first president. After Alkalaj's death in 1929, this office passed to Lazar Avramović, a wealthy Belgrade businessman and active Mason, who was also for a time head of the Yugoslav directory of Keren Hayesod and a non-Zionist delegate to the expanded Jewish Agency. Both these men were ardent supporters of the Sephardic cause.

The Belgrade Organization of Sephardic Jews concerned itself not only with Sephardic cultural matters in the Diaspora but also with the improvement of the status of Sephardim in Palestine. In 1927 Dr. Solomon Alkalaj submitted an article to *Židov* entitled "The Sephardim and the Zionist Executive," in which he vigorously con-

demned the Zionist Organization for its treatment of Sephardic immigrants to Palestine. The Zionist Executive in London expressed its
concern on this issue in extensive correspondence with Yugoslav
Zionist leaders.[32] Eventually a compromise agreement was worked
out between the Belgrade Sephardic Organization and the Yugoslav
Zionist Federation whereby 20 percent of the revenues collected in
Yugoslavia by Keren Hayesod were to be designated specifically for
aid to Sephardic colonies in Palestine.[33]

Surprisingly enough, despite the fact that Sarajevo could boast
of the most vocal Sephardic spokesmen and the foremost Sephardic
intellectuals in the country, such as Dr. Vita Kajon, Dr. Kalmi Baruch, and Dr. Braco Poljokan, the Bosnian center never established
its own branch of the Universal Sephardic Confederation. Hence
Belgrade, not Sarajevo, stood in the forefront of organized Sephardist
activity during the interwar period.

In June 1930 the Belgrade Sephardim were hosts to the Balkan
Conference of Sephardic Jews attended by delegates from Rumania,
Bulgaria, Greece, Italy, France, and Palestine, as well as the various
parts of Yugoslavia. In fact, the Yugoslavs proved to be among the
most active workers of all the Balkan Sephardim. The Bulgarian
Sephardim for the most part did no cooperate with the movement,
since they were staunch Zionists; the Rumanian delegates were participating in the Sephardic conference for the first time, while the
Sephardim of Greece, specifically from Salonika, had neglected to
organize the Diaspora headquarters of the organization, which therefore had to move to Paris. Hence Belgrade, by default, became a very
important center within the Sephardic movement and organized this
conference to try to invigorate its neighbors into participation. The
topics on the agenda included the Sephardic movement in general,
the organization of local Sephardic groups, and the cooperation of the
Sephardim in the Balkans in national, cultural, religioeducational,
social, and economic fields. In addition, they discussed their relationship with the major Jewish institutions, especially the Jewish Agency
and the World Zionist Organization. The Belgrade conference also
made plans for a future international Sephardic conference, which
eventually took place in London in 1935.[34]

These Sephardic efforts never achieved great success either in
Yugoslavia or elsewhere. The Universal Confederation of Sephardic
Jews remained a fairly weak and loosely organized body; as a result
it was largely ignored by the Zionists and the rest of world Jewry.[35]
In retrospect, it would seem that many of the demands and com-
plaints presented by the Sephardim were indeed to a large extent

justified. The general Zionist policy conspicuously favored European immigrants in Palestine, and as a result Oriental settlers were treated as second-class Jews. Elsewhere, the Sephardim also endured "poor relative" status. Sephardic self-awareness remained at a minimum, restricted mainly to a small circle of intellectuals; the Sephardic masses, whether in Palestine or in the Diaspora, enjoyed little opportunity to improve their lot and tended to remain largely apolitical.

The Sephardist ideology in Yugoslavia drew its advocates primarily from among former members of the Sephardic student club named Esperanza. In Vienna in 1898 a group of students from the Balkans decided to form an academic society for Sephardic Jews ("Sociedad academica de judios espanioles," in Ladino), which they called Esperanza (hope). The organization served social and cultural, not political, functions. Its members developed an awareness of their Sephardic heritage by studying its language and history and discussing common problems among themselves. Of the first generation of Sephardic intellectuals who received their education in Vienna before World War I, many, including Dr. Isaac Alcalay, Dr. Solomon Alkalaj, and Dr. Raphael Margulis from Belgrade, and Dr. Moric Levi, Isidor Sumbul, Dr. Vita Kajon, Dr. Jakov Kajon, and Dr. Isak Samokovlija from Sarajevo, played active roles in Esperanza. The younger generation of Sephardim, who studied in Zagreb during the interwar period, started their own Esperanza in 1925, in which such individuals as Avram Pinto, Dr. Samuel Kamhi, Dr. Juda Levi, and Dr. Ješua Kajon served as presidents.[36] The members of Esperanza supplied most of the leadership of the Sephardist movement, and their debates provided its ideological framework. No such Sephardic student organizations ever emerged in Belgrade, despite the increasing number of Sephardic candidates studying there. To develop strong Sephardic consciousness, it would seem that one had to leave the Sephardic milieu.

Attempts on the part of these Sephardists to transmit their special sense of Sephardic pride to the youth back home, in Sarajevo or Belgrade, met with general failure. In 1927 Zagreb Esperanza members sponsored a conference of Sephardic youth in Sarajevo to discuss problems and goals. Out of this meeting came a series of resolutions which included the following statement of purpose:

The Sephardic movement is a nationalist movement and aims at preserving and developing the positive cultural-historical heritage of Sephardic Jewry, which is peculiar to it, and participating in the general Jewish rebirth both in Eretz Israel as well as in the *galut.* The conference of Sephardic youth finds in this movement the true expression of its spirit; it alone is in a position to regenerate the Sephardic element nationally, culturally, and socially from its foundations so that it may become the real bastion of the glorious Sephardic lineage.

The conference sends out a solemn appeal to all Sephardic youth, which is still in a state of expectation, to subscribe to this movement and put their best strength in its service.[37]

These resolutions formulated plans for a Sephardic Youth Organization within the framework of the Universal Sephardic Confederation. Their platform favored the use and study of Ladino, but also advocated the teaching of Hebrew. The seven member associations of the newly formed Sephardic Youth Organization, including Esperanza and several Bosnian youth clubs, such as Jehuda Halevi in Sarajevo, broke away from the Federation of Jewish Youth Associations, with which they had formerly been affiliated.[38] After an initial period of general enthusiasm, during which time the Sephardic youth leaders, especially Dr. Samuel Kamhi, made numerous propaganda trips around the country and distributed brochures on "The Sephardic Movement" and "The Sephardim until Today," the local Sephardic youth clubs gradually disappeared, with the exception of the parent association Esperanza. By the 1930s the Sephardic Youth Organization existed on paper only.[39]

Among the younger generation of Sephardim born and educated in interwar Yugoslavia, a specifically Sephardic ideology had little appeal. In Sarajevo the children of middle-class Sephardic families tended to join Hashomer Hatzair (a left-wing Zionist youth group) in the thirties; those from the lower classes belonged to Matatja, a Jewish working youth association. In Belgrade youth activity never achieved a high degree of organization, but the majority of young people apparently either became Zionists or remained unaffiliated. Clearly, in a society which was gradually becoming less traditional and more westernized, the distinctions between Sephardim and Ashkenazim were beginning to blur and assume less importance in the eyes of the offspring than of their progenitors. One indication of this phenomenon is the relative success of Zionism as opposed to Sephardism among these elements; another might be seen in the increasing number of mixed marriages between members of the two rites. In Sarajevo between 1908 and 1918, there were only 25 such unions, comprising 5 percent of the total marriages in both communities combined. (See table 14.) Between 1919 and 1929, there were 76 mixed marriages, representing 8 percent of all marital ceremonies performed, and in the final decade, 1930 to 1940, the total reached 112, or 14 percent of the Jewish marriages in Sarajevo. This trend is more striking when viewed as percentages of marriages involving Ashkenazim in Sarajevo. From 1908 to 1918 approximately 10 percent of the Ashkenazim marrying in that city chose Sephardic spouses, while between 1919 and 1929 the percentage doubled. During the final decade, almost 40 percent of Ashkenazim contracting marriages did so with Sephardim.[40] Although no equivalent data is available for Belgrade, this trend was perhaps even more pronounced in the capital than in the provinces. Hence, despite the existence of staunch Sephardic movement supporters, primarily among the older intellectuals, and despite the continuation of separate communal institutions and local organizations, B'nai B'rith, Zionism, and youth activities were helping to bring Sephardim and Ashkenazim closer together by minimizing their differences and stressing their common sense of belonging to the Jewish people.

A deep attachment to Palestine formed a basic ingredient within the traditional Sephardic mentality in the Balkans. Rabbis, scholars, and pious men from Sarajevo, for example, went to the Holy Land to die during those centuries when Bosnia was part of the Ottoman Empire. For one hundred and forty years members of the Sarajevo Sephardic community have been making regular pilgrimages to pay homage to their revered spiritual leader, Rav Moše Danon, who died on his way to Jerusalem in 1830. At his remote graveside near Stolac in Hercegovina, they recite the ritual *limudim* in honor of the deceased and recount the almost legendary tale of his miraculous rescue from the hands of an evil Turkish pasha and his tragic death en route to the Promised Land.[41]

Although this phenomenon reflected a religious rather than a political attitude toward Zion and should be classified as medieval Messianism as opposed to modern Zionism, nevertheless, such a climate seemed to provide fertile spiritual conditions for the growth of Zionism on South Slav soil. Jehuda Haj Alkalaj (1798–1878), a forerunner of political Zionism, was born in Sarajevo and served as rabbi in Zemun in Slavonia, across the Danube from Belgrade.[42] Rabbi Alkalaj's granddaughter Rachel and her husband (and cousin) Dr. David M. Alkalaj attended the First Zionist Congress in Basle in 1897. Dr. Alkalaj, a lawyer, subsequently played an important role as Zionist leader in Belgrade and as the second president of the Yugoslav Zionist Federation from 1924 until his death in 1933.[43]

Among the Sephardim most active in Zionist affairs were Dr. Moric Levi, head rabbi of the Sarajevo Sephardic community, who served as vice-president of the Zionist Federation and delegate to Zionist congresses for many years, Dr. David Albala, and David A. Alkalaj of Belgrade, and Leon Kamhi of Bitolj. Nevertheless, despite the fact that a number of Sephardim participated prominently in Yugoslav Zionism, the Sephardic population as a whole did not live up to the expectations of the early Zionist leaders, and Zionist leadership was primarily concentrated in Ashkenazic hands.

Just as the Sephardic movement in the South Slav lands traced its origins back to a student organization in Vienna around the turn of the century, so too did Zionism. In 1902 a group of students from the Balkans founded a second academic society, which they called Bar Giora. Unlike Esperanza, which, although sympathetic to Zionist ideals, concentrated its energies on specifically Sephardic activities, Bar Giora was based entirely on Zionist principles and included both Sephardim and Ashkenazim among its membership. This association defined as its aims "the raising of Jewish nationalist consciousness among Jewish students from the South Slav lands, the cultivation of their national history, language [i.e., Hebrew] and literature, as well as the fostering of good fellowship."[44] Its founders included Johanan Thau (1880–1918) and David Fuhrmann; its active members included Alexander Licht (Zagreb), David Albala (Belgrade), Moric Levi (Sarajevo), and Oskar Grof (Sarajevo), all of whom later participated prominently in Zionist activities.

Prior to World War I, in the South Slav lands as elsewhere, Zionism gained its support primarily from among Jewish youth. During their vacations at home and upon their return to their native country after completing their studies, Bar Giora members helped organize the earliest Zionist associations to appear on the South Slav scene, such as B'ne Zion in Sarajevo (1904), Gideon in Belgrade (1905), and Theodore Herzl in Osijek (1906). In 1908 a student association called Judeja was started in Zagreb.[45] Under the auspices of Bar Giora, and later also with the help of Esperanza and Judeja, Zionist Conferences for Students and Matriculants were held in Osijek in 1904 and 1906, in Zemun in 1908, and in Sarajevo in 1910 to stimulate Jewish national consciousness at least among the younger generation.[46]

In 1909 the National Association of Zionists of the South Slav Lands of the Austro-Hungarian Monarchy was founded in Slavonski Brod (Croatia-Slavonia) with Dr. Hugo Spitzer, head of the Osijek Jewish community, as its first president.[47] Before World War I the association met annually, and after a four-year interlude, it reconstituted itself as the Federation of Zionists of Yugoslavia, which now included Serbia and Macedonia as well as Croatia and Bosnia. The Zionist organ from 1906 to 1914 was *Židovska smotra;* in 1917 the official Zionist journal became *Židov,* published biweekly and later weekly in Zagreb.

In Yugoslavia Zionism never developed into a mass movement due to the size of the Jewish community and the varied nature of local conditions. Instead it became a tightly organized countrywide federation based in Zagreb with branches in nearly all localities containing a Jewish population of any significance. Among European Zionist organizations, the Federation of Zionists of Yugoslavia was considered an exemplary model, since it incorporated within itself all the basic Zionist tenets: membership in local groups, independent fund directorships, its own press organ, concern for youth work, a healthy relationship between volunteer workers and professional officials, unity with respect to parties as well as institutions, good communication among the various groups, and decisive influence in Jewish communal life.

The framework of the Zionist Federation encompassed a variety of subsidiary bodies, each functioning in its own defined field. A secretariat took care of organization and propaganda; the national *shekel* commission collected membership dues; the Palestine Office for Yugoslavia and the national *hakhsharah* commission prepared persons for emigration to Palestine. In addition, under the same umbrella also operated the administration of the newspaper *Židov,* as well as the publications under the same name; the Committee for the Hebrew University; the Central Jewish Bureau for Productive Social Aid; the Federation of Zionist Women of Yugoslavia (WIZO); the Jewish Youth Federation (SŽOU), the Jewish National Fund, and Keren Hayesod.[48] All these departments, with the exception of Keren Hayesod (which moved to Belgrade in the mid-1920s), were located in Zagreb, so that, in effect, the Zagreb Zionists ran practically the entire operation.

The guilding light of Yugoslav Zionism was to be found in the person of Alexander Licht (1884–1948). He was born in a small Croatian town called Lepavina but received nearly his entire education in Zagreb, where he attended elementary school, gymnasium, and eventually the university, from which he graduated in 1909 as doctor of law. He also spent a year studying in Vienna. After serving in the Austro-Hungarian army during the war, he returned to Zagreb to set up a law practice and married a Sephardic woman, Ester Montiljo.

Dr. Licht had been active in Zionist affairs from their inception in the South Slav lands, first as president of Bar Giora, then with his brother Herman as cofounder and coeditor of *Židovska smotra*. With the creation of the Zionist Association in 1909, Licht became secretary of the Action Committee, and shortly after World War I he assumed the position of president of the Action Committee of the newly constituted Federation of Zionists of Yugoslavia, an office which he held until 1933, when he in turn was elected president of the Zionist Federation itself.

Alexander Licht devoted his entire life almost exclusively to the Zionist cause. He was an excellent orator, a prolific writer and a respected leader; nearly all the Yugoslav Zionists were his disciples and owed their allegiance to him personally. By the end of his tenure, however, some considered him a dictator and claimed that he had lost touch with the youth. An ardent admirer of Chaim Weizmann, president of the World Zionist Organization throughout most of the interwar years, Licht was a General Zionist with some leftist leanings and this position determined the course that Yugoslav Zionism was to follow during this period.[49]

The Zionist Federation in Yugoslavia included all Zionists, with the exception of the Revisionists (the right-wing followers of Vladimir Jabotinsky). The older generation of Zionists, namely, those born before the turn of the century, tended to affiliate with General Zionism or the middle-of-the-road policy of supporting the colonization of Palestine and the establishment of a Jewish homeland there by gradual means. Among the leaders who founded the Association of General Zionists of Yugoslavia in 1935 were Lav Stern (president of the association), Dr. Marko Horn (vice-president of the Action Committee of the Zionist Federation), Dr. Marko Bauer (president of JNF for Zagreb), Dr. Nikola Tolnauer (former president of SŽOU), and Dr. Šalom Freiberger (formerly leader of Ahdut Hatzofim), all from Zagreb; Dr. David Albala (president of JNF for Belgrade), Dr. Leon Steindler (president of Keren Hayesod for Yugoslavia), Šime Spitzer (later to become secretary of the SJVO), Dr. Friedrich Pops (president of the SJVO and of the Belgrade Jewish Nationalist Society), David A. Alkalaj, Dr. Žak Kalderon, Moše Demajo, and Avram Koen, all of Belgrade; and Iso Herman (president of the Sarajevo Ashkenazic community) and Dr. Leon Perić (president of the Sarajevo Local Zionist Organization), both of Sarajevo.[50] Their slightly younger cohorts, those born in the twentieth century, were more likely to associate themselves with the moderate left-wing, the Hapoel Hatzair-Palestine Workers-Hitahdut faction, which advocated the development of a socialist society in the Land of Israel. Among the more prominent representatives of Hapoel Hatzair were Hans Hochsinger, Dr. Joel Rosenberger, Dr. Cvi Rothmüller (Cvi Rotem), and Drago Steiner (Yakir Eventov), all of Zagreb; Leon Kamhi of Bitolj; Dr. Moše Schweiger of Subotica; and Dr. Albert Vajs of Belgrade. The two groups generally managed to work together satisfactorily; in fact, the editorship of *Židov* always remained in the hands of the leftists, whereas the top leadership was usually General Zionist in sympathy. The joint Yugoslav delegation to the World Zionist Congresses regularly included at least one representative out of three from the left or later two out of five.[51] Hence, Yugoslav Zionism was not specifically party oriented, but basically federative. (At the international congresses, the Yugoslav deputation was prone to vote with the General Zionists A, a center-left grouping, which included the Czechoslovak and American delegations.)

The Zionist Revisionists, whose platform demanded the immediate creation of a Jewish state on both sides of the Jordan River, first appeared as a separate force on the Yugoslav scene in 1933, when they held a national conference in Osijek and founded the Zionist Revisionist Organization-Vladimir Jabotinsky. Their leader and president was Julije Dohany of Novi Sad, and most of their followers also came from the Vojvodina. The Zionist Federation at first refused to recognize the secession of the Revisionists and waged a bitter campaign against them.[52] The Revisionists in turn directed their vigorous propaganda against the General Zionists. They tried especially to attract the support of the Sephardim, but achieved only moderate (and temporary) success. Originally the Revisionists and their organ, *Malchut Jisrael,* were based in Novi Sad, but in 1938 they shifted to Zagreb, renaming their paper *Jevrejska tribuna,* and finally in 1940, they moved to Belgrade. The New Zionist Organization, as they styled themselves, had a small, but active, youth movement in Yugoslavia called Betar.[53]

Membership in the Yugoslav Zionist organization increased steadily throughout the interwar period. In 1922 there were 4,719 persons who paid the *shekel* fee, which varied from fifteen to twenty-five dinars annually; this number represented about 1 in 13 Jews in the country. In 1930 there were 6,192 people reported who paid the fee, of whom 1,350 were from Zagreb, 778 from Belgrade, and 494 from Sarajevo, that is, 15 percent, 10 percent, and 6 percent respectively of the local Jewish residents.[54] By 1939, however, the total reached 10,233, which meant that 1 in 7 Jews were formally affiliated as Zionists on the eve of World War II. Among them were 1,880 from

Zagreb (28 percent of the total number in the country who paid the *shekel*), 1,209 from Belgrade (19 percent) and 836 from Sarajevo (14 percent).[55] The actual number paying the *shekel* serves as a general indicator of Zionist identification, but it is by no means accurate, since some people probably paid their *shekel* regularly but were really not convinced Zionists, whereas undoubtedly there were others who considered themselves Zionists but did not pay the *shekel*. This ambivalence particularly held true for the Sephardim in such places as Sarajevo or even Belgrade. Nevertheless, the upward trend in *shekel* collections and the remarkably high incidence of contributors among Yugoslav Jewry demonstrates the effectiveness of the Zionist organization and the growing receptiveness of the Jews themselves to the idea of Jewish nationalism and Palestine. For a country with less than 70,000 Jews to be able to send 6 delegates to the Twenty-first World Zionist Congress in 1939 in Geneva was indeed an accomplishment.[56]

Without a doubt, the Zionist Federation proved to be the most strongly organized force within the Jewish community of Yugoslavia as a whole during the interwar period. By the 1930s the Zionists had conquered the local communities, the Federation of Jewish Religious Communities, and almost the entire Jewish youth movement, in addition to virtually monopolizing the Jewish press.

The Zionist cause drew its supporters primarily from the middle class, both among the Sephardim and the Ashkenazim. The leadership was composed mainly of professionals, especially lawyers, with some doctors and intellectuals; the rank and file membership and major contributors came from the business world. The wealthier strata, the industrialists, the bankers, tended to favor integrationism and the status quo and hence never became active Zionists. A few examples will illustrate this point. The wealthiest families in Zagreb, the Deutsch-Maćelskis, the Alexanders, the Marićs, etc., were all non-Zionists; in Belgrade, Geca Kon, the publisher who paid the highest taxes in the Ashkenazic community and served for many years as its vice-president, and in Sarajevo, Avram Majer Altarac, a well-to-do Sephardic businessman and longtime president of the Sephardic community, and Avram Levi-Sadić, a Sephardic manufacturer, all fell into the same category. Many of these people were very prominent in Jewish communal affairs, especially the Hevra Kaddisha and other charitable institutions, but they did not belong to Zionist organizations. Similarly, the poorer class, the Sarajevo workers and artisans, never became directly involved. Although a Poale Cijon group (Socialist-Zionist) formed in Sarajevo shortly after World War I, it gradually abandoned its Zionist precepts and eventually evolved into a burial society. An exception to this general rule can be seen in Bitolj, however. In their extreme economic plight these Macedonian Sephardim adopted Zionism in the hope that they could find a new and better life for themselves in Palestine.[57] Overall, however, the middle class formed the backbone of the Zionist Federation.

The Ashkenazim were more active in Yugoslav Zionism than the Sephardim although, superficially at least, the Sephardic tradition would appear more conducive to fostering Zionist ideology. In neighboring Bulgaria, with a predominantly Sephardic Jewish community, the Sephardim became ardent Zionists.[58] In Yugoslavia, however, with Ashkenazic control over the Zionist organization from Zagreb, many Sephardim evidently became alienated from the central body and never involved themselves in its activities wholeheartedly. Zionist propaganda and programs did not gear themselves to Sephardic interests and needs; instead, more attention was directed toward the more assimilated Ashkenazim, whether in Croatia or in the Vojvodina. In Yugoslavia, as in western Europe, Zionism was to a large extent a postassimilationist phenomenon and attracted to its ranks those who had already broken away from Judaism, who were seeking a solution to their identity crisis in the concept of a Jewish people.[59]

The Jews in the South Slav lands began contributing to the Jewish National Fund shortly after its creation in 1901. In 1906 a collection center for Croatia, Slavonia, and Bosnia was established in Osijek; during the first few years of its existence, over half of its revenues came from Bosnia. The headquarters moved to Zagreb in 1910, and thereafter the contributions of Croatian Jewry far exceeded those of their Bosnian brethren.[60] During the interwar period, Yugoslav Jews contributed a total of 20,400,000 dinars ($364,000). From 1919 to 1933 the annual average amounted to 830,000 dinars ($15,-000), whereas during the last seven years, it increased by 50 percent to 1,200,000 dinars ($21,500).[61] In 1928, for example, the wealthier Jews of Croatia, who comprised 32 percent of Yugoslav Jewry, contributed 58 percent of the national total to the Jewish National Fund; the poorer Jews of Bosnia and Dalmatia, 19 percent of the population, donated 10 percent, and the Jews of Serbia and Macedonia, also 19 percent, paid 12 percent. This pattern appears even more obvious in the individual cities: Zagreb, with approximately 13 percent of the Yugoslav Jewish population, gave 288,472 dinars, or 28.85 dinars per capita (26 percent of the national total), while Belgrade, with about 10 percent, contributed 116,312 dinars, or 16.61 dinars per capita (which amounted to 10 percent of the national total), and Sarajevo, with approximately 11 percent of all Jews, donated 47,834, or 5.98 dinars per capita (4 percent of the entire sum).[62] Hence it is clear that the Jews of Zagreb gave by far the largest share and the Jews of Sarajevo much less, and the Belgrade Jewish community held the median. Considering that the official policy of the Jewish National Fund was based upon collection boxes and small gifts, such a wide divergence between Zagreb and Sarajevo must be attributed to more than the difference in relative wealth between the two communities. That this fund primarily derived its resources from among the believers indicates once again that the major Zionist center in Yugoslavia was indeed Zagreb with respect to financial support as well as membership.

The non-Zionists in Zagreb were also able to contribute a good deal more to Palestine than their counterparts in Belgrade and Sarajevo. Unlike the Jewish National Fund, the Keren Hayesod aimed at collecting a rather substantial sum from each individual and did not confine its efforts to the ranks of the Zionists. Keren Hayesod was first introduced into Yugoslavia in 1921 and had its offices in Zagreb. Following a minor scandal concerning mismanagement of funds by Šime Spitzer, the bureau was shifted to Belgrade four years later in an attempt to attract more support from the Sephardim.[63] In 1928 out of a total of 960,890 dinars ($17,500) collected, 357,181 dinars originated from Zagreb, 279,127 from Belgrade, and 99,693 from Sarajevo.[64] During the 1920s, Yugoslavia ranked twenty-first in the world in its contributions to Keren Hayesod.[65] While this feat in itself might not appear particularly impressive, it was nevertheless a respectable showing for a relatively small Jewish community.

When the Jewish Agency expanded in 1929, with non-Zionists as well as Zionists officially sitting on its council, a problem arose in Yugoslavia concerning how these non-Zionists should be elected. No specifically non-Zionist representative institutions or bodies existed in the country and the definition of who qualified as a non-Zionist was somewhat hazy. Eventually, it was decided that the non-Zionists should be chosen by the Federation of Jewish Religious Communities,[66] but in practice the actual decision most often rested with the Zionist Federation instead. This policy usually resulted in the selection of one Sephardist from either Belgrade or Sarajevo and one wealthy integrationist from Zagreb.

Initially, the name of the chief rabbi, Isaac Alcalay, was proposed for this position, but because he regularly paid his *shekel* and attended Zionist national conferences, it was thought that he might not be suitable. In his stead, the nomination fell to Lazar Avramović, director of Keren Hayesod and president of the Belgrade Organization of Sephardic Jews.[67] He also paid a *shekel* and once served as a member of the Central Committee of the Zionist Federation. Among the other Sephardim who were subsequently named for this post were Avram Majer Altarac and Dr. Vita Kajon of Sarajevo and Rafailo Finci and Dr. Bukić Pijade of Belgrade.[68] In some of these instances, the designation "non-Zionist" does not seem particularly appropriate; presumably such appointments were political rather than ideological in nature. In the case of the integrationists, the choice of candidate generally rested on somewhat firmer ground. Included as members, or their substitutes, were such men as Dr. Julius Mogan, a lawyer and instructor in maritime law at Zagreb University; Otto Heinrich, a Zagreb banker; Bernard Ernst of Novi Sad; Bernard Robiček, a Belgrade senior civil servant; and Dr. Milan Marić, a Zagreb industrialist who converted to Christianity in 1938 during his term of office.[69] In retrospect it would seem that no really outstanding non-Zionist spokesmen per se were to be found in Yugoslavia during this time.

The vast majority of Yugoslav Zionists during the period between the wars, especially those of the older generation who adhered to the General Zionist philosophy, did not have the slightest intention of ever actually settling in Palestine. Like many other Zionists in the western world, they devoted their energies to establishing a Jewish homeland—for others who might need it. A number of Yugoslav Jews did however decide to emigrate to Palestine in the twenties and thirties. The main components of this group consisted of approximately five hundred poor Jews from Bitolj[70], a few leaders of Hapoel Hatzair, the moderate left-wing, such as Drago Steiner (Yakir Eventov) and Cvi Rothmüller (Cvi Rotem),[71] and some of the younger generation, especially those affiliated with Hashomer Hatzair, such as Slavko Weiss (Hillel Livni).[72]

The Yugoslav Zionist Federation set up a Palestine Office in 1920 to aid individuals and groups who wanted emigrate.[73] The efforts of the twenties for the most part ended in failure, however. The first group of *halutzim* (pioneers), seventeen boys and two girls, spent a year in agricultural training at Bjelina (Bosnia), and smaller numbers received their preparation in the Vojvodina and in Mostar (Hercegovina). In 1921 eighteen of these youths, twelve Yugoslavs and six foreign citizens, set off for Palestine; few of them stayed there for long.[74] In 1926 the Zionist Federation initiated an attempt to set up a Yugoslav colony in Djedda in Palestine, but this effort, too, did not succeed.[75]

Substantial permanent emigration began only in the thirties. Between 1932 and 1935, of the 525 persons who left Yugoslavia for Palestine, 386 held Yugoslav citizenship, and the remainder were German refugees or Austrian nationals. Included among the Yugoslav Jews were 290 individuals classified as *halutz* workers.[76] From 1936 to 1939 there were 404 more persons who left Yugoslavia for Palestine; in this contingent only 104 were Yugoslav citizens, the rest being foreign nationals.[77] Emigration continued, albeit on a limited scale, until 1941. Considerably more persons, both Yugoslav and foreign citizens, would have gone to Palestine had enough certificates, or special visas for Jewish immigrants issued by the British authorities, been available for their use.

In 1933 a *hakhsharah* commission to help prepare prospective pioneers for settlement in Palestine was formed within the Zionist Federation, in conjunction with the Federation of Jewish Youth Associations and the Women's Zionist Federation.[78] In subsequent years a network of *hakhsharah* stations grew up in various parts of Yugoslavia to train youth in agriculture and trades before they left for Palestine. The first such enterprise began in the spring of 1933 in Zagreb with six members of Hashomer Hatzair; by fall there were more than forty *halutzim* studying various trades, among them carpentry and locksmithing.[79] Gradually the emphasis shifted more and more toward agriculture. The Yugoslav Zionist Federation, together with the National Federation of Hehalutz for Germany and both the Yugoslav and German B'nai B'rith Grand Lodges, set up an agricultural center in Golenić, where in addition to fifty to sixty trainees from Germany, ten to fifteen Yugoslav Jewish youths received training each session.[80] This station continued to be used primarily for German refugees until 1939, when it was handed over to Yugoslav Hashomer Hatzair. Several other rural and urban training centers were formed in Yugoslavia, but usually lasted only brief periods. These enterprises were sponsored by other youth groups as well, such as Tehelet Lavan (Blue-White) and Akiba, and not limited exclusively to members of Hashomer Hatzair.

Throughout the thirties, Yugoslav Zionists provided a valuable contribution to the Zionist movement as a whole by creating and maintaining these preparatory centers which enabled not only Yugoslav Jews but also many other European Jews to receive proper physical and mental preparation before emigrating to Palestine. On the eve of World War II Yugoslavia was an important transit stop on the escape route from Nazi Europe to Palestine and the Yugoslav Zionists did everything possible to aid their fellow Jews in reaching their destination.

Zionism succeeded in rooting itself firmly on Yugoslav soil, but it took on a number of different forms. In Zagreb the adoption of Zionist principles meant the rejection of the notion of Jews as Croats of the Israelite faith and the opportunity to put forth specifically Jewish lists in municipal elections. For the individual, being a Zionist meant working and contributing money for the Zionist cause. In Belgrade being a Zionist was not incompatible with being a Serb patriot; one could be active in Zionist affairs and at the same time be a member of a Serbian political party. Zionism did not interfere with loyalty to the Yugoslav state, indeed, as far as the regime was concerned, being a Jewish nationalist was certainly preferable to being a Hungarian nationalist, for example. Owing allegiance to Palestine in the interwar period seemed to present no conflict with one's citizenship. In Sarajevo, where a Jewish nationality did not represent a novel idea and where attachment to Zion was traditional, virtually all the Sephardim at least accepted the basic tenets of Zionism even if they did not actively participate in its programs. For the older generation, the transition to Zionism was primarily internal rather than external; Zionism changed their self-definition but not their way of life. Only some of the younger generation of Zionists adopted a Palestine-centered interpretation of Zionism, carrying the theory to its logical conclusion through emigration.

The younger generation of Jews born on South Slav territory in the twentieth century does not appear to have become deeply involved in either Serb or Croat nationalism. Jewish youth in the period between the wars tended to fall into three general categories: the Zionists, the Communists, and the apolitical. The son or daughter of a wealthy integrationist was likely to turn to communism or else become committed to a profession. The children of middle-class parents often became Zionists, especially socialist-Zionists of the Hashomer Hatzair variety; the lower classes for the most part were apolitical.[81] Neither bourgeois integrationism nor the Sephardic movement found too many supporters among this group.

Before World War I, organized Jewish youth activity was only beginning in the South Slav lands. The prime movers in this field were the older students, especially members of Bar Giora and Esperanza in Vienna and later Judeja in Zagreb. These activists sponsored the biennial Zionist youth conferences which were held from 1904 to 1910. In Belgrade the first club for young people was the Serbian-Jewish Youth Group, a literary society which promoted integrationist ideology; it was formed before the turn of the century but did not survive World War I.[82] In the Serbian capital the oldest Zionist youth association for boys in secondary school was called Gideon, while its sister counterpart for girls was Karmel. In addition, a nationalist club for youth out of school, Atehija, also was formed.[83] In Zagreb the organization for high school boys known as Literary Meetings of Jewish Youth began holding sessions in 1898 to discuss Jewish cultural and literary matters; gradually, its programs became more and more Zionist in content.[84] Shortly before the outbreak of the war, a Zionist girls' group, B'not Zion, formed in Zagreb.[85] Sarajevo also manifested two early Zionist youth groups, B'ne Zion for boys and Moriah for girls. These associations were generally rather small and ineffective, but it is worth noting that even prior to 1918 almost all youth organizations in existence exhibited a pro-Zionist orientation.

In 1919 a conference of Jewish youth clubs held in Brod na Savi (Croatia) resolved to establish a Federation of Jewish Youth Associations for the Kingdom of Serbs, Croats, and Slovenes.[86] According to its statutes, this federation aimed at "educating all Jewish youth into a healthy nationalist whole imbued with Jewish knowledge and culture, by means of joint and systematic work on the part of all Jewish youth associations." The means of attaining this goal were: encouraging existing associations to work with material dealing with Jewish knowledge and arts; creating Hebrew courses; enabling the creation and maintenance of gymnastic and sports organizations; advising and helping these institutions in their work and forming new associations in places where they did not already exist. Membership in the federation included all Jewish youth associations, regardless of the sex or class of their members or their particular ideological bent, as long as they recognized the Basle program of 1897 which established the basic Zionist principles.[87]

The youth federation operated as the junior branch of the national Zionist Federation and had its headquarters in Zagreb. It drew its leadership from the younger regular Zionists, sometimes General Zionists, but more often Hapoel Hatzair supporters. In 1920 the organization included 28 clubs with a total of 1,400 members;[88] ten years later, it comprised 41 organizations with 1,089 regular and 1,250 special members;[89] and by the end of the interwar period, close to 3,500 Jewish young people belonged to affiliated associations.[90] The federation published its own periodical *Gideon* from 1919 to 1926 and later *Hanoar* from 1927 to 1937.

The Federation of Jewish Youth Associations served as the coordinating agency for nearly all organized Jewish youth activity in the country. Like the Zionist Federation, its ideological position in the beginning was slightly left-of-center Zionist, but not particularly Palestine centered. Also like its parent organization, the youth federation was beset by difficulties caused by internal factionalism. In 1926 Esperanza and the Sephardic youth clubs in Bosnia, under the influence of the Sephardic movement philosophy, decided to secede from the federation and form their own separate Organization of Sephardic Youth. At about the same time, the sports and gymnastic associations, which were not particularly Zionist, broke away and founded a Makabi Association. And at the other extreme, the Ahdut Hatzofim (scout union) seceded because the federation itself was not Zionist enough. Thus in the course of one year, the federation lost almost half of its membership, temporarily at least.[91]

Ahdut Hatzofim originated in 1924 as a radical subsidiary of the youth federation. At first it comprised only a couple of so-called scout troups, which were located mainly in Zagreb and Sarajevo. Its aims were:

(a) to transform their members into people who want the conscious responsibility that Zionism requires of them to be able to regulate their lives according to nationalist needs; (b) to bring its members closer to Jewry and its values through experience and education; and (c) by physical and spiritual education to create the ideal type of Jew, bearing in himself a synthesis of youth combined with spiritual and bodily strength, which is necessary for a healthy and creative life in Eretz Yisrael.

This group became emphatically Palestine centered; it advocated socialist principles and eventual *aliya* to Palestine. Its official language was Hebrew. Ahdut Hatzofim organized itself on the basis of local branches, called *kibbutzim* (or later *kenim*), which were in turn divided into *kvutzot,* or small groups, each containing five to twelve members. The leadership was also arranged in hierarchical fashion, with each *kvutza* headed by a *rosh kvutza,* a council of local leaders, headed by the *rosh hakibbutz* and a national council, called *hanhagah haroshit,* composed of three members.[92] In 1928 a reconciliation took place between the Ahdut Hatzofim and the youth federation, whereby the former gained a special status and the national scout leaders joined the executive of the federation.[93] Henceforth, the left-wing dominated the federation and imposed its Palestine-centered philosophy upon the entire organization.

In 1931 Ahdut Hatzofim changed into Histadrut Hashomer Hatzair and belonged officially to the international Hashomer Hatzair movement, which was Marxist and radical Zionist in orientation and stressed *halutziut,* or pioneer emigration to Palestine to work primarily in agriculture.[94] One of the most important aspects of the youth program was the annual summer camp experience which several hundred children shared each year, beginning in 1925. In 1932, for example, 310 young people attended three separate but adjacent Hashomer Hatzair camps near Gožde (Slovenia). The youngest group of children, those under thirteen, called *kfirim* (cubs), included 58 campers (of whom 19 were from Zagreb, 15 from Belgrade, and none from Sarajevo). The intermediary group, *tzofim* (scouts), comprised 95 members (25 from Zagreb, 23 from Belgrade, and 22 from Sarajevo); the *bogrim* (adults) over eighteen, with 157, formed the largest contingent (65 from Zagreb, 56 from Belgrade, and 27 from Sarajevo).[95] During the two weeks of camp, the program would consist of a variety of activities, including sports and hikes, but also numerous serious talks and debates and Hebrew classes. A typical list of discussions for the *bogrim* might encompass the following topics: the situation of the Jews in the world; the development of the Zionist Organization; the Arab question in Palestine; the worker in Palestine; the *kibbutz* movement; the youth movement and its problems; Marxism; historical materialism; imperialism and the colonial question; Borochovism and the nationality problem; religion; sexual and erotic questions, and also the women's question.[96] The organization took its educational and propaganda role very seriously, and to a certain extent it succeeded in its mission: in the late thirties, Hashomer Hatzair sponsored several *hakhsharah* stations, the largest of which was at Golenić. A very high percentage of the Yugoslav Jews who went on *aliya* in the thirties were products of the Hashomer Hatzair movement.[97]

By 1938 Hashomer Hatzair had 1,374 members, of whom 831 were boys and 543 girls, organized into 132 *kvutzot* in all parts of Yugoslavia. Interestingly enough, the biggest *ken* was to be found in Sarajevo, with 245 members (126 boys and 119 girls) in 20 *kvutzot.* In Zagreb there were 181 members (118 boys and 63 girls) in 18 *kvutzot,* and in Belgrade, 127 (87 boys and 40 girls), divided into 13 smaller groups.[98] Ironically, Sarajevo, the center with the weakest local Zionist organization and very strong Sephardic feelings, produced the largest and most active Hashomer Hatzair organization in the country. Evidently, the younger generation of Sephardim in Sarajevo, especially those with a middle-class background and high school education, preferred a more radical brand of Jewish nationalism than their elders and turned to left-wing Zionism as the path for the future.

Although Hashomer Hatzair represented the strongest and most important Zionist youth organization in the thirties, it by no means had the entire field to itself. Closest in ideology to Hashomer Hatzair was Kadima, founded in 1935 to provide slightly less intensive Jewish nationalist education for youths in smaller towns. By 1940 it had 40 clubs with some 900 members and ran its own summer camps and programs, placing increasing stress on *halutziut* and *aliya.*[99] Tehelet Lavan was also an offshoot of Hashomer Hatzair, but it was less socialist and less political in orientation. It began its work in Yugoslavia in 1936 and by the outbreak of the war it had 900 members in 15 locations, mainly centered in the Vojvodina. Tehelet Lavan established its own marine *hakhsharah* station in 1938 at Sušak, on the Dalmatian Coast, which trained some 30 youths of both sexes as sailors and fishermen.[100] Akiba provided the only General Zionist youth association in the country. It had no class ideology and placed less emphasis on *halutziut* and Palestine. It was the smallest of the youth organizations with only 250 members in 5 groups, but it had its own tiny *hakhsharah* station for 6 persons.[101] In addition, Betar, the Revisionist youth organization, and Junior WIZO also existed in Yugoslavia, but they did not have any affiliation with the Federation of Jewish Youth Associations.

Although the Zionist youth organizations constituted the dominant factor in organized activity among the younger generation within the Jewish community during the interwar period, the Zionist monopoly was not quite complete. Outside the exclusively Zionist sphere were, for a time, the Sephardic youth clubs and the various sports clubs of the Makabi Association. No traces of active integrationist youth organizations are to be found in the literature available; hence, it must be assumed that non-Zionist youths for the most part associated with youth groups outside the Jewish community. A considerable number of young Jewish left-wing intellectuals, many of whom had formerly belonged to Hashomer Hatzair, joined the Federation of Communist Youth of Yugoslavia (SKOJ) or the Communist Party (KPJ) during the 1930s. These individuals tended to be cosmopolitan rather than Jewish nationalist by ideology. The most important exception to the general rule of Zionist preponderance in Yugoslav Jewish youth organizations can be discovered, however, in Matatja, an association for Jewish working youth in Sarajevo.

Matatja began its existence in 1923, when a group of young Jewish employees and workers decided to form their own club to fulfill their own particular social and cultural needs. Starting with 80 to 100 members, by 1930 the association had grown to 650 and its membership roster continued to increase. Matatja operated on the basis of sections (in which approximately 200 active members took part), including Jewish music, a band, a string orchestra, a drama group, a literary circle, a cultural section, sports teams, an outing club, and a girls' division. The organization frequently presented lectures, concerts, and plays, often in Ladino, all of which were well attended by both members and the general Jewish public. It also maintained its own library.[102]

Matatja rejected the philosophies of the other local Jewish youth organizations, both Zionist and Sephardist, on account of their predominantly middle-class, intellectual orientation. Whereas Kibbutz Haolim and Jehuda Halevi attracted the students at academic high schools, Matatja appealed to the less-educated working-class elements, the young artisans, commercial assistants, and workers. Although overwhelmingly Sephardic in composition, Matatja never identified itself with the Sephardic movement. In the early thirties the large cultural section devoted much of its attention to Zionist topics and tried to increase Jewish nationalist awareness among its members,[103] but toward the end of the decade, the major subject under discussion was most likely to be Marxist doctrine. Claims have been made that Matatja became a Communist cover organization; this is indeed plausible. Some members of the organization were secretly associated with the underground Communist movement and tried to use the club as a basis for operations and propaganda. In 1936 several dozen Matatja members were arrested for suspected Communist activities and thereafter the organization came under constant police surveillance.[104] In 1939 the authorities forced the association to disband, allegedly for not abiding by its statutes but in reality for Communist affiliations; a year later, however, it was allowed to reconstitute itself under the supervision of the Sephardic communal executive.[105]

An organization like Matatja could only have been possible in a town such as Sarajevo, with a large Jewish working-class population and strong Jewish consciousness. The association was Jewish by membership and by conviction; it was not integrationist, not Zionist, and not even Sephardist. This branch of the younger generation seemingly rejected all the ideologies of their elders and, wittingly or not, helped pave the way for the future Yugoslavia.

A substantial percentage of Jewish youth in Yugoslavia during the interwar period belonged ideologically to the left wing. The Communist intellectuals, the working-class members of Matatja and the middle-class members of Hashomer Hatzair (and to a lesser extent Kadima) were all Marxist in orientation, despite their differences on the nationality issue. After the German occupation of Yugoslavia in 1941, the entire Belgrade *ken* of Hashomer Hatzair joined Tito's Partisans, as did many other young Jewish activists. They fought for a Jewish as well as a Yugoslav cause.

The question of the national identity of Yugoslav Jews during the interwar period is complex. If the Jewish population is divided into three age groups, the older generation (born before 1880), the middle generation (born before World War I), and the younger generation (born during the interwar period), a definite pattern seems to emerge. The oldest group, especially in Zagreb and to a lesser extent in Belgrade, often tended toward integrationism—they considered themselves Serbs or Croats of the Mosaic faith—but this philosophy lost ground within the Jewish community by the interwar period. A large proportion of the middle group gradually began to adopt Zionism in its General or moderate socialist form, which meant belief in a Jewish nationality and hope for a future Jewish homeland in Palestine but a personal commitment to living in Yugoslavia. A splinter group of Sephardic intellectuals among this segment of the population stressed the Sephardic aspects of their Jewish national identity and of Zionism and evolved their own philosophy of Diaspora nationalism. The younger generation, however, frequently chose a more extreme solution, either within the Zionist context or outside it, emigration to Palestine and effecting a social revolution there or helping to create a revolution at home.

The multinational complexion of interwar Yugoslavia, which hindered the progress of integrationism, considerably facilitated the acceptance of a Jewish national identity. Where nationality paralleled citizenship and religion was not a major criterion in national identification, Jews were more likely to consider themselves members of the same nationality as their neighbors. Thus, in states with but one major national group, England, France, Germany, Jews could manage to convince themselves that they were Englishmen, Frenchmen, or Germans of the Jewish faith. In a pluralistic society, however, it was more difficult for a Jew to lose his distinct identity, particularly when nationality was closely linked with religion.

In the former Austro-Hungarian Empire, the Jews had been tempted to affiliate themselves with the German or Magyar nationalities, but in the successor states, such as Yugoslavia and Czechoslovakia, this course of action was neither advisable nor desirable. The Jew who retained Hungarian or German loyalties might be regarded as foreign and hence suspect. The trend among Jews to identify themselves with the Slavic nationalities, the Serbs, Croats, and Czechs, developed primarily in the twentieth century. It never succeeded in establishing very deep roots among the Jewish population at large and thus allowed for the growth of Jewish nationalism.

Zionism provided an alternative for Jews who realized that they could never integrate themselves fully into the surrounding culture. In Yugoslavia this applied more to the Ashkenazim, who tried to become Croats and generally failed to be accepted as such, than to the Sephardim, who had carved for themselves a special niche in Serbian or Bosnian society. Jewish nationalism was thus considered a legitimate response for Jews in this multinational environment. Yugoslav Jews were not expected to see themselves as Serbs or Croats, but preferably to identify themselves as Jews by nationality, rather than as members of any other minority ethnic group.

9

THE PRESSURES OF POLITICS

The political heritage of the South Slavs reflected the diversity of their history. On the eve of World War I, Serbia was an independent kingdom under the Karageorgević dynasty. It could boast of a democratic constitution and a national assembly, the Skupština, elected by popular male suffrage based on minimal taxation. Croatia, by contrast, had little tradition of democracy. It possessed a provincial assembly, or Sabor, elected by very limited suffrage on a curial basis, but was administered by a *ban* appointed by Budapest. Bosnia-Hercegovina enjoyed even less political experience because before 1910 it had no legislature whatsoever. Montenegro displayed a brief period of constitutional monarchism and manhood suffrage, but the remaining territories, Slovenia, the Vojvodina, and Macedonia, were merely entitled to elect several representatives to the Austrian or the Hungarian or the Turkish parliaments, respectively.

From these varied models the Kingdom of Serbs, Croats, and Slovenes adopted the Serbian form of government with only slight modifications. The Vidovdan Constitution of 1921 defined the new Yugoslav state as a "constitutional, parliamentary, and hereditary monarchy" and at the same time retained the basic Serbian constitution of 1903, the one-chamber Skupština and the Karageorgević dynasty, along with the old Serbian administrative system. Universal manhood suffrage and a type of proportional representation (the D'Hondt system) designed to foster large parties rather than encourage smaller factions were introduced.

Except for the Communist Party, which was outlawed in 1921, the main Yugoslav political parties were regional in nature and depended upon the support of one particular nationality. The largest

Serbian political group was the Radical Party, whose leaders were in power throughout most of the 1920s. The Democratic Party, which eventually split into two divisions, also had a substantial Serbian following, and there existed, in addition, a small Serbian Agrarian group. The spokesman for the Croats was the Croatian Peasant Party; a smaller, bourgeois Croatian Union initially also attempted to compete for votes but later faded. Among the Slovenes, the predominant party was the Slovenian People's Party, whereas the major representative of the Muslims in Bosnia was the Yugoslav Muslim Organization. These parties, then, were the most important, although by no means the only, political forces in the Yugoslav parliamentary era of the twenties.

The leaders of the different political parties varied considerably in their attitudes toward the Jews. Most sympathetic to Jewish causes were the Radicals, the largest Serbian party. Nikola Pašić, party chief and frequent prime minister until his death in 1926, projected an image of himself as a great friend of the Jews. He adopted as his motto the Serbian proverb, "He is my brother, whatever his faith may be," and thereby gained the loyal support of many Serbian Jews.[1] Much the same could be said for Milan Srškić, the Radical boss in Bosnia. As president of the regional government and later minister of justice and premier of the royal government in the early 1930s, he helped protect the constitutional rights of the Jewish minority. In return he generally received the bulk of the Sarajevo Jewish vote.[2] The leaders of the Democratic Party, such as Ljubomir Davidović, appear to have had a rather neutral record with regard to the Jews, and their party too received a share of the ballots cast by Jews, especially in the Belgrade area.[3]

The leadership of the Croatian Peasant Party, however, in particular Stjepan Radić, one of its founders, occasionally resorted to anti-Semitic demagoguery. As early as 1906 Radić published a polemical article entitled "Jewry as a Negative Cultural Element."[4] He continued to make anti-Semitic remarks part of his campaign rhetoric for opportunistic reasons throughout the 1920s. However, because anti-Semitism was by no means a major plank in his platform, he should not be considered in the same class as other blatantly anti-Semitic politicians elsewhere in Eastern Europe at the time.[5] Nevertheless, Croatian Jews were rarely found among his followers, even though he constantly swept the Croatian electorate for his party. Not unlike Radić was Msgr. Anton Korošec, the moving spirit of the Slovenian People's Party. The party and its leader were devoutly Catholic and had little love for the Jews on religious rather than racial grounds. Although Korošec was rarely openly anti-Semitic in his speeches, he was the initiator of the first anti-Jewish legislation passed in late 1940. Mehmed Spaho, the leader of the Yugoslav Muslim Organization was himself not overtly anti-Semitic; but his party received almost no Jewish backing because it sponsored such programs as a boycott of Jewish stores in Bosnia in 1925. The only other political figure of any significance with respect to the Jews was Dimitrije Ljotić, who was minister of justice for a brief period in 1931 and later head of the tiny Fascist group, called Zbor. This group, centered in the Vojvodina, received 1 percent of the total vote in the 1938 election.[6] Ljotić's anti-Semitism was undisguised and unrestrained; he enjoyed little popularity but nonetheless made his voice heard. The Croatian Fascists, known as the Ustaši, did not participate in the Yugoslav parliamentary system during the interwar period, but operated illegally, primarily in exile in Italy. They apparently were not concerned to any great extent with anti-Semitism before the outbreak of the war.

Yugoslav political life in the interwar period, especially in its first decade, presented a very complex picture of shifting coalitions and bitter feuds. At issue was the nature of the state organization. Despite the efforts of most Croats and Slovenes and some Serbs to find a federal solution, the Vidovdan Constitution, supported by most Serbs and Montenegrins, established a centralized state with all power emanating from Belgrade. This continuing dispute led to parliamentary stagnation and constant governmental crises. Frustration in parliament brought on by the obstructionist tactics of the opposition culminated in the shooting of Stjepan Radić, the Croatian Peasant Party leader, in the Skupština in 1928. Six months later, lacking a viable alternative for restoring order in his chaotic state, King Alexander declared a personal dictatorship. The country was renamed Yugoslavia and redistricted along geographic rather than historic lines in order to blur traditional regional-ethnic loyalties. In 1931 the king promulgated a new constitution and restored limited parliamentary government. No parties were allowed to exist—just the government and opposition blocs. Yugoslavia was somewhat less authoritarian than many countries in Eastern Europe in the thirties, but it could no longer be considered a parliamentary democracy.

The role of the Jews in the political activities of the South Slav lands was a very minor one. Before World War I there was generally one Jewish member in each of the various national assemblies. In the

Serbian Skupština, Avram Ozerović, a fairly assimilated, wealthy Belgrade merchant, served as a Progressive (conservative) deputy in the 1880s and 1890s; later Bencion Buli (1867–1933), a prominent Belgrade banker, held a seat as Radical representative. Both men were very active members of the Belgrade Sephardic community and served as its president for a number of years.[7] In Croatia, Emmanuel Prister and Dr. Ljudevit Schwarz, both leading members of the Zagreb Jewish community, were elected deputies to the Sabor in the late nineteenth and early twentieth centuries.[8] It was only in Bosnia that Jews were appointed and elected to office specifically as Jews and by Jews. In 1877, shortly before the end of Ottoman rule, Javer effendi Baruh and Salamon effendi Salom became representatives of Bosnian Jewry to the Turkish parliament.[9]

For the first elections to the Bosnian Sabor in 1910 after the Austro-Hungarian annexation, the authorities established a separate Jewish electoral curia. Officially the Jews received two seats in the assembly, one for a virilist (or ex officio member) to which the head rabbi of the Sarajevo Sephardic community was appointed and the other for an elected deputy. In the subsequent election, the president of the Sarajevo Sephardic community, Ješua D. Salom, an affluent banker, soundly defeated Dr. Moritz Rothkopf, a well-respected lawyer and president of the rival Ashkenazic community. Unofficially there was a third Jewish member of the Sabor: the president of the local bar association, first Dr. Josip Fischer, the integrationist vice-president of the Ashkenazic community, and later Dr. Rothkopf, also held a virilist seat.[10] Thus Bosnian Jews were much better represented in parliament on the eve of World War I than their Serbian or Croatian counterparts, and, unlike the others, they ran, for the most part, overtly as Jews.

In the interwar period, Jews proved less successful in being elected to national office. No Jewish party came into existence, although Jewish activists suggested the idea several times, especially in the Vojvodina where Jews lived in greatest concentration.[11] Considering the nature of the Yugoslav voting system with its proportional representation and the diverse character of the Jewish population, both geographically and ideologically, the concept of a separate Jewish list was highly impractical, except on the municipal level. As in western European countries, the only hope for a Jewish presence in the legislature was through the established political parties. Since the Jewish vote was nowhere crucial, except perhaps in the city of Sarajevo, it was difficult to make deals with the major parties. As a result, a Jewish candidate had to be nominated on the basis of his merits as a party loyalist, not primarily as a Jew.[12]

No Jewish representative sat in the Constituent Assembly or the first two postwar parliaments, although several Jewish candidates, mainly Radicals and Democrats, but also Socialists, were on electoral lists. In 1927 a Jew was elected to the Skupština as a Radical deputy. He was Šemaja Demajo, a lawyer, who was prominent in Belgrade Radical circles, an active member of the Sephardic community, and a non-Zionist.[13] In the 1930s, the era of dictatorship and limited parliamentary government, few Jews, if any, were interested in running for national office and none was elected during that decade. In 1932 King Alexander appointed the chief rabbi of Yugoslavia, Dr. Isaac Alcalay of Belgrade, as an ex officio member of the newly created Senate;[14] in this capacity he served as permanent representative of all the Jews in the country.

The leading Jewish figures in the Radical Party in Belgrade during the twenties were Šemaja Demajo, Dr. Jakov Čelebonović, a lawyer, Dr. David Albala, a medical doctor, Solomon Azriel (1852–1928), a merchant, and Šalom Ruso, a teacher. These men shared a number of characteristics: except for Ruso, they were all at one time or another during the interwar period president of the Belgrade Sephardic community (Ruso, however, was an active member of the communal executive); all but Albala had been elected members of the Belgrade municipal council (Albala had run for office but been defeated); and, with the exception of Albala again, none of them was a fervent Zionist. Other communal presidents during this interwar period were also politically involved: Rafailo Finci, a merchant, Dr. Solomon Alkalaj and Dr. Bukić Pijade, both physicians, were all active Democrats, as was Dr. Friedrich Pops, a lawyer, president of the Belgrade Ashkenazic community throughout the period and president of the Federation of Jewish Religious Communities after 1933. Pijade and Pops were elected members of the Belgrade municipal council; they were both Zionists, whereas Finci and Alkalaj were prominent in the Belgrade Sephardic Organization. It is clear that those who played an active role in politics stood in the forefront of Jewish affairs as well.

In Sarajevo there was generally more political activity among the Jews around election time than in Belgrade or Zagreb. The Radical Party held large campaign meetings with speeches and propaganda in Ladino.[15] Undoubtedly this was due to the strategic significance of the Jewish vote to the Radicals in the multiethnic city. The Democrats campaigned less among the Sarajevo Jews, and the Croat and Muslim parties hardly at all.[16] The leading Sarajevo Radicals were

Dr. Vita Kajon, a banker, intellectual, and vocal Sephardic champion, Avram Majer Altarac, a wealthy merchant and long-time president of the Sephardic community, Dr. Pepi Baruch, a maverick judge, and Silvio Alkalaj, a Zionist. The spokesman for the Democrats was Dr. Jakov Kajon, a respected lawyer and vice-president of the Sephardic community. In addition, a few Jews were active in the rather small Socialist camp, the most important being Dr. Mojsije Zon (1891–), a physician, originally from Poland.[17] It would appear, however, that the Radicals had fairly solid control over the Sarajevo Jewish vote in the 1920s, especially after a boycott of Jewish stores sponsored by the Yugoslav Muslim Organization in 1925 and the subsequent alliance of the Democrats with the Muslims.[18] By the late thirties the Sarajevo Jews were somewhat less prone to vote for the government; of the 2,234 eligible Jewish voters in the 1938 elections, 403 voted for the Stojadinović dictatorship government, 1,124 for the opposition, none for Ljotić's Fascists, and 808 did not cast ballots at all.[19] Thus, three-quarters of Sarajevo Jews joined the antigovernment forces openly, despite a strong government appeal for their support.

As for municipal politics, Sarajevo differed from Belgrade in that there continued to be a separate Jewish list in local elections. In 1928 in the first elections for city council held since the war, two Jewish lists competed for votes: the Sephardic and Ashkenazic establishment, known as the Political Committee of Jews, headed by Avram Majer Altarac, and a worker-youth coalition, predominantly Sephardic, led by Dr. Pepi Baruch. The former received 945 votes and 3 seats; the latter gained 698 votes and 2 seats. Hence, on the thirty-five member council, there were 5 Jews, all elected on Jewish platforms. The Altarac group aligned itself with the Radical Party and the 2 dissidents with the Muslims, Croats, and splinter groups.[20] More class conflict was in evidence among the Jews in Sarajevo than elsewhere; their election behavior is but one means of demonstrating this fact. Jewish solidarity did not always remain intact when economic and social interests, as well as personality factors, dictated otherwise.

In Zagreb the Jewish political situation looked very different. Jews did not play an active part in Croatian politics on the national level. In local elections, instead of conflict between political parties as in Belgrade or class antagonisms as in Sarajevo, there was a struggle between Zionists and integrationists for control over Jewish representation. The real debate centered around whether to run for office as a Jew on a Jewish ticket or as a Croat of the Israelite faith on a broader platform. Unfortunately for the proponents of the latter view, there was not much choice for Jews within the Croatian political spectrum. The major force was the Croatian Peasant Party, peasantist in orientation and somewhat anti-Semitic. The only possible alternative was the Croatian Union, a more middle-class party, which, however, lacked popular appeal, even among the bourgeois Jews.

The 1920 municipal election was the first in Zagreb with a separate Jewish list, led by two active Zionists, Lav Stern, a bank director, who was to become vice-president of the Jewish community, and Dr. Marko Horn, a lawyer and future communal president in the 1930s. Out of 833 Jewish voters, 496 chose the Jewish list. This marked a decisive defeat for the predominantly integrationist Jewish communal executive, although its president, Dr. Robert Siebenschein, was elected on the Croatian Union ticket. In the next election, at the end of 1921, despite vigorous propaganda on the part of Narodni Rad, the small but vocal integrationist group, the Jewish list won 75 percent of the Jewish vote, putting into office Dr. Hugo Kon, the recently elected president of the community, a lawyer and a Zionist, and Dr. Marko Horn. In 1925 the same two deputies were reelected by 88 percent of the Jewish vote. Two years later Jewish voters elected a third Zionist candidate, Makso Bauer, a lawyer, when 806 out of 983 cast their ballots for the Jewish list.[21] Jewish voter participation in Zagreb municipal elections was fairly low—48 percent and 45 percent in the 1925 and 1927 elections, respectively—but it is apparent that those who did vote clearly preferred the Jewish list under Zionist control to any of the Croatian parties, no matter what Jews happened to be running on the various platforms. Throughout the 1930s, the Jewish list managed to maintain its two mandates, Dr. Hugo Kon and Dr. Marko Bauer, another communal activist, while several other Jews, among them Dr. Robert Siebenschein, elected on other tickets, regularly served on the city council as well.[22] Despite considerable voter apathy, Zagreb remained a Zionist stronghold throughout the interwar period.

When comparing the political scene in the three cities, the differences prove striking, but the similarities are perhaps more significant. Belgrade Jews were much better integrated into Yugoslav political life than the majority of their contemporaries in Zagreb. Serbian and Bosnian Jewry could at least find national parties for which they could, in all conscience, vote and which they felt represented their interests; Croatian Jewry generally lacked this opportunity, being too Croatian in sympathy to vote for any of the ultra-Serbian parties, yet finding the Croatian parties unreceptive to their outlooks and aspirations. In Zagreb and Sarajevo, Jewish lists were put forth in municipal elections and received most of the Jewish vote, whereas, in Belgrade, this was never considered necessary. Such distinctions were produced by the diversity of environments in which the Jews found themselves.

Other parallels can be drawn from within the Jewish context itself. Jews who participated most actively in the general political sphere played a very prominent role in Jewish communal affairs as well. Even the integrationist-oriented politicians generally took an important part, particularly in Jewish philanthropic endeavors, such as the Hevra Kaddisha. The Sephardic activists were the backbone of their respective communities, and the Zionists provided much of the new Ashkenazic leadership, especially in Zagreb. Only in Zagreb did candidates run on an openly Zionist platform; in Sephardic circles, it was neither advantageous nor desirable. In fact, unless elected on a specifically Zionist ticket, Jewish deputies tended to be non-Zionist in sympathy. Another common characteristic was that of wealth. All successful Jewish candidates seem to have belonged to the affluent strata and most of them were professionals. Indeed, very few Jews engaged in Yugoslav politics in the interwar period, and with few exceptions, the primary function of this elite was to defend the interests of their fellow Jews, mainly on the local level. It is hence no coincidence that this narrow circle corresponds almost exactly to the roster of presidents of the various Jewish communities during the same two decades.

In contrast to the rather small number of older Jews who participated in the official political parties, there was a sizable group of younger Jews who played an active role in the illegal Communist Party, which functioned as an underground movement after 1921. The exact number of Jewish Communists in Yugoslavia in the interwar period is difficult to establish, since membership was secret and Jews were not counted separately in their midst. Some indication of left-wing Jewish activity may be taken from the fact that among a list of 89 Communists in jail in Sarajevo in 1929, there were 8 unmistakably Jewish names to be found.[23] As the thirties progressed, more and more Jewish students, especially those studying abroad in such places as Prague but also a growing number at the universities in Zagreb and Belgrade, joined the ranks of Communist sympathizers.[24] Many of these young radicals had formerly been active members of Jewish youth organizations, in particular Hashomer Hatzair. Seventeen Yugoslav Jews, including 5 from Zagreb and 3 each from Belgrade and Sarajevo, fought in the Spanish Civil War.[25] This is surely a remarkable figure, considering that the total number of Jews within the Yugoslav Communist Party could not have been very large at the time.

The most important and best known Jewish representative in the history of Yugoslav Communism was Moše Pijade, who was born in Belgrade's Dorćol. An artist and a journalist, he became the chief ideologist of the movement, translating Marx into Serbo-Croatian while spending most of the interwar years in prison. During and after the war, Pijade was Tito's right-hand man. Designated a National Hero, the highest possible honor granted by the socialist state, he served as vice-president of Yugoslavia until his death in 1955.

Jewish Communists in the interwar period in general no longer took part in Jewish communal life, religious or national. Not denying their Jewish origins, they considered themselves primarily Yugoslavs rather than Jews. Although their contribution to the development of Communism in their country was perhaps not as great as that of Jewish Communists elsewhere in Eastern Europe, nevertheless their role in helping to lay the foundations for the future Yugoslavia was of some significance.

In general, the official attitude of the Yugoslav government toward the Jewish minority until the very end of the interwar period was sympathetic. This, to a large extent, was due to the tradition of tolerance of the Serbian Orthodox church and to the friendly relations maintained between the Serbian people and the native Sephardic Jews. Throughout the 1920s and 1930s the government was essentially controlled by Serbs, and policy reflected their viewpoint.

The Serbs considered the local Jews patriotic citizens because they had served bravely in both the Balkan Wars and World War I. Approximately six hundred Jews fought alongside the Serbs as both soldiers and officers; of these, about one-quarter were killed or died from typhus. Sixty-two Belgrade Jews were included among these victims. Several Jews received high military decorations, and in 1927 the Belgrade Jewish community erected a monument to the Jewish war dead.[26] Bosnian and Croatian Jews had also served in World War I in the Austro-Hungarian army. The newly created Yugoslav state did not regard such behavior with equal favor, however, and tended to question the loyalty of Jews outside Serbia. As a result, Belgrade Jews were regularly chosen as representatives of all Yugoslav Jewry before the king, and de facto, if not de jure, they enjoyed a rather special position.

Although the law recognized the Jews as a religious rather than a national minority, the Serbian, and later the Yugoslav, government at all times displayed sympathy for the Zionist cause. The Serbian government became one of the first to express its official support for the Balfour Declaration of November 2, 1917. A letter dated Washington, December 27, 1917, from Milenko Vesnić, the head of the Serbian War Mission to the United States, to Dr. David Albala, medical captain in the Serbian Army, then on a propaganda campaign for Serbia among American Jewry, contained the following message, in the original English:

I wish to express to your jewish [*sic*] brothers . . . the sympathy of our Government and of our people for the just endeavour of resuscitating their beloved country in Palestine, which will enable them to take their place in the future Society of Nations, according to their numerous capacities and to their unquestioned right. We are sure this will not only be to their own interest, but at the same time, to that of the whole of humanity.

You know, dear Captain Albala, that there is no other nation in the world sympathizing with this plan more than Serbia. Do we not shed bitter tears on the rivers of Babylon in sight of our beloved land lost only a short time ago? How should we not participate in your clamours and sorrows, lasting ages and generations, especially when our countrymen of your origin and religion have fought for their Serbian fatherland as well as the best of our soldiers.

It will be a sad thing for us to see any of our Jewish fellow-citizens leaving us to return to their promised land, but we shall console ourselves in the hope that they will stand [*sic*] as brothers and leave with us a good part of their hearts, and that they will be the strongest tie between free Israel and Serbia.[27]

Undoubtedly the primary purpose of this so-called Vesnić letter was to gain more aid for the Serbian war effort in America, but at the same time it laid the foundation for future policy. Vesnić later represented the Kingdom of Serbs, Croats, and Slovenes at the San Remo Conference in 1920, where he continued to back Jewish nationalist aspirations.[28]

The Karageorgević royal household always maintained a cordial relationship with the Jewish community and its representatives. The Yugoslav chief rabbi, Dr. Isaac Alcalay, was an intimate friend of the family and a confidant of the king.[29] Jewish leaders frequently received civilian decorations from the Crown; the most common were the different degrees of the Order of Sveti Sava (Saint Sava) and the Order of the White Eagle. King Alexander granted audiences to Jewish delegations on such occasions as the visits to Yugoslavia of prominent Zionists, like Nahum Sokolow in 1928 and Menahem Ussishkin two years later. At such times he expressed interest in the Palestine situation, especially with regard to the position of the Orthodox churches, over which he considered himself protector, as successor to the Russian tsar.[30] In 1928 a forest in Palestine was dedicated in the name of the late King Peter, whom the Jews regarded as a strong ally; in 1934, after the assassination of King Alexander, a similar forest was planted in his memory.[31] Later, under the regent, Prince Paul, interviews with Jewish representatives tended to be on the subject of Jewish security and anti-Semitism, rather than discussions of Zionism. The royal family continued to maintain close ties with individual Jews and to express concern for Jewish problems even after the young King Peter went into exile.[32]

Indeed, the general consensus among virtually all government spokesmen until the very end of the interwar period was that no anti-Semitic movement and no "Jewish question" existed in Yugoslavia. This attitude was clearly articulated in 1929 by Dr. Vojislav Marinković, Minister of External Affairs, in an interview with Jakob Landau, director of the Jewish Telegraphic Agency.

Our country does not suffer from the poison of anti-Semitism. On the contrary, we value and love the Jews. And that is no coincidence. The historical development of our nation was in many respects similar to the development of the Jewish nation. We had to undergo so much suffering and misfortune and so many bloody battles in which we bore so many sacrifices for freedom that we have and have always had full understanding for the Jews whose history knows so much hardship and suffering, just because the Jews too faithfully preserved their faith and community. In this regard, the same endurance, stamina and perseverence ties us together, so that it is natural that Serbs and Jews should understand one another.

We value the loyalty which the Jew has for his faith and it is very remote from any thought that we scorn or slight a Jew on this account. . . .[33]

These same themes of common history, patriotism, respect, and toleration constantly repeated themselves, even after the skies had begun to darken over European Jewry. Before the outbreak of World War II, each successive government regularly reassured Jewish deputations that nothing could happen to the Jews in Yugoslavia and that their government would always protect them.[34]

In 1938 and 1939 two books, evidently government sponsored, appeared on the market in defense of the Jews, stressing their patriotism and other positive characteristics.[35] In 1940 a collection of short essays by forty prominent Yugoslavs, mainly Serbs, but including several Jews as well, were published under the title *Our Jews*. In general, the purpose of this volume was to demonstrate how much the local populace loved the native Jews. Foreign Jews, however, did not receive quite such favorable treatment.[36] Until the outbreak of the war, the official policy was that stated by Dr. Anton Korošec, then Minister of the Interior, in a speech in September of 1938:

Among us in Yugoslavia, as everyone can testify, the Jewish question does not exist. Yugoslavia is among the few states which are not bothered by this question. That is the best proof that the Jews among us are treated as citizens with equal rights. All the benefits of the law are extended to Jews just as to other citizens; the same holds true for all obligations of the law as well. As far as the emigration of Jews from other states is concerned, which is today on the agenda, we maintain this principle: No state in the world in present circumstances wishes to increase the number of its minorities, be that minority linguistic, religious or other. . . .[37]

Thus, the country's political leaders continued to deny the existence of anti-Semitism or of a "Jewish problem" in Yugoslavia.

An organized anti-Semitic movement never existed in Yugoslavia before World War II. Nevertheless, with increasing frequency over the years, sporadic incidents occurred in scattered parts of the country, reflecting the influence of foreign currents and events. Here as elsewhere in Europe, anti-Semitism was scarcely a new phenomenon in the twentieth century; it had revived as a force in the 1880s and then seemed to go into eclipse until the interwar period.[38] Such minor anti-Semitic outbreaks as did take place from time to time did not have any official support from the king, the government, or the Serbian Orthodox church.

Despite the general policy of fair treatment toward the Jews and the frequent denials of the existence of anti-Semitism, some instances of bureaucratic discrimination against Jews per se can be cited, especially in the immediate post–World War I era. Antagonism tended to focus on the recent Ashkenazic immigrants, former citizens of the Habsburg Monarchy, whom the native inhabitants often regarded as an alien element and accused of being war profiteers or Communist sympathizers.[39] In May 1919 local authorities began a series of expulsions of such "foreigners," chiefly from Bosnia but also from Croatia. A number of protests ensued, from Serbian sources as well as Jewish organizations, such as the newly created Federation of Jewish Religious Communities, the national Zionist Federation and the Committee of Jewish Delegations at the Paris Peace Conference. Eventually, through their combined efforts, these forces succeeded in

rectifying the matter, but not before a considerable amount of suffering on the part of innocent individuals had resulted.[40]

A similar situation arose regarding the right of Jews to vote for
the Constituent Assembly in 1920. The problem originated out of a
dubious interpretation of the "option clause" for former Austro-
Hungarian citizens which had been included in the various peace
treaties.[41] Since the Jews in nearly all parts of the country except
Serbia were theoretically eligible to choose Austrian or Hungarian
rather than Yugoslav citizenship, it was arbitrarily decided that all
Jews in territories formerly belonging to the Habsburg Empire should
not have the right to vote in the first postwar election. This conclusion was scarcely consistent with the official policy that Jews were a
religious minority but part of the Serb-Croat nationality. The Jews,
especially the Sephardim, raised a clamor in opposition to this administrative decree. In Sarajevo two thousand people attended a protest meeting which resulted in a spirited resolution being sent to the
Ministry of Interior.[42] At the last second, these efforts met with
success; Bosnian Jewry, both Sephardic and Ashkenazic, received the
right to vote for the Constituent Assembly.[43] It is unclear from the
material available whether or not Croatian Jewry was able to vote at
this time. The Jews of the Vojvodina, however, had to wait several
more years before their citizenship and voting rights became clarified.[44]

Such examples do not necessarily imply a deliberate policy of
official discrimination against Jews as such. On the contrary, they
seem to reflect anti-Habsburg xenophobia on the part of local administrative officials rather than concerted anti-Semitism. There was
never any dispute over the citizenship or electoral rights of the native
Jews, the Serbian Sephardim. Questions only arose pertaining to the
legal status of "foreign," or Austro-Hungarian, Jews, especially the
Hungarian or German-speaking Ashkenazim.

In the 1920s there was no clear pattern to the various instances of anti-Semitic activity. In 1920 a petition was signed by
340 Zagreb medical students demanding a numerus clausus for all
"native Jews" and the expulsion of all "foreign" Jews from the
medical faculty of Zagreb University.[45] This appeal, obviously an
imitation of the contemporaneous situation in Hungary, came to
nought. In 1925 the Yugoslav Muslim Organization called for a
boycott against Jewish stores in Bosnia. The motive was primarily
political revenge, because the Jews had voted for the Radical
Party in the recent election, but overtones of religious anti-Semitism developed when the action was proclaimed in mosques as

well as newspapers. The boycott itself was a failure and was sup-pressed by local police.[46] Three years later, a peculiar incident erupted into a minor scandal. An air force general had issued a decree cautioning his officers against marrying Jewish women, lest they be considered subversive. This type of action was so entirely out of keeping with standard policy that it could scarcely be be-lieved—and was, of course, officially denied.[47] Potentially of greater consequence was a blood libel accusation which took place in 1928 in Petrovo Selo, a predominantly Hungarian town in the Vojvodina. This rumor was promptly squelched by the courts, and the furor soon died down.[48] These four isolated events, un-fortunate as they were in their occurrence, created but a mild stir at the time and had little lasting effect on Yugoslav or Jewish life.

In the 1930s, however, there was a dramatic change. Instead of unrelated happenings at infrequent intervals, anti-Semitic phenom-ena appeared more regularly, especially in the press, and could most often be linked with Nazi propaganda sources. In 1933 the National Socialist organ *Völkischer Beobachter* in Munich published in German and Croatian an appeal signed by "Croatian nationalists" for a boy-cott of Jewish shops in Zagreb in response to the Jewish boycott of German goods.[49] Thereafter, articles of an anti-Semitic nature be-came a common sight in certain newspapers, such as *Balkan* and *Vreme* in Belgrade and similar publications in Croatia and Slovenia. The most flagrant proponent of Nazi racist ideology was *Die Erwache,* the paper of the pro-Fascist Ljotić group in the Vojvodina. At the same time, small local groups began to circulate anti-Semitic pamphlets. By 1936 *Protocols of the Elders of Zion* had been translated into Serbo-Croatian and distributed, and tracts on such topics as "Jews and Masons," the "Talmud Jew," "The Jewish Problem" rolled off the anti-Semitic underground press. There was nothing at all original about this literature; it was all merely copied from abroad. As World War II approached, anti-Semitic manifestations grew more and more common.

The Federation of Jewish Religious Communities served as the Yugoslav Jewish defense agency or antidefamation league. Indeed, one of the most important functions of this supracommunal body involved the protection of Jewish rights, both inside and outside Yugoslavia. Even before the federation received formal government recognition, it became active in the struggle to prevent mass expul-sions of Jews with foreign citizenship from Bosnia and Croatia.

Through a series of appeals and interventions, it played an instrumental role in sparing hundreds of Jews from illegal eviction.[50] Similarly, throughout the interwar years, the central Jewish authorities fought to gain Yugoslav citizenship for foreign-born Jews, especially those in the Vojvodina. This issue was particularly crucial to the Jewish community as it pertained to foreign religious functionaries and teachers, who were desperately needed to fill the ranks of these professions due to the serious lack of qualified native Yugoslavs. When actual citizenship was not forthcoming from the government, the communal federation pressed for regular renewal of temporary residence permits.[51] As the mediator between the government and individual Jews or communities, the federation generally met with considerable success. Although the relations between synagogue and state were not always perfect, for the most part, such arrangements worked out satisfactorily.

During the first decade of the interwar period, the federation concentrated on defending the rights of foreign Jews in Yugoslavia and opposing discrimination outside the country's borders, such as in neighboring Hungary and Rumania. By the mid-1930s, however, there was a growing concern within the Jewish community, particularly among its leadership, about the deteriorating situation not only beyond their own frontiers but inside their own territory as well. Yugoslav Jewry was at all times well informed of current events in Germany and elsewhere. Although they expressed confidence that such developments could never happen in their homeland, they were nonetheless determined to take whatever steps they could to curb anti-Semitism and secure their own safety.

In October 1933 the Federation of Jewish Religious Communities issued a memorandum to all its members to be on the alert for any signs of anti-Semitism and to report them immediately.[52] At the federation's Sixth Congress held in Belgrade in March 1936, the central committee passed a unanimous resolution condemning anti-Semitism in Yugoslavia, which stated:

The Congress of the Federation of Jewish Religious Communities of the Kingdom of Yugoslavia is conscious of the significance of the more frequent anti-Jewish attacks which are being conducted in our land without hinderance, although they violate the principle of equality of religious communities. The Congress states that anti-Semitism, as an expression of the most hateful reaction, cannot cause the feeling of civil equality and patriotic duty to waver among the Jews of this land. The Congress considers that anti-Semitism, in addition to being degrading and humiliating for Jews, also brings great moral harm to the reputation of the state. The Jews can pit against anti-Semitic attacks only their own feeling of honor and human dignity.

The Congress states that these occurrences, which until recently were almost unknown among us and which in its deep conviction do not have roots in the broad strata of the people, imbued with traditional kind-heartedness, have created a justifiable and great discomfort in our Jewish community and it seeks and expects from all official factions the respect of full and actual equality.[53]

In addition to making general condemnations, the federation also attempted to take positive action in opposing anti-Semitism, through interventions with various authorities, court cases, and press coverage.

In 1936 there was an unsuccessful attempt to have the *Protocols* banned from Yugoslavia.[54] Later that same year, the communal federation brought a libel charge against the editor of *Die Erwache.* The court acquitted the accused on the somewhat dubious grounds that according to the constitution, the Jews were a religious, rather than a national minority, whereas the newspapers' attacks had been against the Jewish race and not the Jewish religion![55] Hence the Jews were denied protection by the constitution in this instance. Further efforts at prosecution of the anti-Semitic press also ended in failure. Frequent interviews of Jewish representatives with government officials throughout the decade and various appeals to the authorities for help in combating anti-Semitism resulted in empty verbal assurances but little concrete support.

Also arising out of the anti-Semitic fervor spreading throughout Europe, another issue which greatly concerned the communal federation during the thirties was the question of Jewish refugees from Nazi-occupied countries. The first refugees began to arrive from Germany in 1933, soon after Hitler came to power, and immediately Yugoslav Jewry started to organize its resources to help them. In agreement with the federation, the Zagreb Jewish community established a Local Committee for Aid to Jews from Germany, headed by Dr. Makso Pscherhof, vice-president of the Zagreb executive. From the beginning, virtually all Jewish institutions contributed generously to this cause. The Yugoslav volunteers, led by Alexander Klein, the secretary of the Zagreb community, worked in conjunction with the American Jewish Joint Distribution Committee (the JOINT) and the European branch of HICEM, the Hebrew Immigrant Aid Society, based in Paris. In 1933 about 4,400 German refugees reached Zagreb, and the following year 4,200 more. The Zagreb committee managed to collect donations of 1,180,000 dinars ($21,000) the first year and

2,660,000 ($47,500) the second from within the community, plus substantial funds from outside sources.[56] From 1934 to 1937 the number of arrivals fell, but considerable amounts of money were still required to help persons find new homes. Generally, it proved difficult for refugees to establish permanent residence in Yugoslavia. Therefore, most recent emigrés needed to locate opportunities for settling elsewhere, mainly in Palestine. The Federation of Jewish Religious Communities and the Zionist Federation, as well as various other affiliated organizations, were constantly searching for places where these people could go and the means to get them there. In 1936 a Central Committee for Aid to Jews from Germany was organized in Belgrade.[57]

The general situation deteriorated rapidly in 1938 with mass emigration and expulsions of Jews from Austria after the Anschluss. The most publicized incident was the case of eighty Jews from Burgenland, who were evicted from their towns and became stranded on the Yugoslav border, lacking visas. After several months of difficult negotiations, the federation obtained permission from the government for these unfortunates to enter Yugoslavia on a temporary basis with guaranteed support from the Jewish community. As the dismal parade of refugees grew ever longer, it became imperative to erect special facilities to house these unfortunate people. Between 1938 and 1940 the communal federation established fifteen collection centers for 3,210 persons in various parts of the country.[58]

In the late thirties, thousands of Jews succeeded in escaping from Europe by boats along the Danube to the Black Sea with aid from the Belgrade Jewish leaders. The last transport reached the Yugoslav-Rumanian border in October 1939 with 1,100 passengers on board. But the Rumanian authorities refused to allow the ship passage through Rumanian waters, and these refugees were forced to remain in Yugoslavia where they found accommodations in Kladova and later Šabac.[59]

The cost involved in caring for the refugees and finding ways for them to leave the country was enormous. In 1938 the federation proposed a 20–30 percent communal tax increase to cover these expenses, and the various Jewish communities complied with 10–50 percent raises, but by 1940 this allotment had to be raised to 60 percent or higher.[60] Communities which were otherwise often unwilling to contribute their share to the communal federation usually managed to afford this donation to the central aid fund. From 1933 to 1941 Yugoslav Jewry raised 41,575,000 dinars ($742,410) in support of the refugees, while JOINT contributed 21,650,000 dinars

($386,607) and HICEM, 15,520,000 dinars ($277,142). The Federation of Jewish Religious Communities and the Zagreb Jewish community helped some 55,000 Jewish refugees during their stay in Yugoslavia, and the Zionist Federation and many other Jewish organizations gave generously of their time, money, and efforts.[61]

Despite all the aid given to these refugees by the Jewish community, their situation remained extremely precarious, especially after the outbreak of the war.

Throughout the 1930s, Yugoslavia was gradually slipping under the economic and political domination of Germany. The government found itself increasingly under pressure to conform to Nazi policy. Yugoslavia apparently had little difficulty resisting the introduction of anti-Jewish laws before the invasion of Poland. Soon after, however, following the precedents set by virtually every other country in Eastern Europe, the Yugoslav government also succumbed to outside influence.

Yugoslavia proved to be no different from other countries in its unwillingness to accept Jewish refugees in the 1930s. The first discriminatory legislation proposed against the Jews was, predictably enough, directed against foreign Jews, all Jews who lacked Yugoslav citizenship. The real targets, however, were the thousands of refugees who had come from Germany and German-occupied territories since 1933. In October 1939 the Ministry of the Interior formulated a law whereby all Jews who had entered the country, legally or illegally, since 1935 were compelled to leave within three months. All other Jewish noncitizens were required to depart within six months to a year.[62] Apparently, this regulation never actually went into effect, however. No reference to such a law appeared in *Židov* or *Jevrejski glas,* which published all other laws relating to Jews, or in correspondence between the Federation of Jewish Religious Communities and the Ministry of Justice, although the subject of restrictions against refugees was raised repeatedly in the ministry. Hence, it seems fair to conclude that this law was probably never formally promulgated. Unfortunately, there was virtually no place left in the world where these stranded Jews could go.

On October 5, 1940, the Cvetković-Maček government promulgated two laws which signaled the revocation of Jewish emancipation. The first piece of legislation essentially prohibited Jews from engaging in the wholesale food business or related occupations.[63] This was the beginning of an attempt to exclude Jews from the country's economic life. The second act was a numerus clausus, limiting Jewish enrollment at all high schools and universities to their percentage of the total population.[64] Since the number of Jews receiving advanced education greatly exceeded .46 percent, such legislation clearly intended to reduce Jewish cultural and professional participation in Yugoslav society. These laws came as a bitter blow to Yugoslav Jewry. Despite repeated promises by government leaders, they were denied their civil equality and legal protection against discrimination. These decrees, only partially implemented, were the last of the series before the German invasion and occupation of Yugoslavia in April 1941.

The Federation of Jewish Religious Communities reacted to the passage of the anti-Jewish legislation in the fall of 1940 with a declaration of faith in the Jewish people and in Yugoslavia. The Jewish leaders were both shocked and dismayed by this ominous development, but they refused to despair.[65] As the official spokesman of Yugoslav Jewry, the federation tried, as it had in the past, to fight against ill treatment of Jews wherever it occurred. At the same time it expressed loyalty to its host country and confidence in the future of the Jewish community in Yugoslavia.

In general, the political situation in interwar Yugoslavia, as viewed from the perspective of the Jews, was for the most part healthy because the Jews constituted only a very small percentage of the population, and the government's policy was favorable. Anti-Semitism, especially of the racial variety, was an imported phenomenon, stamped Made in Germany; it never struck deep local roots. Such anti-Semitism as did exist was more apparent in the ex-Habsburg territories than in the Serbian or former Ottoman areas. Hence, it was more often directed against Ashkenazim than Sephardim, the former being considered foreign and the latter native.

But Yugoslavia, too, became a victim of the Nazi war machine. The Jews could not defend themselves, and Yugoslavia, in the end, was no longer capable of protecting them, even had the government wished to do so. Yugoslav Jewry was to suffer the fate of the rest of European Jewry. But interwar Yugoslavia is one of the few countries in Eastern Europe that may be remembered for fair treatment of its Jewish minority.

EPILOGUE: THE SURVIVING REMNANT

On March 25, 1941, Yugoslavia signed the Tripartite Pact, allying itself with Hitler. Two days later, however, a bloodless coup d'état took place in Belgrade, led by a Serbian general, Dušan Simović, evidently in opposition to the government's pro-Axis policies. As a result, on April 6, German bombers attacked Belgrade, while the Italians struck Dalmatia; shortly after, Hungarian and Bulgarian troops also invaded the country. Within less than two weeks the Yugoslav armed forces surrendered.

Thus, by May 1941 Yugoslavia had ceased to exist as a state. Much of its territory was divided among the conquering Axis powers. Germany occupied Northern Slovenia and the Banat; Hungary acquired Bačka and Baranja, the remaining two sections of the Vojvodina, and several smaller adjacent areas. Italy annexed Southern Slovenia and most of the Dalmatian littoral and also occupied a considerable portion of the interior regions in the south, bordering on Albania. Bulgaria received most of Macedonia. From the remaining territory were carved the small German puppet state of Serbia and the Independent State (later Kingdom) of Croatia, which also included Bosnia-Hercegovina.

Not only did the country suffer from partition and foreign occupation but also a bloody civil war raged uncontrolled in its midst. The Ustaši (the Croatian Fascists), led by Ante Pavelić, with Muslim help, massacred Serbs by the thousands, and the Serbs, especially the Četnik troops led by General Draža Mihailović, retaliated in kind. But whereas the Četniks began by combating the Germans and the Ustaši, they ended up in a struggle against the Partisans, the Communist forces headed by Josip Broz Tito. During the course of the war, more than a million and a half Yugoslavs, or about 10 percent of the total population, lost their lives.

While the Yugoslav populace as a whole was being decimated, the Jews were being subjected to a process of systematic annihilation. The treatment of the Jews varied slightly from region to region and the timetable for their elimination differed accordingly, but the ultimate effect was the same virtually everywhere: the almost total destruction of the existing Jewish community.

The Jews of Serbia were the first to experience the full impact of Nazi policy. On May 30, 1941, the German military authorities in Belgrade issued a definition of who was a Jew, followed by a series of regulations whereby Jews were removed from public service and the professions, all Jewish property was to be registered, forced labor was introduced, the Serb population was forbidden to hide Jews, and all Jews were order to wear a yellow star.[1] Such measures were merely preliminaries, however, and a more extreme solution to the "Jewish problem" ensued shortly thereafter.

By July of the same year, Jews were being arrested and a number put to death, supposedly in retaliation for Communist activities. In August several concentration camps were set up and a systematic roundup of Jewish men began all over Serbia and in the Banat. In October some 4,000 Jewish men were shot by the German army. Women and children were also rounded up and sent to Sajmište, a special camp erected in Zemun across the river from Belgrade. During the spring and summer of 1942, more than 6,000 of them were killed in gas vans. By August 1942 the Nazis had achieved their ultimate solution to the Jewish question in the area. Serbia was for all intents and purposes *judenrein*.[2]

In the Independent State of Croatia, implementation of the anti-Jewish policy lay largely in the hands of the Ustaši. Discriminatory regulations, similar to those in Serbia and elsewhere, were issued as early as April 30, 1941. Roundups of Croatian and Bosnian Jews began in the summer of 1941 and continued intermittently thereafter. Sarajevo's Jews disappeared by August 1942; Zagreb Jewry managed to remain largely unconfined until as late as 1944. The most notorious among the various labor and concentration camps where Jews and other "undesirable elements" were interned was the torture camp of Jasenovac, in which a large number of Croatian Jews lost their lives. Those Jewish inmates who did not die from starvation, typhus, and maltreatment in the Yugoslav camps were eventually deported to Auschwitz and other death camps beyond the South Slav frontiers. By the end of 1944, the only Jews to remain in

Croatian territory were those who were recognized as "honorary Aryans," Jewish partners in mixed marriages and *Mischlinge* (products of intermarriages).[3]

The entire Jewish community of Bulgaria proper managed to survive the war virtually intact, but the Jews in Bulgarian-controlled Macedonia were not so fortunate. In March of 1943 some 8,000 Jews from Bitolj, Skoplje, and other towns in the area were rounded up and shipped in three transports to Treblinka.[4] Macedonian Jewry was thereby annihilated almost totally.

The Jews in the Hungarian-occupied regions experienced a similar fate. In January 1942 several thousand Jews and Serbs were shot in a bloody massacre which took place in Novi Sad and several of the surrounding towns in the Bačka.[5] Between 1942 and 1944, some 4,000 Jews were mobilized into labor units and sent to the Ukraine, various parts of Hungary, and the local Bor copper mines. Soon after the Germans took control of the Hungarian zone in March 1944, mass roundups of Jews began. At first these Jews were interned in a number of collection or concentration camps in the area or else crowded into the newly created Subotica ghetto. But beginning in May 1944 a majority of the Jews of Bačka and Baranja found themselves on transports heading for Auschwitz.[6] Like the rest of the Jews in the Hungarian provinces, these Jews remained unconfined longer than most of their fellow European Jews under Nazi occupation, but not long enough to outlast the war.

The Jews who managed to escape to those regions under Italian control faired relatively better than Jews in other parts of the former Yugoslav kingdom. While most of these Jews, whether natives of the area or recent refugees, were eventually interned in Italian camps, they appear to have received better treatment. The Italian authorities saved them from deportation to the Reich as long as they were in command.[7] After the capitulation of Italy, those Jews who fell into German hands were transported to death camps. Others, however, succeeded in reaching southern Italy, where they were able to remain alive in such camps as Ferramonte, which the Jewish Brigade later helped to liberate. A considerable number of Jews from the Italian zone, especially those who had been interned on the island of Rab, joined Tito's Partisan forces.[8]

Thus, the Holocaust wiped out an estimated 55- to 60,000 Yugoslav Jews, approximately 80 percent of the prewar Jewish population of the country.[9] Some were shot in the streets, others died in Yugoslav concentration camps; many were sent to the crematoria of Auschwitz and death camps elsewhere. In addition, a relatively small but nevertheless significant number of Jews lost their lives while fighting with the Partisans.

By the end of the war, fewer than 15,000 Yugoslav Jews remained alive. Among these survivors, many had found refuge through emigration, mainly in Italy, but some in Switzerland or the United States. A substantial group had fought with Tito's Partisans. Although exact figures are not available, it would appear that between 2- and 3,000 Jews joined the Partisans during the war, both for ideological and pragmatic reasons. (Eleven Jews, among them 4 from Sarajevo, were later designated National Heroes, the highest possible honor in Socialist Yugoslavia.)[10] About 450 Jewish reserve officers and 200 noncommissioned officers and soldiers, who were in the Royal Yugoslav Army when it surrendered, returned home in 1945. They had spent five years incarcerated in Germany, generally segregated as Jews, but protected by German adherence to the Geneva Convention regarding military prisoners of war. Others had somehow managed to endure the concentration camps, and a few had been successfully hidden by non-Jewish families for the duration of the war.[11]

In 1946 a total of 12,495 Jews were counted on Yugoslav soil. In Belgrade 2,236 Jews were to be found; in Zagreb, 2,126; and in Sarajevo, 1,413.[12] The vast majority of Holocaust survivors had been left with nothing. Their families had perished and their health, both physical and mental, had been destroyed. The future looked bleak indeed.

Soon after the creation of the State of Israel, the Yugoslav authorities permitted Jews to emigrate there freely if they so desired. At first, doctors and other professionals were discouraged from leaving, but later they too were allowed to go with their families. Non-Jewish spouses were also given permission to leave the country. Between 1948 and 1952, in a series of five emigration waves, 7,578 persons departed for Israel.[13] Thereafter, individuals could follow if and when they chose. About 150 Jews returned from Israel to Yugoslavia; others made their way from there to North or South America, where there were several small Yugoslav Jewish emigré colonies. After more than half the surviving population had gone on aliya to Israel, a Jewish community of 6- to 7,000 remained in Yugoslavia.

Since 1952 very little migration by Jews either to or from Yugoslavia has taken place. The overall population of the Jewish community has remained fairly constant. Within the country there has been internal movement of Jews from smaller to larger centers. In 1939 of the total Jewish population, 72 percent lived in ten cities. This figure increased to 77 percent by 1946. By 1958 over 85 percent of Yugoslav Jewry were registered in the ten largest communities. The size of the three major communities has not increased very greatly, however. Between 1952 and 1969, the Belgrade Jewish population grew from 1,380 to 1,602; Zagreb, from 1,287 to 1,341; and Sarajevo, from 1,028 to 1,090.[14]

Yugoslav Jewry today is comprised very heavily of natives of the country. According to a survey conducted in 1971,[15] approximately one-third of the members of the Belgrade and Zagreb communities were born in the city in which they now reside, but almost 60 percent of those living in Sarajevo spent their earliest years there as well. Eighty percent of the Jews in Belgrade and Zagreb claimed Serbo-Croatian as their mother tongue, whereas 93 percent did so in Sarajevo.[16] Nearly 14 percent of those enumerated in the population survey claimed some knowledge of Ladino, but only 4 percent reported it as their native language. Of those respondents age thirty and older, fewer than 5 percent knew Yiddish and only .5 percent considered it their mother tongue. None of the younger generation were familiar with Yiddish and only eight persons in the thirty to forty-four age group were able to speak the language.[17]

The ratio between Sephardim and Ashkenazim in the overall Jewish population has remained relatively constant from the interwar period to the present. The line of demarcation between these two groups no longer exists to the extent which prevailed previously, however. Some Sephardim have crossed over from the poorer and less developed areas of Macedonia and Bosnia to wealthier regions, such as Croatia or even Slovenia. Official distinctions are no longer being made between Ashkenazim and Sephardim, and the differences between them are gradually disappearing, especially among the younger generation. According to the results of the 1971 demographic survey, about one-third of Yugoslav Jews had Sephardic parentage and about one-half, Ashkenazic parentage, while slightly less than 5 percent were of mixed Sephardic-Ashkenazic origin and the remaining 10 percent considered themselves to be Jews without further specification.[18]

The economic condition of the Jewish population in postwar Yugoslavia is, in general, fairly good. The community gives intermittent monetary aid to the elderly and the sick who can no longer support themselves, but poverty is not a major problem among Jews. Their economic well-being is quite uniform in the various parts of the country, unlike before World War II when there were much greater discrepancies between different regions.

In the interwar period most Jews were involved in business, crafts, and private white-collar jobs, and some were engaged in the free professions. Under the Communist regime, the economic structure of the country has changed drastically and the Jews were obliged to adapt themselves to the new circumstances or leave. Consequently, the Jews who remained in Yugoslavia after the war were mainly professionals or civil servants, many holding high positions in these fields. This rather peculiar occupational distribution may be accounted for by the survival of a high percentage of the Jewish professional class who had been reserve officers in the Royal Yugoslav Army and by the policy of the authorities to discourage the emigration of these professionals, especially medical doctors.

Hence, the Jewish population continues to display a high proportion of individuals engaged in professional occupations, such as doctors, lawyers, teachers, professors, engineers, and scientists. (Table 15 presents the occupational structure of Yugoslav Jewry in 1953 and 1970, which may be compared with table 9 for the interwar period.) According to the 1971 demographic survey, in Belgrade, out of 333 persons gainfully employed, 141 (or 42 percent) were considered professionals; of 328 in Zagreb, 161 (or 48 percent) fell into this category; and in Sarajevo, 157 out of 288 (56 percent). Correspondingly, the number of persons with higher education is quite high— approximately one-third of the respondents in Belgrade and Zagreb and close to a quarter in Sarajevo.

The surviving Yugoslav Jewish population have thus managed to rebuild their lives since the Holocaust. The community, too, has succeeded in reconstructing itself to the best of its ability after the devastation of the war years. It has been a long and hard struggle, but the community has emerged considerably more unified than before.

Immediately after the Germans invaded Yugoslavia in 1941, the Federation of Jewish Religious Communities ceased to function. Some local Jewish communities were able to continue their operations temporarily, albeit in a restricted fashion. In Belgrade the separate Sephardic and Ashkenazic communities were abolished and replaced by the Representative Body of the Jewish Community (Vertretung der jüdischen Gemeinschaft). The Jewish council, similar to the Judenräte elsewhere in Nazi Europe but apparently with more limited authority,[19] provided aid to the needy Jews who had lost their jobs, and to those who had been transferred to Belgrade from elsewhere. It set up soup kitchens to feed hungry Jews and even provided food for internees in the collection centers in the area. It also organized a Jewish health service and clinic, as well as a hospital staffed by Jewish doctors and other trained medical personnel.[20] When Belgrade Jewry was destroyed several months later, this body, too, disappeared.

In May 1941 two judges were appointed as commissioners responsible for the property of the Sephardic and Ashkenazic communities of Sarajevo.[21] In the Bosnian center, too, the local Jewish leaders attempted to alleviate the misery of the Jewish population by providing food and other assistance. These efforts achieved only limited, and temporary, success.[22] Soon the Sarajevo Jewish community also ceased to exist. The same tragic story repeated itself in nearly all the other Jewish communities.

In Zagreb, however, the Jewish community somehow managed to continue functioning throughout the war years. It supplied health care and school facilities for the local Jewish population. Together with the Osijek community, the Zagreb Jewish leaders were active in sending food packages to the Jewish internees in the various labor and concentration camps nearby. (Whether many of these parcels actually reached their intended destination is not clear, however.) The Zagreb Jewish executive was also able to arrange for a group of Jewish children to reach Palestine in 1942 with the help of the International Red Cross.[23]

Nevertheless, by 1944, with the exception of Zagreb, organized Jewish life had virtually come to a halt in the Yugoslav lands. During the course of the war, the Germans and their allies had completely destroyed or severely damaged nearly all the Jewish public buildings in the country. The main Sephardic synagogues in Belgrade and Sarajevo as well as the Ashkenazic temple in Zagreb had been totally demolished, and the Ashkenazic houses of prayer in Belgrade and Sarajevo and the four-century-old Sephardic synagogue in Sarajevo were almost beyond repair. Communal treasures had been lost and records had, for the most part, permanently disappeared.

On October 22, 1944, two days after the liberation of Belgrade, Dr. Friedrich Pops, who had spent most of the war years in hiding in Belgrade, returned to the premises of the Federation of Jewish Religious Communities, posted a new sign and set up an improvised office.[24] He thereby symbolically began the work of rebuilding the Jewish community in Yugoslavia through the organization of which he had been a founder and also served as president on the eve of the war.

In the immediate postwar period, the federation occupied itself primarily with humanitarian tasks—taking care of the returnees from the concentration camps, the sick, the elderly, and the orphaned. From 1945 to 1952 the Autonomous Committee for Aid, established in conjunction with the American Joint Distribution Committee, worked with the federation in assisting the Jewish community in its recovery. Another major task of the federation in the late forties and early fifties was to help emigration to Israel.[25] It was only after 1952 that the federation was finally able to consolidate its power and reorganize itself and its activities to correspond to the needs of those Jews who had remained in the country.

By 1946 fifty-six Jewish communities had been reestablished, less than half the number in existence six years earlier. Many of these communities, however, consisted of only a handful of individuals. After the various waves of emigration to Israel, thirty-six organized communities remained.[26] In postwar Yugoslavia, the three largest and most important Jewish communities have once again been located in Belgrade, Zagreb, and Sarajevo. Some Jewish communal activity is also to be found in eight other cities: Subotica, Novi Sad, Osijek, Rijeka (Fiume), Zemun, Split, Ljubljana, and Skoplje. But, for the most part, the remaining twenty-five Jewish communities exist primarily on paper because they do not have enough members to support any kind of real communal life.

In the postwar period, the Yugoslav Jewish community has become very tightly organized both on the countrywide and local levels.[27] All Jewish organizations and institutions are subsidiary to the local community and in turn to the federation. Distinctions between Ashkenazim and Sephardim, Neologues and Orthodox no longer operate. Thus, every community includes all Jews in its vicinity. This situation contrasts sharply with the state of affairs before the war, when separate communities often functioned side by side, each with a wide variety of associated but independent charitable and cultural organizations. Since the war, this multiplicity of local bodies has been eliminated completely, in part due to expediency, considering the small size of the population, but also out of a desire for uniformity and cohesiveness.

The Jewish community in postwar Yugoslavia is officially recognized as both a national and a religious community, although there are no longer any special laws which define its existence, such as the Law on the Religious Community of Jews in Yugoslavia of 1929. The community is allowed to conduct its affairs freely, according to the general law on the legal position of religious communities in Yugoslavia, passed in 1953, and the principle of freedom of religion and conscience as guaranteed in the constitution.

Nonetheless, communal authorities have little control over matters of Jewish status. A functioning *beth din* no longer exists, and the regular courts have complete jurisdiction over Jewish affairs. Marriage and divorce are entirely under civil control; there do not appear to be any Jewish religious marriages or divorces in present-day Yugoslavia. The dietary laws are also not observed. The community itself, however, is to a large extent responsible for the nonobservance of these traditionally Jewish matters, not the state. An explanation for the existing situation can be found in the lack of qualified religious personnel and the strongly secularist attitude of the Jewish leadership.

Indeed, the primary focus of the Jewish community, both on a local and national level, has shifted radically away from the religious sphere. In 1952 the federation deleted the word *Religious* from its official title to indicate this change and to stress that it was concerned with all aspects of communal life, including national, cultural, educational, social welfare, and youth activities as well.[28]

Some religious facilities are maintained for the benefit of those who wish to use them, that is, mainly members of the older generation who have retained a traditional outlook on Judaism. In the major centers services are generally held on Friday evenings and on holidays. In all of the larger communities, Rosh Hashanah and Yom Kippur services attract a sizable crowd.

These services are generally led by knowledgeable laymen, as there are no qualified religious personnel in the country. The last remaining rabbi, Menahem Romano of Sarajevo, died in 1968 at the age of 87. Since then, the federation has been conducting an intensive search for suitable rabbinical candidates. In 1972 a retired diplomat Cadik Danon, who had some formal theological training before the war, returned to Yugoslavia, and he is now acting as the rabbi for the federation.

Holidays continue to be celebrated by the community. Special programs are sponsored by the women's groups and the youth for such occasions as Hanukkah, Purim, and Tu Bi-Shevat. The major communities also hold annual communal seders on the first night of Passover.[29] Matzoth are made available during Passover as a gift from the Joint Distribution Committee, and *lulavim* and *etrogim* as well as other religious articles are supplied from Israel for Sukkot and other occasions. Kosher meat is not readily available and must be imported from Italy or Austria if necessary.

Religious activity, however, is at a minimum and the younger generation displays little or no interest in it. The federation itself provides only limited support for religious endeavors and stresses the secular, cultural side of communal life.

More importance is attached to the communal service sphere. After World War II the Jewish community in Yugoslavia, with the help of the American Joint Distribution Committee, set up a wide network of social welfare institutions to help the poor, the orphaned, the sick, and the elderly in their recovery from the devastations of the war. These facilities, which included orphanages, old age homes, clinics, soup kitchens, and student mensas (dining halls), were administered by the Autonomous Committee for Aid, which operated from 1948 to 1952.[30] When life became more settled and a majority of Yugoslav Jewish survivors left for Israel, these institutions were no longer needed and were gradually phased out.

The most significant social service institution functioning within the Yugoslav Jewish community today is the Home for the Aged in Zagreb. This home, as it will be recalled, has existed in one form or another since 1909. Today it is housed in a modern building, which can accomodate 115 persons. It has its own synagogue, in addition to all other necessary facilities, including an up-to-date hospital wing. The new home was built by the federation with the help of funds from the Joint Distribution Committee and the Jewish Claims Conference. The residents and their families contribute only as much as they can afford to pay for room and board. This institution is considered the finest of its kind in Yugoslavia and compares favorably with Jewish homes for the aged elsewhere in Europe.[31]

The Jewish community provides aid to some 1,100 needy individuals, including monetary assistance to about 500 who are sick, elderly, or no longer able to support themselves. It also gives help to Jewish transients or refugees on their way from Eastern Europe to Israel.[32]

Cultural matters, however, have occupied the position of greatest importance within the communal framework since the war. In the larger centers, lectures, films, and various other programs on Jewish topics are sponsored by the local community. The women's sections of the communities hold regular teas with speakers and discussions on subjects of Jewish interest. The youth groups, too, have cultural programs, talks, and debates on current problems in the Jewish world. In addition, the Belgrade and Zagreb Jewish communities each have their own choir. The Braća Baruh choir in Belgrade (named after three Jewish brothers who were active Partisans in World War II) and Moše Pijade choir in Zagreb (named after the foremost Jewish Communist leader in Yugoslavia) cultivate both Jewish and Yugoslav music, with Hebrew, Yiddish, Ladino, and Serbo-Croatian songs in their repertoire. They perform at Jewish functions, compete in Yugoslav music festivals, give their own concerts, and have toured Europe and Israel several times.[33]

The major Jewish communities have their own Jewish libraries and reading rooms, which contain books and newspapers of general Jewish interest in Serbo-Croatian and foreign languages (mainly German). The most extensive of these facilities is connected with the federation in Belgrade, while the Zagreb Jewish community has a fine private collection of Judaica from the interwar period which belonged to a former Zagreb Jewish lawyer, Dr. Lavoslav Schick.[34] The federation maintains the Jewish Historical Museum and Archive in Belgrade, which amasses and displays materials pertaining to the history of Yugoslav Jewry.[35] In Sarajevo, there is a Jewish museum for Bosnia-Hercegovina run by the state. The federation is responsible for looking after Jewish cemeteries in localities where a Jewish community no longer exists. Some of these cemeteries have been moved elsewhere; others are being maintained at considerable expense. In addition, to preserve its heritage the Jewish community has erected close to thirty memorials around the country to commemorate the Jews who lost their lives during the war.[36]

The federation encourages scholarly research and literary productivity by offering annual awards for works pertaining to the Yugoslav Jewish experience. Between 1955 and 1969 there were 462 entries submitted for this competition, of which 147 won prizes—37 for scholarly research, 106 for literature, and 4 for musical compositions. Most of the literary works submitted have dealt with the Holocaust. Both Jews and non-Jews compete for these monetary awards and many of the works are later published.[37] Every two to three years, *Jevrejski almanah* (Jewish Almanac) appears containing articles on scholarly topics pertaining to Yugoslav Jews and contemporary Yugoslav Jewish literature. It is issued in 1,200 copies and is distributed to various Jewish and other libraries in Yugoslavia and elsewhere. In addition, the federation sponsors publication of books pertaining to Yugoslav Jewish history, the Holocaust, and special events in Jewish life.[38]

The Yugoslav Jewish community also publishes a bimonthly called *Jevrejski pregled* (Jewish Review). Its 3,500 copies are sent to every registered Jewish household in the country and also abroad. Its purpose is above all to supply information on Jewish affairs in Yugoslavia and around the world, especially Israel. The Jewish youth occasionally publish their own periodicals called *Kadima* in Belgrade and *Šalom* in Sarajevo. These issues appear at infrequent intervals. Annually, a Jewish calendar is published, containing Jewish holidays and other important dates, as well as statistical information on Yugoslav Jewry.

Unfortunately, facilities no longer exist for formal Jewish education in Yugoslavia. With the exception of two kindergartens, which scarcely fill any very useful Jewish educational role, the community concentrates its educational efforts on children's, youth, and student club meetings, but especially the summer camp. In fact, the most important activity of the Yugoslav Jewish community on behalf of the younger generation is the summer camp. Almost 300 Jewish youth per year, divided into three age groups, have spent about two weeks each at a community-sponsored camp, usually located along the Adriatic coast. This camp has existed in one form or another since the 1950s. In the 1970s, however, somewhat fewer children have been attending—in 1972, only 193 children participated. In addition to sports, hikes, excursions, and other typical camp activities, this camp tries to provide a Jewish cultural atmosphere for the youth by offering a fairly wide range of lectures, talks and discussions on Jewish subjects, such as the Bible, Jewish history, and current Jewish problems. This cultural emphasis is most apparent among the oldest group, those over 17 years of age. The program is conducted by the federation and the communal leadership, along with some Israelis. A number of Jewish youth from other eastern and western European countries also participate. The camp experience provides many Jewish youth, especially those from the smaller communities, with their only real contact with Jewish life and the opportunity to meet other young Jews. The effectiveness of this activity is difficult to evaluate, but it does help to provide some Jewish awareness.[39]

The most serious challenge facing the Yugoslav Jewish community today is the basic question of its ability to survive. A number of major factors must enter into any prognosis for its continued existence: the size and age of its membership, the problem of intermarriage, the level of involvement in Jewish communal affairs, the supply of young leadership, and finally, the general situation of Jews within socialist Yugoslavia.

Before World War II, membership within the Jewish community was compulsory by state law for all Jews living in Yugoslavia. Since the war, however, membership has become an entirely voluntary matter. Membership is open to all persons of Jewish descent who do not belong to any other religious community and who voluntarily state that they want to become members of the community. The spouse and children of such persons are also eligible for membership if they fulfill the same conditions. Persons who fall under neither of the above categories but wish to become members of the Jewish community may be admitted upon written request at the discretion of the communal leadership.[40]

One thus becomes a member of the community by formally stating that one wishes to do so. Any member can leave the community by submitting a written statement. Membership is generally an individual matter, although families of members of the community are also eligible to join. It often happens, however, that the individual who is of Jewish descent becomes a member of the community, while his or her non-Jewish spouse and their children do not.

An accurate estimate of the total number of individuals eligible for membership in the Jewish community is not available. An indeterminate number of persons of Jewish descent do not acknowledge their Jewish connections and have no affiliation with the community whatsoever. It is assumed, however, that this group is relatively small. In 1965, there were 6,879 persons registered as Jews, that is, they identified themselves as Jews officially, and 6,197 persons were formally members of the Jewish community. Thus 90 percent of the self-acknowledged Jews officially belonged to the community. This ratio has remained fairly stable since 1952.[41]

The number of Jews recorded in the Yugoslav census results is substantially lower than the actual membership within the Federation of Jewish Communities. The 1953 census was the only one in the postwar period which contained a question on religion, as well as one on nationality. In that year, 2,565 persons were enumerated as belonging to the "Mosaic faith," whereas 2,307 individuals declared themselves to be Jews by nationality. Interestingly, approximately half of the Jews by religion claimed to be part of some Slavic nationality (or else Hungarian), whereas almost half of those who considered themselves Jews by nationality did not identify themselves as Jews by religion. The 1961 census reported 2,110 Jews by nationality, approximately one-third of the total membership in the various Jewish communities.[42] Ten years later, the census results showed a phenomenal increase, doubling the number of Jews by nationality to

4,811. According to a critical analysis of the data, however, much of this apparent jump was probably due to computer error.[43] In any event, there are clearly many more Jews living in Yugoslavia than appear in official government statistics.

In 1954 Dr. Albert Vajs, who was then president of the Federation of Jewish Communities, categorized the Jews remaining in Yugoslavia into five types:

a. those who considered themselves Jews by nationality but not members of any religious community;
b. those who considered themselves Jews by nationality and also members of the Jewish (Mosaic) faith;
c. those who considered themselves as Jews by religion but Serbs or Croats by nationality;
d. persons of Jewish descent who considered themselves members of another nationality and who did not belong to any religious community, but still showed a certain interest in Jewish life and participated in some activities; and
e. Jews by descent who did not consider themselves Jews by religion or by nationality and who no longer maintained ties with Jewry or showed interest in the life of the community.

Dr. Vajs pointed out that these variations were not always sharply defined and that individuals often switched back and forth from one category to another. For the community, however, the first two types, which represented the vast majority of the organized Jewish community in Yugoslavia, formed the most important element, and the third type also played a significant role.[44]

The Jewish community considers as Jewish virtually anyone who wishes to be considered as such. Certainly, one Jewish parent is sufficient criterion for an individual to be accepted as a member in good standing of the community. The key to this lenient policy of acceptance within the community lies in the extremely high rate of intermarriage in Yugoslavia.

Of 4,702 communal members responding to the 1971 demographic survey, 3,209 persons, or 68 percent, had two Jewish parents, 1,028 individuals, or 22 percent, had one Jewish parent, and 465 registered members, or 10 percent, reported neither parent to have been Jewish. In the 2,557 households of respondents, 4,199 people out of a possible 6,457, or 65 percent, declared themselves to be Jews.[45] Significantly, of the 102 residents of the Jewish Home for the Aged in Zagreb, 95 reported both parents Jewish and none had only

1 Jewish parent, while 7 had no Jewish parentage.[46] The older generation, then, are rarely, if ever, the products of mixed marriages and are
less likely to have married outside the community. Among the middle and younger generations, however, intermarriage seems to be the
general rule rather than the exception. It has undoubtedly been
steadily on the increase since World War II. The community is small
and scattered throughout the country; hence, the likelihood for one
young Jew to marry another is quite limited.

Conversion does not enter as a factor in these intermarriages.
Even if the non-Jewish partner were willing to convert, there is no
one qualified to perform the conversion. So, too, there are no Jewish
weddings, and religious practices in general are played down. The
Jewish partners to mixed marriages are fully accepted as members of
the Jewish community and their non-Jewish spouses are accepted to
a certain degree as well. Many persons involved in mixed marriages
are fairly active in Jewish affairs, and their families sometimes also
participate in Jewish activities. The Jewish community seems to have
acknowledged that intermarriage is an inevitable feature of Jewish
life in Yugoslavia today and they try to make the best of it and retain
as many of their members as possible. This attitude has enabled the
community to remain reasonably stable in its membership over the
past two decades.

The Jewish population in Yugoslavia is a rapidly aging one,
however, with a very low birth rate. According to the survey conducted in 1971, in each of the three major communities, well over
half the membership were over 45 years of age: in Belgrade, 58
percent; in Zagreb, 67 percent (or 70 percent, if one includes the
Home for the Aged); and in Sarajevo, 53 percent. Less than 10
percent were found to be under 15: 6 percent in Belgrade, 6 percent in Zagreb, and 9 percent in Sarajevo.[47] The Jewish community, then, is an old one, with fewer and fewer children available
to fill the ranks in the future.

Participation in community affairs depends chiefly on age and
interests. The avenues of participation are to be found in the communal administration (the communal councils), the women's sections,
the Home for the Aged, the choirs, and the youth groups, as well as
the synagogue. The communal administration is theoretically open to
all, but it tends to be dominated by older men, with only a few
women and even fewer youth or young adults. The women's sections
are often the largest and most dynamic bodies operating within the
community. Their combined membership across the country was
reported to be over 800, of whom some 100 were considered very

active. Membership tends to be drawn from among the older women (in 1968 only one-third of the members were under 50), although some younger women also participate in its cultural and educational activities.[48] The supporters of the Home for the Aged usually belong to one or the other of the above groups, but are concentrated predominantly in Zagreb. The two choirs, which total around 80 members, have a somewhat better age distribution than the other organizations, but participation is naturally limited on the basis of talent and interest. The youth groups are popular primarily among unmarried students, usually ranging in age from 18 to 25. The young people who are most active in these groups often seem to disappear from communal life after they graduate or marry. The so-called middle generation, the young adults from 25 to 45 with young families, constitutes a lost element in the community and presents a great problem which the leadership has thus far failed to solve satisfactorily.[49]

According to the 1971 survey, in Belgrade, 213 persons over 15 years of age, or 23 percent of those replying to the questionaire, claimed to have participated in Jewish activities since World War II. In Sarajevo, 289 individuals, or 38 percent of the respondents, admitted to taking part in communal life; in Zagreb, only 147, or 17 percent, indicated such activity.[50] It would thus appear that Sarajevo presently has the most vibrant community of the three. The number of participants involved in communal activities, however, is relatively low.

Given the small size of the community, the rapidly rising average age of its membership, the high rate of intermarriage, and the rather low level of active participation in communal life, especially among young adults, it is scarcely surprising that the question of who will provide future Yugoslav Jewish leadership looms ominously on the horizon.

Those presently holding top voluntary leadership positions share many traits in common. They all seem to have been born in Yugoslavia in medium or large Jewish communities, usually before World War I, and their Jewish family background was generally rather traditional. They were often active in the Jewish youth movement during the interwar period, although few held high leadership positions within the Jewish community before World War II. During the war, most of the current leadership cadres were German prisoners-of-war, who had been called up as reserve officers in 1941; others fought as Partisans under Tito or found safety in Italian-occupied territory. Virtually all of them are lawyers, doctors, or professors of some kind; many have held responsible government positions but are now retired. Their average age is at least 60.

A brief biographical sketch of the man occupying the highest position of authority, as of this writing, within the Yugoslav Jewish community, the president of the Federation of Jewish Communities, serves to illustrate this pattern clearly. Lavoslav Kadelburg was born in 1910 in Vinkovci, a town in Croatia-Slavonia with a Jewish population of about six hundred on the eve of World War II. He was active in Jewish affairs since high school, when he was president of the local Jewish youth association and a member of the Steering Committee of the federation of Jewish Youth Associations of Yugoslavia. While studying law in Zagreb, he participated in Jewish student clubs. As a reserve officer in the Yugoslav army, he spent the war in a military prison camp. After 1945 he became a public prosecutor and later held a number of high government positions in both the republic and federal administration, including the post of director of the Federal Institute of Public Administration and assistant general director of the Federal Institute for Social Security, until his retirement in 1966. He is an active member of the League of Communists and several other prestigious Yugoslav organizations. Immediately after World War II, he began to play a leading role in Yugoslav Jewish life. From 1945 to 1952 he was a member and then president of the Autonomous Committee for Aid. In 1945 he became a member of the executive board of the federation; in 1948 he was elected vice-president and in 1964 he succeeded Dr. Albert Vajs as president. Kadelburg's sphere of influence has always been within the federation, rather than on the local communal level. He is Yugoslav Jewry's most important diplomat to the outside world and serves as a member of the World and European executives of the World Jewish Congress and as vice-president of the European Council for Jewish Communal Services.[51]

Dr. Lavoslav Kadelburg and his generation have governed the Yugoslav Jewish community ever since the war. But the problem is who will succeed them. The present leadership does attempt to recruit potential leaders from among the younger and middle generations. This is done primarily by encouraging the youth to participate more in the federation and its activities on a countrywide level and by trying to elect more new people to the communal councils and give these young activists some responsibility. How successful this strategy proves remains to be seen.

Together with the voluntary leadership who actually control the communal institutions, organizations, and decision-making, a small group of professionals also help to run the Jewish community. The main positions occupied by professional leaders in the community are the secretary of the federation, the countrywide youth coordinator, the director of the Home for the Aged, and the curator of the Jewish Historical Museum. In 1970 all these positions were held by women. Although there is no available data on their personal backgrounds, it would appear that the present professional leaders are younger than the volunteer leaders, well educated, but not having quite as strong Jewish family backgrounds. The professional leaders were recruited from the membership at large on the basis of qualifications or skills. They have all received at least a certain amount of specialized training for the positions which they hold. The problem of finding suitable professional leaders to perform the necessary functions within the community poses a very serious dilemma for the community. New cadres must somehow be produced to fill future needs.

In general, relations between the Jewish community and Yugoslav society at large are cordial. There has never been a strong tradition of anti-Semitism in the country, although Nazi propaganda before and during World War II has left its mark. Anti-Semitic incidents, such as vandalism of Jewish cemeteries, occur only rarely and are, as a rule, vigorously opposed by the authorities. The Jewish community does not perceive local anti-Semitism as a major problem and a friendly atmosphere is usually maintained. The community takes pride in this sympathetic ambiance and the more specific manifestations of government support and strives to consolidate both.

The Jewish community and its leadership fully support Tito and the Yugoslav brand of Communism. The top leaders often hold, or have held, high government positions and they are, for the most part, members of the League of Communists. In the early postwar years, the Jewish community even participated in national election campaigns in support of the government, presumably to display its loyalty to the regime. Government representatives regularly attend all major conferences, celebrations, or commemorations held within the community. It is clearly very important for the community to foster these close official ties.[52]

Non-Jews do not concern themselves to any great extent with Jewish communal life; however, individual non-Jews participate in Jewish activities. Thus, non-Jewish children attend the Jewish kindergartens, non-Jewish students are to be found at Jewish student club meetings, and non-Jews take part in the Jewish choirs.

The general media seem to have adopted a double standard regarding Yugoslav Jews and Israel. What little is reported on Jews per se, and Yugoslav Jews in particular, is sympathetic and balanced, but the same cannot be said for reporting on the Middle East. Although Yugoslavia was one of the first countries to recognize the State of Israel in 1948, since then official policy has increasingly tended toward support for the Arab cause. The bias of the Yugoslav press against Israel is very pronounced; such a stand cannot help but influence the Jewish community and its behavior.

The Jewish community is obviously rather sensitive on this issue, since its spokesmen for the most part continue to be openly pro-Israel. But there is little that they can do about the situation. The leadership, however, tends to become quite defensive if any foreign source attacks the Yugoslav press as being anti-Semitic. In 1969 the Federation of Jewish Communities sent a letter of rebuttal to the London *Jewish Chronicle* which had published an article under the headline "Yugoslav Papers Become Anti-Semitic." They accused the *Chronicle* not only of being sensationalist but also of not serving the best interests of Jewry in Yugoslavia or Jewry in general. They concluded the letter by stating: "It is necessary to point out that the Yugoslav state and political organization have always taken a correct stand on the national question in general and especially have also maintained a correct relationship with the Jewish community."[53]

The Yugoslav Jewish community keeps up steady contact with the rest of world Jewry. The Federation of Jewish Communities of Yugoslavia has a long-standing affiliation with the World Jewish Congress, as well as with the European Council on Jewish Communal Services (formerly the Standing Committee). It has also had close ties with the American Jewish Joint Distribution Committee, the Claims Conference and later the Memorial Foundation for Jewish Culture, from whom they have received extensive funds on a regular basis.

In addition to these formal affiliations, the federation and its subsidiary organizations maintain links with other worldwide Jewish organizations, such as the Jewish Agency, the World Federation of Sephardic Jews, the World Union of Jewish Students and the International Council of Jewish Women. In short, it would appear that the community favors friendly relations with nearly all international Jewish institutions.

The federation has also developed a network of informal contacts with other European Jewish communities, particularly those in Eastern Europe. Dr. Kadelburg has made several visits to the Soviet Union, as well as to Hungary and Rumania; in return, Jewish leaders from these countries have visited Yugoslavia. In 1966 Jewish dignitaries from all over the world participated in the four-hundredth anniversary celebration of the settlement of Jews in Bosnia-Hercegovina. In 1969 there was a gala celebration of the federation's fiftieth anniversary, attended by many foreigners from both East and West. The following year a large Soviet delegation came to Belgrade on the occasion of Dr. Kadelburg's sixtieth birthday. Yugoslav Jewish leaders travel extensively in Western Europe as well, attending conferences and meetings of various types. Youth leaders, too, frequently attend Jewish youth and student conventions abroad.[54]

Nearly all the ties existing between the Yugoslav Jewish community and Israel today are of an informal rather than a formal nature. The Yugoslav government severed diplomatic relations with Israel after the Six-Day War, but the two countries continue to maintain trade connections.[55] The Yugoslav authorities have in no way tried to interfere directly with the Jewish community's support of Israel and contacts have never been broken, but the community of its own volition exercises caution with regard to its relationship with Israel.

Yugoslav Jews are allowed to travel to Israel freely as tourists (upon acquiring a visa, usually through the Belgian Embassy). Israelis, too, may visit Yugoslavia with no difficulty. Close personal ties are preserved, especially between Yugoslav Jews and Israeli citizens of Yugoslav origin. Yugoslav Jewish leaders make frequent trips to Israel for official or personal reasons. Every summer, about twenty Jewish students from Yugoslavia spend six weeks in Israel, attending a special seminar.

Israel plays a relatively important role in the life of the community. Most Yugoslav Jews seem to consider themselves Zionists, although many choose not to display this fact openly. The community as a whole is pro-Israel, but shows it in a subtle rather than a blatant manner. The younger generation is very interested in Israel and often ask questions and discuss it in a well-informed fashion with foreign visitors at youth meetings.

Israel does not officially provide the community with technical aid, but de facto, Israeli "visitors," many of whom were born in Yugoslavia, do provide assistance in the role of teachers or *shlichim* at summer camps, with informal talks, and so forth. Israelis of Yugoslav descent form a very important link between Yugoslav Jewry and Israel. They often return to Yugoslavia to see family and friends and they generally keep the community informed of current developments in Israel.[56]

Israel does not provide the community with any financial assistance, but the community does occasionally make contributions to Israel, mainly by planting trees, such as in the Martyrs' Forest in the mid-fifties and the Albert Vajs Memorial Forest near Kibbutz Gat in 1964.[57]

Clearly, the Yugoslav Jewish community today no longer enjoys the strength and the vitality which it displayed during the interwar era. The remnant community is small, about one-tenth its former size, and its members are growing older. The outlook for the future is not promising. Who will take over the leadership in the next generation? Intermarriage and assimilation seriously threaten the community's continued existence. Perhaps Yugoslav Jewry is doomed to death by natural causes. Only its centralized organization and its persistent will to live enable it to survive.

The Jewish community of the post–World War II period demonstrates a unity and cohesiveness which was previously unknown in Yugoslavia. No longer do separate Sephardic and Ashkenazic communities operate; Zionists no longer conduct ideological campaigns against integrationists or vice versa; the Orthodox minority no longer feuds with the Neologue majority; rival charitable or cultural societies no longer compete with one another for support. Instead, there is the all-encompassing Federation of Jewish Communities with its local branch communities. This lack of inner divisions and conflicts within Yugoslav Jewry today is by no means a healthy sign, but rather a definite indication of weakness and desperation.

In the eyes of Yugoslav Jews living today, the period between the wars is sometimes viewed as the Golden Age of Yugoslav Jewry. In retrospect, this evaluation, although tinged with nostalgia, does not totally lack merit. Sephardic and Ashkenazic communities, each with its own background and outlook, functioned side by side but within an overall spirit of cooperation. A multiplicity of Jewish institutions, covering a wide range of activities, flourished both on the local and national levels. Such diversity was the hallmark of the Jewish community of Yugoslavia before the Holocaust.

Jewish communities still exist in Sarajevo, Belgrade, and Zagreb. These three centers continue to provide the major focal points for Yugoslav Jewish life. Today they are, however, but pale reflections of their much more dynamic past. The vibrant Jewish communities of interwar Yugoslavia, well adapted to survival in a multinational state, live on today as memories, not as realities.

Appendixes

APPENDIX 1   TABLES

TABLE 1
Population of Sarajevo by Religion, 1885–1921

Religion	1885[a]		1895[b]		1910[c]		1921[d]	
	No.	%	No.	%	No.	%	No.	%
Muslim	15,787	60.10	17,158	45.06	18,460	35.56	22,474	33.89
Orthodox	4,431	16.86	5,858	15.38	8,450	16.27	16,468	24.82
Catholic	3,326	12.66	10,672	28.02	17,922	34.52	19,242	29.01
Jewish	2,618	9.97	4,058	10.66	6,397	12.32	7,458	11.25
Other	106	0.41	337	0.88	690	1.33	675	1.03
TOTAL	26,268	100.00	38,083	100.00	51,919	100.00	66,317	100.00

a. *Ortschafts-und Bevölkerungs-Statistik von Bosnien und der Herzegowina nach dem Volkszählungs-Ergebnisse vom 1. Mai 1885* (Sarajevo: Landesdruckerei, 1886).

b. Landesregierung für Bosnien und die Herzegowina, *Hauptresultate der Volkszählung in Bosnien und der Herzegowina vom 22. April 1895* (Sarajevo: Landesdruckerei, 1896).

c. Landesregierung für Bosnien und die Herzegowina, *Die Ergebnisse der Volkszählung in Bosnien und der Herzegowina vom 10. Oktober 1910* (Sarajevo: Landesdruckerei, 1912).

d. Kraljevina Jugoslavije Opšta državna statistika (KJ-ODS), *Definitivni rezultati popisa stanovništva od 31 januara 1921 godine* (Sarajevo: Državna štamparija, 1932).

TABLE 2
Jewish Residential Distribution in Sarajevo, 1885–1910

District	1885a	1895b			1910c		
	Jews (%)	Jews (%)	Sephardim (%)	Ashkenazim (%)	Jews (%)	Sephardim (%)	Ashkenazim (%)
Čaršija	1,541	1,418	855	563	2,155	1,558	597
	(58.86)	(34.94)	(27.06)	(62.62)	(33.69)	(31.25)	(42.28)
Koševo	78	109	2	107	322	59	263
	(2.98)	(2.69)	(0.06)	(11.90)	(5.03)	(1.18)	(18.63)
Bjelave	688	1,420	1,294	126	1,788	1,694	94
	(26.28)	(34.99)	(40.96)	(14.02)	(27.95)	(33.98)	(6.66)
Kovači	260	966	946	20	1,230	1,141	89
	(9.93)	(23.80)	(29.96)	(2.22)	(19.23)	(22.89)	(6.30)
Grad	3	4	0	4	13	13	0
	(0.11)	(0.10)	(—)	(0.44)	(0.20)	(0.26)	(—)
Hrvatin/	48	141	62	79	889	520	369
Bistrik	(1.83)	(3.47)	(1.96)	(8.80)	(13.90)	(10.44)	(26.13)
TOTAL	2,618	4,058	3,159	899	6,397	4,985	1,412

a. *Ortschafts- und Bevölkerungs-Statistik von Bosnien und der Herzegowina nach dem Volks-zählungs-Ergebnisse vom 1. Mai 1885.*

b. Landesregierung für BuH, *Hauptresultate der Volkszählung in BuH vom 22. April 1895.*

c. Landesregierung für BuH, *Die Ergebnisse der Volkszählung in BuH vom 10. Oktober 1910.*

TABLE 3
Sarajevo, Belgrade, and Zagreb: Growth of Cities and Jewish Population

Census Year	Sarajevo[a]			Belgrade[b]			Zagreb[c]		
	Total	Jews	%	Total	Jews	%	Total	Jews	%
1880							29,218	1,285	4.40
1885	26,268	2,618	9.97						
1890				55,868	2,599	4.65	38,742	1,942	5.01
1895	38,083	4,058	10.66	59,115	3,097	5.24			
1900							57,690	3,237	5.61
1910	51,919	6,397	12.32				74,703	4,233	5.67
1921	66,317	7,458	11.25	111,739	4,844	4.34	108,674	5,970	5.49
1931	78,173	7,615	9.74	238,775	7,906	3.31	185,581	8,702	4.69

a. *Ortschafts- und Bevölkerungs-Statistik von BuH* (1886); *Hauptresultate der Volkszählung in BuH* (1896); *Die Ergebnisse der Volkszählung in BuH* (1912); *Definitivni rezultati popisa, 1921* (1932); KJ-ODS, *Definitivni rezultati popisa stanovništva od 31 marta 1931 godine,* vol.2 (Belgrade: Državna štamparija, 1938).

b. Arnold Wadler, "Die Juden in Serbien," *Zeitschrift für Demographie und Statistik der Juden,* vol. 2, no.10 (October 1906), pp.147–48; *Statistika Kraljevine Srbije,* vol.12 (Belgrade: Državna štamparija, 1899), pp.58–59; *Definitivni rezultati popisa, 1921; Definitivni rezultati popisa, 1931.*

c. Ljubomir St. Kosier, *Jevreji u Jugoslaviji i Bugarskoj* (Zagreb: Ekonomska Biblioteka Srba, Hrvata i Slovenaca, 1930), p.90; *Statistički godišnjak Kraljevine Hrvatske i Slavonije,* vol.1 (Zagreb: Tisak Kr. zemaljske tiskare, 1913), p.24; *Definitivni rezultati popisa, 1921; Definitivni rezultati popisa, 1931.*

TABLE 4
Linguistic Acculturation of Sarajevo Jewry, 1910–31[a]

Language	1910		1931	
	No.	%	No.	%
Serbo-Croatian			3,216	41.63[d]
Ladino	5,441	75.09[b]	3,950	51.13[e]
German			269	3.48
Hungarian			127	1.64
Other	1,805	24.91[c]	164	2.12
TOTAL	7,246	100.00	7,726	100.00

Sources: *Die Ergebnisse der Volkszählung in BuH* (1912), table 47; Germany, Publikationsstelle Wien, *Die Gliederung der Bevölkerung des ehemaligen Jugoslawien nach Muttersprache und Konfession* (Vienna, 1943), p.140.

a. Includes the city of Sarajevo and the surrounding countryside. The town itself had a Jewish population of 6,397 in 1910 and 7,615 in 1931.

b. I.e., 97.72 percent of the 5,568 Sephardim living in the Sarajevo district.

c. In this case, "Other" includes all languages other than Ladino, and hence what languages were reported by the 1,778 Ashkenazim cannot be determined.

d. This figure includes approximately 40 percent of the local Sephardim and about 45 percent of the Ashkenazic population.

e. I.e., about 60 percent of the Sephardic population.

TABLE 5
Linguistic Acculturation among Serbian Jewry, 1895–1931

Serbia	1895		1900		1931[a]	
	No.	%	No.	%	No.	%
Language						
Serbo-Croatian	141	2.79	2,636	46.02	4,665	48.99
Ladino	4,056	80.35	1,544	26.95	2,843	29.86
German	634	12.56	462	8.06	1,159	12.17
Hungarian	58	1.15	40	0.70	586	6.15
Other	159	3.15	1,047	18.27[b]	269	2.83
TOTAL	5,048	100.00	5,729	100.00	9,522	100.00

Belgrade	1895		1931	
	No.	%	No.	%
Language				
Serbo-Croatian	120	3.88	4,285	54.20[c]
Ladino	2,391	77.20	2,350	29.72[d]
German	527	17.02	653	8.26
Hungarian	40	1.29	399	5.05
Other	19	0.61	219	2.77
TOTAL	3,097	99.99	7,906	100.00

Sources: *Statistika Kraljevine Srbije,* vol. 12, pp.58–59; Wadler, "Die Juden in Serbien,"
p.169; Germany, Publikationsstelle Wien, *Die Gliederung,* pp.11, 16, 22.

a. Includes the Belgrade capital district and the Morava province.

b. Probably mostly Ladino speakers who claimed Hebrew or Jewish as their
mother tongue.

c. Includes about two-thirds of the Sephardic community, but only less than
10 percent of the Ashkenazim in Belgrade–a figure which seems somewhat low.

d. I.e., 35.51 percent of the Sephardic population.

TABLE 6
Linguistic Acculturation among Croatian Jewry, 1880–1931

Croatia	1880 (%)	1890 (%)	1900 (%)	1910 (%)	1931[a] (%)
Language					
Serbo-Croatian	4,085	4,894	7,080	9,755	13,593
	(30.29)	(28.35)	(35.34)	(45.89)	(69.44)
German	7,496	8,949	8,377	6,384	2,788
	(55.58)	(51.86)	(41.82)	(30.07)	(14.24)
Hungarian	1,576	3,001	4,203	4,611	2,077
	(11.68)	(17.38)	(20.98)	(21.72)	(10.61)
Other	331	417	372	481	1,117
	(2.45)	(2.41)	(1.86)	(2.22)	(5.71)
TOTAL	13,488	17,261	20,032	21,231	19,575

Zagreb	1900		1910		1931	
	No.	%	No.	%	No.	%
Language						
Serbo-Croatian	1,751	54.09	2,533	59.84	6,402	73.57
German	742	22.92	784	18.52	1,059	12.17
Hungarian	653	20.17	794	18.76	653	7.50
Other	91	2.81	122	2.88	588	6.76
TOTAL	3,237	99.99	4,233	100.00	8,702	100.00

Sources: *Statistički godišnjak Kraljevine Hrvatske i Slavonije,* vol. 1, 1905 (Zagreb, 1913), p.45; Ljubomir St. Kosier, *Jevreji u Jugoslaviji i Bugarskoj,* pp.120–1; Germany, Publikationsstelle Wien, *Die Gliederung,* pp.17, 304.

a. The 1931 figures pertain to the Sava province, which was about equivalent to former Croatia-Slavonia but not exactly coterminus.

TABLE 7
Jewish Population Distribution by Banovina[a]

Banovina	1921		1931				
	Total	% of Jews	Sephardim	Ashkenazim	Orthodox	Total	% of Jews
Sava[b]	17,438	26.93	238	19,310	27	19,575	28,62
Dunava[c]	19,500	30.12	1,809	13,626	3,083	18,518	27.07
Drava[d]	936	1.45	4	813	3	820	1.20
Belgrade[e]	6,070	9.38	6,921	1,993	22	8,936	13.06
Drina[f]	11,606	17.93	8,009	2,034	0	10,043	14.68
Vardar[g]	5,492	8.48	7,382	122	75	7,579	11.08
Morava[h]	754	1.16	524	50	12	586	.86
Vrbas[i]	1,575	2.43	708	450	2	1,160	1.70
Zeta[j]	508	.78	507	100	3	610	.89
Primora[k]	867	1.34	66	512	0	578	.84
TOTAL	64,746	100.00	26,168	39,010	3,227	68,405	100.00

Sources: KJ-ODS, *Statistički pregled KJ po banovima* (Belgrade: Državna štamparija, 1930), p.4; *Definitivni rezultati popisa stanovništva od 31 marta 1931 godine,* vol.2 (Sarajevo: Državna štamparija, 1940), p. vi–vii.

a. In 1930 a general redistricting occurred in Yugoslavia, replacing the historical names and boundaries of the component regions of the country with geographical names and borders, primarily based on rivers.

b. Sava is more or less equivalent to the former Croatia-Slavonia, including Zagreb as its major center and also the city of Osijek.

c. Dunava is generally equivalent to the former Vojvodina, with Novi Sad and Subotica as its largest cities, as well as many other towns with sizable Jewish populations.

d. Drava is the former Slovenia, with Ljubljana and Maribor as its major cities, but including only two small organized Jewish communities in Dolnja Lendava and Murska Subota.

e. The Belgrade administrative (or capital) district includes the city of Belgrade and the surrounding area, encompassing the towns of Zemun and Pančevo as well.

f. Drina more or less covers the former Bosnia, including Sarajevo as its major center.

g. Vardar is Macedonia (or South Serbia), which included Bitolj and Skoplje.

h. Morava comprises the remainder of Serbia, with no large Jewish communities.

i. Vrbas covers most of the former Hercegovina, with a few small Jewish communities, including Banja Luka and Derventa.

j. Zeta is basically Montenegro, but also includes Dubrovnik.

k. Primora covers most of the Dalmatian coast, as well as parts of Hercegovina, with small Jewish communities in Split and Mostar.

TABLE 8
Rate of Natural Increase per 1,000 in Zagreb Ashkenazic and Sarajevo Sephardic Communities, 1894–1939

Year	Zagreb Ashkenazic[a]			Sarajevo Sephardic[b]		
	Births	Deaths	Natural Increase	Births	Deaths	Natural Increase
1894	33.0	19.6	+13.4	42.6	20.9	+21.7
1899	30.2	14.4	+15.8	33.5	18.0	+15.5
1904	23.6	16.2	+ 7.4	35.2	14.4	+20.8
1909	21.9	15.7	+ 6.2	35.6	16.6	+19.0
1914	15.8	13.8	+ 2.0	33.5	14.8	+18.7
1919	11.3	14.8	− 3.5	18.5	14.3	+ 4.2
1924	15.1	16.3	− 1.2	23.8	14.1	+ 9.7
1929	9.0	13.5	− 4.5	14.2	13.9	+ 0.3
1934	7.3	13.5	− 6.2	10.3	7.2	+ 3.1
1939	6.8	16.6	− 9.8	8.5	8.1	+ 0.4

a. Gavro Schwarz, "Nešto statistike iz zagrebačke jevrejske općine," *Glasnik SJVO,* vol. 3 (October 1933), p. 197; "Statistike zagrebačkog nadrabinata," *Židov,* vol.15, no.11 (March 13, 1931); "Nešto statistike iz zagrebačke jevrejske općine," ibid., vol.20, no.18 (May 1, 1936); "Djelatnost uprave zagrebačke židovske općine," ibid., vol.24, no.30 (July 26, 1940).

b. Sarajevo Jewish Library, Matične knjige rodjenih sefardske opštine jevrejske, Sarajevo, 1894–1941; "Statistike Jevreja Sarajeva, 1904–1924," *Narodna Židovska Svijest,* vol.3, no.90 (January 1, 1926), p. 3; Benjamin Pinto, "O kretanju jevrejske stanovništva u Sarajevu," *Jevrejski narodni kalendar,* vol.5, 1939/40, p. 53; "Malo statistike," *Jevrejski glas,* vol.9, no.28 (July 10, 1936), p. 8.

TABLE 9
Occupational Distribution of Active Population in Yugoslavia

Category of Occupation	1931 General[a] %	1939 Jewish[b] %
Agriculture, forestry, and fishing	76.30	.6
Industry and crafts	10.73	12.7
Commerce, credit, and communications	4.07	58.8
Public services, free professions, and military	4.58	11.6
Other	4.32	16.3
TOTAL	100.00	100.00

a. KJ-ODS, *Definitivni rezultati popisa stanovništva od 31 marta 1931,* vol.4 (Sarajevo: Državna štamparija, 1940), p.vii.

b. SJVO, *Izveštaj Glavnog odbora VII kongresu 23 i 24 aprila 1939 godine* (Belgrade: Štamparija Beletra, 1939), table 2, p.83.

TABLE 10
Yugoslav Jewry by Occupation, 1938[a]

Occupations	Sava (%)	Dunava (%)	Belgrade (%)	Drina (%)	Vardar (%)	Other[b] (%)	Total (%)
Merchants	1,557	1,445	832	597	505	267	5,203
	(28.1)	(32.0)	(24.6)	(23.9)	(27.7)	(36.1)	(28.1)
Commercial	499	243	280	106	166	28	1,322
Agents[c]	(8.9)	(5.4)	(8.3)	(4.2)	(9.1)	(3.8)	(7.1)
Clerks and	1,779	892	1,138	288	345	109	4,551
Employees[d]	(32.1)	(19.8)	(33.7)	(11.5)	(18.9)	(14.7)	(24.6)
Professionals[e]	468	377	188	81	36	55	1,205
	(8.4)	(8.4)	(5.6)	(3.2)	(2.0)	(7.4)	(6.5)
Industrialists	216	139	94	21	33	28	531
and Bankers[f]	(3.9)	(3.1)	(2.8)	(0.8)	(1.8)	(3.8)	(2.9)
Artisans	326	271	346	600	280	105	1,928
	(5.9)	(6.0)	(10.2)	(24.0)	(15.3)	(14.2)	(10.4)
Other[g]	217	239	166	517	355	78	1,572
	(3.9)	(5.4)	(4.9)	(20.7)	(19.4)	(10.5)	(8.5)
None[h]	485	893	335	293	106	70	2,182
	(8.8)	(19.9)	(9.9)	(11.7)	(5.8)	(9.5)	(11.8)
TOTAL	5,547	4,499	3,379	2,503	1,826	740	18,494

Source: SJVO, *Izveštaj Glavnog odbora VII kongresu 23 i 24 aprila 1939 godine* (Belgrade: Stamparija Beletra, 1939), table 2, p.83.

a. Includes all communal taxpayers in the country, except the Orthodox.

b. Includes Drava, Morava, Vrbas, Zeta, and Primora regions. (See table 7 for an explanation of the banovina system.)

c. Includes commercial travelers.

d. Includes civil servants.

e. Includes doctors, lawyers, engineers, veterinarians, and pharmacists.

f. Includes money changers.

g. Includes rabbis and other communal employees (total 268), teachers (107), porters (134), agriculturalists (111), as well as miscellaneous.

h. May also include some women heads of household, pensioners, and others not technically considered unemployed.

TABLE 11
Language Distribution among Yugoslav Jewry by Banovina,
1931[a]

	Serbo-Croatian (%)	Jewish[b] (%)	German (%)	Hungarian (%)	Other[c] (%)	Total (%)
Sava	13,593	185	2,788	2,077	932	19,575
	(69.44)	(0.95)	(14.24)	(10.61)	(4.76)	(100)
Dunava	2,383	2,439[d]	5,303	8,003	390	18,518
	(12.87)	(13.17)	(28.64)	(43.22)	(2.11)	(100)
Drava	145	3	165	222	285[e]	820
	(17.68)	(0.37)	(20.12)	(27.07)	(34.75)	(100)
Belgrade	4,549	2,420	1,142	571	254	8,936
	(50.91)	(27.08)	(12.78)	(6.39)	(2.84)	(100)
Drina	4,600	4,581	429	163	270	10,043
	(45.80)	(45.61)	(4.27)	(1.62)	(2.69)	(100)
Vardar	220	7,269	28	31	31	7,579
	(2.90)	(95.90)	(0.37)	(0.41)	(0.41)	(100)
Morava	116	423	17	15	15	586
	(19.80)	(72.18)	(2.90)	(2.56)	(2.56)	(100)
Vrbas	760	211	87	32	70	1,160
	(65.51)	(18.19)	(7.50)	(2.76)	(6.03)	(100)
Zeta	124	401	33	32	20	610
	(20.33)	(65.74)	(5.41)	(5.25)	(3.28)	(100)
Primora	406	66	34	24	48	578
	(70.24)	(11.42)	(5.88)	(4.15)	(8.30)	(100)
TOTAL	26,896	17,998	10,026	11,170	2,315	68,405
	(39.32)	(26.31)	(14.66)	(16.33)	(3.38)	(100)

Source: Germany, Publikationsstelle Wien, *Die Gliederung der Bevölkerung des ehemaligen Jugoslawien nach Muttersprache und Konfession (nach den unveröffentlichen Angaben der Zählung von 1931)* (Vienna, 1943), pp.10–20.

a. See table 7 for an explanation of the banovina system and Sephardic/Ashkenazic distribution.

b. Primarily Ladino speakers, but this category does include some Yiddish speakers as well, as noted below.

c. "Other" includes Slovenian (especially as noted), foreign Slavic languages, Rumanian, Turkish, and other languages which are not specified.

d. Probably at least half of these are Yiddish speakers (mainly Orthodox).

e. Includes 220 speakers of Slovenian, the local Slavic vernacular.

TABLE 12
Jewish Attendance at Primary and Secondary Schools, 1938/39

Schools	Total Pupils[a]	Jewish Pupils[b]	
		No.	%
Primary Schools	1,428,223	3,206	.22
Secondary Schools	206,896	3,474	1.68
Academic	125,098	2,951	2.36
Commercial	7,389	201	2.72
Technical	2,152	51	2.37
Other	72,257	271	.38

Sources: a. *Statistički godišnjak,* vol.10 (Belgrade: Državna štamparija), 1940, pp.336–37.
　　　　 b. SJVO, *Izveštaj Glavnog odbora VII kongresu 23 i 24 aprila 1939 godine* (Belgrade: Štamparija Beletra, 1939), p.86.

TABLE 13
Jewish Attendance at Universities, 1928/29 and 1938/39

Field of Study	1928/29			1938/39		
	Total	Jewish		Total	Jewish	
		No.	%		No.	%
Law	4,108	218	5.3	5,998	91	1.5
Philosophy	2,801	141	5.0	2,866	80	2.8
Medicine	1,286	92	7.2	2,096	140	6.7
Technology	2,889	59	2.0	2,671	143	5.4
Economics	239	30	12.6	986	34	3.4
Other	1,211	29	2.4	3,117	46	1.5
TOTAL	12,534	569	4.5	17,734	534	3.0

Source: *Statistički godišnjak,* vols.1, 10 (Belgrade: Državna štamparija), 1929 and 1940.

TABLE 14
Marriages Between Sephardim and Ashkenazim in Sarajevo, 1908–40

Couples	1908–18		1919–29		1930–40		Total	
	No.	%	No.	%	No.	%	No.	%
Rite								
Seph.-Seph.	333	72.5	672	74.3	591	74.4	1,596	73.9
Ashk.-Ashk.	101	22.0	157	17.3	91	11.5	349	16.2
Seph.-Ashk.	25	5.5	76	8.4	112	14.1	213	9.9
TOTAL	459	100.0	905	100.0	794	100.0	2,158	100.0

Individuals	1908–18		1919–29		1930–40		Total	
	Seph.	Ashk.	Seph.	Ashk.	Seph.	Ashk.	Seph.	Ashk.
Rites								
Sephardim	666	25	1,344	76	1,182	112	3,192	213
%	96.6	11.0	94.7	19.4	91.3	38.1	93.7	23.4
Ashkenazim	25	202	76	314	112	182	213	698
%	3.4	89.0	5.3	80.6	8.7	61.9	6.3	76.6
TOTAL	691	227	1,420	390	1,294	294	3,405	911

Source: Sarajevo Jewish Library, Marriage Registries of Sephardic and Ashkenazic communities in Sarajevo, 1908–40.

TABLE 15

Occupational Distribution of Yugoslav Jewry in Postwar Period

Occupations	1953[a]		1971[b]	
	Total	%	Total	%
White-collar workers[c]	875	37.1	363	22.9
Craftsmen and industrial workers[d]	277	11.7	230	14.5
Commercial employees[e]	247	10.5	92	5.8
Physicians, pharmacists, and other medical personnel	262	11.1	203	12.8
Professors, teachers, and other instructors	102	4.3	183	11.5
Lawyers and economists[f]	72	3.0	113	7.1
Construction engineers, architects, etc.	82	3.5	59	3.7
Physicists, chemists, mathematicians, etc.[g]			91	5.7
Biologists, agronomists, veterinarians, etc.	25	1.1	21	1.3
Managers			62	3.9
Army officers[h]	78	3.3		
Journalists and media personnel	31	1.3	34	2.2
Artists and writers	33	1.4	43	2.7
Other[i]	277	11.7	93	5.9
Grand Total	2,361 100	100.0	1,587	100.0

a. Source: Albert Vajs, "Jevreji u novoj Jugoslaviji," *Jevrejski almanah* (N.S.), 1954, p.36; Institute of Jewish Affairs of the World Jewish Congress, *European Jewry Ten Years After the War* (New York, 1956), pp.190–91.

b. Source: Marko Perić, "Demographic Study of the Jewish Community in Yugoslavia, 1971–72," *Papers in Jewish Demography 1973* (Jerusalem: Institute of Contemporary Jewry, 1977), p.282.

c. In 1953 listed under "civil servants" and in 1971 listed under "clerical, financial, and kindred."

d. In 1953 listed separately as "artisans" and "(factory) technicians."

e. In 1953 listed as "in economic fields."

f. In 1953 included lawyers, judges, and other legalists, but not economists.

g. Not listed as separate category in 1953.

h. Not listed as separate category in 1970.

i. Includes "unknown" also.

APPENDIX 2 MINORITIES TREATY, 1919*

The United States of America, The British Empire, France, Italy, and Japan, The Principal Allied and Associated Powers, on the one hand; And the Serb-Croat-Slovene State on the other hand;

Whereas since the commencement of the year 1913 extensive territories have been added to the Kingdom of Serbia, and

Whereas the Serb, Croat, and Slovene peoples of the former Austro-Hungarian Monarchy have of their own free will determined to unite with Serbia in a permanent union for the purpose of forming a single sovereign independent State under the title of the Kingdom of the Serbs, Croats, and Slovenes, and

Whereas the Prince Regent of Serbia and the Serbian Government have agreed to this union and in consequence the Kingdom of the Serbs, Croats, and Slovenes has been constituted and has assumed sovereignty over the territories inhabited by these peoples, and

Whereas it is necessary to regulate certain matters of international concern arising out of the said additions of territory and of this union, and

Whereas it is desired to free Serbia from certain obligations which she undertook by the Treaty of Berlin of 1878 to certain Powers and to substitute for them obligations to the League of Nations, and

Whereas the Serb-Croat-Slovene State of its own free will desires to give to the populations of all territories included within the State, of whatever race, language, or religion they may be, full guarantees that they shall

*"Kingdom of the Serbs, Croats, and Slovenes, III, Extract from the Treaty between the United States of America, The British Empire, France, Italy, and Japan, and the Serb-Croat-Slovene State done at St.-Germain-en-Laye on September 10th, 1919," from League of Nations, *Protection of Linguistic, Racial, and Religious Minorities by the League of Nations, C.L.110.1927.I.Annexe, August 1927* (Publications de la Societé des Nations I.B, Minorités, 1927, I.B.2), pp. 60–63.

continue to be governed in accordance with the principles of liberty and justice;

For this purpose the High Contracting Parties have appointed as their Plenipotentiaries: [Here follow the names of the plenipotentiaries.]

Who, after having exchanged their full powers, found in good and due form, have agreed as follows:

The Principal Allied and Associated Powers, taking into consideration the obligations contracted under the present Treaty by the Serb-Croat-Slovene State, declare that the Serb-Croat-Slovene State is definitely discharged from the obligations undertaken in Article 35 of the Treaty of Berlin of July 13, 1878.

Article 1.

The Serb-Croat-Slovene State undertakes that the stipulations contained in Articles 2 to 8 of this Chapter shall be recognised as fundamental laws, and that no law, regulation, or official action shall conflict or interfere with these stipulations, nor shall any law, regulation, or official action prevail over them.

Article 2.

The Serb-Croat-Slovene State undertakes to assure full and complete protection of life and liberty to all inhabitants of the Kingdom without distinction of birth, nationality, language, race, or religion.

All inhabitants of the Kingdom of the Serbs, Croats, and Slovenes shall be entitled to the free exercise, whether public or private, of any creed, religion, or belief, whose practices are not inconsistent with public order or public morals.

Article 3.

Subject to the special provisions of the Treaties mentioned below the Serb-Croat-Slovene State admits and declares to be Serb-Croat-Slovene nationals ipso facto and without the requirement of any formality Austrian, Hungarian, or Bulgarian nationals habitually resident or possessing rights of citizenship [*pertinenza, Heimatsrecht*] as the case may be at the date of the coming into force of the present Treaty in territory which is or may be recognised as forming part of the Serb-Croat-Slovene State under the Treaties with Austria, Hungary, or Bulgaria respectively, or under any Treaties which may be concluded for the purpose of completing the present settlement.

Nevertheless, the persons referred to above who are over eighteen years of age will be entitled under the conditions contained in the said Treaties to opt for any other nationality which may be open to them. Option by a husband will cover his wife and option by parents will cover their children under eighteen years of age

Persons who have exercised the above right to opt must within the succeeding twelve months transfer their place of residence to the State for which they have opted. They will be entitled to retain their immovable property in the territory of the Serb-Croat-Slovene State. They may carry with them their movable property of every description. No export duties may be imposed upon them in connection with the removal of such property.

Article 4.

The Serb-Croat-Slovene State admits and declares to be Serb-Croat-Slovene nationals ipso facto and without the requirement of any formality persons of Austrian, Hungarian, or Bulgarian nationality who were born in the said territory of parents habitually resident or possessing rights of citizenship [*pertinenza, Heimatsrecht*] as the case may be there, even if at the date of the coming into force of the present Treaty they are not themselves habitually resident or did not possess rights of citizenship there.

Nevertheless, within two years after the coming into force of the present Treaty, these persons may make a declaration before the competent Serb-Croat-Slovene authorities in the country in which they are resident, stating that they abandon Serb-Croat-Slovene nationality, and they will then cease to be considered as Serb-Croat-Slovene nationals. In this connection a declaration by a husband will cover his wife, and a declaration by parents will cover their children under eighteen years of age.

Article 5.

The Serb-Croat-Slovene State undertakes to put no hindrance in the way of the exercise of the right which the persons concerned have, under the Treaties concluded or to be concluded by the Allied and Associated Powers with Austria, Bulgaria, or Hungary, to choose whether or not they will acquire Serb-Croat-Slovene nationality.

Article 6.

All persons born in the territory of the Serb-Croat-Slovene State who are not born nationals of another State shall ipso facto become Serb-Croat-Slovene nationals.

Article 7.

All Serb-Croat-Slovene nationals shall be equal before the law and shall enjoy the same civil and political rights without distinction as to race, language, or religion.

Difference of religion, creed, or confession shall not prejudice any Serb-Croat-Slovene national in matters relating to the enjoyment of civil or political rights, as for instance admission to public employments, functions, and honors, or the exercise of professions and industries.

No restriction shall be imposed on the free use by any Serb-Croat-Slovene national of any language in private intercourse, in commerce, in religion, in the press or in publications of any kind, or at public meetings.

Notwithstanding any establishment by the Serb-Croat-Slovene Government of an official language, adequate facilities shall be given to Serb-Croat-Slovene nationals of other speech than that of the official language for the use of their own language, either orally or in writing, before the courts.

Article 8.

Serb-Croat-Slovene nationals who belong to racial, religious, or linguistic minorities shall enjoy the same treatment and security in law and in fact as the other Serb-Croat-Slovene nationals. In particular they shall have an equal right to establish, manage, and control at their own expense charitable, religious, and social institutions, schools and other educational establishments, with the right to use their own language and to exercise their religion freely therein.

Article 9.

The Serb-Croat-Slovene Government will provide in the public educational system in towns and districts in which a considerable proportion of Serb-Croat-Slovene nationals of other speech than that of the official language are resident adequate facilities for ensuring that in the primary schools the instruction shall be given to the children of such Serb-Croat-Slovene nationals through the medium of their own language. This provision shall not prevent the Serb-Croat-Slovene Government from making the teaching of the official language obligatory in the said schools.

In towns and districts where there is a considerable proportion of Serb-Croat-Slovene nationals belonging to racial, religious, or linguistic minorities, these minorities shall be assured an equitable share in the enjoyment and application of the sums which may be provided out of public funds under the State, municipal, or other budget for educational, religious, or charitable purposes.

The provisions of the present Article apply only to territory transferred to Serbia or the Kingdom of Serbs, Croats, and Slovenes since January 1, 1913.

Article 10.

The Serb-Croat-Slovene State agrees to grant to the Musulmans in the matter of family law and personal status provisions suitable for regulating these matters in accordance with Musulman usage.

The Serb-Croat-Slovene State shall take measures to assure the nomination of a Reiss-Ul-Ulema.

The Serb-Croat-Slovene State undertakes to ensure protection to the mosques, cemeteries, and other Musulman religious establishments. Full recognition and facilities shall be assured to Musulman pious foundations [Wakfs] and religious and charitable establishments now existing, and the Serb-Croat-Slovene Government shall not refuse any of the necessary facilities for the creation of new religious and charitable establishments guaranteed to other private establishments of this nature.

Article 11.

The Serb-Croat-Slovene State agrees that the stipulations in the foregoing Articles, so far as they affect persons belonging to racial, religious, or linguistic minorities, constitute obligations of international concern and shall be placed under the guarantee of the League of Nations. They shall not be modified without the consent of the Council of the League of Nations. The United States, the British Empire, France, Italy, and Japan hereby agree not to withhold their assent from any modification in these Articles which is in due form assented to by a majority of the Council of the League of Nations.

The Serb-Croat-Slovene State agrees that any Member of the Council of the League of Nations shall have the right to bring to the attention of the Council any infraction, or any danger of infraction, of any of these obligations, and that the Council may thereupon take such action and give such directions as it may deem proper and effective in the circumstances.

The Serb-Croat-Slovene State further agrees that any difference of opinion as to questions of law or fact arising out of these Articles between the Serb-Croat-Slovene State and any one of the Principal Allied and Associated Powers or any other Power, a Member of the Council of the League of Nations, shall be held to be a dispute of an international character under Article 14 of the Covenant of the League of Nations. The Serb-Croat-Slovene State hereby consents that any such dispute shall, if the other party thereto demands, be referred to the Permanent Court of International Justice. The decision of the Permanent Court shall be final and shall have the same force and effect as an award under Article 13 of the Covenant.

APPENDIX 3 CONSTITUTION OF THE KINGDOM OF SERBS, CROATS, AND SLOVENES, 1921* *(Excerpts)*

Article 4.

Only one citizenship exists in the entire Kingdom. All citizens are equal before the law. All enjoy the same protection of the authorities.

Article 12.

Freedom of religion and conscience is guaranteed. Accepted religions are equal before the law and may exercise their religion publicly.

The enjoyment of civil and political rights is not dependent upon the exercise of one's religion. No one may be freed from his civic and military duties and obligations by invoking the precepts of his religion.

Those religions are accepted which, in whatever part of the Kingdom, have already received legal recognition. Other religions may only be recognized by law. Accepted and recognized religions regulate their internal religious affairs autonomously and administer their endowments and funds within the limits of the law.

No one is obligated to practice his religion publicly. No one is obligated to participate in religious acts, ceremonies, practices, and exercises, except with regard to state holidays and ceremonies and insofar as the law regulates it for persons who are subject to paternal, guardian, or military authority.

Accepted and recognized religions may maintain ties with their supreme religious leader even outside the border of the state, insofar as the spiritual prescriptions of certain religions require. The manner in which these relations will be maintained will be regulated by law.

Insofar as resources in the state budget are provided for religious pur-

*Constitution of the Kingdom of Serbs, Croats, and Slovenes (June 28,1921). Source: Djordje Jelenić, *Nova Srbija i Jugoslavija* (Belgrade: Državna štamparija, 1923), pp. 425–27; Nikodie Yovanovitch, *Étude sur la Constitution du Royaume des Serbs, Croates et Slovènes du 28 juin 1921* (Paris: Ernest Sagot et Cie, 1924), pp. 357–58. Identical wording also is to be founded in Articles 4 and 11 of the Constitution of the Kingdom of Yugoslavia (September 3, 1931). See Deyan Loutzitch, *La Constitution du Royaume de Yougoslavie du 3 septembre 1931* (Paris: Éditions Pierre Bossuet, 1933), pp. 263–64.

poses, they must be divided among the various accepted and recognized religions in proportion to the number of their adherents and actual demonstrated needs.

Religious officials may not use their spiritual authority for partisan purposes, whether in places of worship or writings of a religious character or otherwise in the conduct of their official duties.

APPENDIX 4 LAW ON THE RELIGIOUS COMMUNITY OF JEWS IN THE KINGDOM OF YUGOSLAVIA, 1929*

We, Alexander I, by the grace of God and the will of the People, King of Yugoslavia, upon the proposal of Our Minister of Justice and in agreement with the President of Our Ministerial Council order and proclaim: the Law on the Religious Community of Jews in the Kingdom of Yugoslavia.

1. The religious community of Jews in the Kingdom of Yugoslavia is composed of all members of the Jewish faith who live in the Kingdom of Yugoslavia. Its members have full freedom of public exercise of their religion.

Religious Communities and Their Central Representations

2. Members of the religious community of Jews are organized according to religious communities [parishes] which have the task of taking care of the religious and cultural needs of their members. All religious communities, except the Orthodox, form the Federation of Jewish Religious Communities, and the Orthodox form the Union of Orthodox Jewish Religious Communities.

The internal organization of the Federation of Jewish Religious Communities and the Union of Orthodox Jewish Religious Communities, as well as individual religious communities, their rights and duties are regulated according to statutes which the Federation of Jewish Religious Communities or the Union of Orthodox Jewish Religious Communities, as well as each community, draws up for itself, and the Minister of Justice ratifies, upon the suggestion of the Federation of Jewish Religious Communities or the Union of Orthodox Jewish Religious Communities for the communities. The same is also valid with regard to revision of statutes.

3. The Jewish religious communities, as well as the Federation of Jewish Religious Communities or the Union of Orthodox Jewish Religious Com-

*Zakon o verskoj zajednici Jevreja u Kraljevini Jugoslavije (Belgrade: Štamparija Feniks, 1930).

munities, are autonomous bodies which independently administer their own religioadministrative, cultural, and charitable institutions, as well as religious property and religious funds, but under the supreme authority of the state. They decide independently on the acceptance of endowments which are intended for religious purposes, and administer them under the supervision of the authorities on religious endowments, according to the Law on Religious Endowments.

The Federation of Jewish Religious Communities, the Union of Orthodox Jewish Religious Communities, and the religious communities are legal persons and according to regulations of the Law are able to acquire and possess both movable and immovable property and to exercise all rights which belong to them.

4. Jewish religious communities and their Federation and Union independently exercise control over their own revenues and expenses, including the handling of all bookkeeping, which the Minister of Justice will regulate by decree, and submit them, according to the decree of the second paragraph of Article 2 of the Law on Central Control, insofar as Central Control is empowered to control expenditure of revenues in review, according to decreed needs, whether at the request of the Minister of Justice or the religious communities and their Federation or Union themselves.

5. Each religious community of the one or the other religious rite has its own district, and its members are all the Jews of both sexes who live in that district and belong to its rite.

One part may separate from the district of one religious community for the purpose of creating a new community of the other religious rite or uniting with an already existing community of the other religious rite, if at least twenty members of the community who are of age and self-supporting demand this and if it is proven that the separation is being conducted only out of religious motivation and that in the event of the formation of a new community there will be sufficient means for the support of its functionaries and the work of its institutions.

Religious communities which lack sufficient means for the work of the necessary institutions and the support of functionaries may be dissolved and their property and territory given over to the neighboring communities or to one of them, but only to those which are of the same rite.

Decisions on the founding, dividing, uniting, and dissolving of communities are made by the Minister of Justice upon the recommendation of the Federation or Union, in agreement with the interested communities, or in the case of the formation of a new community, in agreement with the members who seek to form that new community.

6. The Federation and Union are the central organs and representatives of all Jewish religious communities of all religious rites in the Kingdom of Yugoslavia. They mediate in official communication between the central state authorities and the religious communities and represent them before those authorities. Upon the request of the Minister of Justice, they give opinions on proposed laws and decrees which pertain to the Religious Community of Jews.

In the statutes of the Federation and Union, which will be drawn up according to the regulations of the second paragraph of Article 2, the organization of the Administration of the Federation and the Union and their sphere of action will be regulated.

7. All organizations of the Religious Community of Jews execute their own decisions themselves and collect their own revenues.

At their request, the state and self-governing authorities will give their administrative assistance in the executing of their decisions and judgments issued with authority and based on full power according to law and will settle all properly assessed taxes.

8. The statutes of religious communities, provided for in the second paragraph of Article 2, must include these basic provisions:

1) district and residence of the community, communal representation, and authorized registry bureau;

2) rights and duties of communal members, especially with regard to electoral rights;

3) composition and manner of election of the administration and length of its term of office, as well as the sphere of activity of its individual organs;

4) manner of hiring (electing) rabbis, regulations on their rights and duties, and further the means of hiring other functionaries, as well, with definition of their rights and duties, and disciplinary regulations for functionaries;

5) manner of carrying out instruction in religious knowledge;

6) regulations on private prayerhouses and religious gatherings;

7) regulations on material support for religious institutions of members of special rites, if such exist within the community;

8) manner of assessing contributions and collecting means to support the community and its institutions;

9) pension statute for functionaries and their families;

10) procedure for revision of statutes.

Property, Revenues, and Expenses of Jewish Religious Communities and Their Federation and Union

9. The material means which are needed by the Jewish religious communities and their Federation and Union for the implementation of their tasks are defrayed by:

1) revenues from their property;

2) religious taxes and contributions;

3) donations and gifts, as well as incomes from [religious] endowments and funds and future assessment of this property;

4) future donations of political-administrative bodies [municipalities];

5) regular state subsidies.

State aid will be established by special decree of the Minister of Justice in conjunction with the Minister of Finance, upon consultation with the Federation and the Union, and on the basis of actual need and the appropriation provided for in the state budget of expenses for the year 1929/30. This subsidy will be paid out via the Federation and Union proportionally according to the number of members in all their communities.

The political-administrative municipalities which in their annual budgets provide regular subsidies for religious purposes will allot such a subsidy proportionally to the Jewish religious communities which are to be found there as well.

10. Buildings intended for the service of God, religious, religioeducational, and charitable institutions, communal buildings in which are located religious authorities, institutions, or the apartments of the clergy, and Jewish cultural-historical monuments are freed from all public taxes.

11. Official correspondence and related mail of the Jewish religious communities and their Federation and Union, as well as rabbinical authorities and the Chief Rabbi, are freed from paying postal and telegraph taxes.

12. All Jews of both sexes who have their own property or income, as well as those who are capable of supporting themselves by earning a living, are obligated to pay all types of religious contributions and taxes to cover the needs of their religious community and its institutions.

Also those Jews of both sexes who do not live in the territory of the religious community of their rite but own property in it or lease some property or engage in some artisan, commercial, or industrial enterprise there are obliged to pay these contributions and taxes.

In the event that a member withdraws from his community and joins another Jewish community which exists in the same place, he is obligated until the end of five budget years after the year of his withdrawal to pay the communal contributions and taxes of that community from which he withdrew, in the amount to which he was indebted at the time of withdrawal. This holds valid also in the case of paragraph 2 of Article 5.

Spiritual and Religious Autonomous Representatives and Functionaries

13. The spiritual head of the Religious Community of Jews in the Kingdom of Yugoslavia is the Chief Rabbi with headquarters in Belgrade. He is appointed by Royal Decree upon the recommendation of the Minister of Justice from among three candidates chosen by the joint Central Committees of the Federation and Union, the presidents of the religious communities of all religious rites in Belgrade, Zagreb, Skoplje, Sarajevo, Novi Sad, Subotica, and Osijek, insofar as they are not represented in the Central Committees, and all rabbis who are employed in Jewish religious institutions in the Kingdom.

If the position of Chief Rabbi is vacated, within a period of six months at the most the election of candidates for the new Chief Rabbi must be executed. Until the election of this Chief Rabbi, his office will be conducted by a rabbi appointed by the Minister of Justice upon the recommendation of the Central Committees of the Federation and Union, made in agreement with both Rabbinical Synods.

The salary of the Chief Rabbi and the personal and material expenses of the Chief Rabbinate are established in the subvention which the state gives to the Religious Community of Jews, set apart from the remaining sum of that subvention.

The Chief Rabbi has the right to the pension of civil servants in group

1, category 1. His personal pension, as well as the family pension after his death, will be paid from the state budget according to the regulations of the Law on Civil Servants and Other State Employees of civilian rank.

14. The Chief Rabbi is the president of both Rabbinical Synods, of which one is composed of three members and two substitutes, elected among the rabbis of the Orthodox religious rite, and the other of five members and three substitutes, elected among the remaining rabbis. They are elected by an assembly of rabbis of the one and the other religious rite.

The rabbinical synods under the presidency of the Chief Rabbi give opinions on all questions of a religious character which are conveyed by the Central Committees of the Federation and Union.

If the Central Committee of the Federation does not adopt the opinion of its Rabbinical Synod, the final decision is made by a special committee to which belong the six members of the Rabbinical Synod, including the Chief Rabbi, and six nonrabbinic members of the Central Committee of the Federation who are appointed by the administration of the Federation. The Chief Rabbi presides over the special committee and a decision is reached by a simple majority of votes.

15. The spiritual heads of the religious communities are the rabbis. In the communities belonging to the Federation, they are virilist [or ex officio] members of the communal councils whenever they are deciding religious questions. In Orthodox communities, rabbis are virilist members of communal councils in general. The communal council decides religious questions in the first stage.

16. Rabbis and other religious functionaries are appointed by decree of the executive of the religious communities permanently or temporarily. Provisional status may not last longer than three years for rabbis and five years for other functionaries.

A permanently hired rabbi or other religious functionary may not be dismissed from service, except on the basis of an executed disciplinary judgment, pronounced according to the disciplinary procedure in the statutes of the community concerned and the Federation or Union.

17. The rabbis and other spiritual persons are not obligated personally to carry out those public duties which according to Jewish religious codes are not in accord with their rank and calling.

18. Official religious functions, whether in the religious community or in state service, may be performed by persons who have those qualifications which the Chief Rabbi prescribes and evaluates along with the Rabbinical Synod concerned.

Foreign citizens may be hired as officials and functionaries of the religious communities only on a temporary basis and only with permission of the Minister of Justice.

19. The functions of the executives of the Federation and Union, as well as of individual communities, are honorary.

Persons who are convicted or are under criminal investigation for criminal activity of a dishonorable nature, as well as those who go into bankruptcy or are under guardianship, may not be elected or carry out their duties during the duration of this hinderance.

20. Disciplinary misconducts of rabbis and other functionaries of reli-

gious communities are treated according to the statutes of the religious community concerned and the statutes of the Federation and Union.

The religious communities belonging to the Federation decide on the disciplinary misconducts of their own religious functionaries, except rabbis.

The Federation decides in the second and final stage on complaints about the decisions of its religious communities, and in the first and final stage about the disciplinary misconducts of the rabbis of its communities.

The Orthodox Rabbinical Synod judges the disciplinary misconducts of Orthodox rabbis and other religious functionaries of Orthodox communities.

The Rabbinical Synod in its official duties may also originate disciplinary procedures against rabbis and other religious functionaries.

State authorities which conduct criminal investigations against religious-autonomous functionaries will report on the matter, as well as on the final results of the investigation, to the Chief Rabbi and the Federation or Union.

Religious Education and Theological Schools

21. In all state and private schools attended by pupils of the Jewish faith, Jewish education is taught in agreement with the responsible Jewish religious communities on the part of their religious organs and according to the regulations of the legal statutes on these schools.

Educational plans and programs for teaching religious knowledge are prescribed by the competent Minister, taking into consideration the needs of religious education according to the recommendations of the Federation and with regard to the followers of the Orthodox Jewish religious rite, according to the recommendation of the Synod of Orthodox Rabbis. The regulations of the law on textbooks will be in force for textbooks of religious knowledge. The Federation and Synod of Orthodox Rabbis will give their approval on all textbooks with regard to their religious content.

Qualified clergy may teach religious knowledge in state elementary schools as religious teachers in the sense of the regulations of the Law on Public Schools.

The Minister of Education appoints as religious teachers in all public schools clergy from the ranks of candidates proposed by the Federation or Synod of Orthodox Rabbis. The competent Minister appoints religious teachers in state secondary and technical schools among candidates who bear the approval of the Federation or the Synod of Orthodox Rabbis that they may teach religious knowledge in secondary schools. The Minister transfers or dismisses religious teachers from duty according to the regulations of the school law.

The administration of the school hires and transfers religious teachers in all private schools with the approval of the authorized Jewish religious community. The regulations of the school laws are also in force for these religious teachers.

The Federation or Synod of Orthodox Rabbis may rescind approval already granted from those religious teachers who do not teach religious knowledge as prescribed by the Jewish faith or who, otherwise, in their life and work do not fulfill their duties as religious teachers.

22. The Jewish Middle Theological Seminary is a recognized institution administered by the Federation.

In the event that such a seminary be founded for the Orthodox religious rite, it will be administered by the Union.

Insofar as such institutions do not provide the conditions for the training of rabbis, it is permitted to acquire preparation in foreign seminaries. The competent Rabbinical Synod will evaluate the qualification of these.

General Provisions

23. The official language of the Jewish religious communities and their central institutions is the official state language. In this language are kept both the religious records and all documents abstracted from them. These abstracts have the character of public documents.

24. No Jewish religious community may perform religious rites for members of another Jewish religious community of this Kingdom unless the [person] concerned presents evidence that he has fulfilled all his obligations to the community to which he belongs. The case of burial is excepted when due to distance and time it is not possible to wait for the submitting of these proofs.

25. The Jewish religious holidays on which state and municipal employees, the military, and students have exemptions according to law are:

1) Pesah [Passover], the first two days and the last two days;

2) Shavuoth [Pentecost], two days;

3) Rosh Hashanah [New Year], two days;

4) Yom Kippur [Day of Atonement], one and a half days (half day on the eve of Yom Kippur);

5) Sukkot [Tabernacles], first two days and last two days.

Temporary Provisions

26. The provision of the first paragraph of Article 5 in which it is provided that in one place there may not be more than one community of the same religious rite is not in force in those communities which already exist in any place on the day when this law goes into effect.

27. All Jewish religious communities must, on the basis of this law, within three months from when it goes into effect, draw up new statutes in conformity with the law, which they will submit to the Federation or Union for approval and in turn to the Minister of Justice for ratification.

28. When this law goes into effect, all laws, decrees, and other regulations regarding the subject of this law lose their validity.

29. This law goes into effect when the King signs it and it receives authoratative power when it is made public in the Official Gazette. (December 14, 1929, No.103860, Belgrade.)

APPENDIX 5 ANTI-JEWISH LEGISLATION, OCTOBER 1940*

Regulation concerning the measures which relate to Jews with respect to the operation of businesses involving objects of human sustenance

The Royal Government has prescribed the Regulation concerning measures which relate to Jews with respect to the operation of businesses involving human foodstuffs. The text of this Regulation reads:

Article 1

Commercial businesses which deal in wholesale trade with human foodstuffs, regardless of whether their owners are material or legal persons, are to be submitted to review if the owners of the businesses are Jews.

All those businesses are to be considered as businesses of Jews whose owners or co-owners are Jews on the day when this Regulation goes into effect or whose capital in whole or the majority thereof is in the hands of Jews.

Joint stock companies, companies with limited liability, and co-operatives are to be considered Jewish if the management, directors, and confidential clerks of the companies or co-operatives are, in the majority, Jews.

The competent general administrative authorities of the second grade or the Belgrade municipal authorities will carry out the review in their district.

Article 2

The competent authority in Article 1, paragraph 4 of this Regulation will make the decision as to which of the commercial businesses which are submitted to review according to Article 1 are forbidden further operation and which of them may be permitted to continue operation.

*"Uredbe i o uredbama protiv Jevreja," *Jevrejski glas,* vol. 13, no. 31 (October 16, 1940), pp. 1–3.

Against this decision there is no place for legal redress in administrative-judicial proceedings or for demands for any kinds of damages.

On the basis of the decision on forbidding further operation of commercial businesses from Article 1, paragraph 1, this Regulation issues authorization or permission for the operation of the respective businesses to be taken away and the businesses to erase their official indebtedness from the registry of businesses. The competent authority which will have made the decision on forbidding further operation will prescribe for the liquidation of current affairs of the respective businesses a set period which may not be longer than two months.

The competent courts, on the basis of the reports of the competent authorities on the banning of further operation, will carry out the cancellation from official indebtedness in the commercial registry or protocol of those businesses whose further operation is forbidden in paragraph 1 of this article.

Article 3

With regard to those industrial enterprises which deal in the production of wholesale human foodstuffs, which according to paragraphs 2 and 3 of Article 1 of this Regulation are to be considered as Jewish, the Ban (or Manager of the City of Belgrade) may assign commissaries at the expense of the enterprise, whose task will be to concern themselves with the correctness of the operation of the enterprise.

The injunctions which the commissary will issue in carrying out his duty will be binding on the management and employees of the firm.

The management and employees of the firm are obligated to give to the commissary on his demand all necessary information and to enable him to examine the business records, documents, and transcripts of the firm, as well as the business premises. The commissary is obligated to keep as an official secret all data which he discovers in the conduct of his task.

Article 4

Whoever, contrary to the decision of the competent authority on the banning of further operation of commercial businesses of Article 1 of this Regulation, continues with the operation of a forbidden business will be punished with imprisonment for two years and a monetary fine of 500,000 dinars [$10,000].

So too will be punished those Jews who make use of other persons merely as fictitious owners for the operation of commercial businesses in wholesale human foodstuffs, as well as persons who enable them on the basis of their right to operate such a commercial business.

The regular courts will pronounce the judgments.

The monetary fines paid will go for the use of the regional fund for the aid to vocational schools of Law No. 406 on businesses, or for the use of the corresponding fund for the administrative district of the City of Belgrade.

Article 5

The general administrative authorities of the first class may interrogate persons who contrary to the decision of the competent authority on the banning of further operation of commercial businesses of Article 1 of this

Regulation continue in the operation of the forbidden businesses, upon coerced stay in a second place, and persons who have already been convicted by one authorized body regarding Article 4, paragraph 1 of this Regulation may be interrogated regarding the coerced stay and the coerced operation.

With regard to the initiation of coerced stay, the appropriate prescription of the Regulation concerning the initiation of unscrupulous speculators in coerced stay and coerced work will be applied.

Article 6

From the day on which this Regulation goes into effect, permits may not be issued to Jews or companies with Jewish capital nor permission to operate commercial businesses dealing in wholesale human foodstuffs.

Article 7

This Regulation goes into effect on the day it appears in print in the Official Gazette.

Regulation on the limitation of schooling of persons of Jewish origin

The Ministerial Council has prescribed the Regulation on the enrollment of persons of Jewish origin as students of universities, high schools on the rank of universities, higher, middle, normal and other vocational schools. Text:

Article 1

At universities, high schools with the rank of universities, higher, middle, normal, and other vocational schools may be enrolled only a fixed number of pupils of Jewish origin. This number will be determined in such a way that they will be in proportion to the number of other pupils of this school in that ratio in which citizens of Jewish origin are to be found in proportion to the number of other citizens.

The highest school authority responsible for each individual type of school will determine according to paragraph 1 of this article how many pupils of Jewish origin, beginning with the school year 1940/41, may be enrolled in the first year for the first class in each faculty or other school. Paragraph 1 of this article will not be applied to pupils of Jewish origin enrolled in other years or classes.

Article 2

Persons of Jewish origin whose parents have served the fatherland may with the approval of the competent highest school authority enroll as students of universities and other schools mentioned in Article 1, paragraph 1, regardless of the limitation contained in the same regulation.

Article 3

Foreigners of Jewish origin may not enroll as students at universities or other schools listed in Article 1, paragraph 1 of this regulation.

Article 4

The competent highest school authorities are authorized to issue the necessary guidelines and explanations applicable to Articles 1, 2, and 3 of this Regulation.

Article 5

This Regulation goes into effect on the day it is published in the Official Gazette.

Abbreviations,
Bibliography, Notes,
and Index

ABBREVIATIONS

ABH   Arhiv Bosne i Hercegovine (Archive of Bosnia and Hercegovina)

AH   Arhiv Hrvatske (Archive of Croatia)

AJ   Arhiv Jugoslavije (Yugoslav National Archive)

ašk. (or Ashk.)   aškenaski (Ashkenazic)

BB   B'ne Brit (B'nai B'rith)

BG   Beograd (Belgrade)

BG-JL   Belgrade Jewish Library

BG-JM   Belgrade Jewish Museum

BiH (or BuH)   Bosna i Hercegovina (Bosnia and Hercegovina)

BL   Banja Luka

bog.   bogoštovni (religious)

br.   broj (number)

crk.-škol.   crkveno-školski (church-school)

CZA   Central Zionist Archives

F   fascicle

GP   Gradsko poglavarstvo (Municipal Government)

gosp.   gospojinsko (women's)

hrv.   hrvatski (Croatian)

IBO   izraelitska bogoštovna općina (Israelite Religious Community)

IFK   Izraelska ferijalna kolonija (Israelite Vacation Colony)

IRPH   Institut za radnički pokret Hrvatske (Institute for the Workers' Movement of Croatia)

Izr.   Izraelska or Izraelitska (Israelite)

jevr.   jevrejski (Jewish) (mainly eastern variant)

JO   jevrejska opština (Jewish Community)

JVO   jevrejska veroispovedna opština (Jewish Religious Community)

JSTZ	Jevrejski srednji teološki zavod (Jewish Middle Theological Seminary)
JŽD	Jevrejsko žensko društvo (Jewish Women's Society)
KBU (DB)	Kraljevinska banska uprava (drinske banovine) (Royal Provincial Administration of the Drina Province)
KH	Keren Hayesod (The Palestine Fund)
KJ	Kraljevina Jugoslavije (Kingdom of Yugoslavia)
KKL (or JNF)	Keren Kayemet L'israel (Jewish National Fund)
KPJ	Komunistička partija Jugoslavije (Yugoslav Communist Party)
kr(alj).	kraljevinski (royal)
KSHS	Kraljevina Srba, Hrvata i Slovenaca (Kingdom of Serbs, Croats, and Slovenes)
MCO	Mesna cionistička organizacija (Local Zionist Organization)
MP	Ministarstvo pravde (Ministry of Justice)
MPVO	Ministarstvo pravde versko odeljenje (Ministry of Justice, Religious Section)
MV	Ministarstvo vera (Ministry of Religions)
NCO	Nova cionistička organizacija (New Zionist Organization)
NOBB	Nezavisni orden B'ne Brit (Independent Order of B'nai Brith)
NS	Novi Sad
ODS	Opšta državna statistika (General State Statistics Bureau)
OS	Osijek
Pov.	povjerlino (Confidential)
prez.	prezidijal (Praesidium)
SA	Sarajevo
SA-JL	Sarajevo Jewish Library
SCKSHS	Savez cionista Kraljevine Srba, Hrvata i Slovenaca (Federation of Zionists of Kingdom of Serbs, Croats, and Slovenes)
SCJ	Savez cionista Jugoslavije (Federation of Zionists of Yugoslavia)
sef. (or Seph.)	sefardski (Sephardic)
SJO(J)	Savez jevrejskih opština Jugoslavije (Federation of Jewish Communities of Yugoslavia)
SJSPSP	Središnja jevrejska stanica za produktivnu socijalnu pomoć (Central Jewish Bureau for Productive Social Aid)
SJVO	Savez jevrejskih veroispovednih opština (Federation of Jewish Religious Communities)
SU	Subotica
SŽOU	Savez židovskih omladinskih udruženja (Federation of Jewish Youth Associations)
UOJVO	Udruženje ortodoksnih jevrejskih veroispovednih opština (Union of Orthodox Jewish Religious Communities)
VŽSO	Veliki župan sarajevske oblasti (Grand Prefect of the Sarajevo District)
VŽZ	Veliki župan Zagreba (Grand Prefect of Zagreb)

zagr. zagrebački (Zagreb)
ZG Zagreb
ZG-JL Zagreb Jewish Library
ZGU Zagreb University Library
ZO Zionist Organization (London or Jerusalem)
ZV(S) Zemaljska vlada (Regional Government) (Sarajevo)
žid. židovski (Jewish)(western variant)
ŽND Židovsko nacionalno (or narodno) društvo (Jewish Nation-
alist Society)

BIBLIOGRAPHY

Archives and Archival Collections

Arhiv Bosne i Hercegovine, Sarajevo
    Fond Zemaljske vlade Sarajeva (1919–20)
    Fond Pokrajinske uprave Sarajeva (1923)
    Fond Velikog župana sarajevske oblasti (1924–29)
    Fond Kraljevinske banske uprave drinske banovine (1929–40)
Arhiv grada Sarajeva, Sarajevo
    Fond Laura Bohoreta Papo
Arhiv grada Zagreba, Zagreb
    Fond Alexander Licht
    Fond Gradskog poglavarstva
Arhiv Hrvatske, Zagreb
    Fond Zemaljske vlade (JU-103) (1892–1925)
Arhiv Instituta za radnički pokret Hrvatske, Zagreb
    Fond Velikog župana Zagreba (VI/S, K38)
Arhiv Jugoslavije, Belgrade
    Fond Masonskih loža našoj zemlje (100, 18–24)
    Fond Ministarstva pravde (1929–41)
    Fond Ministarstva pravde versko odeljenje (F 182–85)
    Fond Ministarstva prosvete (66, F 74)
    Fond Ministarstva vera (69) (1921–29)
Central Zionist Archives, Jerusalem
    Z4–Correspondence of Zionist Organization, London
    S5–Correspondence of Organization Department, Jerusalem
    S6–Correspondence of Immigration Department, Jerusalem
    KH1–Keren Hayesod, Head Office, London (1920–26)
Jewish Historical Museum, Belgrade
    Entire Interwar Collection
Jewish Library, Belgrade
Jewish Library, Sarajevo

Jewish Library, Zagreb
Zagreb University Library, Zagreb

Primary Sources

GOVERNMENT AND OFFICIAL PUBLICATIONS

Bosnische Bote. Vols. 2–21. Sarajevo, 1898–1917.

C. i kr. zajedničko ministarstvo financija. *Izvještaj o upravi BiH.* [Report on the administration of B–H.] Sarajevo: Zemaljska štamparija, 1907–11.

Direkcija državne statistike u Beogradu. *Prethodni rezultati popisa stanovništva u KSHS od 31 januara 1921 godine.* [Preliminary results of the 1921 census.] Sarajevo: Državna štamparija, 1924.

Germany. Publikationsstelle Wien. *Die Gliederung der Bevölkerung des ehemaligen Jugoslawien nach Muttersprache und Konfession (nach den unveröffentlichen Angaben der Zählung von 1931).* Vienna, 1943.

K. u k. gemeinsames Finanzministerium. *Bericht über die Verwaltung von BuH.* Vienna: K.K. Hof- und Staats-Druckerei, 1906, 1913, 1917.

Ko je ko u Jugoslaviji. [Who's who in Yugoslavia.] Belgrade: Jugoslovenski godišnjak and Zagreb: Nova Evropa, 1928.

Kraljevina Jugoslavije, Ministarstvo inostranih dela. *La Yougoslavie d'Aujourd'-hui.* Belgrade, 1935.

Kraljevina Jugoslavije, Opšta državna statistika. *Definitivni rezultati popisa stanovništva od 31 januara 1921 godine.* [Definitive results of the 1921 census.] Sarajevo: Državna štamparija, 1932.

―――. *Definitivni rezultati popisa stanovništva od 31 marta 1931 godine.* vol.2: Prisutno stanovništvo po veroispovesti. [Present population by religion.] Belgrade: Državna štamparija, 1938.

―――. *Definitivni rezultati popisa stanovništva od 31 marta 1931 godine.* vol.4: Prisutno stanovništvo po glavnom zanimanju. [Present population by principal occupation.] Sarajevo: Državna štamparija, 1940.

―――. *Prethodni rezultati popisa stanovništva od 31 marta 1931 godine.* Belgrade: Državna štamparija, 1931.

―――. *Statistički godišnjak.* vols. 1–11. Belgrade: Državna štamparija, 1929–40.

―――. *Statistički pregled Kraljevine Jugoslavije po banovima.* Belgrade: Državna štamparija, 1930.

Landesregierung für BuH. *Die Ergebnisse der Volkszählung in BuH vom 10. Oktober 1910.* Sarajevo: Landesdruckerei, 1912.

―――. *Hauptresultate der Volkszählung in BuH vom 22. April 1895.* Sarajevo: Landesdruckerei, 1896.

Ortschafts- und Bevölkerungs-Statistik von BuH. Sarajevo: K. u K. Regierungsdruckerei, 1880.

Ortschafts- und Bevölkerungs-Statistik von BuH nach dem Volkszählungs-Ergebnisse vom 1. Mai 1885. Sarajevo: Landesdruckerei, 1886.

Statistički godišnjak Kraljevine Hrvatske i Slavonije. [Statistical annual of the Kingdom of Croatia and Slavonia.] vol.1 (1905). Zagreb: Kr. zemaljska tiskara, 1913.

Statistički godišnjak Kraljevine Srbije 1907–8. Belgrade: Državna štamparija Kraljevine Srbije, 1913.

Statistika industrije Kraljevine Jugoslavije. [Statistics of industry in the Kingdom of Yugoslavia.] Belgrade: Ministarstvo trgovine i industrije, 1941.

Statistika Kraljevine Srbije. vol.12: Popis stanovništva u Kraljevini Srbiji od 31 decembra 1895 godine. Belgrade: Ministarstvo narodne privrede, 1899.

Trgovačka i obrtnička komora u Zagrebu. *Izvještaj o poslovanju Trgovačke i obrtničke komore u Zagrebu.* [Report on the activities of the Chamber of Trade and Commerce in Zagreb.] Zagreb: Tisak Hrvatskog štamparskog zavoda, 1923–37.

Who's Who in Central and East Europe. 1st and 2nd eds. 1933/34, 1935/36. Zurich. 2 vols.

Yugoslavia Trade Year Book. Belgrade: Beletra, 1935.

BROCHURES, PAMPHLETS, AND PUBLICATIONS

Alkalaj, D. *O cionizmu, njegov značaj i razvitak.* [On Zionism, its significance and development.] Belgrade: Štamparija Milorada Stefanovica, 1910.

Altaraz, I. *Cijonizam, njegovo biće i njegova organizacija.* [Zionism, its nature and its organization.] 2nd ed. Zagreb: Tiskara Merkur, 1919.

———. *Omladinski pokret, ideje i smjernice.* [The youth movement, ideas, and directions.] Zagreb: Judeja, 1919.

Atijas, S. *Jevreji, državna politika i Ustavotvorna skupština.* [The Jews, state politics, and the Constituent Assembly.] Sarajevo: Štamparija Daniel A. Kajon, 1920.

Balkanska konferencija sefardskih Jevreja. [Balkan conference of Sephardic Jews.] Belgrade: Štamparija Karić, 1930.

Ciljevi NOBB. [The goals of the Independent Order of B'nai Brith.] Belgrade: Štamparija Dositije Obradović, 1911.

Delić, Rista St. *Jevreji u Jugoslaviji.* [The Jews in Yugoslavia.] Belgrade: Prosveta, 1939.

Dimitrijević, Mica, ed. *Naši Jevreji, Jevrejsko pitanje kod nas.* [Our Jews, the Jewish question among us.] Belgrade: Štamparija Minerva, 1940.

Društveni propisi Izraelske ferijalne kolonije u Zagrebu. [Statutes of the Society Israelite Vacation Colony in Zagreb.] Zagreb: Tisak Adolf Engel, 1924.

Gajić, E. B. *Jugoslavija i "jevrejski problem".* [Yugoslavia and the Jewish problem.] Belgrade: Štamparija Drag. Gregorića, 1938.

Godišnjak izdaju Jevrejsko kulturno-prosvetno društvo La Benevolencia u Sarajevu i Dobrotvorno društvo Potpora u Beogradu. [Annual published by the Jewish cultural-educational society La Benevolencia and charitable society Potpora.] Sarajevo: Štamparija Menahem Papo, 1933.

Godišnjak Izraelitske bogoštovne opcine zagrebačke. [Annual of the Israelite Religious Community of Zagreb.] Zagreb: Jugoslavenska štampa, 1928.

Godišnje izvještje Izrajelitske glavne učione u Zagrebu. [Annual report of Israelite school in Zagreb.] Zagreb, 1869–74.

Godišnje izvješće obospolne Javne izraelitske pučne škole u Zagrebu. Zagreb, 1880–81.

Godišnje izvješće obospolne Izraelitske konfesionalne škole u Zagrebu. Zagreb, 1884–1914.

Grünbaum, Jichak. *Naša doba, Doba odluka.* [Our times, times of decisions.] Zagreb: Biblioteka Židov, 1936.

Gur-Ari, Jichak. *Rabi Jehuda (ben Salomon) Haj Alkalaj.* Zagreb: Biblioteka Židov, 1931.

Hašomer Hacair. Zagreb: Biblioteka Hanoar, 1932.

Hinković, Hinko. *The Jugoslav Problem.* Reprinted from *The World Court,* 1918.

Informativna biblioteka WIZO. *Omladina.* [Youth.] Zagreb: Savez cionističkih žena, 1940.

Istine i zablude o cijonismu. [Truths and misconceptions on Zionism.] Belgrade: Mesna cijonistička organizacija, 1936.

Izraelitički molitvenik. Trans. Gavro Schwarz. Zagreb: Knjižara Lav. Hartmana, 1902.

Izraelski molitvenik. Zagreb: Knjižara Lav. Hartmana, 1892.

Izvještaj Bar Giora društva Židova akademičara iz jugoslavenskih zemalja u Beču. [Report of Bar Giora, society of Jewish students from the South Slav lands in Vienna.] Vienna, 1904, 1906, 1907, 1912.

Izvještaj Izraelitskog hrvatskog literarnoga društva u Zagrebu za godine 1904, 1905 i 1906. [Report of the Israelite Croatian Literary Society in Zagreb.] Ed. G. Schwarz. Zagreb: Tisak Ign. Granitza, 1907.

Izvještaj Izraelske ferijalne kolonije. [Report of the Israelite Vacation Colony.] Zagreb: Tiskara Merkur, 1921, 1923.

Izvještaj Judeje, Židovskog akademskog kulturnog kluba u Zagrebu za godinu 5670–1909/10. [Report of Judeja, Jewish academic cultural club in Zagreb.] Zagreb: Dionička tiskara, 1910.

Izveštaj o radu Uprave crkveno-školske jevrejske opštine u Beogradu za period 1922–23. [Report on the work of the administration of the Church-school Jewish Community in Belgrade.] Belgrade: Štamparija M. Karića, 1924.

Izveštaj o radu Uprave crkveno-školske jevrejske opštine u Beogradu za period vremena od 11 juna 1924 do 27 juna 1926 godine. Belgrade: M. Karić, 1926.

Izveštaj o radu Uprave crkveno-školske jevrejske opštine u Beogradu za period vremena od 27 juna 1926 do 26 maja 1929 godine. Belgrade: Štamparija Planeta, 1929.

Izveštaj o radu Uprave crkveno-školske jevrejske opštine u Beogradu za period vremena od 10 juna 1929 do 20 maja 1932. Belgrade: Štamparija Merkur, 1932.

Izveštaj sa svečanosti o prijemu dužnosti novoizabrane Uprave i Odbora crkveno-školske jevrejske opštine u Beogradu, 3 jula 1932. [Report on the ceremony of the taking of office of the newly elected board and council of the Belgrade Jewish community.] Belgrade: Štamparija Polet, 1932.

Jacobi, H. *Biblijska povjesnica za izraelsku mladež pučkih i nižih srednjih škola.* [Biblical history for Israelite youth in elementary and lower secondary schools.] Zagreb: Pokrajinska uprava za Hrvatsku i Slavoniju, 1884, 1901, 1923.

————. *Derech hakodeš, Katekizam mojsijeve vjere.* [The holy way, a catechism of the Mosaic religion.] Zagreb: Pokrajinska uprava za Hrvatsku i Slavoniju, 1886, 1900, 1923.

Jevrejsko žensko društvo u Beogradu, 1874–1924. [Jewish women's society in Belgrade.] Belgrade: Uprava Jevrejskog ženskog društva, 1924.

Kadima i njen rad. [Kadima and its work.] Zagreb: SŽOU, 1938.

Kalderon, Solomon and Levi, Juda. *Istorija jevrejskog naroda.* vol. 2: Od izgona Jevreja sa Pirinejskog poluostrva do najnovijeg vremena. [History of the Jewish people. From the expulsion of the Jews from the Iberian peninsula to modern times.] Belgrade: SJVO, 1935.

Kajon, J.A. *Sefardi do danas.* [The Sephardim until today.] Zagreb: Biblioteka Esperanza, 1927.

Kamhi, S. *Sefardi i sefardski pokret.* [The Sephardim and the Sephardic movement.] Zagreb: Biblioteka Esperanza, 1927.

Koen, D.A. *Besede posvećene Srpskoj omladini mojsijeve vere.* [Addresses dedicated to the Serbian youth of the Mosaic faith.] Belgrade: Štamparija Sv. Nikolića, 1897.

Kraus, Oton. *Židovsko pitanje i sionizam.* [The Jewish question and Zionism.] Zagreb: Knjižara Gjure Trpinca, 1904.

Licht, Aleksandar. *O mržnji i o izbavljenju.* [On hatred and on deliverance.] Zagreb: Biblioteka Židov, 1937.

———. *Potrebe i zahtevi.* [Needs and demands.] Zagreb: Tiskara Merkur, 1919.

Molitvenik. [Prayerbook.] Trans. and ed. Šalom M. Freiberger. Zagreb: Tiskara Merkantile, 1938.

Palestine Foundation Fund [Keren Hajesod], Centralna uprava za Jugoslaviju. *Izveštaj o radu u 1926–27 godine.* Belgrade, 1927.

———. *Izveštaj o radu u 1927–28 godine.* Belgrade, 1928.

———. *Izveštaj o radu u 1929–30 godine.* Belgrade, 1930.

Pravila Chevre Kadiše aškenaskih Židova u Sarajevu. [Statutes of the Hevra Kaddisha of the Ashkenazic Jews in Sarajevo.] Sarajevo: Štamparija B. Buchwald, 1928.

Pravila crkveno-školske jevrejske opštine u Beogradu. Belgrade: Štamparija S. Horovica, 1894.

Pravila crkveno-školske jevrejske opštine u Beogradu. Belgrade: Štamparija M. Karića, 1926.

Pravila Društva Bet Tefila. Sarajevo: Zadružna tiskara, 1913.

Pravila Društva Hesed Šel Emet (1910). Belgrade: Štamparija M. Karića, 1923.

Pravila Društva Oneg Šabat i Gemilut Hasadim. Belgrade: Štamparija Dositije Obradović, 1921.

Pravila Društva Potpora. Belgrade, 1936.

Pravila Društva Rehica Gedola u Beogradu. Belgrade: Štamparija M. Karića, 1919.

Pravila Hevre Kadiše u Zagrebu. Zagreb: Tiskara A. Engel, 1924.

Pravila Jevrejskog društva Milosrdje za pomaganje bednih. Belgrade: Štamparija Merkur, 1928.

Pravila Jevrejskog kulturnog i humanog društva Šemaja Demajo u Beogradu. Belgrade: Štamparija Drag. Gregorica, 1933.

Pravila Jevrejske veroispovedne opštine aškenaskog obreda u Sarajevu. Sarajevo: Štamparija B. Buchwald, 1923.

Pravila Jevrejske veroispovedne opštine sefardskog obreda u Sarajevu. Sarajevo, 1922.

Pravila kreditne zadruge Melaha. Sarajevo: Menahem Papo, n.d.

Pravila za Chebra Kadischa u Zagrebu. Zagreb: Tiskara Weiser, 1913.

Prvi izvještaj Jevrejskog srednjeg teološkog zavoda u Sarajevu za školske godine 1928–29 i 1929–30. [First report of the Jewish Middle Theological Seminary in Sarajevo.] Ed. Moric Levi. Sarajevo: Štamparija Papo, 1930.

Radić, Stjepan. *O Židovima.* [On Jews.] Zagreb: Kamnik, 1938.

Sachs, Vladimir. *Izraeličani i kršćansko-socijalni kulturni program.* [The Israelites and the Christian-Socialist cultural program.] Varaždin, 1910.

Savez cijonista. *Izveštaj Saveznog odbora vijeću Saveza cijonista u KSHS u Subotici, dne*

4 i 5 decembra 1927. [Report of the central committee to the conference of the Federation of Zionists.] Zagreb, 1927.

———. *Izveštaj Glavnog odbora Saveznom vijeću SCKSHS u Beogradu dne 31 marta i 1 aprila 1929.* Zagreb, 1929.

———. *Izveštaj Glavnog odbora Saveznom vijeću SCJ u Novom Sadu dne 7 i 8 decembra 1930.* Zagreb, 1930.

———. *Izveštaj SCJ Saveznom vijeću u Novom Sadu 12 i 13 maja 1935.* Zagreb, 1935.

———. *Izveštaj SCJ Saveznom vijeću u Banjoj Luci 24, 25 i 26 decembra 1939.* Zagreb, 1939.

Savez jevrejskih veroispovednih opština. *Izveštaj Glavnog i Izvesnog odbora i Izveštaj blagajne, IV redovan kongres, dne 25 i 26 decembra 1930.* [Report of the central and executive committees and report of treasurer, IV Regular Congress of SJVO.] Belgrade: Štamparija Karić, 1930.

———. *Izveštaj Glavnog i Izvršnog odbora i Izveštaj blagajne, V redovan kongres, dne 2 i 3 aprila 1933.* Belgrade: Štamparija Polet, 1933.

———. *Izveštaj o radu u godinama 1933–1936, VI kongres.* Belgrade: Prosveta, 1936.

———. *Izveštaji Izvršnog odbora za sednicu Glavnog odbora 23, 24 i 25 januara 1938 u Zagrebu.* Belgrade: Štamparija Beletra, 1938.

———. *Izveštaj Glavnog odbora VII kongresu 23 i 24 aprila 1939 godine.* Belgrade: Štamparija Beletra, 1939.

Schwarz, Gavro. *Obredi izraelske vjere.* [Customs of the Israelite faith.] Zagreb: Tiskara Narodnih novina, 1916, 1924.

———. *Prilozi k povjesti Židova u Hrvatskoj iz starina zagrebačke općine (1805–1845).* [Supplements to the history of Jews in Croatia from the old days of the Zagreb community.] Zagreb: Kr. zemaljska tiskara, 1903.

———. *Sedamdesetgodišnjica Josipa Siebenscheina, predsjednika bog. izr. općine u Zagrebu.* [Seventieth birthday of Josip Siebenschein, president of the Zagreb Jewish community.] Zagreb, 1906.

Šik, Lavoslav. *Slovenci i Židovi.* [The Slovenes and the Jews.] Zagreb: Tiskara Merkur, 1919.

Spitzer, Samuel. *Die Gemeinde-Ordnung bei den alten Israeliten verglichen mit den diesfälligen neuesten Bestimmungen in Oesterreich-Ungarn.* Osijek, 1873.

Spomenica dobrotvornog bazara u korist šume kralja Petra Oslobodioca u Palestini. [Commemorative volume for the charity bazaar in honor of the Forest of King Peter the Liberator in Palestine.] Zagreb: 1930.

Spomenica Gospode Estire S. Ruso učiteljice na dan proslave 32 godine prosvetnog, nacionalnog i humanog rada, 1 juna 1924. [Commemorative volume to Estira S. Ruso, teacher, on the day of celebrating 32 years of educational, national, and humanitarian work.] Belgrade: Štamparija M. Karića, 1924.

Spomenica Izraelske ferijalne kolonije u Zagrebu prigodom 25-godišnjice opstanka društva, 1914–1939. [Commemorative volume of the Israelite Vacation Colony in Zagreb in honor of the twenty-fifth anniversary of the founding of the society.] Zagreb, 1940.

Spomenica Kuratorija doma zaklade Lavoslav Schwarza u Zagrebu prigodom 30-godišnjice opstanka 1909–1939. [Commemorative volume of the curatorium of the Schwarz Home in Zagreb in honor of the thirtieth anniversary of its founding.] Ed. Gavro Schwarz. Zagreb: Naklada Društva prijatelja Schwarzovog doma u Zagrebu, 1940.

Spomenica Lože Zagreba 1090 NOBB, 1927–1932. Zagreb, 1932.
Spomenica o židovskom kantoru. [Commemorative volume on the Jewish cantor.] Ed. Josip Rendi. Zagreb: Tisak Richard Furst, 1908.
Spomenica poginulih i umrlih srpskih Jevreja u Balkanskom i svetskom ratu 1912–1918. [Memorial to the Serbian Jews who died in the Balkan Wars and the World War.] Belgrade: Štamparija M. Karića, 1927.
Spomenica povodom 50-godišnjice Doma staraca SJOJ (Zaklada Švarca) u Zagrebu 1910–1960. [Commemorative volume on the fiftieth anniversary of the Home for the Aged of the SJOJ—Schwarz Home—in Zagreb.] Ed. David A. Levi-Dale. Belgrade: Srboštampa, 1960.
Spomenica prigodom 50-godišnjeg opstanka jevrejske veroispovjedne opčine aškenaskog obreda u Sarajevu. [Commemorative volume on the fiftieth anniversary of the founding of the Ashkenazic community in Sarajevo.] Ed. Oskar Grof. Sarajevo: Štamparija Bosanska posta, 1930.
Spomenica prigodom osvećenja novog hrama Jevrejske vjeroispovjedne opčine sefardskog obreda u Sarajevu, 14 septembra 1930. [Commemorative volume on the occasion of the dedication of the new synagogue of the Sephardic community in Sarajevo.] Sarajevo, 1930.
Spomenica proslavi 30-godišnjicu sarajevskoga kulturno-potpornoga Društva La Benevolencija, maja 1924. [Commemorative volume on the 30th anniversary of the Sarajevo cultural-charitable society La Benevolencia.] Ed. Stanislav Vinaver. Belgrade: Vreme, 1924.
Spomenica svečane instalacije Velike lože u Beogradu, 27 oktobra 1935. [Commemorative volume in honor of the installation of the B'nai Brith Grand Lodge in Belgrade.] Belgrade: Državna štamparija, 1936.
Statuten der Vereinigung jüdischer Hochschüler aus den südslavischen Ländern Bar Giora in Wien. Vienna: 1902.
Universal Confederation of Sephardi Jews, Executive Committee in Jerusalem. *Financial Report and General Administrative Report for the Year 5687 (1926–1927).* Jerusalem: Haibri Press, 1927.
Wertheim, Pavao, ed. *Naše omladinstvo, Članci i govorci.* [Our youth, articles and addresses.] Zagreb: Biblioteka Hanoar, 1930.
Zapisnik svečane instalacije Lože Zagreb NOBB br.1090 obavljene u Zagrebu, 20 novembra 1927 godine. [Minutes of the installation ceremony of B'nai Brith Lodge Zagreb.] Zagreb, 1927.
Zemaljska uprava Keren Kajemeta. *Omladina i Keren Kajemet Lejisrael.* [Youth and the Jewish National Fund.] Zagreb, 1936.
Židovska Masonerija. [Jewish Masonry.] Moderna Socijalna Kronika. Zagreb: Mosk, 1935.

NEWSPAPERS AND PERIODICALS

Beogradske jevrejske novine. [Belgrade Jewish Paper.] 1936–37.
Beogradski jevrejski glasnik. [Belgrade Jewish Herald.] 1924.
Bilten. [Bulletin.] 1952–58.
Cionij, List opće cionističke omladine Jugoslavije. [The Zionist, paper of the General Zionist Youth of Yugoslavia.] Osijek, 1937.
Ever Hajarden, Betarski mesečnik. [Over the Jordan, Betar monthly.] Novi Sad, 1934–37.

Gideon, Vijesnik SŽOU. [Gideon, gazette of SŽOU.] Monthly. Zagreb, 1919–26.

Glasnik jevrejske aškenaske veroispovedne opštine. Monthly. Belgrade, 1941.

Glasnik SJVO. Belgrade, 1933.

Haaviv, List jevrejske djece. [Spring, paper for Jewish children.] Zagreb, 1922–41.

Hanoar, List jevrejske omladine Jugoslavije. [Youth, paper of Jewish youth of Yugoslavia.] Monthly. Zagreb, 1926–37.

Herut, Vjesnik SŽOU KJ. [Freedom.] Zagreb, 1930–31.

Hozer, Ahdut Haolim. [Review.] Zagreb, 1928–30.

Israel, Jüdische Wochenschrift von Marthef. Subotica and Novi Sad, 1925–28.

Jevrejska tribuna, Nezavisni kulturni-politički list Jevreja KSCS. [Jewish Tribune, independent cultural-political paper of the Jews of KSCS.] Sarajevo, 1921.

Jevrejska tribuna. Weekly. Zagreb and Belgrade, 1937–41.

Jevrejski almanah. (O.S.) [Jewish Almanac.] Annual. vols. 1–5. Vršac, 1925–30.

Jevrejski almanah. (N.S.) Belgrade, 1954–70.

Jevrejski glas. [Jewish Voice.] Weekly. Sarajevo, 1928–41.

Jevrejski list. Zagreb, 1934.

Jevrejski narodni kalendar. [Jewish National Calendar.] Annual. vols.1–6. Belgrade, 1935–41.

Jevrejski pregled. [Jewish Review.] 1959–76.

Jevrejski vjesnik. Osijek, 1934–37.

Jevrejski život. [Jewish Life.] Weekly. Sarajevo, 1924–27.

Jüdische Rundschau. 1909–36.

Jüdische Zeitung. Vienna, 1907–20.

Malchut Jisrael, Cijonističko-revizionistički organ. [Kingdom of Israel, Zionist-Revisionist organ.] Weekly. Novi Sad, 1933–37.

Medura šel Kibuc Hacofim. [Campfire.] Zagreb, 1930–31.

Mjesečnik jevrejskih kantora. [Monthly of the Jewish Cantors.] Karlovac, 1928–30.

Narodna židovska svijest. [National Jewish Conscience.] Weekly. Sarajevo, 1924–28.

Omanut, Mjesečnik jevrejske kulture. [Art, Jewish cultural monthly.] Zagreb, 1936–41.

Službeni list SJVO KJ. [Official paper.] Belgrade, 1936–39.

Vesnik jevrejske sefardske veroispovedne opštine. [Gazette of the Sephardic community.] Monthly. Belgrade, 1939–41.

Vesnik Keren Hajesod. Belgrade, 1939.

Vjesnik SŽOU. Zagreb, 1924–31.

Die Welt. Vienna, 1897–1914.

Židov-Hajehudi. [The Jew.] Weekly: Zagreb, 1917–41.

Židovska smotra. [Jewish Review.] Bimonthly. Zagreb and Osijek, 1906–14.

Židovska svijest. [Jewish Conscience.] Weekly. Sarajevo, 1919–23.

Secondary Sources

UNPUBLISHED MATERIALS

Albala, Paulina. "O dr Albali." [On Dr. Albala.] Los Angeles, 1943.
————. "Dr. David Albala as a Jewish National Worker." Leo Baeck Institute, New York, n.d.
Arnon, Aleksa (Aleksandar Klein). "10 godina rada u korist jevrejskih izbjeglica u Jugoslaviji (1933–42)." [Ten years of work on behalf of Jewish refugees in Yugoslavia.] Tel Aviv, n.d.
Ivanović, Lazar. "Pojava antisemitisma u Jugoslaviji i beogradski Jevreji." [The appearance of anti-Semitism in Yugoslavia and Belgrade Jews.] Belgrade, n.d.
Kostić, Milivoj. "Zapisi starog Beogradjanina, Milivoja Kostića, o Jevrejima na Dorćolu i ostalim delovima starog Beograda." [Memoirs of an old Belgrader, Milivoj Kostić, on the Jews in Dorćol and other writings of old Belgrade.] Jewish Historical Museum, Belgrade, 1958–59.
(Levi, Mihael.) "40 godina Keren Kajemet u Jugoslaviji." [Forty years of Jewish National Fund in Yugoslavia.] Jewish Historical Museum, Belgrade, n.d.
Pinto, Avram. "Protujevrejski zakoni za vrijeme vlade dra Anton Korošeca, ministra prosveta." [Anti-Jewish laws at the time of the government of Dr. Anton Korošec, minister of education.] Sarajevo, n.d.
Tajtacak, David I. "Beogradski-srpski Jevreji i njihova zanimanja do drugog svetskog rata." [Belgrade Serbian Jews and their occupations to World War II.] Jewish Historical Museum, Belgrade, 1971.
Veith, Robert. "Cionistički pokret u Jugoslaviji." [The Zionist movement in Yugoslavia.] Jewish Historical Museum, Belgrade, n.d.

ARTICLES

Albala, David. "Royalty in Palestine." *The New Palestine,* May 2, 1941, pp.8–10.
Albala, Paulina. "Dr David Albala kao jevrejski nacionalni radnik." [Dr. David Albala as a Jewish nationalist worker.] *Jevrejski almanah* (N.S.), 1957–58, pp.94–108.
————. "Our Jewish Sisters of Yugoslavia." *Congress Weekly,* November 5, 1943, p.19.
Alcalay, I. "The Jews of Serbia." *American Jewish Year Book,* vol.20 (1918–19), pp.75–87.
————. "Arhivski gradja o Jevrejima u Srbiji." *Jevrejski almanah* (O.S.), vol. 3 (1927–28), pp.21–44, vol. 4 (1928–29), pp.28–40.
————. "Jevrejske knjige štampane u Beogradu." [Jewish books published in Belgrade.] *Jevrejski almanah* (O.S.), vol. 1 (1925–26), pp.133–43.
Alkalaj, Aron. "Dr. Bukić Pijade." *Jevrejski almanah* (N.S.), 1968–69, pp.49–54.
————. "Dvanaest godina Jevrejske čitaonice u Beogradu, 1929–1941."

[Twelve years of the Jewish Reading Room in Belgrade.] *Jevrejski almanah* (N.S.), 1955–56, pp.113–16.

———. "Mladoturci i Staroturci u Beogradu, Spor oko zidanja nove sinagoge Bet Israel." [Young Turks and old Turks in Belgrade, the dispute over the building of the new synagogue Bet Israel.] *Jevrejski almanah* (N.S.), 1965–67, pp.105–14.

———. "Purim u jevrejskoj mahali." [Purim in the Jewish quarter.] *Jevrejski almanah* (N.S.), 1954, pp.146–49.

———. "Život i običaji u nekadašnjoj jevrejskoj mahali." [Life and customs in the former Jewish quarter.] *Jevrejski almanah* (N.S.), 1961–62, pp.82–97.

Alkalaj, David. "Nova sinagoga Bet Israel." [The new synagogue Bet Israel.] *Jevrejski almanah* (O.S.), vol. 1 (1925–26), pp.73–82.

———. "Sefardska opština u Beogradu u 1860 godinama." [The Sephardic community in Belgrade in the 1860s.] *Jevrejski narodni kalendar,* vol.3 (1937–38), pp.101–11.

Alkalaj, Samuilo. "Klub Zajednica." *Jevrejski almanah* (N.S.), 1961–62, pp.110–14.

Almuli, Sofija. "Jelena Demajo." *Jevrejski almanah* (N.S.), 1955–56, pp.149–53.

Atijas, Jakov. "Esperansa, Jevrejski sefardski studentski klub u Zagrebu." [Esperanza, the Jewish Sephardic student club in Zagreb.] *Jevrejski almanah* (N.S.), 1955–56, pp.110–12.

Baron, Salo W. "Freedom and Constraint in the Jewish Community." Israel Davidson, ed. *Essays and Studies in Memory of Linda R. Miller.* New York: Jewish Theological Seminary, 1938, pp.9–23.

Bejtić, Alija. "Jevrejske nastambe u Sarajevu." [Jewish settlement in Sarajevo.] *Spomenica 400 godina od dolaska Jevreja u Bosnu i Hercegovinu,* pp.23–32.

Breyer, Mirko. "Glas srca i savjesti." [The voice of heart and conscience.] *Nova Evropa,* vol.5, nos.9–10 (July 21, 1922), pp.280–83.

Demajo, Samuilo. "Sećanja na Jaliji." [Memories of Jalija.] *Jevrejski narodni kalendar,* vol.4 (1938–39), pp.49–55.

Despot, Miroslava. "Protužidovski izgredi u Zagorju i Zagrebu godine 1883." [The anti-Jewish disturbances in Zagorje and Zagreb of 1883.] *Jevrejski almanah* (N.S.), 1957–58, pp.75–85.

Dimitrijević, Vojo. "Slikari Jevreji u Sarajevu izmedju dva rata." [Jewish artists in Sarajevo between the wars.] *Spomenica 400,* pp.315–17.

Djordjević, T. R. "Jevreji Balkanskog poluostrva." [The Jews of the Balkan peninsula.] *Spomenica La Benevolencija,* 1924.

———. "Jevreji u Srbiji za vreme prve vlade kneza Miloša." [Jews in Serbia duringthefirstreignofPrinceMiloš.] *Godišnjica N.Čuprica,* vol.35, 1923.

Djurić, Olivera. "Slikar Leon Koen, 1859–1934." *Jevrejski almanah* (N.S.), 1954, pp.121–26.

Djurić-Klajn, Stana. "Začetnik srpskog muzičkog života u XIX veka." [The founder of Serbian musical life in the 19th century.] *Jevrejski almanah* (N.S.), 1961–62, pp.68–73.

Djurić-Zamolo, Divna. "Jevrejski amam u Beogradu." [The Jewish mikvah in Belgrade.] *Jevrejski almanah* (N.S.), 1968–70, pp.187–97.

———. "Stari jevrejski četvrt i jevrejska ulica u Beogradu." [The old Jewish quarter and Jewish street in Belgrade.] *Jevrejski almanah* (N.S.), 1965–67, pp.41–76.

Esref, Camfara. "Laura Papo Bohoreta." *Jevrejski almanah* (N.S.), 1965–67, pp.137–44.

Eventov, Jakir. "Nostalgije Evropljanina, Uz 10-godišnjicu smrti Aleksandra Lichta." [Nostalgia for a European, ten years after the death of Alexander Licht.] *Jevrejski almanah* (N.S.), 1957–58, pp.197–205.

Finci, Moni. "U avangardi društvenog progresa." [In the avant-garde of social progress.) *Spomenica 400*, pp.189–204.

Fisher, Jack C. "Urban Analysis: A Case Study of Zagreb, Yugoslavia." *Annals of the Association of American Geographers*, vol.53, no.1 (September 1963), pp.266–84.

Freidenreich, Harriet Pass. "Yugoslav Jewry: A Community that Rests on its Organization." [Hebrew.] *Tefutsot Israel*, vol.12, no.2 (March–April 1974), pp.41–74.

Gaon, Solomon. "Rabbi Jehuda Hai Alkalai." in *A Memorial Tribute to Paul Goodman*. Ed. Israel Cohen. London: Edward Goldston and Son, 1952, pp.138–47.

Gelber, N. M. "Jewish Life in Bulgaria." *Jewish Social Studies*, vol.8, no.2 (April 1946), pp.103–26.

Hahamović, Julije. "Aškenazi u BiH." [The Ashkenazim in B-H.] *Spomenica 400*, pp.141–53.

Helfgott, Herman. "Bombardovanja Beograda, 1862." [The bombardment of Belgrade in 1862.] *Jevrejski narodni kalendar*, vol.4 (1938–39), pp.56–61.

Hersch, Liebman. "Jewish Population Trends in Europe." in *The Jewish People Past and President*, vol.2. New York: Jewish Encyclopedic Handbooks, 1948, pp.1–24.

Kadelburg, Lavoslav. "Položaj i perspektive jevrejske zajednice u Jugoslaviji." [The position and perspective of the Jewish community in Yugoslavia.] *Jevrejski almanah* (N.S.), 1968–70, pp.9–17.

Kajon, Vita D. "Jevrejski gradjani Jugoslavije i njihov odnos prema državi." [The Jewish citizens of Yugoslavia and their relation to the state.] *Nova Evropa*, vol.5, nos.9–10 (July 21, 1922), pp.264–70.

———. "M. Srškić i Jevreji." [Milan Srškić and the Jews.] in *Milan Srškić* (1880–1937). Sarajevo, 1938, pp.199–204.

Kamhi, Aron and Levinger, Mirko. "Pokret otpora medju Jevrejima Bosne i Hercegovine interniranim na Lopudu i Rabu." [The resistance movement among the Jews of Bosnia and Hercegovina interned on Lopud and Rab.] *Spomenica 400*, pp.255–62.

Kamhi, Haim. "400 godišnjica jevrejske opštine u Sarajevu." [Four-hundredth anniversary of the Jewish community in Sarajevo.] *Jevrejski almanah* (N.S.), 1961–62, pp.15–24.

———. "Jevreji u privredi BiH." [Jews in the economy of B-H.] *Spomenica 400*, pp.55–70.

———. "Jevrejska publicistika u BiH." [Jewish journalism in B-H.] *Spomenica 400*, pp.167–73.

———. "Sarajevski rabini." [The rabbis of Sarajevo.] *Spomenica 400*, pp.273–78.

Kamhi, Samuel. "Jezik, pjesme i poslovice bosansko-hercegovačkih

Sefarada." [The language, songs, and folk sayings of the Bosnian-Hercegovinian Sephardim.] *Spomenica 400,* pp.105–22.

Kann, Robert A. "Hungarian Jewry During Austria-Hungary's Constitutional Period, 1867–1918." *Jewish Social Studies,* vol.7, no.4 (October 1945), pp.357–86.

Katzburg, Nathaniel. "Hungarian Jewry in Modern Times: Political and Social Aspects." in *Hungarian-Jewish Studies,* .vol.1. Ed. Randolph L. Braham. New York: World Federation of Hungarian Jews, 1966, pp.137–70.

————. "The Jewish Congress of Hungary, 1868–69." Ibid., vol.2, 1969, pp.1–33.

Konforti, Josef. "Doprinos ljekara Jevreja zdravstvenoj zaštiti i kulturi BiH." [The contribution of Jewish doctors to health protection and culture in B-H.] *Jevrejski almanah* (N.S.), 1968–70, pp.105–23.

————. "Jevreji u unutrašnjosti BiH." [Jews in the interior of B-H.] *Spomenica 400,* pp.131–40.

Kovačević, Božidar. "O Jevrejima u Srbiji." [On the Jews in Serbia.] *Jevrejski almanah* (N.S.), 1959–60, pp.105–12.

Kruševac, Teodor. "Društvene promene kod bosanskih Jevreja za austrijskog vremena." [Social changes among Bosnian Jews during the Austrian period.] *Spomenica 400,* pp.71–98.

Laszlo, Erno. "Hungarian Jewry: Settlement and Demography, 1735–38 to 1910." *Hungarian-Jewish Studies,* vol.1. Ed. Randolf L. Braham. New York: World Federation of Hungarian Jews, 1966, pp.68–124.

Lažić, Ivan. "Pravni i činjenični položaj konfesionalnih zajednica u Jugoslaviji." [The legal and actual position of religious communities in Yugoslavia.] *Vjerske zajednice u Jugoslaviji.* Zagreb: NIP Binoza, 1970, pp.45–77.

Lestschinsky, Jacob. "The Economic and Social Development of the Jewish People." *The Jewish People Past and Present,* vol.1. New York: Jewish Encyclopedic Handbooks, 1946, pp.361–90.

Levi, Isak and Konforti, Josef. "Jedan stari statut jevrejske sefardske opštine u Sarajevu." [An old statute of the Sarajevo Sephardic community.] *Jevrejski almanah* (N.S.), 1968–70, pp.83–98.

Levi, Moric. "David Pardo, sarajevski haham." *Jevrejski almanah* (O.S.), vol.1 (1925–26), pp.118–26.

————. "Fragmenti iz života Sefarada." [Fragments from the life of the Sephardim.] *Spomenica La Benevolencija,* 1924, pp.16–24.

Levntal, Zdenko. "Iz responza Josefa Almoznina." [From the responsa of Josef Almoznino.] *Jevrejski almanah* (N.S.), 1965–67, pp.29–40.

Maestro, Jakov. "Naš stari meldar." [Our old Jewish school.] *Spomenica La Benevolencija,* 1924, pp.103–6.

Matkovski, Aleksandar. "The Destruction of Macedonian Jewry in 1943." *Yad Vashem Studies on the European Catastrophe and Resistance,* vol.3 (1959).

Mevorah-Petrović, Luci. "Abraham Kapon." *Jevrejski almanah* (N.S.), 1961–62, pp.74–81.

Milošević, Mihajlo. "Hajim S. Davičo." *Jevrejski almanah* (N.S.), 1965–67, pp.129–35.

Mosbacher, Eduard. "Jugoslovenski Jevreji u svetlosti statistike." [Yugoslav Jewry in the light of statistics.] *Jevrejski narodni kalendar,* vol.6 (1940–41), pp.122–34.

Perera, David. "Neki statistički podaci o Jevrejima u Jugoslaviji u periodu od 1938 do 1965 godine." [Some statistics on Jews in Yugoslavia in the period from 1938 to 1965.] *Jevrejski almanah* (N.S.), 1968–70, pp.135–47.

Perić, Marko. "Demographic Study of the Jewish Community in Yugoslavia, 1971–1972." *Papers in Jewish Demography 1973.* Jerusalem: Institute of Contemporary Jewry, 1977.

———. "Jugoslovenski Jevreji—Španski borci." [Yugoslav Jews—Spanish fighters.] *Jevrejski almanah* (N.S.), 1963–64, pp.96–102.

———. "Prvi rezultati našeg demografskog istraživanja." [First results of our demographic survey.] *Jevrejski pregled,* vol. 23, nos. 11–12 (November–December 1972), pp.2–7.

———. "Dalnji rezultati našeg demografskog istraživanja." [Further results . . .] *Jevrejski pregled,* vol. 24, nos. 1–2 (January–February 1973), pp.16–21; nos. 3–4 (March–April 1973), pp.31–34; nos.5–6 (May–June 1973), pp.2–7; nos.7–8 (July–August 1973), pp.3–6.

Pijade, Bukić. "Iz nedavne prošlosti jevrejske sefardske opštine u Beogradu." [From the recent past of the Belgrade Sephardic community.] *Jevrejski narodni kalendar,* vol.4 (1938–39), pp.33–48.

Pinto, Avram. "Prosvjeta i prosvjetni radnici Jevreji u Bosni." [Education and Jewish educational workers in Bosnia.] *Jevrejski almanah* (N.S.), 1968–70, pp.99–104.

———. "Jevrejska društva u Sarajevu." [Jewish societies in Sarajevo.] *Spomenica 400,* pp.173–87.

———. "Jevrejska gimnazija u Sarajevu 1939/40 godine." [The Jewish gymnasium in Sarajevo in 1939/40.] *Jevrejski pregled,* vol.25, nos.11–12 (November–December 1974), pp.20–26.

Pinto, Benjamin. "O kretanju jevrejskog stanovništva u Sarajevu." [On the growth of the Jewish population in Sarajevo.] *Jevrejski narodni kalendar,* vol.5 (1939–40), pp.52–65.

Pinto, Samuel. "Položaj bosanskih Jevreja pod turskom vladavinom." [The position of Bosnian Jews under Turkish rule.] *Jevrejski almanah* (N.S.), 1954, pp.48–59.

———. "Prosvjetne prilike bosanskih Jevreja za turskoj vladavine." [Educational conditions of Bosnian Jewry under Turkish rule.] *Jevrejski almanah* (N.S.), 1955–56, pp.64–70.

Radej, Slavko. "Hinko Gotlib." *Jevrejski almanah* (N.S.), 1954, pp.127–31.

Rotem, Cvi. "The Jews of Yugoslavia in Our Day." [Hebrew.] *Gesher,* vol.10, no.3 (September 1964), pp.45–49.

Segall, Jacob. "Die Juden in BuH." *Zeitschrift für Demographie und Statistik der Juden,* vol.9, nos.7–8 (July–August 1913), pp.104–10.

Šik, Lavoslav. "O potrebi povjesnice Jevreja u Jugoslaviji." [On the need for a history of Jews in Yugoslavia.] *Jevrejski almanah* (O.S.), vol.1 (1925–26), pp.89–101.

———. "Židovi u slovenskim zemljama, nekad i sad." [Jews in Slavic lands, past and present.] *Nova Evropa,* vol.5, nos.9–10 (July 21, 1922), pp.271–79.

Sindik, Dušan. "Na jevrejskim školama u Beogradu u 19. veku." [At Jewish schools in Belgrade in the nineteenth century.] *Jevrejski almanah* (N.S.), 1960–61, pp.98–105.

Skarić, Vladislav. "Iz prošlosti sarajevskih Jevreja." [From the past of Sarajevo Jewry.] *Spomenica La Benevolencija,* 1924, pp.29–33.

Stajić, Aleksandar and Papo, Jakov. "Ubistva i drugi zločini izvršeni nad Jevrejima u Bosni i Hercegovini u toku neprijateljske okupacije." [Murders and other crimes committed against the Jews in Bosnia-Hercegovina in the time of enemy occupation.] *Spomenica 400,* pp.205–48.

Štajner, Aleksandar. "Jehuda Haj Alkalaj (1798–1878)." *Jevrejski almanah* (N.S.), 1968–70, pp.55–66.

Steiner, Miriam. "Yugoslav Jewry." *Dispersion and Unity,* nos.13–14, pp.223–35 (also in Hebrew in *B'tfuzot Hagola,* vol 13, nos.3–4, 1971–72, pp.142–53).

Sućeska, A. "Položaj Jevreja u BiH za vrijeme Turaka." [The position of Jews in B-H in the time of the Turks.] *Spomenica 400,* pp.47–54.

Vajs, Albert. "Jevreji u novoj Jugoslaviji." [Jews in the new Yugoslavia.] *Jevrejski almanah* (N.S.), 1954, pp.5–47.

———. "Na kraju prve i na početku druge decenije." [At the end of the first and the beginning of the second decade.] *Jevrejski almanah* (N.S.), 1955–56, pp.7–16.

Vajs, Maks. "Prethodni rezultati popisa Jevreja u Jugoslaviji." [Preliminary results of the census of Jews in Yugoslavia.] *Jevrejski almanah* (N.S.), 1957–58, pp.162–66.

Vinaver, Stanislav. "La Benevolencija." *Spomenica La Benevolencija,* 1924, pp.3–6.

Vinaver, Vuk. "Jevreji u Srbiji početkom 19. veka." [The Jews in Serbia at the beginning of the nineteenth century.] *Jevrejski almanah* (N.S.), 1955–56, pp.28–34.

Vucinich, Wayne S. "Interwar Yugoslavia." *Contemporary Yugoslavia, Twenty Years of Socialist Experiment.* Ed. Wayne S. Vucinich. Berkeley: University of California Press, 1969.

Wadler, Arnold. "Die Juden in Serbien." *Zeitschrift für Demographie und Statistik der Juden,* vol.2, no.10 (October 1906), pp.145–48; vol.2, no.11 (November 1906), pp.168–73.

Wischnitzer, Mark. "Jewish Communal Organization in Modern Times." *The Jewish People Past and Present,* vol.2. New York: Jewish Encyclopedic Handbooks, 1948, pp.201–16.

Zitron, S. L. "Zur Geschichte der Zionsliebe, Rabbi Jehuda Alkalai." *Der Jude,* vol.3, no.3 (June 1918), pp.116–21.

Zon, Mojsije. "O socijalnoj diferencijaciji sarajevskih Jevreja." [On the social stratification of Sarajevo Jews.] *Godišnjak La Benevolencia i Potpora.* Sarajevo: Štamparija Menahem Papo, 1933, pp.130–36.

BOOKS

Auty, Phyllis. *Yugoslavia.* London: Walker & Company, 1965.

Babić, Vladimir. *Historija naroda Jugoslavije.* [A history of the peoples of Yugoslavia.] Vol.2. Zagreb: Skolska knjiga, 1959.

Baron, Salo Wittmayer. *The Jewish Community.* Vols.1–3. Philadelphia: Jewish Publication Society, 1942.

Beard, Charles A. and Radin, George. *The Balkan Pivot: Yugoslavia.* New York: Macmillan Company, 1929.

Berliner Büro der Zionistischen Organisation. *Warum gingen wir zum ersten Zionistenkongress?* Berlin: Jüdischer Verlag, 1922.

Benardete, Mair Jose. *Hispanic Culture and Character of the Sephardic Jews.* New York: Hispanic Institute in the United States, 1952.

Besarević, Risto, ed. *Kultura i umjetnosti u BiH pod austro-ugarskom upravom—Gradja.* [Culture and the arts in B-H under Austro-Hungarian rule—Sources.] Sarajevo: Arhiv Bosne i Hercegovine, 1968.

Böhm, Adolf. *Die Zionistische Bewegung.* Vol.2. Berlin: Jüdischer Verlag, 1937.

Čelebija, Evlija. *Putopis odlomci o jugoslovenskim zemljama.* [Travelogue fragments on the South Slav lands.] Trans. Hazim Sabanović. Sarajevo: Sjvetlost, 1954.

Clissold, Stephen. *A Short History of Yugoslavia.* Cambridge: Cambridge University Press, 1966.

Čulinović, Ferdo. *Jugoslavija izmedju dva rata.* [Yugoslavia between the two wars.] 2 vols. Zagreb: Zavod Jugoslovenske akademije znanosti i umetnosti, 1961.

Dawidowicz, Lucy. *The War against the Jews.* New York: Holt, Rinehart and Winston, 1975.

Dedijer, Vladimir; Božic, Ivan; Čirković, Sima; and Ekmečić, Milorad. *History of Yugoslavia.* New York: McGraw-Hill Book Company, 1974.

Djordjević, Tihomir R. *Iz Srbije kneza Miloša: Stanovništvo-naselja.* [From the Serbia of Prince Miloš: Population settlement.] Belgrade: Uzdavačko Geca Kona, 1924.

Emmanuel, I. S. *Histoire des Israélites de Salonique.* Vol.1. Paris: Thonon, 1936.

Eventov, Yakir. *A History of Yugoslav Jews* [Hebrew]. Vol.1. Tel Aviv: Hitahdut Olej Yugoslavia, 1971.

Finci, Moni. *Djelovanje KPJ u kulturnim i sportskim društvima i organizacijama u BiH izmedju dva rata.* [The activities of the YCP in cultural and sports associations and organizations in B-H between the wars.] Sarajevo: Akademija nauka i umjetnosti BiH, 1970.

Galanté, Abraham. *Documents officiels turcs concernant les Juifs de Turquie.* Istanbul: Haim, Rozio & Company, 1931.

Gavrilović, B. N.; Pandurović, S.; and Parežanin, R. *Beograd.* Belgrade: Beletra, 1940.

Ginić, Ivanka. *Dinamika i struktura gradskog stanovništva Jugoslavije.* [The dynamics and structure of the urban population of Yugoslavia.] Belgrade: Institut društvenih nauka, 1967.

Goodblatt, Morris S. *Jewish Life in Turkey in the XVI Century.* New York: Jewish Theological Seminary of America, 1952.

Gordon, Milton M. *Assimilation in American Life.* New York: Oxford University Press, 1964.

Great Britain. Naval Intelligence Division. *Jugoslavia.* Vol. 2: History, Peoples and Administration. Vol.3: Economic Geography, Ports and Communications. London: Geographical Handbook Series, 1944, 1945.

Gross, Mirjana. *Vladavina Hrvatsko-Srpske koalicije 1906–1907.* [The regime of the Croat-Serb coalition, 1906–1907.] Belgrade: Institut društvenih nauka, 1960.

Guldescu, Stanko. *The Croatian-Slavonian Kingdom 1526–1792.* The Hague: Mouton, 1970.

Hilberg, Raul. *The Destruction of the European Jews.* Chicago: Quadrangle Books, 1961.

Hitahdut olej Jugoslavija. *Za Spomen dra Aleksandra Lichta.* [In memory of Dr. Alexander Licht.] Tel Aviv: Tiskara Gaon, 1955.

Hoptner, J. B. *Yugoslavia in Crisis, 1934–1941.* New York: Columbia University Press, 1962.

Ivanović, Lazar, and Vukmanović, Mladen. *Dani smrti na Sajmištu.* [Days of death at Sajmište.] Novi Sad: Dnevnik, 1969.

Iz istorije Jugoslavije 1918–1945, Zbornik predavanja. [From the history of Yugoslavia, 1918–1945, a collection of lectures.] Belgrade: Nolit, 1958.

Janković, Dragoslav. *O političkim strankama u Srbiji XIX veka.* [On the political parties in Serbia of the XIXth century.] Belgrade: Prosveta, 1951.

Janowsky, Oskar I. *The Jews and Minority Rights, 1898–1919.* New York: Columbia University Press, 1933.

————. *People at Bay, The Jewish Problem in East Central Europe.* New York: Oxford University Press, 1938.

Jevrejski istorijski muzej. *Zbornik.* I: Studije i gradja o Jevrejima Dubrovnika. [Studies and sources on the Jews of Dubrovnik.] Belgrade: SJOJ, 1971.

————. *Zbornik.* II: Studije i gradja o učešću Jevreja u narodnooslobodilačkom ratu. [Studies and sources on the participation of Jews in the War of National Liberation.] Belgrade: SJOJ, 1973.

Jovanović, Živorad P. *Iz starog Beograda.* [From old Belgrade.] Belgrade: Turistička štampa, 1964.

Kečkemet, Duško. *Vid Morpurgo i narodni preporod u Splitu.* [Vid Morpurgo and the national reawakening in Split.] Split: Muzej grada Splita, 1963.

————. *Židovi u povijesti Splita.* [The Jews in the history of Split.] Split, 1972.

Kerner, R. J., ed. *Yugoslavia.* Berkeley: University of California Press, 1949.

Kirk, Dudley. *Europe's Population in the Interwar Years.* Princeton: Princeton University Press, 1946.

Kosier, Ljubomir St. *Jevreji u Jugoslaviji i Bugarskoj.* [The Jews in Yugoslavia and Bulgaria.] Zagreb: Ekonomska biblioteka Srba, Hrvata i Slovenaca, 1930.

————. *Jevreji u trgovini Jugoslavije i Bugarske.* [The Jews in the commerce of Yugoslavia and Bulgaria.] Zagreb, 1930.

————. *Statistika Jevreja u Jugoslaviji i Bugarskoj.* [Statistics of Jews in Yugoslavia and Bulgaria.] Zagreb, 1930.

Kreševljaković, Hamdija. *Esnafi i obrti u starom Sarajevu.* [Guilds and trades in old Sarajevo.] Sarajevo: Narodna prosvjeta, 1958.

————. *Sarajevo za vrijeme austrougarske uprave, 1878–1918.* [Sarajevo at the time of Austro-Hungarian rule.] Sarajevo: Arhiv grada Sarajeva, 1969.

Kruševac, Todor. *Sarajevo pod austro-ugarskom upravom, 1878–1918.* [Sarajevo under Austro-Hungarian administration.] Sarajevo: Narodna štamparija, 1960.

Laqueur, Walter. *A History of Zionism.* New York: Holt, Rinehart and Winston, 1972.

Lederer, Ivo J. *Yugoslavia at the Paris Peace Conference.* New Haven: Yale University Press, 1963.

Lenski, Gerhard. *The Religious Factor.* New York: Doubleday Anchor Books, 1963.

Leven, Narcisse. *Cinquante Ans d'Histoire: L'Alliance Israélite Universelle, 1860–1910.* Paris: Librairie Félix Alcan, 1911.

Levin, Nora. *The Holocaust.* New York: Schocken Books, 1973.

Levy, Moritz. *Die Sephardim in Bosnien.* Sarajevo: A. Kajon, 1911. (Also translated into Serbo-Croatian: *Sefardi u Bosni.* Belgrade, 1969.)

Lockwood, William G. *European Moslems: Economy and Ethnicity in Western Bosnia.* New York: Academic Press, 1975.

Loeb, Isidore. *La Situation des Israélites en Turquie, en Serbie et en Roumanie.* Paris: Joseph Baer et Cie., 1877.

Loutzitch, Deyan. *La Constitution du Royaume de Yougoslavie du 3 septembre 1931.* Paris: Éditions Pierre Bossuet, 1933.

Löwenthal, Zdenko, ed. *The Crimes of the Fascist Occupants and Their Collaborators against Jews in Yugoslavia.* Belgrade: Federation of Jewish Communities of FPRY, 1957.

Macartney, C. A. *Hungary and Her Successors.* London: Oxford University Press, 1937.

―――. *National States and National Minorities.* London: Oxford University Press, 1934.

Markert, W., ed. *Jugoslawien.* Cologne, 1954.

May, Arthur. *The Habsburg Monarchy 1867–1914.* Cambridge: Harvard University Press, 1965.

Medding, P. Y. *From Assimilation to Group Survival.* New York: Hart Publishing Company, 1969.

Mezan, Saul. *Les Juifs Espagnols en Bulgarie.* Vol.1. Sofia: Imprimerie Amichpat, 1925.

Mirković, Mijo. *Ekonomska historija Jugoslavije.* Zagreb: 1958.

Mirkovitch, Borivoie B. *La Yougoslavie Politique et Économique.* Paris: Pierre Bossuet, 1935.

Molho, Michael. *Usos y costumbres de los Sefardies de Salonica.* Trans. F. Perez Castro. Madrid-Barcelona: Instituto Arias Montano-Consejo Superior de Investigaciones Cientificas, 1950.

Moskovits, Aron. *Jewish Education in Hungary, 1848–1948.* New York: Bloch Publishing Company, 1964.

Mousset, Albert. *Le Royaume Serbe-Croate-Slovène, son Organisation, sa Vie Politique et ses Institutions.* Paris: Éditions Bossards, 1926.

Mousset, Jean. *La Serbie et son Église, 1830–1904.* Paris: Librairie Droz, 1938.

Novak, G. *Židovi u Splitu.* Split, 1920.

Nehama, Joseph. *Histoire des Israélites de Salonique.* 4 vols. Salonika: Librairie Molho, 1935.

Oren, Uri. *A Town Called Monastir.* Trans. Mark Segal. Tel Aviv: Dror Publications, 1971.

Patton, Kenneth S. *Kingdom of Serbs, Croats and Slovenes (Yugoslavia): A Commercial and Industrial Handbook.* Washington: U.S. Government Printing Office, 1928.

Pavlowitch, Stevan K. *Yugoslavia.* London: Ernest Benn Limited, 1971.

Philipson, David. *The Reform Movement in Judaism.* New York: Macmillan Company, 1931.

Popović, Dušan J. *Beograd kroz vek⌐ve.* [Belgrade through the centuries.] Belgrade: Turistička štampa, 1964.

———. *Beograd pre 200 godina.* [Belgrade two hundred years ago.] Belgrade: Geca Kon, 1935.

Rado, Mirko, and Mayor, Josif. *Istorija novosadskih Jevreja.* [A history of the Jews of Novi Sad.] 1st ed., 1930. 2nd expanded edition, Tel Aviv: Odbor za spomen novosadske racije u Izraelu, 1972.

Reitlinger, Gerald. *The Final Solution.* New York: A. S. Barnes and Company, 1953.

Renard, Raymond. *Sepharad: Le monde et la langue judéo-espagnole des Séphardim.* Mons: Annales Universitaires de Mons, 1966.

Robinson, Jacob. *Were the Minorities Treaties a Failure?* New York: Institute of Jewish Affairs, 1943.

Roth, Cecil. *The Sarajevo Haggadah.* London: W. H. Allen, 1963.

Rosanes, Salomon A. *A History of the Jews in Turkey* [Hebrew]. 5 vols. Tel Aviv and Sofia: Imprimerie Amichpat, 1930–38.

Rühlmann, Paul. *Das Schulrecht der deutschen Minderheit in Jugoslawien.* Vol.5. *Das Schulrecht der europaischen Minderheiten.* Berlin: Reimar Hobbin, 1932.

Ruppin, Arthur. *The Jewish Fate and Future.* London: Macmillan and Company, 1940.

———. *The Jews in the Modern World.* London: Macmillan and Company, 1934.

———. *Die Soziologie der Juden.* 2 vols. Berlin: Jüdischer Verlag, 1930, 1931.

Sachar, Abram Leon. *Suffrance Is the Badge.* New York: Alfred A. Knopf, 1939.

Samokovlija, Isak. *Sabrana djela.* [Collected works.] 3 vols. Sarajevo: Svjetlost, 1967.

Šik, Lavoslav. *Jüdische Ärzte in Jugoslawien.* Trans. Lujo Thaller. Zagreb: Tiskara Eugen Sekler, 1931.

Schwarz, Gavro. *Povijest zagrebačke židovske općine od osnutka do 50-tih godina 19. vijeka.* [A history of the Zagreb Jewish community from its founding to the 1850s.] Zagreb: Štamparija Gaj, 1939.

Simeunović, Vladimir. *Stanovništvo Jugoslavije i Socijalističkih Republika 1921–1961, Ukupno stanovništvo, polna i starosna struktura.* [The population of Yugoslavia and the Socialist republics from 1921 to 1961, total population, sex, and age structure.] Belgrade: Savezni zavod za statistiku, 1964.

Skarić, Vladislav. *Sarajevo i njegova okolina od najstarijih vremena do austro-ugarske okupacije.* [Sarajevo and its environs from ancient times to the Austro-Hungarian occupation.] Sarajevo: Bosanska pošta, 1937.

Skarić, Vladislav; Nuri-Hadić, Osman; and Stojanović, Nikola. *BiH pod austro-ugarskom upravom.* [B-H under the Austro-Hungarian administration.] Belgrade: Geca Kon A.D., n.d.

Skoplje-Sarajevo, oktobar 1966. Ed. Luci Mevorah-Petrović. Belgrade: SJOJ-Srbo-štampa, 1966.

Šlang, Ignjat. *Jevreji u Beogradu.* [The Jews in Belgrade.] Belgrade: M. Karić, 1926.

Society for the History of Czechoslovak Jews. *The Jews of Czechoslovakia: Historical Studies and Surveys.* 2 vols. Philadelphia: Jewish Publication Society, 1968, 1971.

Spomenica 400 godina od dolaska Jevreja u Bosnu i Hercegovinu, 1566–1966. [Commemorative volume on the 400th anniversary of the arrival of Jews in Bosnia–Hercegovina] Ed. Samuel Kamhi. Sarajevo: Božidar Sekulić, 1966.

Spomenica Saveza jevrejskih opština Jugoslavije, 1919–1969. [Commemorative volume for the Federation of Jewish Communities of Yugoslavia.] Ed. David Levi-Dale. Belgrade: SJOJ-Srboštampa, 1970.

Stavrianos, L. S. *The Balkans since 1453.* New York: Holt, Rinehart and Winston, 1958.

Steckel, Charles W. *Destruction and Survival.* Los Angeles: Delmar Publishing Company, 1973.

Stein, Leonard. *The Balfour Declaration.* New York: Simon and Schuster, 1961.

Stoianovich, Traian. *A Study in Balkan Civilization.* New York: Alfred A. Knopf, 1967.

Stojković, Ljubiša, and Martić, Miloš. *National Minorities in Yugoslavia.* Belgrade: Jugoslavija, 1952.

Sugar, Peter F. *Industrialization of Bosnia-Hercegovina, 1878–1918.* Seattle: University of Washington Press, 1963.

Szabo, Gjuro. *Stari Zagreb.* [Old Zagreb.] Zagreb: Knjižara Vasić i Horvat, 1941.

Tadić, Jorjo. *Jevreji u Dubrovniku do polovina XVII stoljeće.* [The Jews in Dubrovnik to the mid-17th century.] Sarajevo: La Benevolencia, 1937.

Tomasevich, Jozo. *Peasants, Politics and Economic Change in Yugoslavia.* Stanford: Stanford University Press, 1955.

Turosienski, Severin K. *Education in Yugoslavia.* Washington: U.S. Government Printing Office, 1939.

West, Rebecca. *Black Lamb and Grey Falcon, A Journey through Yugoslavia.* New York: Viking Press, 1964 (reprint).

Wolf, Lucien. *Notes on the Diplomatic History of the Jewish Question.* London: Jewish Historical Society, 1919.

Wolff, Robert Lee. *The Balkans in Our Time.* New York: W.W. Norton and Company, 1967.

Yovanovitch, Nikodie. *Étude sur la Constitution du Royaume des Serbes, Croates et Slovènes du 28 juin 1921.* Paris: Ernest Sagot and Company, 1924.

Zimmels, H. J. *Ashkenazim and Sephardim: Their Relations, Differences and Problems as Reflected in the Rabbinical Responsa.* London: Oxford University Press, 1958.

Interviews

Rabbi Isaac Alcalay, Sephardic Home for the Aged, Brooklyn. Chief rabbi of Yugoslavia from 1923 to 1941. Discussed office of chief rabbinate; relations between Sephardim and Ashkenazim and between Orthodox and Neologues; ties between the Jewish community and the Yugoslav government and royal family.

Aron Alkalaj, Belgrade. Former secretary of B'nai Brith Grand Lodge for Yugoslavia and president of Belgrade Jewish Reading Room, 1929–1941. Information on religious life of Belgrade Sephardic community and B'nai Brith activities.

David A. Alkalaj, Jerusalem. Active member of Belgrade Sephardic community and Jewish Nationalist Society between the wars and president of

Belgrade Jewish community immediately following World War II. Discussed Yugoslav Zionist Federation, Sephardic movement and Sephardic Zionists, and Belgrade Sephardic community.

Michael Agmon (Šmule Engelmann), Tel Aviv. Zionist youth leader in the twenties. Discussed Federation of Jewish Youth Associations and emigration to Palestine.

Vladimir Brajković, Ramat Gan, Israel. Discussed Narodni Rad and Jewish political activity in Zagreb.

Moni Finci, Sarajevo. Active member of Matatja and later Partisan. Discussed Matatja and political activity among Sarajevo Jews in interwar period.

Professor Andrija Gams, Belgrade. Discussed Jews in the Vojvodina and the legal status of Yugoslav Jews in the period between the wars.

Bata Gedalja, Jerusalem. Secretary of Federation of Jewish Religious Communities in the thirties. Discussed Jewish student life in Belgrade, leadership of the Belgrade Sephardic community, and operations of the Federation of Jewish Religious Communities.

Dr. Lavoslav Glesinger, Zagreb. Coeditor of literary journal, *Omanut.* Discussed early years of Jewish community in Zagreb and activities during the interwar period.

Daniel and Ella Ichaki (Papo), Kibbutz Sha'ar Ha'amakim, Israel. Discussed Jewish life in Sarajevo.

Isak Kabiljo, Sarajevo. Present secretary of the Sarajevo Jewish community. Discussed synagogues and religious life of Sarajevo Sephardic community and its educational facilities.

Professor Samuel Kamhi, Sarajevo. Sephardic youth leader in interwar period and active member of Sarajevo Sephardic community. Discussed Sephardic movement and Jewish community in Sarajevo, as well as general problems concerning Yugoslav Jewry.

Dr. Haim Kamhi, Sarajevo. President of Sarajevo Jewish community in postwar period. Discussed Sephardic way of life.

Rosa Kronenberger (née Israel), Kibbutz Sha'ar Ha'amakim. Youth leader in Hashomer Hatzair in Sarajevo and Zagreb. Discussed Jewish family life in Sarajevo and Zionist youth activities in Yugoslavia.

David Levi-Dale, Zagreb. Editor of *Židovska Svijest* in Sarajevo and later secretary of the Federation of Jewish Religious Communities. Discussed the Federation of Jewish Religious Communities and the Federation of Zionists.

Mihael Levi, Tel Aviv. Zionist activist in Sarajevo Sephardic community. Discussed Zionists in Sarajevo and Belgrade and relations between Sephardim and Ashkenazim.

Hillel Livni (Slavko Weiss), Kibbutz Sha'ar Ha'amakim. Zionist youth leader in the 1920s and early 1930s. Discussed development of Ahdut Hatzofim and Hashomer Hatzair, youth leadership, and other Zionist youth organizations.

Avram and Johanan Omri (Steindler), Kibbutz Sha'ar Ha'amakim. Discussed Belgrade Ashkenazic community; relations between Sephardim and Ashkenazim; and Jewish youth activity in Belgrade.

Avram Pinto, Sarajevo. Discussed Jewish artisans in Sarajevo, Jewish cultural and charitable organizations, and education.

Cvi Rotem (Rothmüller), Tel Aviv. Zionist activist and youth leader. Discussed Yugoslav Zionism, Sephardic movement, youth activities, the Zagreb Jewish community, and integrationists.

Jichak and Sarina Talmi (Pinto), Kibbutz Sha'ar Ha'amakim. Discussed relations of Sarajevo Jews with their Serb, Croat, and Muslim neighbors, youth activity, and *hakhsharah.*

Mile Weiss, New York. Secretary of the Association of Yugoslav Jews in the United States. Discussed Ashkenazic community in Belgrade and Jews in Yugoslav political life.

Yakir Eventov (Drago Steiner), Haifa. Zionist activist and youth leader in interwar period and presently in charge of the archive of Hitahdut Olej Jugoslavije. Discussed general problems of Yugoslav Jewry in the interwar period.

NOTES

Introduction

1. From 1918 to 1929, the official name of the country was the Kingdom of Serbs, Croats, and Slovenes, after the three major South Slav nationalities. Thereafter, it became Yugoslavia (*Jugo* meaning south). As an introduction to the history of Yugoslavia, the following works are available in English: L. S. Stavrianos, *The Balkans since 1453* (New York: Holt, Rinehart and Winston, 1958); Robert Lee Wolff, *The Balkans in Our Time* (New York: W.W. Norton and Co., 1967); Stephen Clissold, *A Short History of Yugoslavia* (Cambridge: Cambridge University Press, 1966); Phyllis Auty, *Yugoslavia* (London: Walker and Co., 1965); R. J. Kerner, ed., *Yugoslavia* (Berkeley: University of California Press, 1949); Jozo Tomasevich, *Peasants, Politics, and Economic Change in Yugoslavia* (Stanford: Stanford University Press, 1955).

2. The standard work in English on the Bogomils, mainly dealing with Bulgaria, is D. Obolensky, *The Bogomils: A Study in Balkan Neo-Manichaeism* (Cambridge, 1946). See also D. Talbot Rice, *The Bogomils* (London, 1962).

3. The ruins of two fourth-century synagogues have been discovered in Stobi, Macedonia and Solin, Dalmatia, near Split. The main Jewish center in Slovenia was Maribor, especially in the fourteenth and fifteenth century. The Jews were expelled from Slovenia in 1496 and never returned in any significant numbers. For information on the Jews in the South Slav lands from the earliest times to the end of the nineteenth century, see Yakir Eventov, *A History of Yugoslav Jews,* vol.1 [Hebrew] (Tel Aviv: Hitahdut Olej Yugoslavia, 1971).

4. For background material on the Sephardim in the Balkans, see Salomon A. Rosanes, *A History of the Jews of Turkey,* 5 vols. [Hebrew] (Sofia: Imprimerie Amichpat, 1930–38); Morris S. Goodblatt, *Jewish Life in Turkey in the Sixteenth Century* (New York: Jewish Theological Seminary of America, 1952); Joseph Nehama, *Histoire des Israélites de Salonique,* 4 vols. (Salonika: Librairie Molho, 1935); I. S. Emmanuel, *Histoire des Israélites de Salonique,* vol.1 (Paris:

Thonon, 1936); Saul Mezan, *Les Juifs Espagnols en Bulgarie,* vol.1 (Sofia: Imprimerie Amichpat, 1925). Regarding their language and customs, see Michael Molho, *Usos y costumbres de los Sefardies de Salonica* (Madrid: Institute Arias Montano–Consejo Superior de Investigaciones Cientificas, 1950) and Mair Jose Benardete, *Hispanic Culture and Character of the Sephardic Jews* (New York: Hispanic Institute, 1952).

5. Yugoslav scholars have studied the early history of the Sephardic communities in Dubrovnik and Split extensively in such works as Jorjo Tadic, *Jevreji u Dubrovniku do polovine XVII stoljeća* (Sarajevo: La Benevolencia, 1937); G. Novak, *Židovi u Splitu* (Split, 1920); and Duško Kečkemet, *Židovi u povijesti Splita* (Split, 1972).

6. For more detail on the Orthodox-Neologue conflict in Hungary, see David Philipson, "Reform in Hungary" in *The Reform Movement in Judaism* (New York: Macmillan Co., 1931); Nathaniel Katzburg, "The Jewish Congress of Hungary, 1868–1869" in Randolph L. Braham, ed., *Hungarian-Jewish Studies,* vol.2 (New York: World Federation of Hungarian Jews, 1969), pp. 1–33; and Aron Moskovits, *Jewish Education in Hungary, 1848–1948* (New York: Bloch Publishing Co., 1964).

7. "Statistika Jevrejstva Kraljevine Srba, Hrvata i Slovenaca," *Jevrejski almanah* (O.S.), 1929–30, p.225.

8. For a discussion of the differences between these two groups, see H. J. Zimmels, *Ashkenazim and Sephardim* (London: Oxford University Press, 1958).

Chapter 1

1. Moritz Levy, *Die Sephardim in Bosnien* (Sarajevo: A. Kajon, 1911), p.3; Vladislav Skarić, "Iz prošlosti sarajevskih Jevreja," *Spomenica La Benevolencija* (Belgrade: Vreme, 1924), p.30.

2. Levy, *Die Sephardim in Bosnien,* pp.8, 86–87.

3. Ibid., p.87: Evlija Celebija, *Putopis odlomci o jugoslovenskim zemljama,* trans. Hazim Sabanović, (Sarajevo: Svjetlost, 1954), pp.117, 131; Alija Bejtić, "Jevrejske nastambe u Sarajevu," *Spomenica 400 godina od dolaska Jevreja u Bosnu i Hercegovinu* (Sarajevo: Božidar Sekulić, 1966), p.27.

4. Moric Levi, "Fragmenti iz života Sefarada," *Spomenica La Benevolencija,* pp.16–17.

5. Ibid., p.18; Samuel Kamhi, "Jezik, pjesme i poslovice bosansko-hercegovačkih Sefarada," *Spomenica 400,* pp.111–13; Todor Kruševac, "Društvene promene kod bosanskih Jevreja za austrijskog vremena," *Spomenica 400,* p.94.

6. The chief sources of information concerning the early Jewish community of Sarajevo were the communal minute books, called *pinakes* or *pinkes,* dating from 1720 to 1888, which were preserved in the archives of the Sarajevo Sephardic community until World War II. These records contained administrative reports, communal statutes, tax lists, accounts of annual income and expenses, as well as other data on communal leaders, rabbis, and other officials. They were written in Hebrew cursive (so-called Rashi script), partly in Ladino and partly in Hebrew. Since these records did not survive the war, the only communal documents from this period which presently

exist are those, including the revised communal statute of 1731, which were translated and included in the book *Die Sephardim in Bosnien* by Rabbi Moric Levi (Moritz Levy) of Sarajevo, published in 1911.

7. Levy, *Die Sephardim in Bosnien,* pp.22–25.

8. Ibid., pp.12–16; Vladislav Skarić, *Sarajevo i njegova okolina od najstarijih vremena do austro-ugarske okupacije* (Sarajevo: Bosanska Pošta, 1937), p.108.

9. Moric Levy, "David Pardo, sarajevski haham," *Jevrejski almanah* (O.S.), 1925–26, pp.122–25.

10. Levy, *Die Sephardim in Bosnien,* pp.52–57; Skarić, *Sarajevo i njegova okolina,* p.153.

11. A. Sućeska, "Položaj Jevreja u Bosni i Hercegovini za vrijeme Turaka," *Spomenica 400,* pp.48, 52.

12. Samuel Pinto, "Položaj bosanskih Jevreja pod turskom vladavinom," *Jevrejski almanah* (N.S.), 1954–55, pp.48–49; Levy, *Die Sephardim in Bosnien,* pp.35–36.

13. Ibid., pp.42–48.

14. Pinto, "Položaj bosanskih Jevreja," p.53; Abraham Galanté, *Documents officiels turcs concernant les Juifs de Turquie* (Istanbul: Haim, Rozio & Co., 1931), pp.4–7, Isidore Loeb, *La Situation des Israélites en Turquie, en Serbie et en Roumanie* (Paris: Joseph Baer et Cie., 1877), pp.15–16.

15. Isak Levi and Josef Konforti, "Jedan stari statut jevrejske sefardske opštine u Sarajevu," *Jevrejski almanah* (N.S.), 1968–70, pp.86–97.

16. Julije Hahamović, "Aškenazi u Bosni i Hercegovini," *Spomenica 400,* pp.142, 147–50; Oskar Grof, "Naš prilog o proslavi jevrejske aškenaske općine," *Jevrejski glas,* vol.3, no.2 (January 17, 1930), pp.5–6.

17. AJ, MPVO, F 185, Izveštaj SJVO u Beogradu po traženju Ministarstva pravde, Pov. br. 1235/39–15, November 4, 1939.

18. The remaining population of Čaršija was 37 percent Catholic, 22 percent Orthodox, and 6 percent Muslim; in the case of Bjelave, it was 39 percent Catholic, 13 percent Orthodox, and 26 percent Muslim; in Kovači, there were 52 percent Muslims, 24 percent Orthodox, and 9 percent Catholics. The numbers of persons of "other" religions in this breakdown were of little significance. Todor Kruševac, *Sarajevo pod austro-ugarskom upravom 1878–1918* (Sarajevo: Narodna štamparija, 1960), pp.25–26.

19. Haim Kamhi, "Jevreji u privredi Bosne i Hercegovine," *Spomenica 400,* pp.57–60; Levy, *Die Sephardim in Bosnien,* pp.72–75; Skarić, "Iz prošlosti sarajevskih Jevreja," pp.31–33; Jorjo Tadić, *Jevreji u Dubrovniku do polovine XVII stoljeća* (Sarajevo: La Benevolencija, 1937), pp.202–3.

20. Hamdija Kreševljaković, *Esnafi i obrti u starom Sarajevu* (Sarajevo: Narodna prosvjeta, 1958), p.118; Kamhi, "Jevreji u privredi," p.58; Skarić, *Sarajevo i njegova okolina,* p.134.

21. Kreševljaković, *Esnafi i obrti,* p.49; Skarić, *Sarajevo i njegova okolina,* pp.134–35.

22. Kruševac, "Društvene promene kod bosanskih Jevreja," p.80.

23. Hahamović, "Aškenazi u Bosni i Hercegovini," pp.143–47.

24. Kamhi, "Jevreji u privredi," pp.62–63.

25. Peter F. Sugar, *Industrialization of Bosnia-Hercegovina 1878–1918* (Seattle: University of Washington Press, 1963), p.214.

26. Kamhi, "Jevreji u privredi, pp.66–68, 70; BG-JM, Box 20, Sarajevo,

Samuel Pinto, List of Jewish lawyers, judges, and officials in Sarajevo (hand-written manuscript, n.d.); Josef Konforti, "Doprinos ljekara Jevreja zdravst-venoj zaštit i kulturi Bosne i Hercegovine," *Jevrejski almanah* (N.S.), 1968–70, pp.110–11, 122; SA-JL, Marriage registry of Sarajevo Sephardic community, 1894–1940.

27. Mojsije Zon, "O socijalnoj diferencijaciji sarajevskih Jevreja," *Godišnjak La Benevolencia i Potpora* (Sarajevo: Štamparija Menahem Papo, 1933), pp.130–32, 135.

28. "Rad sarajevske jevrejske opštine sefardskog obreda u minuloj godine," *Jevrejski glas,* vol.1, no.36 (September 21, 1928), pp.2–3.

29. In 1938 the average Jewish household size in the Drina province, which included Sarajevo, was reported to be 4.49, the highest in the country. Source: SJVO, *Izveštaj Glavnog odbora VII kongresu 23 i 24 aprila 1939 godine* (Belgrade: Štamparija Beletra, 1939), table 1, p.82.

30. Isak Samokovlija, "Jevrejski sirotinji i bijeda," *Jevrejski glas,* vol.1, no.6 (February 17, 1928), p.1.

31. Zon, "O socijalnoj diferencijaciji," p.135; Samuel Kamhi, *Jevrejski glas,* vol.8, no.49 (December 20, 1935).

32. Jakov Maestro, "Naš stari 'Meldar'," *Spomenica La Benevolencija,* pp.103–5; Samuel Pinto, "Prosvjetne prilike bosanskih Jevreja za turske vladavine," *Jevrejski almanah* (N.S.), 1955–56, pp.67–69; Kruševac, "Društvene promene kod bosanskih Jevreja," p.89.

33. Ibid., p.90.

34. Ibid.

35. Pinto, "Položaj bosanskih Jevreja," p.57; Landesregierung für Bos-nien und die Herzegowina, *Die Ergebnisse der Volkszählung in Bosnien und der Herzegowina vom 10 Oktober 1910* (Sarajevo: Landesdruckerei, 1912).

36. Germany, Publikationsstelle Wien, *Die Gliederung der Bevölkerung des ehemaligen Jugoslawien nach Muttersprache und Konfession* (Vienna, 1943), pp.14, 140; Kraljevina Jugoslavije, Opšta državna statistika (KJ-ODS), *Definitivni rezultati popisa stanovništva od 31 marta 1931 godine,* vol.2 (Belgrade: Državna štamparija, 1938), pp.vi–vii.

37. See Stanley Lieberson, "Language Questions in Censuses" in S. Lieberson, ed., *Explorations in Sociolinguistics* (Bloomington: Indiana Univer-sity Press, 1969), pp.134–51; Dudley Kirk, *Europe's Population in the Interwar Years* (Princeton: Princeton University Press, 1946), pp.224–26; and L. Tesnière, "Statistique des Langues de l'Europe" in A. Meillet, *Les Langues dans l'Europe nouvelle* (Paris: Payot, 1928), pp.293–304, 426.

38. A more exact breakdown is available for the Drina province as a whole, which included Sarajevo as its major city. The 1931 census results show 58 percent of the Ashkenazim in the province Serbo-Croatian speakers, 21 percent as German speakers, 8 percent as Hungarian speakers, and 13 percent as speakers of other languages. Source: Germany, Publikationsstelle Wien, *Die Gliederung,* pp.14, 140; *Definitivni rezultati popisa 1931,* vol.2, pp.vi–vii; see also table 11 in app. It is not immediately clear why a higher percentage of Ashkenazim claimed Serbo-Croatian as their native tongue in smaller towns as opposed to Sarajevo.

39. The observations which follow are based on a study of the birth registries of both the Sephardic and Ashkenazic communities in Sarajevo in

the late nineteenth and twentieth centuries. SA-JL, Matične knjige rodjenih sefardske opštine jevrejske, Sarajevo, 1894–1941, Matične knjige rodjenih aškenaske opštine, Sarajevo, 1880–1941.

Chapter 2

1. Ignjat Šlang, *Jevreji u Beogradu* (Belgrade: M. Karić, 1926), p.4; Salomon A. Rosanes, *A History of the Jews of Turkey* [Hebrew] (Sofia: Imprimerie Amichpat, 1938), vol.2, p.3.

2. Šlang, p.19; Rosanes, vol.2, p.123.

3. Šlang, p.22; Divna Djurić-Zamolo, "Stari jevrejski četvrt i jevrejska ulica u Beogradu," *Jevrejski almanah* (N.S.), 1965–67, p.42.

4. Šlang, p.22; Rosanes, vol.2, p.123; Djurić-Zamolo, p.44.

5. Djurić-Zamolo, p.44.

6. Ibid., p.47.

7. Šlang, p.22.

8. Aron Alkalaj, "Život i običaji u nekadašnjoj jevrejskoj mahali," *Jevrejski almanah* (N.S.), 1961–62, pp.83–85.

9. Ibid., pp.88–90; Aron Alkalaj, "Purim u jevrejskoj mahali," *Jevrejski almanah* (N.S.), 1954, pp.146–49.

10. Aron Alkalaj, "Život i običaji," p.87.

11. Šlang, pp.26–41; Rosanes, vol.3, p.189, vol.4, p.22; Zdenko Levntal, "Iz responza Josefa Almoznina," *Jevrejski almanah* (N.S.), 1965–67, pp.30–31.

12. Šlang, p.50.

13. Šlang, pp.51–54; Djurić-Zamolo, pp.46–48.

14. Šlang, pp.58–59.

15. Djurić-Zamolo, p.48; Vuk Vinaver, "Jevreji u Srbiji početkom XIX veka," *Jevrejski almanah* (N.S.), 1955–56, p.29.

16. Šlang, p.64.

17. Ibid., pp.65–66.

18. L. S. Stavrianos, *The Balkans since 1453* (New York: Holt, Rinehart and Winston, 1958), p.251. See also Tihomir R. Djordjević, *Iz Srbije kneza Miloša* (Belgrade: Geca Kon, 1924), pp.152–64.

19. Stana Djurić-Klajn, "Začetnik srpskog muzičkog života u XIX veka," *Jevrejski almanah* (N.S.), 1961–62, pp.68–73; Viktor Novak, "Josif Šlezinger," *Jevrejski glas,* vol.2, no. 2 (January 11, 1929), pp.1–2; Šlang, pp.73–74.

20. Šlang, p.71.

21. Isidore Loeb, *La Situation des Israélites en Turquie, en Serbie et en Roumanie* (Paris: Joseph Baer et Cie., 1877), p.22; Narcisse Leven, *Cinquante Ans d'Histoire: L'Alliance Israélite Universelle 1860–1910* (Paris: Librairie Félix Alcan, 1911), p.94; Šlang, p.80.

22. Loeb, p.31.

23. Loeb, pp.22–23, 32–33, 41–44; Šlang, pp.81–82; Jean Mousset, *La Serbie et son Église, 1830–1904* (Paris: Librairie Droz, 1938), p.253.

24. Loeb, pp.33–34; Mousset, p.254; Šlang, p.82.

25. Leven, p.101; Mousset, pp.254–55.

26. Loeb, pp.23–24.

27. Loeb, p.29; Šlang, pp.96–97.

28. Božidar Kovačević, "O Jevrejima u Srbiji od XVIII do početka XX veka," *Jevrejski almanah* (N.S.), 1959–60, p.110; Loeb, pp.25–26; Šlang, p.95.

29. Lucien Wolf, *Notes on the Diplomatic History of the Jewish Question* (London: Jewish Historical Society, 1919), p.33.

30. Loeb, p.18.

31. As quoted in Loeb, p.25.

32. Šlang, pp.68–70.

33. David Alkalaj, "Sefardska opština u Beogradu u 1860 godinama," *Jevrejski narodni kalendar,* vol.3, 1937–38, p.105.

34. Ibid., p.104.

35. Šlang, p.84.

36. Kraljevina Jugoslavije-Opšta Državna Statistika, *Definitivni rezultati popisa stanovništva od 31 januara 1921 godine* (Sarajevo: Državna štamparija, 1932), p.4.

37. AJ, MPVO, F 185, Izveštaj SJVO u Beogradu po traženju Ministarstva pravde, Pov.br.1235/39–15, November 4, 1939.

38. Aron Alkalaj, "Život i običaji," p.82.

39. KJ-ODS, *Definitivni rezultati popisa, 1921.*

40. Belgrade Jewish Museum [BG-JM], Reg. br. 217/10, F dok K11, Spisak obveznika verskog prinosa jevrejske aškenaske veroispovedne opštine u Beogradu za 1941 godinu; Spisak razreza glavnog opštinskog verskog prinosa i vanrednog prireza za 1940 godinu.

41. Ibid.

42. Ibid.

43. *Izveštaji sa svečanosti o prijemu dužnosti novoizabrana Uprave i Odbora crkveno-školske jevrejske opštine u Beogradu 3 jula 1932 godine* (Belgrade: Štamparija Polet, 1932), pp.19–20.

44. BG-JM, Spisak obveznika, 1941.

45. Dušan Sindik, "Na jevrejskim školama u Beogradu u XIX veku," *Jevrejski almanah,* 1961–62, p.99; Djordjević, p.110; Dušan J. Popović, *Beograd pre 200 godina* (Belgrade: Geca Kon, 1935), p.41; I[saac] Alcalay, "Arhivski gradja o Jevrejima u Srbiji," *Jevrejski almanah* (O.S.), 1928, pp.28–41.

46. Sindik, pp.99–102, 106–9; Šlang, p.92.

47. Sindik, p.98; Šlang, pp.88–89.

48. Sindik, p.102.

49. David Alkalaj, "Sefardska opština," p.109.

50. Sindik, p.133.

51. Jelena de Majo, "O kulturnih razvitaka jevrejskih žena u Srbiji," *Jevrejsko žensko društvo u Beogradu, 1874–1924* (Belgrade, 1924), pp.54–58.

52. I[saac] Alcalay, "The Jews of Serbia," *American Jewish Year Book,* vol. 20, 1918–19, p.79–81.

53. Šlang, pp.85–88.

54. Ibid., p.102.

55. *Statistika Kraljevine Srbije,* vol.12 (Belgrade: Državna štamparija, 1899), pp.58–59; Arnold Wadler, "Die Juden in Serbien," *Zeitschrift für Demographie und Statistik der Juden,* vol.2, no.10 (October 1906), p.169.

56. Germany, Publikationsstelle Wien, *Die Gliederung der Bevölkerung des ehemaligen Jugoslawien nach Muttersprache und Konfession* (Vienna, 1943), pp.11, 22.

57. Ibid.; KJ-ODS, *Definitivni rezultati popisa 1931,* vol.2, pp.vi–vii. The evidence on the Sephardic community is corroborated by a 1929 municipal survey, which reported 2,256 Ladino speakers out of 7,443 Jews, or 30 percent. Source: Ljubomir St. Kosier, *Jevreji u Jugoslaviji i Bugarskoj* (Zagreb: Ekonomska biblioteka Srba, Hrvata i Slovenaca, 1930), pp.120–21. The Ashkenazic figure appears somewhat out of line with linguistic data for Ashkenazim elsewhere in the country, see table 11 in app.

58. BG-JM, Spisak razreza 1940 godinu.

59. BG-JM, Spisak obveznika 1941 godinu.

60. Šlang, pp.108–14; I[saac] Alcalay, "The Jews of Serbia," p.76.

Chapter 3

1. An excellent source of information on the growth and development of the city of Zagreb may be found in an article by Jack C. Fisher, "Urban Analysis: A Case Study of Zagreb Yugoslavia," *Association of American Geographers Annals,* vol.53, no.3 (September 1963), pp. 266–84.

2. Arthur May, *The Habsburg Monarchy 1867–1914* (Cambridge: Harvard University Press, 1965), p.72.

3. Gavro Schwarz, *Povijest zagrebačke židovske opĉine* (Zagreb: Štamparija Gaj, 1939), p.7.

4. Ibid., pp.7–8.

5. Traian Stoianovich, *A Study in Balkan Civilization* (New York: Alfred A. Knopf, 1967), p.166.

6. Schwarz, p.9.

7. Ibid., p.11.

8. Ibid., pp.14–15

9. Ibid., pp.17–18.

10. Ibid., p.23.

11. Ibid., pp.26–27; Djoko Milojčić, "Nekoliko priloga u povijesti Jevreja Jugoslavije," *Židov, Kulturni i literarni prilog,* vol.1, no.15 (July 23, 1937), p.66.

12. Milojčić, p.67.

13. Schwarz, p.16.

14. Nathaniel Katzburg, "Hungarian Jewry in Modern Times," in Randolph L. Braham, ed., *Hungarian-Jewish Studies,* vol.1 (New York: World Federation of Hungarian Jews, 1966), p.142.

15. Arhiv Hrvatske, Fond Zemaljske vlade, JU-103, IX-7-1892-6; Document from Kralj. odjelni predstojnik, No. 1759, November 23, 1870; Letter from Ministerialni savietnik Bogović to Ban Ivan Mazuranić, No. 1849, October 25, 1873; "Zur Entstehungsgeschichte des Gesetzes über die Gleichstellung der Juden," *Židovska smotra,* vol.2, no.7 (July 1908), pp.163–64.

16. BG-JM, Box 16, Zagreb, No. 34, Reg. br. 1211/55, Osnova zakona o vjeroispovjednim odnosima from Prilog 18 k. stenograf. zapisnikom sabora kralj. Hrvatske, Slavonije i Dalmacije, g. 1905, p.1.

17. Ibid., p.4.

18. Obrazloženje osnovi zakona o vjeroizpoviednim odnosima, ibid., p.12.

19. BG-JM, Box 16, Zagreb, No. 29, Reg. br. 1208/55, Zapisnik o skup-

štini predstavnika izraelitičkih bogoštovnih obćina u kraljevinama Hrvatskoj i Slavoniji; Nos.37, 38, Reg. br. 1212/55, Preporuka kr. hrvatsko-slavonsko-dalmatinskoj vladi k osnovi zakona o vjeroispovjednim odnosima; Hugo Kon, "Izraelitska bogoštovna općina u Zagrebu u godini 1926," in *Godišnjak Izraelitske bogoštovne općine zagrebačke.* (Zagreb: Jugoslavenska štampa, 1928), pp.21–22.

20. A similar situation had also existed in Hungary until a law on the equality of the Jewish religion was passed in 1895. See Katzburg, "Hungarian Jewry in Modern Times," pp.142–43.

21. Schwarz, p.32. Goldman resigned from his office in 1849 and subsequently converted to Christianity, causing quite a scandal in the Jewish community.

22. Ibid., p.33.

23. Ibid., pp.34–35.

24. Ibid., pp.35–36.

25. Ibid., pp.37–38, 72–73; "Nešto arhivske gradje za povijest Jevreja u Jugoslaviji," *Omanut,* vol.1, no.7 (March 1937), p.228.

26. Schwarz, pp.80–82; Milojčić, "Nekoliko priloga u povijesti Jevreja Jugoslavije," p.100; AH, ZV, JU-103, IX-7-1892-6, Correspondence and reports on the Orthodox community.

27. BG-JM, Box 16, Zagreb, No. 16, Reg. br. 1210/55, "Zakon od 7 veljače 1906 o uredjenju israelitskih bogoštovnih obćina," in *Sbornik zakona i naredaba valjanih za Kraljevine Hrvatsku i Slavoniju,* vol.4, no.9 (1906), p.146.

28. See Salo W. Baron, "Freedom and Constraint in the Jewish Community" in Israel Davidson, ed., *Essays and Studies in Memory of Linda R. Miller* (New York: Jewish Theological Seminary, 1938), pp.9–23; Nathaniel Katzburg, "The Jewish Congress of Hungary, 1868–1869," *Hungarian-Jewish Studies,* vol.2, pp.1–33, and "Hungarian Jewry in Modern Times," ibid., vol.1, pp. 137-70.

29. "Zakon od 7 veljače 1906," p.147; (Ben Benjamin Zef), "Die Regelung der Kultusgemeinde in Kroatien," *Židovska smotra,* vol.1, nos. 9–10 (July-August 1907), p.238.

30. "Zakon od 7 veljače 1906," p.150.

31. (Ben Benjamin Zef), "Die Regelung der Kultusgemeinde in Kroatien," pp.236–37; AJ, MV, 69, 5-98-28, Pravila udruženja starovjerica članova izraelitske bogoštovne obćine u Zagrebu (1913); "Izraelitska bogoštovna općina u Zagrebu u godini 1926," pp.28–30.

32. Ibid., pp.30, 36.

33. AJ, MPVO, F 185, Izveštaj SJVO u Beogradu po traženju Ministarstva pravde, Pov. br. 1235/39-15, November 4, 1939, Statistika ortodoksne jevrejske zajednice, November 10, 1939.

34. Aleksandar Klein, "Nešto statistike o zagrebačkim Jevrejima," *Židov,* vol.18, no.7 (February 2, 1934), p.3.

35. "Uspješni financijski rad uprave zagrebačke židovske općine," *Židov,* vol.24, no.26 (June 28, 1940), p.5.

36. "Socijalni rad uprave zagrebačke židovske općine," *Židov,* vol.24, no.27 (July 7, 1940), p.6.

37. Schwarz, p.39.

38. Ibid., p.40; Aleksandar Klein, "Naša osnovna škola," *Židov,* vol.20, no.43 (October 23, 1936), p.9.

39. Ibid.

40. Klein, "Naša osnovna škola," p.9.

41. ZG-JL, *Godišnje izvještje Izrajelitske glavne učione u Zagrebu,* 1869–74; *Godišnje izvješće obospolne Javne izr. pučke škole u Zagrebu,* 1880–89; *Godišnje izvješće obospolne Izr. konfesionalne škole,* 1889–1914.

42. Klein, "Naša osnovna škola," p.9; "Upisi u zagrebačku konfesionalnu školu," *Židov,* vol.6, nos.40–41 (September 12, 1922), p.14; "IBO u Zagrebu u 1926," *Godišnjak IBO Zagreb,* p.39; "Intervju s predsjednikom g. dr Hugo Konom," *Židov,* vol.12, nos.37–38 (September 14, 1928), p.3; "Intervju s ravnateljim g. M. Margelom," ibid., vol.13, no.40 (October 4, 1929), p.7; "Rad jevrejske vjeroispovjedne općine u Zagrebu u g. 1934," ibid., vol.19, no.16 (April 17, 1935), p.9; "Nešto statistike iz zagrebačke jevrejske općine," ibid., vol.20, no.18 (May 1, 1936), p.9; "Važna sjednica Pretstojništva JVO u Zagrebu," ibid., vol.21, no.17 (April 23, 1937), p.7; "Rad u prošloj godini JVO u Zagrebu," ibid., vol.22, no.17 (April 29, 1938), p.8; "Djelatnost uprave zagrebačke židovske općine," ibid., vol.24, no.30 (July 26, 1940), p.5.

43. Ibid.

44. "Statistisches über die kroatischen Mittelschulen im Schuljahre 1907–8," *Židovska smotra,* vol. 2, no. 8 (August 1908), pp.205–6.

45. "Osnovna škola JVO u Zagrebu," *Židov,* vol.18, no.28 (July 13, 1934), p.6.

46. "Važna sjednica Pretstojništva JVO u Zagrebu," *Židov,* vol. 20, no. 17 (April 23, 1937), p.7.

47. BG-JM, Box 16, Zagreb, No. 8, Reg. br. 1215/55, Statuten des Agramer israelitischen Kranken-Unterstützung- und Beerdigungs-Vereines (Chebra Kadischa), Agram, 1859; Statuten der Israelitischen Cultus-Gemeinde in Agram (1867).

48. Lavoslav Šik, "Pojavi dr Hozeja Jacobia," *Židov,* vol.9, nos.17–18 (April 24, 1925), p.3.

49. David Spitzer, "Reminiscences," *Omanut,* vol.3, nos.4–5 (April–May 1939), p.57.

50. M. Ekmečić, "Profiles of Societies in the Second Half of the Nineteenth Century," in Vladimir Dedijer, et al., *History of Yugoslavia* (New York: McGraw-Hill Book Co., 1974), p.359.

52. "Svakako, samo ne hrvatski," *Židov,* vol.2, no.19 (October 1, 1918), p.1.

52. *Statistički godišnjak Kraljevine Hrvatske i Slavonije,* vol.1, 1905 (Zagreb, 1913), p.45; Ljubomir St. Kosier, *Jevreji u Jugoslaviji i Bugarskoj,* pp.120–21.

53. Ibid.

54. Germany, Publikationsstelle Wien, *Die Gliederung der Bevölkerung des ehemaligen Jugoslawien nach Muttersprache und Konfession,* p.304.

Chapter 4

1. Oscar I. Janowsky, *The Jews and Minority Rights 1898–1919* (New York: Columbia University Press, 1933), p.155.

2. Minorities Treaty, art. 2. For the complete text of this agreement, see app. 2.

3. In the Yugoslav and Bulgarian treaties, however, special provisions were made for the sizable Muslim minority. Janowsky, *Jews and Minority Rights,* pp.372–73 and C. A. Macartney, *National States and National Minorities* (London: Oxford University Press, 1934), pp.249–52, 405. See Minorities Treaty, art.10 in app.2.

4. See app.3 for a translation of the relevant articles of the Yugoslav constitutions.

5. KJ-ODS, *Statistički pregled Kraljevine Jugoslavije po banovima* (1930), pp.4–5.

6. Minorities Treaty, art.8. See app.2.

7. See Constitution of 1921, art.12, para.6, in app.3.

8. Borivoie B. Mirkovitch, *La Yougoslavie Politique et Économique* (Paris: Pierre Bossuet, 1935), p.50.

9. Minorities Treaty, arts. 7, 9. See app.2.

10. Art. 9. See also Jacob Robinson, *Were the Minorities Treaties a Failure?* (New York: Institute of Jewish Affairs, 1943), pp. 154–58.

11. According to the 1931 census, 18,044 individuals reported as their mother tongue languages which were officially classified as Jewish. The overwhelming majority of these persons were clearly Ladino-speaking Sephardim, although this category undoubtedly also included some number who claimed to speak Yiddish, and perhaps even Hebrew as well. Source: Germany, Publikationsstelle Wien, *Die Gliederung der Bevölkerung des ehemaligen Jugoslawien nach Muttersprache und Konfession* (Vienna, 1943,) p.10.

12. This regulation was apparently aimed more against the Hungarians than against Jews per se in an attempt to reduce the total number of the Hungarian minority. See C. A. Macartney, *Hungary and Her Successors* (London: Oxford University Press, 1937) pp. 408–25.

13. In this case, the Zionists, the only likely protagonists for Jewish national rights, sided with the government in pushing for the use of Serbo-Croatian instead of Hungarian.

14. Arhiv grada Zagreba, Fond Alexander Licht, Alexander Licht to Leo Motzkin, Paris, Answers to questionaire of Conseil pour les droits des minorités juives, 1930.

15. Ibid.

16. "Svetkovanje subote i jevrejskih praznika u školama," *Službeni list SJVO,* vol.1, no.2 (December 15, 1936), pp.1–2; Law on the Religious Community of Jews in the Kingdom of Yugoslavia, art. 25, see app. 4.

17. "Pitanje svetkovanja subote u Sarajevu," *Židov,* vol.9, no.49 (November 13, 1925), p.5; Arhiv Jugoslavije, Fond Ministarstva vera, 69, 55-65-25, Letter from SJVO to MV, No. 759, October 20, 1925.

18. Kraljevina Jugoslavije Opšta Državna Statistika, *Definitivni rezultati popisa stanovništva od 31 marta 1931 godine,* vol.2 (Belgrade: Državna štamparija, 1938), pp.viii–xii; Great Britain, Naval Intelligence Division, *Jugoslavia,* vol.3 (London: Geographical Handbook Series, 1945), p.54; Dudley Kirk, *Europe's Population in the Interwar Years* (Princeton: Princeton University Press, 1946) table 2, p.15.

19. See Arthur Ruppin, *The Jewish Fate and the Future* (London: Macmillan and Co., 1940), pp. 62–68.

20. Kirk, *Europe's Population in the Interwar Years,* table 3, p.24; Jozo Tomasevich, *Peasants, Politics and Economic Change in Yugoslavia* (Stanford: Stanford University Press, 1955), p.289.

21. SJVO, *Izveštaj Glavnog odbora VII kongresu 23 i 24 aprila 1939 godine* (Belgrade: Štamparija Beletra, 1939), table 1, p.82.

22. By 1939 the Jewish birth rate had declined to 8.2 per 1,000, while the death rate remained at 12.6. The birth and death rates among the general population had also fallen during this period, but only to 25.9 and 15.0 respectively. KJ-ODS, *Statistički godišnjak* (Belgrade: Državna štamparija KJ, 1929–1940); Eduard Mosbacher, "Jugoslovenski Jevreji u svetlosti statistike," *Jevrejski narodni kalendar,* vol.6, 1940–41, p.130.

23. Kirk, *Europe's Population in the Interwar Years,* p.58; Great Britain, Naval Intelligence Division, *Jugoslavia,* vol.3, pp.49–51; Tomasevich, *Peasants, Politics and Economic Change,* p.302.

24. KJ-ODS, *Statistički godišnjak,* 1929–40.

25. *Izveštaj o radu uprave crkveno-školske jevrejske opštine u Beogradu za period vremena od 11 juna 1924 do 27 juna 1926 godine* (Belgrade: M. Karić, 1926); *Izveštaj . . . od 10 juna 1929 do 20 maja 1932* (Belgrade: Štamparija Merkur, 1932); Matične knjige rodjenih aškenaske jevrejske opštine u Sarajevu, 1880–1941; "Statistike Jevreja Sarajeva, 1904–24," *Narodna židovska svijest,* vol.3, no.91 (January 1, 1926), p.3; "Statistički podaci," *Židov,* vol.18, no.36 (September 7, 1934); Braco Poljokan, "Relativno opadanje naše zajednice," *Jevrejski glas,* vol.3, nos.15–16 (April 11, 1930), p.12.

26. Ruppin, *The Jewish Fate and the Future,* p.101.

27. KJ-ODS, *Definitivni rezultati popisa, 1921* (1932), pp.4, 190, 262; AJ, MPVO, F 185, Izveštaj SJVO u Beogradu po traženju Ministarstva pravde, Pov.br.1235/39-15, November 4, 1939; Statistika ortodoksne jevrejske zajednice, November 10, 1939.

28. KJ-ODS, *Definitivni rezultati popisa stanovništva od 31 marta 1931 godine,* vol. 4 (Sarajevo: Državna štamparija, 1940), pp.106–7; SJVO, *Izveštaj VII kongresu,* p.83.

29. Jacob Lestschinsky, "The Economic and Social Development of the Jewish People," *The Jewish People Past and Present,* vol.1 (New York: Jewish Encyclopedic Handbooks, 1946), pp.379–80. For further comparative data on Jewish occupational distribution in the interwar period, see Ruppin, *The Jewish Fate and the Future,* pp.145–71.

30. Aleksandar Klein, "Nešto statistike o zagrebačkim Jevrejima," *Židov,* vol.18, no.7 (February 2, 1934), p.3; BG-JM, Spisak razreza glavnog opštinskog verskog prinosa i vanrednog prireza za 1940 godinu and Spisak obveznika verskog prinosa jevrejske aškenaske veroispovedne opštine u Beogradu za 1941 godinu.

31. Sarajevo Birth and Marriage Registries; Haim Kamhi, "Jevreji u privredi BiH," *Spomenica 400 godina od dolaska Jevreja u Bosnu i Hercegovinu, 1566–1966* (Sarajevo: Božidar Sekulić, 1966), pp.66–69.

32. KJ-ODS, *Definitivni rezultati popisa, 1931,* vol.2, pp.vi–vii; Germany, Publikationsstelle Wien, *Die Gliederung,* pp.22, 140, 304.

33. For a critique on the pitfalls of linguistic statistics, see Kirk, *Europe's Population in the Interwar Years,* pp.224–26.

34. KJ-ODS, *Statistički godišnjak,* vol.1 (1929), pp.84–85.

35. Arhiv Bosne i Hercegovine, Fond Kraljevine banske uprave, DZ, pov.1931, List of students studying abroad, Sarajevo, 1930/31 and 1931/32.

36. KJ-ODS, *Statistički godišnjak*, vol.1 (1929), pp.378-79; ibid., vol.10 (1940), p.359.

37. Lavoslav Šik, "Poljski Jevreji na medicinskom fakultetu u Ljubljani," *Židov*, vol.18, no.4 (January 26, 1934), p.1.

38. KJ-ODS, *Statistički godišnjak*, vol.10 (1940), p.359.

39. SJVO, *Izveštaj VII kongresu*, table 4, p.86.

40. KJ-ODS, Statistički godišnjak, vol.1 (1929), pp.378–79; ibid., vol. 10 (1940), p.359.

41. Ruppin, *The Jewish Fate and the Future*, p.274.

42. KJ-ODS, *Statistički godišnjak*, vol.3 (1931); *Definitivni rezultati popisa 1931*, vol. 2 (1938).

Chapter 5

1. For a complete translation of this law see app.4.

2. A debate on the future of Sephardic and Ashkenazic relations was presented in a series of articles in *Židov* in May and June of 1926.

3. AJ-MPVO, F 184, Predlog zakona o verskoj zajednici mojsijevaca u KSHS (n.d.-1926?); Statut za jevrejsku veroispovest u KSHS (n.d.-1928?); Projekt zakona o pravnom uredjenju i odnosu ortodoksnog Jevrejstva u KSHS (n.d.-1928?).

4. Law on the Religious Community of Jews, arts. 5, 26.

5. Ibid., arts. 9, 10, 11.

6. Ibid., art. 7.

7. Ibid., art. 2.

8. Ibid., arts. 13, 14. These institutions will be discussed further in the next chapter.

9. Ibid., arts. 21, 25.

10. Ibid., arts. 2, 3. The subsequent discussion is based upon the following statutes:

a. for Zagreb: Statuten der Israelitischen Cultus Gemeinde in Agram (1867)(found in the Zagreb University Library); Pravila izraelitske bogoštovne općine u Zagrebu (1912)(ZGU); ibid. (1923)(ZGU); Pravila jevrejske veroispovjedne općine u Zagrebu (1931)(BG-JM); Pravila jevrejske veroispovjedne općine sefardskog obreda u Zagrebu (1927)(AJ-MV); Pravila izraelitske ortodoksne bogoštovne općine u Zagrebu (1925)(AJ-MV).

b. for Belgrade: Pravila crkveno-školske jevrejske opštine u Beogradu (1893)(Zagreb Jewish Library); ibid. (1926) (ZG-JL); Pravila jevrejske sefardske veroispovedne opštine u Beogradu (1936)(AJ-MPVO); Pravila jevrejske veroispovedne opštine eškenaskog obreda u Beogradu (1930, 1933)(AJ-MPVO).

c. for Sarajevo: Statutes of the Sephardic Community of Sarajevo (1731) (Moritz Levy, *Die Sephardim in Bosnien* [German], pp.21–25); Statutes of the Spanish Israelite Community in Sarajevo (1882)(in original Ladino, transliterated, and in Serbo-Croatian translation in Isak Levi and Dr. Josef Konforti, "Jedan stari statut jevrejske sefardske op-štine u Sarajevu," *Jevrejski almanah* [N.S.], 1968–70, pp.86–97); Pravila jevrejske veroispovedne opštine sefardskog obreda u Sarajevu (1922, 1929, 1935)(AJ-MPVO)(1913 missing); Statuten der Österreichischen-Ungarischen Israelitischen Kultusgemeinde in Sarajevo (1907) (BG-JM); Pravila jevrejske veroispovedne opštine aškenaskog obreda u Sarajevu (1923)(Sarajevo Jewish Library). The Zagreb Sephardic and Orthodox communities, both of which were very small, are not included in this analysis except when specifically mentioned.

11. Law on the Religious Community of Jews, arts. 1–3.

12. KJ-ODS, *Statistički pregled Kraljevine Jugoslavije po banovima* (1930), pp. 4,8,16,26.

13. The Belgrade Sephardic community had an eleven-member board (1926 statutes, art. 10); Belgrade and Sarajevo Ashkenazic, a twelve-member board (BG-Ashk., 1933, art. 9 and SA-Ashk., 1922, art. 7); Sarajevo Sephardic, eighteen (1922, art. 5); and Zagreb, forty-five (1923, art. 5).

14. The Zagreb Jewish community had three such committees in 1912 and four in 1923: religious, educational, administrative, and social-charitable (art. 14). The Belgrade Sephardic and Ashkenazic councils were also divided into committees: financial, cultural-educational, social-charitable, religious, etc. (BG-Seph., 1926, art. 14; BG-Ashk., 1933, art. 15). Both Sarajevo communities developed similar systems as well. The Sephardic council was split into synagogue, administrative-legal, financial, *gabelle* (kosher meat), school, social welfare, and property sections ("Svečana sjednica novog Vijeća sefardske opštine," *Jevrejski glas,* vol.6, no.47 [November 31, 1933], p.6), while the Ashkenazim had financial, school, social welfare, and synagogue committees. (BG-JM, Box 45, Arhiva jevrejske veroispovedne opštine aškenaskog obreda u Sarajevu, Prijava rezultata izbora i konstituiranja odbora, Sarajevo, May 12, 1937, No. 145/1937.)

15. BG-Seph., 1926, arts. 82, 83; BG-Ashk., 1933, art. 10.

16. The Zagreb communal council contained ninety members, forty-five elected to it specifically, plus the forty-five members of the board of directors (1923, art. 5). In the Belgrade Sephardic community, the council consisted of twenty-five members plus the eleven-man board (1926, art. 14), while the Belgrade Ashkenazic council included twenty plus twelve (1933, art. 10). The Sarajevo Sephardim had provisions for neither a communal meeting nor a representative council, but governed itself with one eighteen-man board including a five-member executive (1922, art. 5).

17. In Zagreb, women and students received the right to vote in 1923 (art. 91), while in Belgrade women had to wait until 1933 in the Ashkenazic community (art. 32) and 1936 in the Sephardic community (art. 30), before they were permitted to cast ballots.

18. ZG-Orth., 1925 statutes, arts. 5, 6.

19. BG-Seph., 1893, art. 17, but not in 1926, 1936 versions; BG-Ashk., 1933, art. 29.

20. ZG-Ashk. 1923, 1931, art. 111.

21. Law on the Religious Community of Jews, art. 15.

22. AJ, MV, 69, 23-41-29, Letter from Crkveno-školska jevrejska op-ština, No.853, to MV, September 9, 1926; "Izbori za sefardsku opštinu u

Beogradu," *Židov,* vol.16, no.21 (May 27, 1932); "Izbori u sefardskoj opštini," ibid., vol.22, no.22 (June 3, 1938), p.9; "Izbori za crkveno-školsku jevrejsku opštinu u Beogradu," ibid., vol.19, no.22 (May 31, 1935), p.6.

23. "Izbori za jevrejsku sefardsku općinu," ibid., vol.13, no.1 (January 4, 1929), p.6; "Izbori za sefardsku opštinu u Sarajevu," *Jevrejski glas,* vol.2, no.1 (January 4, 1929), p.3; "Rezultat izbora za sefardsku općinu," *Židov,* vol.17, no.47 (November 24, 1933), p.5.

24. "Izbori u zagrebačkoj bogoštovnoj općini," *Židov,* vol.8, no.5 (February 1, 1924), p.6; "Izbori u zagrebačkoj židovskjoj općini," ibid., vol.14, no.12 (March 20, 1930), p.4; "Izbori za jevrejsku veroispovjednu općinu u Zagrebu," ibid., vol.19, no.49 (November 29, 1935), p.6.

25. After World War II, Dr. Vajs was to succeed Dr. Pops as president of the Federation of Jewish Communities from 1948 until his death in 1964.

26. "Izbori u židovskoj bogoštovnoj općini," *Židov,* vol.14, no.10 (March 3, 1930), p.7.

27. "Svečana sednica nove uprave u opštinskoj salu," *Židov,* vol.16, no.27 (July 8, 1932).

28. "Izbori za sefardsku opštinu u Beogradu," *Židov,* vol.16, no.21 (May 27, 1932).

29. "Izbor u sefardskoj opštini," *Židov,* vol.22, no.22 (June 3, 1938), p.9.

30. "Dvije liste za izbore Vijeća sefardske općine," *Židov,* vol.17, no.45 (November 10, 1933), p.7; "Rezultat izbora za sefardsku općinu," ibid., no.47 (November 24, 1933), p.5.

31. Zagreb statutes of 1923 and Belgrade and Sarajevo statutes of 1936.

32. "Službena saopštenja jevrejske aškenaske veroispovedne opštine," *Glasnik jevrejske aškenaske veroispovedne opštine,* no.1 (January 15, 1941), p.14; BG-JM, Spisak obveznika verskog prinosa jevrejske aškenaske veroispovedne opštine u Beogradu za 1941 godinu.

33. AJ, MV, 69, 4-62-22, Letter from Crkveno-školska jevrejska opština, No.561, to MV, June 25, 1922; MPVO, F 184, Letter No.548, June 12, 1924; "Izbori za beogradsku sefardsku opštinu," *Židov,* vol.16, no.20 (May 20, 1932), p.5; ibid., no.21 (May 27, 1932); "Izbori za crkveno-školsku jevrejsku opštinu u Beogradu," ibid., vol.19, no.22 (May 31, 1935), p.6; "Izbori u sefardskoj opštini," ibid., vol.22, no.22 (June 3, 1938), p.9.

34. "Izbori u zagrebačkoj židovskoj općini," *Židov,* vol.14, no.11 (March 13, 1930), p.2.

35. "Službena saopštenja jevrejske aškenaske veroispovedne opštine," *Glasnik jevr. ašk. VO,* no.1 (January 15, 1941), pp.14–15; "Sadašnja Uprava jevrejske veroispovedne opštine aškenaskog obreda u Sarajevu," *Jevrejski glas,* vol.3, no.2 (January 17, 1931), p.11.

36. "Rezultat izbora u sefardskoj opštini," *Narodna židovska svijest,* vol.3, no.35 (December 5, 1924), p.3.

37. BG-Seph., 1926, art. 105. Similar clauses appeared in most of the other statutes as well.

38. "Izraelitska bogoštovna općina u Zagrebu u 1926," *Godišnjak Izraelitske bogoštovne općine zagrebačke,* vol.1 (Zagreb: Jugoslovenska štampa, 1928),

pp.38–39; annual reports in *Židov* on the work of the Zagreb Jewish community and its budget to 1940.

39. "Budžet 1921–31," *Izveštaj o radu uprave crkveno-školske jevrejske opštine u Beogradu, 1929–32,* pp.62–63; Moše de Majo, "Budžet naše opštine za 1940," *Vesnik,* vol.2, no.14 (February 1, 1940), p.11.

40. David Levi-Dale, "Iz sarajevske sefardske općine," *Narodna židovska svijest,* vol.1, no.21 (August 22, 1924), pp.3–4; *Spomenica jevrejske vjeroispovjedne opštine sefardskog obreda u Sarajevu* (1930), pp.11–12; AJ-MP, 229-5-30, Budget for 1934; "Sa budžetske sjednice jevrejske sefardske opštine u Sarajevu," *Jevrejski glas,* vol.13, no.1 (January 5, 1940), p.7.

41. BG-Seph., 1926, art. 88. Parallel situations existed in other communities as well.

42. See notes 39 and 40 above.

43. BG-Seph., 1926, arts. 89, 94–96.

44. AJ, MP, 229-5-30, "Protokol plenarne sjednice od 18 decembra 1933," and other documents and correspondence from 1933 to 1935.

45. "Sa budžetske sjednice jevrejske sefardske opštine u Sarajevu," *Jevrejski glas,* vol.13, no.1 (January 5, 1940), p.7.

46. AJ, MP, 102-39-34, Izvod iz zapisnika sedme redovne sednice Veća jevr. sef. VO u BG, 18 decembra 1939; BG-JM, Spisak razreza glavnog opštinskog verskog prinosa i vanrednog prireza za 1940 godinu, p.60; Moše de Majo, "Budžet naše opštine za 1940," *Vesnik,* vol.2, no.14 (February 1, 1940), p.11; AJ, MFVO, F 184, Izvod iz zapisnika sednice odbora jevr. ašk. VO u BG, 11 aprila 1940; "Službena saopštenja jevr. ašk. VO," *Glasnik jevr. ašk. VO,* no.1 (January 15, 1941), p.15; BG-JM, Spisak obveznika 1941.

47. "Budžetska rasprava zagr. bogoštovne općine," *Židov,* vol.8, no.50 (November 28, 1924); "Sjednica pretstojništva jevr. općine u ZG," ibid., vol.17, no.4 (January 27, 1933), p.3; "Socijalni rad uprave zagr. židovske općine," ibid., vol.24, no.27 (July 5, 1940), p.6.

48. ZG, 1912, art. 22; BG-Seph., 1926, art. 50; BG-Ashk., 1933, art. 54; SA-Seph., 1929, Art. 19.

49. Law on the Religious Community of Jews, art. 18.

50. Interview with Chief Rabbi Alcalay at the Sephardic Home for the Aged in Brooklyn, January 8, 1971; *Židov,* vol.7, no.50 (December 8, 1923), p.6.

51. Moritz Levy, *Die Sephardim in Bosnien* (Sarajevo: A. Kajon, 1911); translated into Serbo-Croatian and reprinted as *Sefardi u Bosni* (Belgrade, 1969).

52. Samuel Pinto, "O pitanjima Židova u BiH," *Židov,* vol.1, no.3 (October 15, 1917), p.1; "Dr Moric Levi," *Jevrejski glas,* vol.3, no.35 (September 12, 1930), p.3.

53. "Dr Hosea Jacobi," *Židov,* vol.9, nos.17–18 (April 24, 1925), p.3.

54. "Nadrabin dr Gavro Schwarz," *Židov,* vol.15, no.5 (January 30, 1931), p.3; *Izraelitički molitvenik,* Gavro Schwarz, trans. (Zagreb: Lav Hartman, 1902); Gavro Schwarz, *Obredi izraelske vjere* (Zagreb: Tiskara Narodnih novina, 1st ed. 1916, 2nd ed. 1924).

55. Gavro Schwarz, *Povijest zagrebačke židovske općine od osnutka do 50-tih godina 19. vijeka* (Zagreb: Stamparija Gaj, 1939).

56. "Instalacija rabina zagr. jevrejske opštine dra Miroslava Frei-

bergera," *Službeni list SJVO,* vol.2, no.3 (January 15, 1937); Šalom M. Freiberger, ed. and trans., *Molitvenik* (Zagreb: Biblioteka Jevrejskog narodnog kalendara, 1938); Šalom Freiberger, "Reforme u zagr. bogoštovnoj općini," *Židov,* vol.9, no.26 (June 19, 1925).

57. Ignjat Šlang, *Jevreji u Beogradu* (Belgrade: M. Karić, 1926).

58. "Nadrabin dr Samuel Weszel," *Jevrejski glas,* vol.1, no.14 (April 20, 1928), p.1; H. Urbach, "Dr Samuel Weszel," *Jevrejski almanah* (O.S.), 1928–29, pp.20–22; Rudolf Buchwald, "Nadrabin dr Samuel Weszel," *Jevrejski glas,* vol.3, no.2 (January 17, 1930), p.8.

59. Arhiv grada Zagreba, Fond Alexander Licht, Letter from Alexander Licht, Zagreb, to Dr. L. Neuer, Sarajevo, July 20, 1928; "Novi nadrabin ašk. opštine u Sarajevu," *Jevrejski glas,* vol.1, no.47 (December 7, 1928), p.2.

60. BG-Seph., 1936, art. 79.

61. ZG, 1912, arts. 25–29; BG-Seph., 1926, arts. 48, 49, 54–63, 65–80; SA-Seph., 1922, arts. 17–18, 24–28.

62. BG-JM, Box 4, Synagogues, Hajim Kamhi, "The Ancient Sephardic Temple—Part of the City Museum," [English and Serbo-Croatian], March 22, 1963.

63. Luci Mevorah-Petrović, "Abraham Kapon," *Jevrejski almanah* (N.S.), 1961–62, p.79.

64. David Alkalaj, "Nova sinagoga Bet Israel," *Jevrejski almanah* (O.S.), 1925–26, pp.73–82; Aron Alkalaj, "Mladoturci i Staroturci u Beogradu," *Jevrejski almanah* (N.S.), 1965–67, pp.105–14.

65. *Izveštaj o radu 1929–32,* p.11; "Beogradska pisma—Kroz Fišekliju," *Židov,* vol.18, no.52 (December 28, 1934), p.5.

66. "Avram Majer Altarac," *Jevrejski glas,* vol.6, no.47 (November 31, 1933), p.5.

67. "Istorijat gradnje Velikog sefardskog hrama," *Jevrejski glas,* vol.3, no.35 (September 12, 1930), p.2; R. Lubynski, "Nova sefardska sinagoga u Sarajevu," *Spomenica JVO sef. obreda u SA* (1930), pp.21–23.

68. AJ, MP, 230-128-31, Correspondence between Avram Majer Altarac and Ministry of Justice on the subject of Bet Tefila, June, 1931.

69. The Ashkenazic synagogue was the only one left standing in Belgrade after World War II. In Sarajevo, the Ashkenazic synagogue remained intact and is also still in use, while the only surviving Sephardic temple, Il Kal Grandi, has been turned into a Jewish museum. In Zagreb, no synagogue building now exists.

70. Oskar Heim, "Reforme u hramu," *Židov,* vol.3, no.6 (February 10, 1919), p.4.

71. Šalom Freiberger, "Reforme u zagrebačkoj bogoštovnoj općini," *Židov,* vol.9, no.26 (June 19, 1925), pp.2–3.

72. "Oko autonomne općine zagr. ortodoksa," *Židov,* vol.9, no.52 (December 4, 1925), p.9; "IBO u ZG u 1926," *Godišnjak IBO ZG* (1928), p.30; AJ, MV, 69, 5-98-28, Correspondence and documents interchanged between the Zagreb Orthodox community, Zagreb Neologue community, UOJVO, SJVO, and Ministry of Religions, 1925–26.

73. "Oko autonomne općine zagrebačkih ortodoksa," *Židov,* vol.9, no.52 (December 4, 1925), p.9; J. Levi, "Oko osnivanja sefardske opštine u Zagrebu," *Jevrejski život,* vol.2, no.86 (December 11, 1925), p.2.

74. Arhiv grada Zagreba, Gradsko poglavarstvo, 141386-1-1930, Orthodox Jewish community in Zagreb to GP, October 13, 1930.

75. Andor Engelmann, "Razgovor s pretsednikom sefardske općine u Zagrebu," *Jevrejski glas,* vol.5, no.2 (January 8, 1932), p.2.

76. Ivo Andrić, "Na jevrejskom groblju u Sarajevu," *Spomenica 400 godina od dolaska Jevreja u Bosnu i Hercegovinu, 1566–1966,* ed. Samuel Kamhi (Sarajevo: Božidar Sekulić, 1966), pp.99–104; "Beogradska pisma," *Židov,* vol.12, no.28 (July 13, 1928), p.6.

77. Schwarz, *Povijest,* p.41.

78. Arhiv grada Zagreba, GP, 109798-1933-VI, Letter from Orthodox Hevra Kaddisha in ZG to GP, July 16, 1933.

79. The Zagreb Sephardic Hevra Kaddisha, more correctly burial fund under the wing of the Zagreb Hevra Kaddisha, was not established until 1939. "Sefardska Hevra Kadiša," *Jevrejska tribuna,* vol.3, no.22 (June 30, 1939), p.5.

80. BG-JM, 69a, Jevrejske organizacije i udruženje pre rata, No.2, Pravila Hevre-Kadiše u Zagrebu (Zagreb: Tiskara A. Engel, 1924).

81. Compulsory membership was characteristic of the Belgrade Ashkenazic community (1933, art. 5). Otherwise, membership was varied. There were 984 members of the Zagreb Hevra Kaddisha in 1926 ("Izvještaj Hevre Kadiše za 1926," *Godišnjak IBO ZG,* p.50); 176 members of the Sarajevo Ashkenazic Hevra Kaddisha in 1929 ("Aškenaska Hevra Kadiša u SA," *Jevrejski glas,* vol.3, no.2 (January 17, 1930), p.7); and approximately 300 members of the Sarajevo Sephardic Hevra Kaddisha in 1926 ("Glavna skupština Hevre Kedoše," *Jevrejski život,* vol.3, no.93 [January 29, 1926], p.3.)

82. SA-JL, Zapisnik Pogrebnog fonda Jevreja u SAu od 6 septembra 1931.

83. Jakov Maestro, "Naš stari meldar," *Spomenica La Benevolencia* (1924), pp.103–5; Samuel Pinto, "Prosvjetne prilike bosanskih Jevreja za turskoj vladavini," *Jevrejski almanah* (N.S.), 1955–56, pp.67–69.

84. Dušan Sindik, "O jevrejskim školama u Beogradu u XIX veku," *Jevrejski almanah* (N.S.), 1961–62, pp.98–104.

85. Jakov Maestro, "Iz prošlosti jevrejske škole u Sarajevu," *Jevrejski glas,* vol.9, nos.37–38 (September 16, 1936), p.16 and ibid., no.39 (September 39, 1936), p.4.

86. "Jevrejska škola," *Židov,* nos.8–9 (March 5, 1921).

87. Aleksandar Klein, "Naša osnovna škola," *Židov,* vol.20, no.43 (October 23, 1936), p.9; Aleksandar Klein, "O štogodišnju jevrejske osnovne škole u Zagrebu," *Glasnik jevr. ašk. VO,* vol.1, no.2 (February 15, 1941), p.7.

88. "Maušel kao Herostrat," *Židov,* vol.6, nos.38–39 (September 9, 1922), p.9.

89. "Rad JVO u ZG u g.1934," *Židov,* vol.19, no.16 (April 17, 1935), p.9; "Djelatnost uprave zagr. žid. općine," ibid., vol.24, no.30 (July 26, 1940), p.5.

90. *Izveštaj o radu uprave crkveno-školske jevr. opštine u Beogradu, 1924–26* (Belgrade: M. Karić, 1926), p.3; *Izveštaj o radu 1926–29,* p.12; *Izveštaj o radu 1929–32,* pp.11–20; "Vjerska nastava sefarada u Sarajevu," *Jevrejski glas,* vol.7, no.2 (January 12, 1934), p.5.

91. Aleksandar Klein, "Gan Hajeladim u Zagrebu," *Omanut,* vol.1, no.4

(December 1926), pp.129–33; "Gan Hajeladim u Zagrebu i u Beogradu," *Jevrejski narodni kalendar,* vol.1, 1935–36, pp.113–17; "Vjerska nastava Sefarada u SA," *Jevrejski glas,* vol.7, no.2 (January 12, 1934), p.5.

92. Kalmi Baruh, "Rad hebrejske škole 'Safa Berura'," *Jevrejski život,* vol.2, no.56 (April 24, 1925), p.5.

93. See section on anti-Jewish legislation in chapter 9 below.

94. Solomon Kalderon, "Jevrejska gimnazija u Beogradu," *Jevrejski almanah* (N.S.), 1954, pp.150–52; Avram Pinto, "Protujevrejski zakoni za vrijeme vlade dra Anton Korošeca, ministra prosveta," (Sarajevo); Avram Pinto, "Jevrejska gimnazija u Sarajevu 1939/40 godine," *Jevrejski pregled,* vol.25, nos.11–12 (November–December 1974), pp.20–26.

Chapter 6

1. Hugo Spitzer, "Povijest pokreta za osnutak SJO," *Židov,* vol.5, no.36 (November 20, 1921), pp.1–3; "Bundestag der jüdischen Kultusgemeinde in Kroatien-Slavonien," *Židovska smotra,* vol.2, no.7 (July 1908), pp.173–78; AH, ZV, JU-103, II-1908-50-396, Correspondence between Osijek Jewish community, Zagreb Jewish community, and ZV, 1909–10; "Osnivanje Saveza," in David Levi-Dale, ed., *Spomenica SJO Jugoslavije 1919–1969* (Belgrade: Srbo-štampa, 1969), pp.23–26.

2. Friedrich Pops, "Osnivanje SJVO," *Glasnik SJVO,* vol. 1 (1933), pp.4–7.

3. Nikola Tolnauer, "Dr Hugo Spitzer," *Židov,* vol.6, nos.4–5 (January 20, 1922), p.1; "Dr Hugo Spitzer," ibid., vol.18, no.33 (August 17, 1934), p.1; "Dr Hugo Spitzer," *Jevrejski narodni kalendar,* vol.1, 1935–36, p.34; *Spomenica SJOJ,* pp.187–89.

4. "Dr Fridrih Pops, šezdesetgodišnjak," *Židov,* vol.18, no.48 (November 30, 1934), p.2; David A. Alkalaj, "Dr Fridrih Pops," *Vesnik,* vol.2, no.15 (March 1, 1940), pp.2–3; Bata (Naftali) Gedalja, "Dr Fridrih Pops," *Jevrejski almanah* (N.S.), 1955–56, pp.138–45; *Spomenica SJOJ,* pp.190–92.

5. "Resolucija predstojništva," *Židov,* vol.3, nos.12–13 (April 14, 1919), pp.2–5; *Spomenica SJOJ,* pp.28–29.

6. "Izveštaj o kongresu židovskih općina," *Židov,* vol.3, nos.22–23 (July 22, 1919), pp.7–9; BG-JM, 5b, Rad SJVO pre rata, First circular of SJVO to the executives of all Jewish-Israelite religious communities, August 15, 1919; *Spomenica SJOJ,* pp.29–31.

7. AJ, MPVO, F 184, Letter from UOJVO to MV, signed by Herman Deutsch and Sandor Pollak, May 8, 1924.

8. Art. 2 of "Pravila SJVO u KSHS," *Židov,* vol.5, nos.31–32 (September 30, 1921), p.17.

9. Arts. 11, 12 of "Pravila SJVO," ibid. In 1936 these provisions were revised so that the central committee consisted of thirty-six members: twenty-nine laymen, of whom at least six had to have their residence in Belgrade, the chief rabbi, five rabbis, and one cantor, with eleven substitutes, eight lay, and three rabbinic. BG-JM, Box 11f, Izmene i dopune u Pravilima SJVO, April 24, 1939.

10. AJ, MP, 214-218-33, Attendance records of central committee and executive board meetings of SJVO, 1921–33.

11. BG-JM, Box 30, Makedonija-Kosmet, Circular from SJVO to all Jewish communities, January 20, 1922; Ivan Kon, "Najvažniji momenti u radu SJVO," *Glasnik SJVO,* vol.1, (1933), pp.11–12.

12. AJ, MV, 69, 4-61-23, Letter from SJVO to MV, No.12343, June 26, 1923; "SJVO," *Židov,* vol.7, no.48 (November 24, 1923), p.5.

13. AJ, MPVO, F 184, Zapisnik kongresa SJVO KSHS and Zapisnik II redovnog kongresa; BG-JM, Box 30, Makedonija-Kosmet, Memorandum from SJVO to all Jewish communities, No.885, September 16, 1924.

14. "Kongres SJVO," *Židov,* vol.5, nos.37–38 (December 1, 1921), p.8; AJ, MPVO, F 184, Zapisnik sednice Glavnog odbora SJVO, Zagreb, January 25, 1938.

15. *Izveštaj Glavnog i Izvršnog odbora V redovnog kongresa SJVO, 2 i 3 aprila 1933* (Belgrade: Polet, 1933); "V kongres SJVO u Beogradu 2–3 aprila 1933," *Židov,* vol.17, no.14 (April 7, 1933), pp.3–8; *Hanoar,* vol.6, nos.6–8 (March-May, 1933), p.218.

16. "Konferencija u Beogradu," *Židov,* vol.18, no.29 (July 20, 1934), p.1; Bukić Pijade, "Za snošljivost u jevrejstvu," ibid., pp.1–2; "Povodom beogradske konferencije—Asimilacija?" *Malchut Jisrael,* vol.2, no.15 (August 1, 1934), p.5.

17. "Sjednica Glavnog odbora SJVO," *Židov,* vol.20, no.36 (September 4, 1936), p.8; "Sjednica Glavnog odbora SJVO u Beogradu," *Jevrejski glas,* vol.9, no.36 (September 4, 1936), pp.1–3; "Kriza u Savezu općina," ibid., pp.2–3; as well as a lengthy series of articles in both papers in subsequent editions, lasting until 1939.

18. "VII kongres SJVO u Beogradu, 23 i 24 aprila 1939," *Židov,* vol. 23, no.17 (April 28, 1939), pp.5–7; "I ovaj kongres SJVO dokazao da imamo pravo," *Jevrejski glas,* vol.12, no.17 (April 28, 1939), p.1; "23–24 aprila održan je u Beogradu VII kongres SJVO," ibid., pp.5–7.

19. "Sistematsko eliminisanje sefardskih prvaka iz javnog jevrejskog života," *Jevrejski glas,* vol.12, no.19 (May 12, 1939), p.3.

20. This dispute is dealt with very polemically in a long series of articles in *Malchut Jisrael* and later *Jevrejska tribuna,* 1937–39; "Povodom kongresa SJVO," *Jevrejska tribuna,* vol.3, no.12 (April 21, 1939), pp.4–5.

21. Salo Baron, *The Jewish Community,* vol.1 (Philadelphia: Jewish Publication Society of America, 1942), pp.12–13.

22. AJ, MPVO, F 183, MPVO to Pretsednik Ministarskog saveta, No. 44696/30–15, (n.d. 1930); F 184, MPVO, Uredba o stalnoj godišnjoj pomoći verskoj zajednici Jevreja u KJ, No. 30497/30-15, March 29, 1930.

23. Borivoie B. Mirkovitch, *La Yougoslavie Politique et Économique* (Paris: Pierre Bossuet, 1935), p.50. A second source, which was somewhat more anti-Serb, reported that, according to the 1929 budget, the Orthodox received a total of 61,561,613 dinars (made up of 46,312,613 dinars in ordinary subsidy and 15,240,000 dinars in special contributions), the Catholics were given 35,612,363 dinars; the Muslims, 19,983,952, and the Protestants, 1,-155,000 dinars, whereas the Jewish figure was the only one to correspond exactly at 1,131,220. According to these tabulations, the Orthodox as well as the Muslims also received much more than their equitable share, while the Catholics and the Protestants were worse off. Nevertheless, the Jewish com-

munity still emerges on top on a per capita basis. See C. A. Macartney, *Hungary and Her Successors,* (London: Oxford University Press, 1937), p.425.

24. AJ, MPVO, F 183, Letter from SJVO to MPVO, No.1640, March 18, 1935; also SJVO to MPVO, No.1913, April 8, 1927; No.2160, April 2, 1938; No.2419, April 18, 1939; No.2124, April 8, 1940; UOJVO to MPVO, No.366, May 10, 1931; No.60, May 5, 1933; Budget UOJVO for 1934/35, May 6, 1934; to 1940.

25. AJ, MPVO, F 184, MPVO, Uredba, March 29, 1930; F 183, SJVO to MPVO, No.1130, May 15, 1931.

26. "Državna pomoć jevrejskoj zajednici i njena upotreba," *Službeni list SJVO,* vol.2, no.4 (February 15, 1937), pp. 5–6.

27. Defense activities will be discussed in chapter 9.

28. Law on the Religious Community of Jews, art. 13.

29. Similarly, there existed an Orthodox rabbinical synod with three members, associated with the Orthodox Union, which was also headed by the chief rabbi. Law on the Religious Community of Jews, art. 14.

30. BG-JM, 58a, *Pravila SJVO u KJ* (Belgrade: Štampa Merkur, 1930), arts. 22–24.

31. AJ, MPVO, F 184, Zapisnik III kongres SJVO KSHS, 25 decembra 1927 u Beogradu; "Iz života SJVO," *Glasnik SJVO,* vol.3 (1933), p.223; SJVO, *Izveštaj VI kongresa* (Belgrade: Prosveta, 1936), p.18.

32. AJ, MPVO, F 184, SJVO to MPVO, No.42, January 4, 1937; "Značajna sednica Glavnog odbora SJVO," *Židov,* vol.22, no.4 (January 28, 1938), pp.4–5; "Definitivno utvrdjivanje teritorijalne nadležnosti JVO u KJ," *Službeni list SJVO,* vol.3, no.22 (October 15, 1938), p.2; "Iz izveštaja Glavnog odbora—Rabinski sinod," *Židov,* vol.23, no.16 (April 21, 1939), p.5.

33. "Kongres jevrejskih općina," *Židov,* vol.5, no.36 (November 20, 1921), p. 3; AJ, MPVO, F 184, Zapisnik II redovnog kongresa; Gavro Schwarz, "Izobrazba vjeroučitelja i kantora," *Židov,* vol.12, no.23 (June 8, 1928), p.2.

34. *Prvi izvještaj Jevrejskog srednjeg teološkog zavoda u SA za školske godine 1928/29 i 1929/30,* ed. Moric Levi (Sarajevo: Stamparija Papo, 1930), pp.6–11, 25; "Rad u JSTZ u školskoj godine 1928/29," *Jevrejski glas,* vol.2, no.26 (July 5, 1929), p.2; "JSTZ u Sarajevu," ibid., vol.3, no.32 (August 15, 1930), p.3.

35. *Prvi izvještaj JSTZ,* pp.22–23; art. 17 in "Statut o ustrojstvu i nastavnom planu JSTZ," *Službeni list SJVO,* vol.2, no.3 (January 15, 1937), pp.3–7.

36. The SJVO regularly allotted approximately 200,000 dinars of its annual subvention to the seminary. AJ, MPVO, F 183, SJVO to MPVO, No.1130, May 15, 1931, No.1913, April 8, 1937.

37. *Prvi izvještaj JSTZ,* p.11; art. 4, "Statut JSTZ," *Službeni list SJVO,* vol.2, no.3 (January 15, 1937), p.3.

38. *Prvi izvještaj JSTZ,* p.36.

39. AJ, MPVO, F 184, SJVO to MPVO, No.6486, December 15, 1934.

40. "Iz izveštaja Glavnog odbora—JSTZ," *Židov,* vol.22, no.16 (April 21, 1939), p.6; *Izveštaj Glavnog odbora VII kongresu 23 i 24 aprila 1939 godine,* pp.27–28.

41. *Izveštaj o radu u godinama 1933–1936 VI kongresa,* p.17; *Izveštaj VII kongresa* (1939), p. 28.

42. Samuel Kamhi, "O potrebi jedinstvenog uredjenja sudbenosti u

bračnim stvarima Jevreja u Jugoslaviji," *Jevrejski glas,* vol.4, no.50 (November 21, 1931), p.6; Samuilo S. Demajo, "Jevrejsko bračno pravo u KJ," *Godišnjak La Benevolencija i Potpora,* pp.198–228; Rafailo Finci, "Jevrejski duhovni sud," *Glasnik SJVO,* vol.1 (1933), pp.30–31: "Jevrejski duhovni sud," *Izveštaj o radu uprave crkvene-školske jevrejske opštine u Beogradu, 1929–32,* pp.53–54. For a general discussion on the legal system in interwar Yugoslavia, see Charles A. Beard and George Radin, *The Balkan Pivot: Yugoslavia* (New York: Macmillan Co., 1929), pp.266–78 and Great Britain, Naval Intelligence Division, *Jugoslavia,* vol.2, History, Peoples and Administration (London, 1944), pp.345–50.

43. AJ, MP, 31-212-34, 194-246-31, Documents and correspondence, 1931–1933; "V kongres SJVO," *Židov,* vol.17, no.14 (April 7, 1933); "Nadležnost jevrejskih duhovnih sudova, Bet Din, u brakorazvodnim parnicima," *Glasnik SJVO,* vol.3 (1933), pp.218–19.

44. BG-JM, Box 16, Zagreb, "Obrazloženje osnovi zakona o vjeroispoviednim odnosima" (1905), art. 14.

45. "Die Regelung der Kultusgemeinde in Kroatien," *Židovska smotra,* vol.1, nos.9–10 (July–August 1907), p.236.

46. Gavro Schwarz, "Nešto statistike iz Zagreba," *Glasnik SJVO,* vol.3 (1933), pp.199–200.

47. AJ, MPVO, F 184, Zapisnik IV redovnog kongresa SJVO, Resolution 2; "Kongres SJVO," *Židov,* vol.14, no.53 (December 26, 1930), p.6; "Nakon kongresa Saveza općina," ibid., vol.15, no.1 (January 2, 1931), p.2; "Mišljenja predsjednika i potpredsjednika ZG JVO o kongresu SJVO u BG," *Jevrejski glas,* vol.4, no.2 (January 9, 1931), p.5.

48. SJVO, *Izveštaj VII kongresu,* table 3c, p.85; "Djelatnost uprave ZG židovske općine," *Židov,* vol.24, no.30 (July 26, 1940), p.5; "Godišnja glavna skupština SA ašk. opštine," *Jevrejski glas,* vol.12, no.25 (June 30, 1939), p.8.

49. "Istupi iz židovstva u Zagrebu," *Židov,* vol.22, no.49 (December 9, 1938), p.7; ibid., vol.22, no.52 (December 30, 1938), p.6; "Istupi iz židovstva u godini 1938," ibid., vol.22, no.51 (December 23, 1938), p.7.

50. "Dezerteri su gorje od neprijatelja," *Jevrejska tribuna,* vol.2, no.45 (December 9, 1938), p.5.

51. "Bjegunci, otpadnici," *Židov,* vol.22, no.49 (December 9, 1938), p.7; "Odmetnici," ibid., no.51 (December 23, 1938), p.7.

52. Ibid.

53. Martef [pseud.], "Rabinski savez u Jugoslaviji," *Židov,* vol.7, no.22 (May 25, 1923), p.6; Martef, "Konferencija rabina u Vinkovci," ibid., no.29 (July 13, 1923), pp.5–6; Martef, "Konstituiranje Rabinskog saveza KSHS," ibid., no.44 (October 27, 1923), p.2.

54. "Konferencija Glavnog odbora SJVO," *Židov,* vol.10, no.4 (January 22, 1926), p.4; "III kongres Saveza rabina KSHS," ibid., no.26 (June 6, 1926), p.5; AJ, MPVO, F 184, Letter from Chief Rabbinate to MP, February 28, 1930.

55. AJ, MV, 69, 9-31-27, Letter from Cantor Josip Rendi to MV, March 12, 1924.

56. AJ, MV, 69, 9-31-27, Statut Saveza kantora u KSHS, September 24, 1924, arts. 2, 3.

57. AJ, MV, 69, 8-31-27, Zapisnik glavne skupštine Saveza jevrejskih

kantora u KSHS, November 16, 1926; "Mitteilungen des Kantoren-Verbandes," *Mjesečnik jevrejskih kantora,* vol.1, no.1 (January 1928), p.3; ibid., no.2 (February 1928); "Generalversammlung des Verbandes der jüdischen Kantoren in KSHS," ibid., no.3 (March 1928).

58. Jakov Maestro, "Za organizaciju jevrejskih vjeroučitelja," *Glasnik SJVO,* vol.3 (1933), pp.211–13.

59. Arhiv Instituta za radnički pokret Hrvatske, Fond Velikog župana Zagreba, VI/3, K 18, Pravila Udruženja prosvjetnih i administrativnih službenika jevrejskih ustanova u KJ, June 26, 1938.

60. "O osiguranju službenika JVO," *Službeni list SJVO,* vol.2, no.4 (February 15, 1937), pp.3–4; "Kongres rabina, kongres kantora i sastanak ostalih službenika jevrejskih ustanova u Zagrebu," *Židov,* vol.21, no.47 (November 5, 1937), p.8; "Statut centralnog penzionog fonda," *Službeni list SJVO,* vol.3, nos.20–21 (July 15, 1938), pp.3–11; "Sastav uprave Centralnog penzionog fonda," *Židov,* vol.22, no.43 (October 28, 1938), p.9.

Chapter 7

1. Discussion in this chapter will be limited to local charitable and cultural associations. Zionism and the Sephardic movement, with their affiliated organizations, as well as youth activities, will be dealt with in chapter 8.

2. Braco Poljokan, "O ustanovama u jevrejskom Sarajevu i o njihovom radu," *Jevrejski glas,* vol.2, nos.17–18 (April 24, 1929), p.10; Dragutin Tolentino, "Reformacija i ujedinjenje naših društava," *Židovska svijest,* vol.2, no.57 (January 23, 1920), p.2; as well as reports on annual meetings of the various organizations in *Jevrejski glas* and *Židov* to 1941.

3. Julije Hahamović, "Aškenazi u BiH," *Spomenica 400 godina od dolaska Jevreja u Bosnu i Hercegovinu, 1566–1966,* ed. Samuel Kamhi (Sarajevo: Božidar Sekulić, 1966) pp.148–50; *Spomenica prigodom 50 godišnjeg opstanka JVO ašk. obreda u SA,* ed. Oskar Grof (Sarajevo: Stamparija Bosanska pošta, 1930); "Društvenost i karitativan rad—Iz istorije Ahdusa," *Jevrejski glas,* vol.3, no.2 (January 17, 1930), p.9; "25-godišnjica kulturno-humanitarnog društva Ahdusa," ibid., vol.5, no.3 (January 15, 1932).

4. Stanislav Vinaver, "La Benevolencija," in *Spomenica proslavi tridesetgodišnjica sarajevskoga kulturno-potpornoga društva La Benevolencija, maja 1924,* ed. Stanislav Vinaver (Belgrade: Vreme, 1924), pp.3–5; Avram Pinto, "Jevrejska društva u Sarajevu," *Spomenica 400,* pp.174–75.

5. Vinaver, "La Benevolencija," pp.5–6, 8; Pinto, "Jevrejska društva u Sarajevu," pp.174–75.

6. Vinaver, "La Benevolencija," pp.5, 7.

7. Vita Kajon, "La Benevolencia u posljednjih deset godina (1923–33)," *Godišnjak La Benevolencia i Potpora* (1933), tables 1–5.

8. Ibid., pp.8–12; Pinto, "Jevrejska društva u Sarajevu," pp.177–79; "Rad La Benevolencije za naučnike," *Jevrejski glas,* vol.2, no.11 (March 15, 1929); Kalmi Baruh, "La Benevolencija mora da nadje novu orijentaciju u svom radu," *Jevrejski glas,* vol.5, no.43 (October 21, 1932), pp.4–5.

9. *Spomenica proslavi tridesetgodišnjice sarajevskoga kulturno-potpornoga društva La Benevolencija, maja 1924,* ed. Stanislav Vinaver (Belgrade: Vreme, 1924);

Godišnjak izdaju Jevrejsko kulturno-prosvetno društvo La Benevolencia u Sarajevu i Dobrotvorno društvo Potpora u Beogradu (Sarajevo: Štamparija Menahem Papo, 1933); Jorjo Tadić, *Jevreji u Dubrovniku do polovine XVII stoljeca* (Sarajevo: La Benevolencia, 1937).

10. Kajon, "La Benevolencia," pp.13–18.

11. Ibid., pp.20–25.

12. "Glavna skupština društva La Benevolencije," *Jevrejski glas,* vol.4, no.21 (June 5, 1931), pp.4–5.

13. Rafael Margulis, "Istorija dobrotvornog društva Potpora," *Godišnjak La Benevolencia i Potpora,* pp.33–45; "Godišnja skupština dobrotvornog društva Potpora," *Jevrejski glas,* vol.4, no.17 (April 24, 1931), p.3.

14. Moše de Majo, "Jevrejske ustanove u Beogradu," *Godišnjak La Benevolencia i Potpora,* pp.49–59.

15. "Beogradska pisma—Malo kod Aškenaza," *Židov,* vol.19, no.3 (January 18, 1935), p.4.

16. "Izveštaj odbora akcije za zimsku pomoć," *Vesnik,* vol.2, no.16 (April 1, 1940), p.13.

17. Gavro Schwarz, "Socialni i karitativni rad u židovskim općinama u Beču i u Zagrebu," *Židov,* vol.14, no.30 (September 22, 1930), pp.21–22.

18. David Fuhrmann, "Potreba proširenja produktivnog socijalnog rada," *Židov,* vol.19, no.1 (January 4, 1935), p.5; ibid., vol.19, no.2 (January 11, 1935), p.11; David Fuhrmann, "Glavna skupština Središnje jevrejske stanice za produktivnu socijalnu pomoć," ibid., vol.22, no.9 (March 4, 1938), p.6; ibid., vol.22, no.10 (March 11, 1938), p.8; "SJSPSP," ibid., vol.23, no.50 (December 18, 1939), p.6. Along much the same line of reasoning, an Association for Jewish Artisans and a credit union, called Ezra, were established in Zagreb to allow small Jewish businessmen and craftsmen to help themselves and each other. "Ezra, Jevrejska zadruga zaštednju i zajmove u Zagrebu," *Židov,* vol.16, no.26 (July 1, 1932), p.3; "Činovnici i nameštenici," ibid., vol.16, no.44 (November 4, 1932), p.5.

19. AJ, Fond Masonskih loža, 100-20-95, Circular from SJSPSP, December 1936; Letter from Lodge Zagreb to Grand Lodge, B'nai Brith, December 22, 1936; SJSPSP to Grand Lodge, April 8, 1937.

20. BG-JM, Box 16, Zagreb, No.1216/55, Legacy of Lavoslav Schwarz, Zagreb, May 4, 1905, and other materials pertaining to the Schwarz Home; "Schwarzov Dom," *Godišnjak IBO ZG* (1928), pp.51–55; Schwarz, *Povijest,* pp.47–48; *Spomenica Kuratorija doma zaklade Lavoslava Schwarza u Zagrebu prigodom 30-godišnjice opstanka 1909–1939,* ed. Gavro Schwarz (Zagreb, 1940).

21. Arhiv grada Zagreba, GP, No.2292, 1930, Letter from Društvo Židovska bolnica u Zagreba (Society for a Jewish Hospital in Zagreb) to GP.

22. AJ, Fond Masonskih loža našoj zemlje (1890–1945), 100-23-103, Adresar članova loža B'ne Brith Srbija (No.676); Zagreb (No.1090); Sarajevo (No.1141), 1933.

23. A number of Yugoslav Jews, including Dr. Hugo Kon of Zagreb and Lazar Avramović of Belgrade, did belong to the Masonic Order, but as a general rule these individuals were not members of B'nai B'rith. In August 1940 a decree by the Ministry of the Interior dissolved all B'nai B'rith lodges, as well as all Masonic lodges in the country. ("Lože B'ne Brit obustavile rad," *Židov,* vol.24, no.34 [August 23, 1940], p.5.) Their records, however, have

been preserved and are presently being kept in the Yugoslav National Archive in a collection called Masonic Lodges, under the subheading Jewish Masonic Lodges. Other evidence to this effect is to be found in: "Jevrejske slobodnožidarske lože u Jugoslaviji," *Jevrejski glas,* vol.7, no.8 (February 23, 1934), p.5; and *Židovska Masonerija* (Zagreb: Mosk, 1935).

24. AJ, Fond Masonskih loža, 100-18-64; *Spomenica Lože Zagreba 1090 NOBB, 1927–1932,* pp.44–46.

25. Ibid., pp.46–50; S. J. Alkalaj, "NOBB Loža Srbija u Beogradu," *Jevrejski život,* vol.1, no.9 (May 23, 1924), p.6; "Jevrejski muzej u Beogradu," *Židov,* vol.8, no.11 (March 14, 1924), p.5.

26. *Spomenica Lože Zagreba NOBB 1927–32,* pp.30–35.

27. AJ, Fond Masonskih loža, 100-18-57, Letter from Lodge Serbia to Grand Lodge 11 District Istanbul, December 26, 1931; 100-18-58, Correspondence between Lodge Serbia and Sarajevo, 1932; 100-23-103, Adresar članova Loža BB KJ, Sarajevo, 1933.

28. NOBB Velika loža za KJ 18 Distrikt, *Spomenica svečane instalacije Velike lože u Beogradu, 27 oktobra 1935.*

29. AJ, Fond Masonskih loža, 100-21-99, 100-21-100, 100-21-101, Correspondence between the Yugoslav Grand Lodge and Jewish organizations abroad, 1935–1940.

30. AJ, Fond Masonskih loža, 100-19-78, Correspondence between Grand Lodge and Lodge Sarajevo, 1936–37.

31. "Proslava 50-godišnjice Jevrejskog ženskog društva u Beogradu," *Židov,* vol.8, no.47 (November 7, 1924), p.5; "Savez jevrejskih ženskih udruženja," *Jevrejski narodni kalendar,* vol.1 1935–36, p.182; Sofija Almuli, "Jelena Demajo," *Jevrejski almanah* (N.S.), 1955–56, pp.149–53.

32. "Osnutak Saveza cijonističkih žena u KSHS," *Židov,* vol.12, no.16 (April 20, 1928); "Sedma zemaljska konferencija Saveza cijonističkih žena," ibid., vol.24, no.2 (January 12, 1940).

33. Jelena de Majo, "O kulturnih razvitka jevrejske žene u Srbiji," *Jevrejsko žensko društvo u Beogradu, 1874–1924* (Belgrade, 1924), pp.53–61.

34. Sofija Almuli, "Jelena Demajo," pp.149–53.

35. "Kratka istorija JŽD," *Jevrejsko žensko društvo u Beogradu, 1874–1924,* pp.7–16.

36. Ibid., p.17.

37. Ibid., pp.19–35; "O radu JŽD u Beogradu," *Jevrejski glas,* vol.1, no.49 (December 21, 1928), p.1; "Beogradska kronika—JŽD," *Židov,* vol.14, no.7 (February 14, 1930), p.6; AJ, Fond Masonskih loža, 100-18-55, article on JŽD, 1939; Sofija Almuli, "Jelena Demajo," pp. 150–53.

38. "JŽD Dobrotvor," *Glasnik jevrejske aškenaske VO,* vol.1, no.2 (February 15, 1941), p.19.

39. "Glavna skupština La Humanidad," *Jevrejski glas,* vol.5, no.12 (March 18, 1932), p.6; "Glavna godišnja skupština La Humanidad," *Jevrejski glas,* vol.13, no.11 (March 14, 1940), pp.8–9; "Glavna godišnja skupština Societad de vizitar dolientes," ibid., p.7.

40. ABH, VZSO, pov.1926–210, Historijat Jevr. ašk. gospojinskog društva u Sarajevu, 1926; "Glavna skupština Ašk. gosp. društva," *Jevrejski glas,* vol.2, no.37 (November 8, 1929); A. Benau, "Jevr. ašk. gosp. društvo u Sarajevu," ibid., vol.3, no.2 (January 17, 1930), p.8.

41. "30-godišnjica rada zagr. izr. gosp. društva Jelena Prister u Zagrebu," *Židov,* vol.1, no.4 (November 1, 1919), p.4; "Izraelsko gospojinsko društvo Jelena Prister," *Godišnjak IBO ZG,* pp.56–58; Arhiv grada Zagreba, GP, 87330-VI-1929, Izr. gosp. društvo Jelena Prister u Zagrebu, August 8, 1929.

42. *Društveni propisi Izraelske ferijalne kolonije u Zagrebu* (Zagreb: Tisak Adolf Engel, 1924); *Izvještaj IFK, 1919–1920* (Zagreb, 1921); *Izvještaj IFK, 1921–1922* (Zagreb, 1923); "Dječki dom ferijalne kolonije u Crkvenici," *Židov,* vol.9, no.37 (August 28, 1925), pp.5–6; Arhiv grada Zagreba, GP, 87330-VI-1929, Društvo IFK, August 14, 1929; Gavro Schwarz, "IFK," *Godišnjak IBO ZG,* pp.59–62; Gavro Schwarz, "Rad IFK prošlih 25 godina," *Spomenica IFK u Zagrebu* (Zagreb, 1940), pp.19–25; Iso E. Papo, "25-godišnjica plemenitog i humanog rada IFK u Zagrebu," *Jevrejski glas,* vol. 13, no.4 (January 26, 1940), p.5.

43. Moše de Majo, "Jevrejska ustanova u Beogradu," *Godišnjak La Benevolencia i Potpora,* pp.52–54; "Skupština Srpskojevrejskog pevačkog društva," *Vesnik,* vol.2, no.16 (April 1, 1940), p.13; Mika Mevorah, "Srpskojevrejsko pevačko društvo," *Glasnik jevr. ašk. VO,* vol.1, no.3 (March 15, 1941), p.13; BG-JM, Box 11, Belgrade, Aron Alkalaj, Beleške o kulturnim životu Jevreja u Beogradu, n.d.

44. Avram Altarac, "Razvoj i rad Lire Jevrejskog pevačkog društva u Sarajevu od 1900 do 1921," *Židovska svijest,* vol.3, no.124 (May 20, 1921), pp.2–3; "Godišnja glavna skupština Lire," *Jevrejski glas,* vol.1, no.44 (November 16, 1928), p.3; Avram Pinto, "Jevrejska društva u Sarajevu," *Spomenica 400,* pp.179–83.

45. Arhiv Instituta za radnički pokret Hrvatske, Fond Veliki župan Zagreba, VI/S, K 38, Pravila Jevrejskog pjevačkog društva Ahdut u Zagrebu, June 21, 1933; "Koncert Ahduta," *Židov,* vol.22, no.10 (March 11, 1938), p.8.

46. Arhiv IRPH, VŽŽ, VI/S, K 38, Pravila Omanut, August 31, 1932; "Izvještaj o radu društva od 24 juna 1937 do 20 avgusta 1938," *Omanut,* vol.2, nos.11–12 (July–August 1938); "Zapisnik V redovite glavne skupštine održane 26 septembra 1939," ibid., vol.3, no.10 (October 1939), p.163; "Omanut, Društvo za promicanje jevrejske umjetnosti u Zagrebu," *Židov,* vol.24, no.39 (September 27, 1940), p.8; "Omanut," *Omanut,* vol.4, no.12 (December 1940), p.190; Slavko Radej, "Hinko Gotlib," *Jevrejski almanah* (N.S.), 1954, pp.127–31.

47. Moše de Majo, "Jevrejska ustanova u Beogradu," p.54.

48. "Jedan plodan i konstruktivan rad—Godišnja skupština Matatje," *Jevrejski glas,* vol.9, no.7 (February 18, 1938), pp.7–8; "25-godišnjica kulturno-humanitarnog društva Ahdus," ibid., vol.5, no.3 (January 15, 1932), pp.4–6.

49. *Spomenica Lože Zagreba NOBB, 1927–1932,* p.35.

50. Samuilo Alkalaj, "Klub Zajednica," *Jevrejski almanah* (N.S.), 1961–62, pp.110–14.

51. "Nekoliko podataka o Literarnim sastancima židovske omladine u ZG," *Gideon,* vol.4, no.7 (April 1923), p.242; "Literarni sastanci židovske omladine," *Godišnjak IBO ZG,* pp.63–64; "Literarni sastanci židovske omladine, 1898–1928," *Hanoar,* vol.2, nos.6–7 (1928), p.215.

52. *Izvještaj izr. hrv. literarnoga društva u Zagrebu za godine 1904, 1905 i 1906,* ed. Gavro Schwarz (Zagreb: Tisak Ign. Granitza, 1907); Gavro Schwarz, "Izr. hrv. literarno društvo u Zagrebu," *Židov,* vol.2, no.11 (June 1, 1918), p.1.

53. "Skupština Jevrejske čitaonice," *Jevrejski glas,* vol.4, no.7 (February 13, 1931); Moše de Majo, "Jevrejska ustanova u Beogradu," pp.54–55; AJ, Fond Masonskih loža, 100-19-89, List of lecture topics, 1938–39; "10 godine rada Jevrejske čitaonice," *Židov,* vol.24, no.6 (February 9, 1940), p.6; BG-JM, Box 11, Belgrade, Aron Alkalaj, Beleske o kulturnim životu Jevreja u Beogradu; Aron Alkalaj, "Dvanaest godina Jevrejske čitaonice u Beogradu, 1929–1941," *Jevrejski almanah* (N.S.), 1955–56, pp.113–16.

54. David A. Alkalaj, "Hajim Davičo, književnik sa Jalije," *Gideon,* vol.6, nos.4–5 (November 15, 1925), pp.77–81; Mihailo B. Milošević, "Hajim S. Davičo, 1854–1918," *Jevrejski almanah* (N.S.), 1965–67, pp.129–37.

55. Ibid.

56. Since Laura Papo received her education in Istanbul and in France, her Ladino contains a number of foreign admixtures as well as spelling peculiarities. This, however, does not negate her cultural contribution to Bosnian Sephardic literature. Arhiv grada Sarajeva, Ostavštite Laura Bohoreta Papo; Rikica Ovadija, "Laura Papo Bohoreta," *Spomenica 400,* pp.305–8; Camfara Esref, "Laura Papo Bohoreta," *Jevrejski almanah* (N.S.), 1965–67, pp.136–44.

57. Isak Samokovlija, *Sabrana djela,* 3 vols. (Sarajevo: Svjetlost, 1967); Marko Marković, "Pripovjedački lik Isaka Samokovlije," *Jevrejski almanah* (N.S.), 1955–56, pp.225–26; Slavko Mićanović, "Isak Samokovlija," *Spomenica 400,* pp.279–88.

58. "Pedesetgodišnjica dra Hinka Gottlieba," *Židov,* vol.20, no.18 (May 1, 1936), p.7; Slavko Radej, "Hinko Gotlib," *Jevrejski almanah* (N.S.), 1954, pp.127–31.

59. Kalmi Baruch wrote studies on Lope de Vega, Calderon, Miguel de Unamuno, as well as works entitled "Jews in the Balkans and Their language" and "Spanish Romances of Bosnian Jewry." Samuel Kamhi, "Dr Kalmi Baruh," *Spomenica 400,* pp.289–95.

60. Juda Levi, article in *Naši Jevreji,* ed. Mica Dimitrijević (1940), pp.46–49; David S. Pijade, "Naši slikari," *Godišnjak La Benevolencia i Potpora,* pp.106–9; Olivera Djurić, "Slikar Leon Koen, 1859–1934," *Jevrejski almanah* (N.S.), 1954, pp.121–26; Aleksa Celebonović, "Bora Baruh," ibid., pp.139–42; Vojo Dimitrijević, "Slikari Jevreji u Sarajevu izmedju dva rata," *Spomenica 400,* pp.315–17; Aleksa Celebonović, "Danijel Ozmo," *Jevrejski almanah* (N.S.), 1954, pp.143–45.

61. *Kultura i umjetnosti u BiH,* ed. Risto Besarević (Sarajevo, 1968), pp.152–53, 227–28; Luci Mevorah-Petrović, "Abraham Kapon," *Jevrejski almanah* (N.S.), 1961–62, pp.77–79; Haim Kamhi, "Jevrejska publicistika u BiH," *Spomenica 400,* p.168.

62. *Židovska smotra* (1906–1914); Joel Rosenberger, *"Židovska smotra,* 1906–1931," *Židov,* vol.15, no.49 (December 4, 1931), p.1.

63. *Židov* (1917–1941); "Službeno glasilo *Židov,"* *Židov,* vol. 10, no.41 (October 8, 1926), p.3.

64. *Židovska svijest* (1919–1924); *Narodna židovska svijest* (1924–1928); *Jevrejski život* (1924–1927); *Jevrejski glas* (1928–1941); Haim Kamhi, "Jevrejska publicistika u BiH," *Spomenica 400,* pp. 169–70.

65. "Beogradska pisma," *Židov,* vol.12, no.39 (September 28, 1928), p.3; *Beogradski jevrejski glasnik* (1924); *Glasnik SJVO* (1933); *Službeni list SJVO*

(1936–1939); *Vesnik jevrejske sefardske veroispovedne opštine* (1939–1941); *Glasnik jevrejske aškenaske veroispovedne opštine* (1941).

66. *Haaviv, List jevrejske djece* (1922–1941); *Gideon, Vijesnik SŽOU* (1919–1926); *Hanoar, List jevrejske omladine Jugoslavije* (1926–1937).

67. *Jüdisches Volksblatt* (1921–1925); *Israel, Jüdische Wochenschrift von Marthef* (1925–1928); *Malchut Jisrael Cijonistički-revizionistički organ* (1933–1937); *Jevrejska tribuna* (1937–1941).

Chapter 8

1. See C. A. Macartney, *Hungary and Her Successors* (London: Oxford University Press, 1937), p.433.

2. See, for example, Rebecca West, *Black Lamb and Grey Falcon* (New York: Viking Press, 1956), p.192.

3. Vladimir Sachs, *Izraeličani i kršćansko-socijalni kulturni program* (Varaždin, 1910), p.9.

4. Lavoslav Glesinger, "Ilirski pokret i Jevreji," *Jevrejski narodni kalendar,* vol.2, 1936–37, pp.59–71; Duško Kečkemet, *Vid Morpurgo i narodni preporod u Splitu* (Split, 1963).

5. Hinko Hinković, *The Jugoslav Problem,* reprinted from *The World Court* (1918); Lavoslav Šik, "Obraćanje dra Hinka Hinkovića," *Židov,* vol. 18, no.36 (June 7, 1934), pp.5–6.

6. "O patriotizmu naših Židova," *Židov,* vol.2, no.8 (April 16, 1918), p.2; Nikola Tolnauer, "Nekoliko riječi k jugoslavenskom problemu," ibid., vol.2, no.16 (August 16, 1918), pp.1–2.

7. "Zagrebačka bogoštovna općina protiv pomoćne akcije za Palestinu," *Židov,* vol.2, no.13 (July 1, 1918), p.3.

8. AH, ZV, JU-103, V-1919-27, Letter from Zagreb Jewish Community, No.135-19/R-26 to Dr. Ivan Paleček, ban of Croatia-Slavonia, April 9, 1919.

9. "Rezolucija predstojništva," *Židov,* vol.3, nos. 12–13 (April 14, 1919), pp.2–5.

10. "Prilog k prirodnoznaštvu asimilanata," *Židov,* vol.6, no.18 (April 21, 1922), p.5.

11. Mirko Breyer, "Glas srca i savjesti," *Nova Evropa,* vol.5, nos.9–10 (July 21, 1922), pp.280–83.

12. "Prilog k prirodnoznaštvu asimilanata," *Židov,* vol.6, no.18 (April 21, 1922), p.5; *Ko je ko u Jugoslaviji* (Belgrade: Jugoslovenski godišnjak, 1928).

13. Gavro Schwarz, "Nešto statistike iz Zagreba," *Glasnik SJVO,* vol.3 (1933), pp.196–200.

14. Gavro Schwarz, "Nekoliko interesantnih statističkih podataka iz zagr. JVO," *Službeni list SJVO,* vol.2, no.13 (November 15, 1937), p.4; Gavro Schwarz, "Malo statistike zagr. žid. općine iz godine 1937," *Židov,* vol.22, no.1 (January 7, 1938), p.5; "Djelatnost uprave zagr. žid. općine," ibid., vol.24, no.30 (July 26, 1940), p.5.

15. D. A. Koen, *Besede posvečene Srpskoj omladini mojsijeve vere* (Belgrade: Štamparija Sv. Nikolića, 1897).

16. "Svečana sednica nove uprave u opštinskoj salu," *Židov,* vol.16, no.27 (July 8, 1932).

17. "G. Avram Lević o 'nacionalističkom pokretu' beogradskih Mojsijevaca," *Jevrejski glas,* vol.7, no.28 (July 20, 1934), p.2.

18. Paulina Albala, "O dr Albali" (Los Angeles, 1943), p.66.

19. Paulina Albala, "O dr Albali"; Paulina Albala, "Dr. David Albala as a Jewish National Worker" (Leo Baeck Institute, New York, n.d.); "Dr David Albala kao jevrejski nacionalni radnik," *Jevrejski almanah* (N.S.), 1957–58, pp.94–108.

20. "Izjava Židova BiH," *Židov,* vol.2, no.22 (November 17, 1918), p.6.

21. Šumbul Atijas, *Jevreji, državna politika i Ustavotvorna skupština* (Sarajevo: Štamparija Daniel i A. Kajon 1920), pp.4–5.

22. Aleksandar Licht, "Protiv separatizma," *Židov,* vol.8, no.6 (February 8, 1924), p.1; "Izvještaj o Saveznom vijeću u Beogradu," ibid., no.27 (June 27, 1924), pp.3–4; "K dopisu Egzekutive," ibid., no.43 (October 10, 1924), pp.7–8.

23. "Iz Židovskog nacionalnog društva u Sarajevu," *Židov,* vol.8, no.11 (March 14, 1924), p.5; "Što se dogadja u Sarajevu," ibid., no.13 (March 28, 1924), p.5; "Spor medju sarajevskim Jevrejima u svijetu istine," *Jevrejski život,* vol.1, no.1 (March 28, 1924), pp.2–4.

24. "Zadna skupština ŽND," *Jevrejski život,* vol.1, no.4 (April 18, 1924), pp.4–5.

25. "Jevrejski klub u Sarajevu," *Narodna židovska svijest,* vol.1, no.28 (October 17, 1924), pp.4–5.

26. CZA, Z4-2029-II, SCJ to ZO, Report on conference held June 15–16, 1924, July 9, 1924; "Izveštaj o Saveznom vijeću u Beogradu," *Židov,* vol.8, no.27 (June 27, 1924), pp.2–8; "K dopisu Egzekutive," ibid., no.43 (October 10, 1924), pp.7–8; "Loše politike SCJ," *Jevrejski život,* vol.2, no.68 (July 17, 1925), pp.1–2; "Sarajevski spor," *Židov,* vol.9, no.32 (July 24, 1925), pp.5–6; "Izvješće o Saveznom vijeću," ibid., nos.45–47 (October 16, 1925), pp.18–19; CZA, Z4-3568, SCJ to ZO, Report on annual conference, December 12, 1927.

27. "Izvještaj o Saveznom vijeću u Beogradu," *Židov,* vol.8, no.22 (June 27, 1924), p.3.

28. "Rezolucije Saveznog vijeća," ibid., p.7; Aleksandar Licht, "Protiv separatizma," ibid., no.6 (February 8, 1924), p.1.

29. "Skupština šekelista u Sarajevu," *Jevrejski glas,* vol.1, no.5 (February 10, 1928); "Glavna skupština MCO," *Židov,* vol.12, no.7 (February 17, 1928).

30. "Druga Svjetska sefardska konferencija," *Židov,* vol.9, no.36 (August 21, 1925), p.3; Solomon J. Alkalaj, "O sefardskom pokretu," ibid., vol.10, no.16 (April 15, 1926), p.5; Aron Alkalaj, "Sefardi, sefardski pokret i njegov značaj," *Glasnik SJVO,* vol.2 (1933), pp.83–90.

31. "Beogradska organizacija sef. Jevreja," *Jevrejski život,* vol.2, no.86 (December 11, 1925), p.3.

32. CZA, Z4-3568-I, Letter from Federation of Zionists of Yugoslavia to Zionist Organization, London, November 28, 1927, with German translation of article; Z4-3579-II, Response, February 8, 1928; "Die Lage der Sephardischen Juden in Erec Israel," n.d.; and ZO to Palestine Executive, Jerusalem, March 15, 1928; Arhiv grada Zagreba, Fond Alexander Licht, Letters from Licht to Dr. Solomon Alkalaj, 1928, 1929.

33. Arhiv grada Zagreba, Fond Alexander Licht, Letter from Licht to Leo Herman, general secretary, Keren Hayesod, Jerusalem, December 31, 1931; CZA, Z4-3568, Memorandum to Keren Hayesod, April 4, 1932; Correspondence between the Federation of Zionists of Yugoslavia and Zionist Organization, London, on Sephardim, 1931–32.

34. *Balkanska konferencija sefardskih Jevreja* (Belgrade: Štamparija Karić, 1930); Benjamin Pinto, "BGska sefardska konferencija," *Jevrejski glas*, vol.3, no.22 (June 1, 1930), pp.1–3; Braco Poljokan, "Rad sefardske konferencije u BG," ibid., no.23 (June 6, 1930), p.1; "Sefardska konferencija u BG," *Židov*, vol.14, no.23 (June 6, 1930), pp.2–6.

35. Universal Confederation of Sephardic Jews, *Financial Report and General Administrative Report for the year 5687 (1926/1927)* (Jerusalem: Haibri Press, 1927); CZA, Z4-3579-II, Summary of Report of World Union of Sephardic Jews; Org. Dept. der Exec., London, Memo an der Exec. betreffend Weltkonfederation der Seph. Juden, February 2, 1928; plus further correspondence between SCJ and ZO; "Stav BG sef. organ.," *Židov*, vol.21, no.23 (June 4, 1937), p.5; "O skupštini BG organ. sef. Jevreja," ibid., vol.18, no.13 (March 29, 1940), p.4.

36. *Die Welt*, vol.6, no.45 (November 7, 1902), p.10; ibid., vol.13, no.13 (March 26, 1909), pp.291–92; "10 semestara rada zagr. Esperanze," *Jevrejski glas*, vol.2, no.9 (March 1, 1929); Jakov Atijas, "Esperansa, Jevrejski sefardski studentski klub u ZG," *Jevrejski almanah* (N.S.), 1955–56, pp.110–12.

37. "Izveštaj sa Sef. konferencije," *Jevrejski život*, vol.3, no.169 (August 26, 1927), p.4.

38. SCJ, *Izveštaj Saveznog odbora vijeću SC u KSHS u Subotici, dne 4 i 5 decembra 1927;* "Saveznom vijeću SŽOU," *Hanoar*, vol.2, nos.2–3 (December 1927), p.94.

39. Ješua Kajon, "Omladina i sarajevski sporazum," *Jevrejski glas*, vol.1, no.1 (January 13, 1928), p.4; Samuel Kamhi, "O Organizaciji sefardske omladine u KSHS," ibid., vol.1, no.2 (January 20, 1928), p.4; "Konferencija Šireg odbora Organ. sef. omladine u ZG," *Jevrejski glas*, vol.1, no.14 (April 20, 1928), p.3; *Izvještaj Saveznog odbora vijeću SCKSHS, BG, 1929;* Pavao Wertheim, "SŽOU i Organ. Sef. Omladine," *Hanoar*, vol.4, no.2 (January–March 1931), p.162.

40. SA-JL, Marriage registries of Sarajevo Sephardic and Ashkenazic communities, 1908–1941. See table 14.

41. Moric Levi, "Rav Danon i Ruždi-paša," *Godisnjak La Benevolencia i Potpora* (1933) and reprinted in *Spomenica 400 godina od dolaska Jevreja u Bosnu i Hercegovinu, 1566–1966*, ed. Samuel Kamhi (Sarajevo: Božidar Sekulić, 1966), pp.327–35. The author had the privilege of participating in this pilgrimage to Stolac in June 1971.

42. Arthur Hertzberg, *The Zionist Idea* (New York: Atheneum, 1971), pp.103–4; Solomon Gaon, "Rabbi Jehuda Hai Alkalai," in *A Memorial Tribute to Paul Goodman*, ed. Israel Cohen (London: Edward Goldston and Son, 1952), pp.138–47; Jichak Gur-Ari, *Rabi Jehuda (ben Salomon) Haj Alkalaj* (Zagreb: Biblioteka Židov, 1931); Aleksandar Štajner, "Jehuda Haj Alkalaj," *Jevrejski almanah* (N.S.), 1968–70, pp.55–66. Less importance however should be placed on the fact that Herzl's paternal grandparents also came from Zemun and his father grew up there. Alex Bein, *Theodore Herzl, A Biography* (Philadelphia: Jewish Publication Society, 1962), pp.3–5; Gaon, "Rabbi Jehuda Hai Al-

kalai," p.147; Lavoslav Šik, "Herzlovi predji u Zemunu," *Židov Kulturni i literarni prilog,* vol.1, no.18 (September 3, 1937), pp.79–82.

43. Berliner Büro der Zionistischen Organisation, *Warum gingen wir zum ersten Zionistenkongress?* (Berlin: Jüdischer Verlag, 1922), pp.10–13; Jakov H. Kalderon, "Dr David Alkalaj," *Židov,* vol.16, no.12 (March 25, 1932), p.1; "Dr David Alkalaj 1862–1933," *Godišnjak La Benevolencia i Potpora,* pp.71–74.

44. BG-JM, Box 5, Cionizam, Razna, Dok.1, 1587/73, Statuten der Vereinigung jüdischer Hochschüler aus den südslavischen Ländern Bar Giora in Wien (1902).

45. *Izvještaj Judeje Židovskog akademsko-kulturnog kluba u Zagrebu za godinu 5670–1909/10* (Zagreb: Dionička tiskara, 1910), p.54.

46. *Die Welt,* vol.8, no.32 (August 5, 1904), p.9; ibid., no.33 (August 12, 1904), pp.8–10; ibid., no.35 (August 26, 1904), p.14; ibid., vol.10, no.32 (August 24, 1906), p.19; *Jüdische Zeitung,* vol.2, no.31 (July 31, 1908), p.4; *Die Welt,* vol.12, no.32 (August 28, 1908), p.10; ibid., vol.14, no.35 (September 2, 1910), pp.850–51; "40-Semestara Bar Giore, 1902–1922," *Gideon,* vol.3, nos.9–11 (June 1922), p.169.

47. *Die Welt,* vol.13, no.22 (May 25, 1909), p.486; ibid., no.36 (September 3, 1909), p.795.

48. CZA, S5-450, Bericht der Exekutive der ZO an den XXII Zionistenkongress Landes- und Sonderverbaende: Jugoslavien, 1946.

49. Arhiv grada Zagreba, Fond Alexander Licht, Personal Papers of Alexander Licht; "Dr Aleksandar Licht," *Židov,* vol.15, no.49 (December 4, 1931), p.2; "Aleksandar Licht uz pedesetgodišnjicu života," *Židov,* Prilog, vol.18, no.14 (April 6, 1934), p.7; Hitahdut Olej Jugoslavija, *Za spomen dra Aleksandra Lichta* (Tel Aviv: Tiskara Gaon, 1955); Jakir Eventov, "Nostalgije Evropljanina, Uz desetgodišnjicu smrti Aleksandra Lichta," *Jevrejski almanah* (N.S.), 1957–58, pp.197–205.

50. "Organizovanje opštih cionista Jugoslavije," *Židov,* vol.19, no.3 (January 18, 1935), p.2; "Zemaljska konferencija Udruženja općih cionista u BG," ibid., vol.20, no.17 (April 24, 1936), p.7.

51. CZA, Z4-3735, Wahlen von Delegereten zum XIV Zionistenkongress, July 15, 1925; Z4-218/30, Letter from SCJ to ZO, July 12, 1927; Z4-222/44, Hauptwahlkommission für die Wahl der Delegierten für den XVI Zionistenkongress, June 20, 1929; "Izbori delegata za XVIII Svjetski cionistički kongres," *Židov,* vol.17, no.27 (July 7, 1933), p.3.

52. CZA, Z4-3568-II, Correspondence between Alexander Licht and Julije Dohany and Viktor Stark, November 1933.

53. "Dajte ostavku," *Malchut Jisrael,* vol.4, no.18 (April 20, 1936); "Grandiozan uspeh osnivačkog kongresa NCO," ibid., vol.4, no.1 (January 3, 1936), pp.1–8; "Zemaljska konferencija u ZGu," *Jevrejska tribuna,* vol.1, no.1 (December 31, 1937), pp.2–3; CZA, S5-556, Letter from SCJ to ZO on Revisionists, February 1, 1938; "Koncentracija svih ustanova NCO u BGu," *Jevrejska tribuna,* vol.4, no.1 (February 23, 1940), p.5; "Kinus arci šel Betar be Jugoslaviji," ibid., vol.3, no.19 (July 9, 1939), pp.1–3.

54. *Izvještaj Saveznog odbora vijeću SCJ u Novom Sadu, 8 decembra 1930* (Zagreb, 1930).

55. *Izvještaj Saveznom vijeću SCJ u Banji Luci, 24, 25 i 26 decembra 1939* (Zagreb, 1939).

56. CZA, S5-1715, Report of Central Electoral Commission for Yugoslavia, 1939; "Izbori delegata za XXI Svjetski cionistički kongres," *Židov,* vol.23, no.28 (July 14, 1939), p.1.

57. Cvi Rothmüller, "Bitoljski Židovi i njihove potrebe," *Židov,* vol.13, no.10 (March 8, 1929), p.1; Leon Kamhi, "Deset godine cijonističkog rada u Bitolju," ibid., no.18 (May 3, 1929), p.6; Avram Romano, "Nekoliko podataka o bitoljskim Jevrejima," *Vesnik,* vol.2, no.14 (February 1, 1940), pp.7–8.

58. For comparative data on the Bulgarian Jewish community, see N. M. Gelber, "Jewish Life in Bulgaria," *Jewish Social Studies,* vol.8, no.2 (April 1946), pp.103–26 and Saul Mezan, *Les Juifs Espagnols en Bulgarie,* vol.1 (Sofia, 1925).

59. Shaul Esh, "Kurt Blumenfeld on the Modern Jew and Zionism," *Jewish Journal of Sociology,* vol.6, no.2 (December 1964), p.236.

60. BJ-JM, Box 5, Cionizam, Mihael Levi, "40 godina Keren Kajemet u Jugoslaviji," (n.d.), pp.3–7.

61. Ibid., p.27.

62. "Izveštaj o radu povjereništva KKL-a za KSHS," *Židov,* vol.13, no.11 (March 15, 1929), p.5.

63. CZA, KH1-29, Felix Rosenblueth, Bericht über meine Reise nach Jugoslawien in November 1922; KH Report to Annual Conference in Carlsbad, September 1921; KH1-29-A-2, Report of Dr. Hantke to KH, December 5, 1925.

64. *Izvještaj Saveznog odbora vijeću SCKSHS u BG, 1929.*

65. Keren Hayesod, *Izvještaj o radu u godini 1929/30.*

66. CZA, Z4-3371, SCJ to ZO, April 17, 1929.

67. CZA, Z4-3371, Alexander Licht to Felix Rosenblueth, July 3, 1929 and September 26, 1929.

68. Ibid., Correspondence 1931, 1933, 1935; "Necionistički pretstavnici jugoslovenskih Jevreja u Jevrejskoj agenciji," *Službeni list SJVO,* vol.2, no.8 (July 15, 1937); "Necionistički pretstavnici jugoslovenskih Jevreja u Jevrejskoj agenciji," *Židov,* vol.23, no.29 (July 21, 1939).

69. Ibid.

70. Avram Romano, "Nekoliko podataka o bitoljskim Jevrejima," pp.7–8.

71. Cvi Rothmüller, "Hitahdut ole Jugoslavije," *Židov,* vol.18, no.46 (November 16, 1934), p.1.

72. "Palestinski ured za Jugoslaviju," *Izvještaj Saveza cionista Jugoslavije Saveznom vijeću u Banji Luci, 24, 25 i 26 decembra 1939* (Zagreb, 1939).

73. "Savezno vijeće cijonističke organizacije u Jugoslaviji," *Židov,* vol.4, nos.31–32 (November 24, 1920), p.5.

74. Ibid.; "Naš prvi halucgrupa," ibid., no.10 (April 13, 1920); CZA, Z4-1506, Letter from Palestinski ured to ZO, London, March 19, 1921.

75. CZA, Z4-2029-III, Gen. Sect. of ZO, London to Gen. Sect. of the Jewish National Fund, Jerusalem, May 4, 1926; Z4-2301, Bericht über die Jahreskonferenz des Zionistenverbandes in KSHS, October 17–19, 1926; Arhiv grada ZG, Fond Alexander Licht, Letter from Alexander Licht to Dr. F. Pops, BG, January 20, 1928; *Izvještaj Saveznog odbora vijeću SCKSHS u BG dne 31 marta i 1 aprila 1929.*

76. Rikard Kohn, "Rad Palestinskog ureda za Jugoslaviju," *Židov,* vol.19, no.16 (April 17, 1935), p.7.

77. "Palestinski ured o svome radu," *Židov,* vol.23, no.50 (December 8, 1939), p.6; *Izvještaj SCJ Saveznom vijeću u Banjoj Luci 24–26 decembra 1939.* Many of the Yugoslav halutzim of the early thirties established themselves in Sha'ar Ha'amakim, a MAPAI kibbutz near Haifa, while those who arrived in the late thirties helped form Kibbutz Gat, a Hashomer Hatzair-MAPAM settlement north of Be'er Sheva; others took up residence in Kibbutz Afikim (Kibbutz Me'uhad) and in different cities and towns. In 1934 the Yugoslav settlers in Palestine founded Hitahdut ole(j) Jugoslavije (association of emigrés from Yugoslavia) in Tel Aviv to help their fellow Yugoslav Jews acclimatize themselves to their new life. Cvi Rothmüller, "Hitahdut ole Jugoslavije," *Židov,* vol.18, no.46 (November 16, 1934), p.1.

78. *Izvještaj SCJ Saveznom vijecu, NS, 1935.*

79. Ibid.

80. Ibid.

81. Interview with Dr. Cvi Rotem (Rothmüller), journalist and active moderate left-wing Zionist leader in Yugoslavia in the twenties and early thirties, Tel Aviv, September 7, 1971.

82. Koen, *Besede posvečene Srpskoj omladini mojsijeve vere;* Samuilo Alkalaj, "Klub Zajednica," *Jevrejski almanah* (N.S.), 1961–62, pp.110–14. It is unclear whether these two sources are discussing the same organization or two different clubs with similar names which followed one another.

83. *Židov,* vol.3, no.7 (February 2, 1919), p.6.

84. "Nekoliko podataka o Literarnim sastancima židovske omladine u ZG," *Gideon,* vol.4, no.7 (April 1923), p.242; "Literarni sastanci židovske omladine," *Godišnjak IBO ZG* (1928), pp.63–64; "Lit. sast. židovske omladine, ZG, 1898–1928," *Hanoar,* vol.2, nos.6–7 (1928), p.215.

85. "O radu B'not Cijona u ZG," *Židov,* vol.2, no.15 (June 1, 1918), p.4.

86. "Izveštaj o konferenciji židovskih omladinskih društava," *Židov,* vol.3, no.26 (August 20, 1919), pp.3–5.

87. "Statut SŽOU KSHS," *Gideon,* vol.1, no.2 (December 1919), p.33.

88. "Omladinski slet u Osijeku," *Židov,* vol.4, nos.22–23 (August 19, 1920), p.10.

89. *Vjesnik SŽOU,* June 1930.

90. "SŽOU," *Izveštaj SCJ Saveznom vijeću, BL, 1939.*

91. Joško Rosenberg, "Saveznom vijeću SŽOU, 1927, OS," *Hanoar,* vol.2, nos.2–3 (December 1927), p.94; "SŽOU," *Izvještaj Saveznom odbora vijeću SCKSHS, SU, 1927.*

92. Rikard Kohn and Slavko Weiss, "Ahdut Hacofim," *Židov,* vol.10, no.6 (February 5, 1926), p.5; "Ahdut Hacofim," *Izveštaj Saveznom vijeću SCKSHS, SU, 1927;* "Kratko povijest Ahduta Hacofim," *Hozer,* no.2 (January 15, 1929).

93. "Izveštaj o izvanrednom Saveznom vijeću, ZG, 1928," *Hanoar,* vol.2, nos.9–10 (August 1928), p.271; *Izvještaj Saveznog odbora vijeću SCKSHS, BG, 1929.*

94. "Prva veida Hašomer hacaira u Brodu," *Židov,* vol.15, no.36 (September 4, 1933), p.4.

95. "Mahane 1932 u Goždu," *Židov,* vol.16, no.29 (July 22, 1932), p.4.

96. BG-JM, Material on Hashomer Hatzair from Kibbutz Merhavia, Sichot für Bogrim (1931?).

97. "Hahšara," *Izvještaj SCJ Saveznom vijeću, BL, 1939.*

98. Josef Indig, "Perspektive naše odgoje u svijetlu brojaka," *Iton hatnua,* vol.2, no.1 (October 1938).

99. "Kadima i njen rad—Pregled za I veidu Kadima," (1938); "Kadima," *Izvještaj SCJ Saveznom vijeću, BL, 1939;* "Kadima," WIZO, *Omladina* (1940), p.22.

100. "Tehelet Lavan," ibid., p.23.

101. "Akiba," ibid., p.28.

102. Jozef Levi, "O Matatji," *Jevrejski glas,* vol.3, nos. 36–37 (September 23, 1930), p.10; Eliezer Levi, "Matatja," *Jevrejski glas,* vol.6, no.3 (January 20, 1933), p.2; "Jedan plodan i konstruktivan rad—Godišnja skupština Matatja," ibid., vol.9, no.7 (February 18, 1938), pp.7–8.

103. Ibid.

104. Moni Finci, "U avangardi društvenog progresa," *Spomenica 400,* p.201; Moni Finci, *Djelovanje KPJ u kulturnim i sportskim društvima i organizacijama u BiH izmedju dva rata* (Sarajevo: Akademija nauka i umjetnosti BiH, 1970), pp.182–83.

105. ABH, KBUDB, pov.1939-7685, Correspondence between Sarajevo police directory, local administration, Matatja, and Sephardic community, 1939–40.

Chapter 9

1. David Albala, "Moje uspomene na Nikole Pašiću," *Židov,* vol.10, no.52 (December 17, 1926), p.3.

2. Vita Kajon, "M. Srškić i Jevreji," in *Milan Srškić, 1880–1937* (Sarajevo, 1938), pp.199–203.

3. "Oko izbora," *Židov,* vol.11, nos.38–39 (September 26, 1927), p.12; "Izbori za skupštinu i Židovi," ibid., vol.7, no.5 (February 2, 1923), p.5; "I demokrati kandidovat će Jevreji," ibid.; "Jevreji i opštinski izbori," ibid., vol.10, no.35 (August 8, 1926), p.5.

4. Stjepan Radić, *O Židovima* (Zagreb: Kamnik, 1938).

5. Stanislav Vinaver, "G. Radić i Jevreji," *Jevrejski život,* vol.2, no.71 (August 7, 1925), p.1.

6. Ferdo Čulinović, *Jugoslavija izmedju dva rata,* vol.2 (Zagreb, 1961), p.132.

7. Solomon Alkalaj, "Sahrana posmrtnih ostataka Avrama Ozerovića," *Židov,* vol.12, no.27 (July 6, 1928), p.6; Nikola Stanarević, "Avram Ozerović kao privredni političar," *Jevrejski almanah* (N.S.), 1959–60, pp.113–15; J. H. Kalderon "Bencion Buli," *Židov,* vol.17, no.34 (August 25, 1933), p.7; BG-JM, Box 11, 'Beograd,' Memoirs of Milovoj Kostić, 1958–59.

8. Lavoslav Šik, "Židovi i izbori," *Židov,* vol.11, no.25 (June 24, 1927), p.3.

9. Moritz Levy, *Die Sephardim in Bosnien,* (Sarajevo: A. Kajon, 1911) pp.83–84.

10. "Rezultat izbora u židovskoj kuriji," *Židovska smotra,* vol.4, no.11

(May 25, 1910), pp.1–5; "Jedna antisemitska ensinuacija u bosanskom saboru," ibid., vol.6, nos.4–5 (April 15, 1912), p.65.

11. "Poziv Jevrejima u Vojvodini da se organizuju u političku stranku," *Židov,* vol.6, no.8 (February 10, 1922), p.5; "Izbori za Parlament," ibid., vol.7, no.2 (January 12, 1923).

12. Lavoslav Šik, "Židovi i izbori," p.3.

13. Moša S. de Majo, "Prvi Židov u parlamentu," *Židov,* vol.11, no.32 (October 21, 1927), p.4; David A. Alkalaj, "Smrt Šemaje Demajo," ibid., vol.16, no.30 (July 29, 1932), p.2. According to one source, Šemaja Demajo was placed on the Belgrade list of the Radical Party as an alternate candidate to the former Minister of the Interior Božidar Maksimović, who later renounced his mandate in the name of his substitute. Rista St. Delić, *Jevreji u Jugoslaviji* (Belgrade: Prosveta, 1939), p.93.

14. "Prvi sastanak Narodnog pretstavništva u Beogradu," *Jevrejski glas,* vol.5, no.5 (January 29, 1932), p.1.

15. ABH, Fond Velikog župana sarajevske oblasti, pov.1927-1810, Policijska direkcija za BiH to VZSO, pov.br. 1219/1927, September 9, 1927.

16. "Oko izbora," *Židov,* vol.11, nos.38–39 (September 26, 1927), p.12.

17. ABH, VZSO, pov.1926-2762, Kandidatske liste u sarajevskoj oblasti za izbor.

18. ABH, VZSO, pov.1925-615, Series of memoranda to police and Ministry of Interior, February–April 1925; "Oko izbora," *Židov,* vol.11, nos.38–39 (September 26, 1927), p.12.

19. ABH, Fond Kraljevine banske uprave drinske banovine, pov.DZ1938-7490, KBUDB to Ministar unutrašnjih poslova, Odeljenje za državnu zaštitu I, December 28, 1938.

20. "Nemile pojave," *Jevrejski glas,* vol.1, no.37 (September 28, 1928), p.1; "Gradski izbori i Jevreji," ibid., vol.1, no.38 (October 5, 1928), p.1; "Rezultati općinskih izbora u Sarajevu," ibid., vol.1, no.43 (November 9, 1928), p.5.

21. "Izbori za gradsko zastupstvo u ZG"; *Židov,* vol.9, no.21 (May 15, 1925), p.6; "Nakon gradskih izbora u Zagrebu," ibid., vol.11, no.36 (September 9, 1927), p.7.

22. Arhiv grada Zagreba, Zapisnici sjednica gradskog vijeća, 1919–39.

23. ABH, VZSO, pov.1929-2171, List of Communists Imprisoned.

24. ABH, KBUDB, pov.1935-3151, List of Communists.

25. Marko Perić-Velimir Drechsler, "Jugoslovenski Jevreji—Španski borci," *Jevrejski almanah* (N.S.), 1963–64, pp.96–102.

26. *Spomenica poginulih i umrlih srpskih Jevreja u Balkanskom i svetskom ratu 1912–1918* (Belgrade: Štamparija M. Karića, 1927).

27. Photostat copy of original in Lavoslav Šik, *Jüdische Ärzte in Jugoslawien* (Zagreb: Tiskara Eugen Sekler, 1931), p.75.

28. "Vesnićevo pismo," *Židov,* vol.3, nos.4–5 (January 31, 1919), p.1; CZA, Z4-727, 1920 Report, "Jugoslavija."

29. Rumor had it that he regularly played bridge with King Alexander, but this was denied by the chief rabbi himself during an interview at the Sephardic Home for the Aged in Brooklyn on January 8, 1971.

30. CZA, Z4-3568-I, SCJ to ZO, London, Report on Visit of President of Executive Nahum Sokolow to KSHS, April 26, 1928; Z4-3568-II, SCJ to ZO, London, August 17, 1930.

31. Editorial in *Židov,* vol.22, no.3 (January 20, 1928), p.1; ibid., vol.18, no.50 (December 14, 1934), p.1.

32. David Albala, "Royalty in Palestine," *The New Palestine,* May 2, 1941, p.8.

33. "G. dr V. Marinković o našim Jevrejima," *Politika,* vol.26, no.7599 (July 1, 1929).

34. BG-JM, Box 30, "Makedonija-Kosmet," Memorandum from SJVO to all Jewish communities and members of central committee, No.5735, October 31, 1938, Re: Audience of Dr. Bukić Pijade with President of Royal Government and Minister of Interior Dr. Milan Stojadinović.

35. E. B. Gajić, *Jugoslavija i "jevrejski problem"* (Belgrade: Štamparija Drag. Gregorića, 1938); Rista St. Delić, *Jevreji u Jugoslaviji* (Belgrade: Prosveta, 1939).

36. Mica Dimitrijević, ed., *Naši Jevreji, Jevrejsko pitanje kod nas* (Belgrade: Štamparija Minerva, 1940).

37. "Uredbe i o uredbama protiv Jevreja," *Jevrejski glas,* vol.13, no.31 (October 16, 1940), p.4.

38. Jean Mousset, *La Serbie et son Église, 1830–1904* (Paris: Librairie Droz, 1938), pp. 352–53; Miroslava Despot, "Protužidovski izgredi u Zagorju i Zagrebu godine 1883," *Jevrejski almanah* (N.S.), 1957–58, pp.75–85.

39. ABH, Fond Zemaljske vlade Sarajeva, prez. 1919–3783, Memorandum from ZVS to Stepa Stepanović, komandant II armiske oblasti u Sarajevu, May 5, 1919.

40. ABH, ZVS, prez.1919-5675, Policijska direkcija za Bosnu i Hercegovinu to ZV za BiH, No.892 praes.19, May 8, 1919; ZVS to Svetozar Pribićević, ministar unutrašnjih dela, June 2, 1919; ZVS, prez.1920-2032, Ministar inostranih dela to Alaupović, MV, Pov.br.678, January 19, 1920. David Levi-Dale, ed., *Spomenica Saveza jevrejskih opština Jugoslavije 1919–1969* (Belgrade: Srbo-štampa, 1970), p.37.

41. See Minorities Treaty, art. 3 in app.2.

42. "Židovi nemaju pravo glasa" and "Biračko pravo Jevreja," *Židovska svijest,* vol.3, no.93 (October 15, 1920), pp.1–2; "Velika protestna skupština Židova u Sarajevu," ibid., pp.4–5; ABH, ZVS, prez.1920-10367, Protestna skupština to dr Milan Srškić, predsjednik ZVS, Resolution, October 15, 1920.

43. "Protest uspio," *Židovska svijest,* vol.2, no.94 (October 22, 1920), pp.1–4.

44. "Službeni antisemitizam," *Židov,* vol.6, no.30 (July 7, 1922), pp.6–7; "Izbori za Parlament," *Židov,* vol.7, no.2 (January 12, 1923).

45. "Numerus clausus," *Židov,* vol.4, no.15 (June 1, 1920), p.1; "Hortyevci saveznici na zagrebačkom universitetu," *Židovska svijest,* vol.2, no.77 (June 11, 1920), p.1.

46. ABH, VZSO, pov.1925-615, Policijska direkcija za BiH to VZSO, No.390 pov.ad., March 10, 1925.

47. "Jedan nečuveni skandal," *Jevrejski glas,* vol.1, no.40 (October 19, 1928), p.2.

48. "Aveti u Bačkom Petrovomselu," *Židov,* vol.12, no.39 (September 28, 1928), p.2.

49. "Hrvatski nacionalni bojkot Židova," *Völkischer Beobachter,* April 18, 1933.

50. AJ, MPVO, F 184, Izveštaj Privremene uprave SJVO za kongres, 1921; *Spomenica SJOJ,* pp.33–36.

51. Ivan Kon, "Najvažniji momenti u radu SJVO," *Glasnik SJVO,* vol.1, (1933), p.12; AJ, MP, 91-137-31, SJVO to MP, No. 4946, December 15, 1930; 102-32-34, SJVO to MP, No. 3862, July 13, 1934; MPVO, F 185, SJVO to MPVO, No. 4782, September 2, 1936; F 184, SJVO to Ministry of Interior, September 12, 1938.

52. BG-JM, Box 30, "Makedonija-Kosmet," SJVO to all Jewish communities and central committee SJVO, No. 4772, October 29, 1933.

53. AJ, MPVO, F 184, Zapisnik VI kongresa SJVO, održanog u Beogradu, 29 i 30 marta 1936.

54. AJ, Fond Ministarstva pravde, 93-42-34, SJVO to MP, No. 3214, February 11, 1936; 93-42-34, Više državno tužiostvo, Split, Ks319/36 to MP, July 24, 1936.

55. "Antisemitska propaganda pred sudom," *Židov,* vol.20, no.49 (December 4, 1936), p.9.

56. Aleksa Arnon (Aleksandar Klein), "10 godina rada u korist jevrejskih izbjeglica u Jugoslaviji (1933–1942)" [Tel Aviv, n.d.], pp.1–3.

57. Ibid., pp.3–4; Aleksandar Klein, "Sadanje stanje njemačke emigracije," *Židov,* vol.20, no.13 (March 26, 1937), p.9.

58. Arnon, "10 godina rada," pp.4–6; "Iz izveštaja Glavnog odbora—Zbrinjavanje izbeglica," *Židov,* vol.23, no.16 (April 21, 1939), p.6.

59. Arnon, "10 godina rada," pp.8–9; BG-JM, 68e, Letter to Dr. David Albala, N.Y., Spor oko zaposjedanja prostorija u Kladovu, March 21, 1940.

60. AJ, MPVO, F 184, SJVO to MP, No.4457, July 1, 1940.

61. Arnon, "10 godina rada," app.1, 2; *Spomenica SJOJ,* p.80.

62. AJ, Ministarstvo prosveta, 66-74-204, KJ Ministarstvo unutrašnjih poslova Upravno odeljenje to Ministarstvo Prosveta, Pov. III, br. 1885, October 21, 1939, Regulation on Foreign Jews—Proposal. An article by Aleksandar Matkovski claims that this law was issued on July 27, 1939, but this statement runs contrary to archival sources, which indicate that the law was still in its preparatory stages in October of that year. Aleksandar Matkovski, "The Destruction of Macedonian Jewry in 1943," *Yad Vashem Studies on the European Catastrophe and Resistance,* vol.3 (1959), p.206.

63. "Uredbe o mjerama koji se odnose na Jevreje u pogledu obavljanja radnja sa predmetima ljudske ishrane," *Jevrejski glas,* vol.13, no.31 (October 16, 1940), pp.1–3; "Veličina i dekadenca emancipacije," *Židov,* vol.24, no.41 (October 9, 1941), pp.3–4; "Povodom uredaba o 'reguliranju' položaja Židova," ibid.; "Uredbe o ograničenju prava Židova na području privrede i školstva," ibid., p. 7; "Uredba o trgovačkim i industrijskim poduzecima," ibid., no. 46 (November 8, 1940), p. 8. For a complete translation of this law, see app. 5.

64. "Uredba o ograničenju školovanja lica jevrejskog porjekla," *Jevrejski glas,* vol.13, no.31 (October 16, 1940), pp.1–3. For a complete translation of this law, see app. 5.

65. "Povodom uredbi protiv Jevreja," *Jevrejski glas,* vol.13, no.31 (October 16, 1940), p.1; "Deklaracija," *Židov,* vol.24, no.41 (October 9, 1940), p.1; *Spomenica SJOJ,* pp. 69–72.

Epilogue

1. Raul Hilberg, *The Destruction of the European Jews* (Chicago: Quadrangle Books, 1967), p.435.

2. Ibid., pp.436–42. For further information on the fate of Serbian Jewry, see also Gerald Reitlinger, *The Final Solution* (New York: A.S. Barnes and Co., Inc., 1953), pp.359–64; Nora Levin, *The Holocaust* (New York: Schocken, 1973), pp.510–14; Zdenko Löwenthal, ed., *The Crimes of the Fascist Occupants and Their Collaborators against Jews in Yugoslavia* (Belgrade: Federation of Jewish Communities of Federative People's Republic of Yugoslavia, 1957), pp.1–9 [English], 1–53 [Serbo-Croatian]; Lazar Ivanović and Mladen Vukmanović, *Dani smrti na Sajmištu* (Novi Sad: Dnevnik, 1969), pp.6–30.

3. Hilberg, pp.453–58. See also Reitlinger, pp.364–69; Levin, pp.514–17; *The Crimes of the Fascist Occupants,* pp.10–20 [English], 54–114 [Serbo-Croatian]; Aleksandar Stajić and Jakov Papo, "Ubistva i drugi zločini izvršeni nad Jevrejima u Bosni i Hercegovini u toku neprijateljske okupacije," *Spomenica 400 godina od dolaska Jevreja u Bosnu i Hercegovinu, 1566–1966,* ed. Samuel Kamhi (Sarajevo: Božidar Sekulić, 1966), pp.214–47.

4. Levin, pp.554–57. See also *The Crimes of the Fascist Occupants,* pp.38–39 [English], 189–95 [Serbo-Croatian]; Aleksandar Matkovski, "The Destruction of Macedonian Jewry in 1943," *Yad Vashem Studies on the European Catastrophe and Resistance,* vol.3 (1959).

5. Hilberg, p.521. See also *The Crimes of the Fascist Occupants,* pp.28–30 [English], 143–58 [Serbo-Croatian]; Vladislav Rotbart, "Ciji je delo novosadska racija," *Jevrejski almanah* (N.S.), 1965–67, pp.168–88.

6. *The Crimes of the Fascist Occupants,* pp.31–37 [English], 163–88 [Serbo-Croatian].

7. Hilberg, pp.456–57; Levin, pp.515–16; Reitlinger, p.368; *The Crimes of the Fascist Occupants,* pp.22–24 [English], 117–35 [Serbo-Croatian].

8. Aron Kamhi and Mirko Levinger, "Pokret otpora medju Jevrejima Bosne i Hercegovine interniranim na Lopudu i Rabu," *Spomenica 400,* pp.255–61.

9. Estimates range as high as 60,000 or more, but that assumes a prewar population of 75,000, rather than less than 70,000. See Levin, pp.715–18, for various estimates.

10. See Nisim Albahari, "Borbi se i sagorjeli u revolucionarno-oslobodilačkoj borbi naroda Jugoslavije," *Spomenica 400,* pp.249–54, 263–69; David Levi-Dale, "Bitoljski Jevreji u narodno-oslobodilačkoj borbi," *Jevrejski almanah* (N.S.), 1957–58, pp.109–16; *Spomenica SJOJ,* pp.108–12.

11. *Spomenica SJOJ,* pp.104–14. Of 3,130 Jewish survivors born before 1930 and still living in Yugoslavia in 1971, approximately two-thirds had been in concentration camps, one-third were refugees and in hiding, one-quarter fought with the Partisans, 6.5 percent were prisoners-of-war and about 8 percent survived by other means. (Some individuals underwent as many as two or more of these experiences.) Source: Marko Perić, "Demographic Study of the Jewish Community in Yugoslavia, 1971–1972," *Papers in Jewish Demography 1973* (Jerusalem: Institute of Contemporary Jewry, 1977), p.283.

12. David Perera, "Neko statistički podaci o Jevrejima u Jugoslaviji u

periodu od 1938 do 1965 godine," *Jevrejski almanah* (N.S.), 1968–70, pp.136, 140. According to a preliminary list of survivors compiled in 1946 by the Federation of Jewish Communities, 690 of the survivors listed had been born in Belgrade, 571 in Zagreb, and 1,049 in Sarajevo. (The figure for Zagreb, however, is probably much too low.) Figures from the same source show about one-third of those living in Belgrade in 1946 had been born there and two-thirds of those who returned to Sarajevo were natives of the city. An accurate estimate for Zagreb cannot be reached from the data available. Source: SJVO, "Automni odbor za pomoć, Spiskovi preživelih Jevreja u Jugoslaviji," Belgrade, 1946 (courtesy of Dr. Helen Fein, New Paltz, New York).

13. Perera, p.142; *Spomenica SJOJ,* pp.144–46; Joseph Gordon, "Yugoslavia," *American Jewish Year Book,* vol.51 (1950), pp.377–78.

14. Perera, p.140; *Spomenica SJOJ,* p.208.

15. In 1971 the Federation of Jewish Communities conducted a demographic survey of all registered Jewish households in the country. Out of some 5,696 registered members, 4,702 individuals (or 85 percent) were interviewed in person and detailed questionaires were completed. In Belgrade 1,010 members of the community (or 63 percent) were involved; in Zagreb 1,122 (or 84 percent) were contacted (of whom 102 lived in the Jewish Home for the Aged, 959 lived elsewhere in Zagreb proper and the rest in outlying towns); in Sarajevo 825 (or 76 percent) participated. The preliminary results of this study, organized by city, appeared in a series of articles written by Marko Perić, "Prvi rezultati našeg demografskog istraživanja," *Jevrejski pregled,* vol.23, nos.11–12 (November-December 1972), pp.2–7; "Dalji rezultati našeg demografskog istraživanja," ibid., vol.24, nos.1–2 (January-February 1973), pp.16–21; ibid., nos.3–4 (March-April 1973), pp.31–34; ibid., nos.5–6 (May-June 1973),pp.2–7; ibid., nos.7–8 (July-August 1973), pp.3–6. The final results were subsequently published in Marko Perić, "Demographic Study of the Jewish Community in Yugoslavia, 1971–1972," *Papers in Jewish Demography 1973* (Jerusalem: Institute of Contemporary Jewry, 1977), pp.267–87.

16. Perić, "Prvi rezultati," *Jevrejski pregled,* vol.23, nos.11–12, p.3; Perić, "Dalnji rezultati," ibid., vol.24, nos.1–2, p.17; ibid., nos.3–4, p.31.

17. Perić, "Demographic Study," pp.281, 284.

18. Ibid., p.277.

19. Some light is shed on this matter in Charles W. Steckel, *Destruction and Survival* (Los Angeles: Delmar Publishing Co., 1973), pp.41–43, but the role of the official Jewish communities in the former Yugoslav state during the war has not yet been fully explored.

20. *Spomenica SJOJ,* pp.85–86.

21. Steckel, pp.23–26.

22. *Spomenica SJOJ,* pp.90–93.

23. Ibid., pp.87–89.

24. Ibid., p.115.

25. Ibid., pp.115–17, 132–35.

26. Perera, p.138

27. For further detail on the nature and organization of the postwar Yugoslav Jewish community, see an article by the author, "Yugoslav Jewry —A Community that rests on Its Organization," [Hebrew] in *Tefutsot Israel,* vol.12, no.2 (March–April 1974), pp.41–74.

28. Albert Vajs, "Jevreji u novoj Jugoslaviji," *Jevrejski almanah* (N.S.), 1954, p.45.

29. *Spomenica SJOJ,* pp.166–67; Leon Shapiro, "Yugoslavia," *American Jewish Year Book,* vol.65 (1964), p.295.

30. *Spomenica SJOJ,* pp.132–35; Vajs, pp.30–33.

31. *Spomenica SJOJ,* pp.150–57; David Levi-Dale, ed., *Spomenica povodom 50-godišnjice Doma staraca—Zaklada Lavoslav Švarca u Zagrebu, 1910–1960* (Belgrade: SJOJ, 1960); "Dom staraca u 1965," *Jevrejski pregled,* vol.17, nos.1–2 (January–February 1966), p.7.

32. Leon Shapiro, "Yugoslavia," *American Jewish Year Book,* vol. 72 (1971), pp.423–26.

33. Lavoslav Kadelburg, "Neka aktuelna pitanja," *Jevrejski pregled,* vol. 21, nos.11–12 (November–December 1970), pp.1–6; Leon Shapiro, "Yugoslavia," *American Jewish Year Book,* vol.62, (1961), pp.297–98; Aleksandar Levi, "Naši horovi," *Jevrejski almanah* (N.S.), 1959–60, pp.201–9; "Desetgodišnjica hore jevreske opštine u Beogradu," *Jevrejski pregled,* vol.18, nos.3–4 (March–April 1962), pp.13–16; "Petnaestgodišnjica Jevrejskog pjevačkog zbora Moša Pijade," ibid., vol.21, nos.5–6 (May–June 1970), pp.1–6; *Spomenica SJOJ,* pp.172–76.

34. *Spomenica SJOJ,* pp.181–82.

35. Ibid., pp.167–72.

36. Ibid., pp. 135–41.

37. *Spomenica SJOJ,* pp.179–81; Luci Mevorah-Petrović, "Deset godina nagradnog konkursa za jevrejsko naučno, književno i umetničko stvaralaštvo," *Jevrejski almanah* (N.S.), 1963–64, pp.145–47.

38. Among these volumes, all of which are published in Serbo-Croatian, the following have appeared: *Crimes of the Fascist Occupants and Their Collaborators against Jews in Yugoslavia* (1952); *A Short History of the Jewish People* by Simon Dubnow (1962), *Old Jewish Art in Palestine* by Dr. Vidosava Nedomački, curator of the Jewish Historical Museum (1964), *The Sephardim in Bosnia* by Moric Levi (1969), as well as several special commemorative editions.

39. *Spomenica SJOJ,* pp.157–63; "Savetovanje o radu omladine u Jugoslaviji," *Jevrejski almanah* (N.S.), 1957–58, pp.156–61; Miriam Steiner, "Yugoslav Jewry," *Dispersion and Unity,* nos.13/14, pp.233–34.

40. Zapisnik VIII konferencije Saveza jevrejskih opština Jugoslavije, Belgrade, December 26–27, 1959 (YIVO, New York).

41. Perera, p.141.

42. Perić, "Demographic Study," pp.270–77.

43. Ibid., pp.284–86.

44. Vajs, p.43.

45. Perić, "Demographic Study," pp.275–78

46. Perić, "Dalji rezultati," *Jevrejski pregled,* vol.24, nos.1–2, p.20.

47. Perić, "Prvi rezultati," ibid., vol. 23, nos. 11–12, p.3; "Dalji rezultati," ibid., vol.24, nos.1–2, p.17, and nos.3–4, p.31.

48. "Sastanak koordinacionog odbora ženskih sekcija," *Jevrejski pregled,* vol.19, nos.3–4 (March–April 1968), pp.16–19; Edita Vajs, "Učešće žena u jevrejskom javnom radu u Jugoslaviji," *Jevrejski almanah* (N.S.), 1957–58, pp.148–55.

49. "Naša 'srednja generacija,'" *Jevrejski pregled,* vol.19, nos.3–4 (March–April 1968), pp.19–21.

50. Perić, "Prvi rezultati," *Jevrejski pregled,* vol.23, nos.11–12, p.6; "Dalnji rezultati," ibid., vol.24, nos.1–2, p.19 and nos.3–4, p.33.

51. Aleksandar Levi, "60-godišnjica dra Lavoslav Kadelburga," *Jevrejski pregled,* vol.21, nos.7–8 (July–August 1970), pp.5–8.

52. A. Vajs, pp.27–29, 42; *Spomenica SJOJ,* pp.130–32; Steiner, p.230.

53. *Jevrejski pregled,* vol. 20, nos. 7–8 (July–August 1969).

54. *Spomenica SJOJ,* pp.120–27; *Jevrejski pregled,* vol. 21, (September–October 1970), p.30.

55. Zvi Locker, "Yugoslavia—Relations with Israel," *Encyclopedia Judaica* (1971), vol. 16, pp.883–84.

56. *Spomenica SJOJ,* pp.127–30.

57. Ibid., pp.147–50.

INDEX

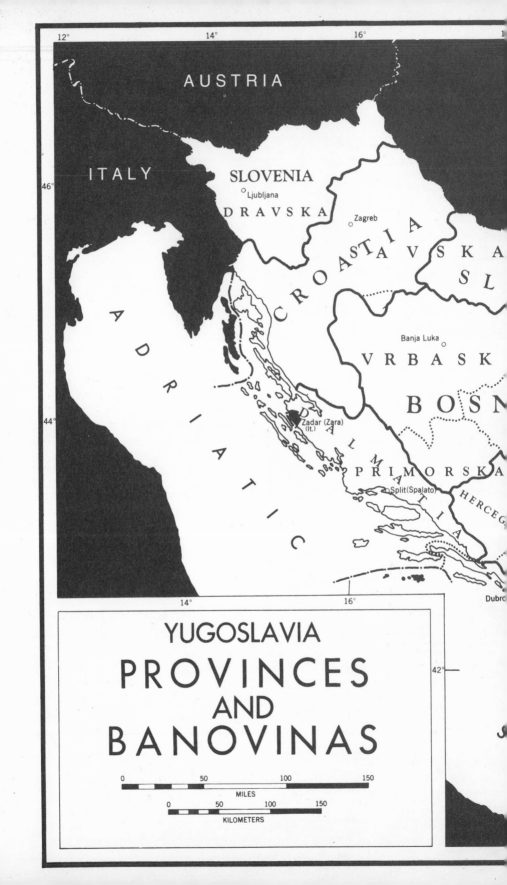

AUSTRIA

ITALY

SLOVENIA
Ljubljana

DRAVSKA

Zagreb

CROATIA

AVSKA
SL

Banja Luka

VRBASK

BOSN

ADRIATIC

Zadar (Zara)
(It.)

DALMATIA

PRIMORSKA

Split (Spalato)

HERCEG

Dubro

YUGOSLAVIA
PROVINCES
AND
BANOVINAS

0   50   100   150
MILES

0   50   100   150
KILOMETERS

42°

46°

44°

12°   14°   16°

14°   16°